ADVERTISEMENTS
FOR MYSELF

NORMAN MAILER

ADVERTISEMENTS FOR MYSELF

Harvard University Press

Cambridge, Massachusetts

London, England

1992

Copyright © 1959 by Norman Mailer
All rights reserved
Printed in the United States of America
10 9 8 7 6 5 4 3 2 1

First Harvard University Press paperback edition, 1992

Library of Congress Cataloging-in-Publication Data

Mailer, Norman.
 [Selections. 1992]
 Advertisements for myself / Norman Mailer.
     p.   cm.
 ISBN 0-674-00590-2
 I. Title.
PS3525.A4152A65   1992   92-13292
813'.54—dc20   CIP

I dedicate this book
to the memory of
ANNE MAILER KESSLER (1889–1958)
and to
DAVID KESSLER
and to my father
ISAAC BARNETT (Barney) MAILER

A NOTE TO THE READER

There are two Tables of Contents. The First lists each piece in sequence, and anyone wishing to read my book from beginning to end may be pleased to hear that the order is roughly chronological. The author, taken with an admirable desire to please his readers, has also added a set of advertisements, printed in italics, which surround all of these writings with his present tastes, preferences, apologies, prides, and occasional confessions. Like many another literary fraud, the writer has been known on occasion to read the Preface of a book instead of a book, and bearing this vice in mind, he tried to make the advertisements more readable than the rest of his pages.

Since such a method is discursive, and this is a time in which many hold a fierce grip on their wandering attention, a Second Table of Contents is offered to satisfy the specialist. Here all short stories, short novels, poems, advertisements, articles, essays, journalism, and miscellany are posted in their formal category.

For those who care to skim nothing but the cream of each author, and so miss the pleasure of liking him at his worst, I will take the dangerous step of listing what I beileve are the best pieces in this book.

In order of appearance they might be:

> The Man Who Studied Yoga
> The White Negro
> The Time Of Her Time
> Dead Ends
> Advertisements For Myself On The Way Out
> and
> some of the writing in italics.

7

Advertisements For Myself On The Way Out is the title to the Prologue of a long novel. Since one of the purposes of this collection is the intention to clear a ground for that novel, I have taken the opportunity to use a part of the title as a name for this book.

Acknowledgment is made to Cross-Section, Story *magazine,* The Harvard Advocate, New World Writing, New Short Novels, The Independent, One Magazine, The Village Voice, *the* N. Y. Post, Modern Writing, The Provincetown Annual, Discovery, Esquire, Partisan Review, Western Review *and* Dissent, *where many of these pieces first appeared. Acknowledgment is also made to* Time *magazine and* Newsweek *for permission to quote from their reviews of* The Deer Park.

The date which comes at the end of some of these writings refers to the year in which the piece was written. Where a date does not appear, the material is new and was written during 1958 and 1959 for this book.

FIRST TABLE OF CONTENTS

SECOND TABLE OF CONTENTS

FICTION

ESSAYS AND ARTICLES

JOURNALISM

INTERVIEWS

POETRY

FIRST ADVERTISEMENT FOR MYSELF

Like many another vain, empty, and bullying body of our time, I have been running for President these last ten years in the privacy of my mind, and it occurs to me that I am less close now than when I began. Defeat has left my nature divided, my sense of timing is eccentric, and I contain within myself the bitter exhaustions of an old man, and the cocky arguments of a bright boy. So I am everything but my proper age of thirty-six, and anger has brought me to the edge of the brutal. In sitting down to write a sermon for this collection, I find arrogance in much of my mood. It cannot be helped. The sour truth is that I am imprisoned with a perception which will settle for nothing less than making a revolution in the consciousness of our time. Whether rightly or wrongly, it is then obvious that I would go so far as to think it is my present and future work which will have the deepest influence of any work being done by an American novelist in these years. I could be wrong, and if I am, then I'm the fool who will pay the bill, but I think we can all agree it would cheat this collection of its true interest to present myself as more modest than I am.

The reader who is curious to test my claims this instant is advised to turn to the pages of "The White Negro," and to the portion from my new novel which ends this book. He can then decide after a few hours of his finest attention if he is likely to agree. But those of you who want a sense of clear focus, like to know left from right, and up from not-so-up, may find it more restful to enter this book by degrees.

There was a time when Pirandello could tease a comedy of pain out of six characters in search of an author, but that is only a whiff of purgatory next to the yaws of conscience a writer learns to feel when he sets his mirrors face to face and begins to jiggle his Self for a style which will have some relation to him. *I would suspect it is not possible, no more than one can remake oneself signature for signature, but I have to admit I am not suited for this sort of confrontation despite two novels put down in the first person and a bloody season of overexpressed personal opinions as a newspaper columnist. To write about myself is to send my style through a circus of variations and postures, a fireworks of virtuosity designed to achieve . . . I do not even know what. Leave it that I become an actor, a quick-change artist, as if I believe I can trap the Prince of Truth in the act of switching a style.*

For instance, when the invitation came, not so very long ago, to make out my fifteenth anniversary report to the Harvard Class of 1943 I thought first of not answering, and then I considered an abbreviated and (by inference) disdainful few lines, and finally I thought, fuck it, let's have something in this class report which is a little less predictable than:

> We are now living in the country, and find to our surprise that we like it, although the children miss the ambiguities and partial unshelterings of a New York public school education. Suburban life is great, qualifiedly great—I find to my perhaps overstructured horror that I rather enjoy the high-pressured rubber of bridge on the evening rocket back—wife and I are working you see with local PTA to initiate Master Point tournaments. These activities do not quite satisfy my programmatic ambitions of fifteen years ago, but still if I will be granted my enthusiasm for one cliché, the little realities of the graying poll and the burgeoning paunch are bracing realities.

And so, foreseeing (correctly) that ninety per cent of my class's answers to the report would have that inimitable lead-kitten charm of Harvard prose, I wrote my reply with the desire to be destructive and therefore useful:

> For the last few years I have continued to run in that overcrowded mob of unconscionable egotists who are all determined to become the next great American writer. But, given the brawl, the wasting of the will, and the sapping of one's creative rage by our most subtle and dear totalitarian time, politely called the time of conformity, I do not know that I would be so confident as to place the bet on myself any longer nor indeed on any of my competitive peers.

Yes, I wanted to say, my creative rage is being sapped, I have been dying a little these fifteen years, and so have a good many of you, no doubt—none of us are doing quite so much as we once thought we would. But then this has been a bad time, we've all been flattened by the dead air of this time, dinched and tamped into a flat-footed class.

Much of this meaning depended on the word "sapping" with its connotations of weakening, enervating, deadening—that word was the nerve of my paragraph. Unfortunately, the "sapping of one's creative rage" was printed in the Class Report as the "slapping of one's creative rage," an interesting montage of words, but my meaning was tricked. As the years go by and I become a little more possible for Ph. D. mills, graduate students will begin to write about the slapping of my creative rage, of Mailer's vision of his rage as his shield, when what I was trying to say was simply, "The shits are killing us."

Now, in the writing of our days, when no ache of evidence can ever be believed unless it is presented by a Doctor of Jargon, a remark like "the shits are killing us" is so declarative that fifty pages of closely reasoned argument should follow in support. I would rather not make the attempt. My mood has shifted, and I prefer to unload some bitter end of overchewed opinions which will show the churl in me, and beef up a drunken bruise or two, but at least will clear the air for us to go ahead.

So, mark you. Every American writer who takes himself to be both major and macho must sooner or later give a faena which borrows from the self-love of a Hemingway style. Any reader who will let me circle back later, in my own way, via the whorls and ellipses of my knotted mind, to earlier remarks, will be entertained en route by a series of comments I have to make (not altogether out of the rhythms of Hemingway) on the man, on my contemporaries and on myself. Brief remarks, absolutely not exhaustive, but still an historic moment.

For you see I have come finally to have a great sympathy for The Master's irrepressible tantrum that he is the champion writer of this time, and of all time, and that if anyone can pin Tolstoy, it is Ernest H. Somewhere in Hemingway is the hard mind of a shrewd small-town boy, the kind of boy who knows you have a real cigar only when you are the biggest man in town, because to be just one of the big men in town is tiring, much too tiring, you inspire hatred, and what is worse than hatred, a wave of cross-talk in everyone around you. You are considered important by some and put down by others, and every time you meet a new man, the battle is on: the latest guest has to decide if you are

a) stronger than he, and
b) smarter than he, and
c) less queer.

And if you pass on all three counts, if you win the arm-wrestle, culture derby, and short-hair count, well then if he is a decent sort he usually feels you should run for President. But all this has happened in the first place because your reputation is uncertain, your name is locked in the elevators of publicity and public fashion, and so your meetings with every man and woman around become charged and overcharged.

There is a time when an ambitious type should fight his way through the jungle and up the mountain—it is the time when experience is rich and you can learn more than you ever will again, but if it goes on too long, you wither from the high tension, you drop away drunk or a burned-out brain, you learn what it is to lose seriously in love, or how it goes when your best friend and you are no longer speaking; it is inevitable that a bad fall comes to the strong-willed man who is not strong enough to reach his own peak.

Hemingway knows this: for years he has not written anything which would bother an eight-year-old or one's grandmother, and yet his reputation is firm—he knew in advance, with a fine sense of timing, that he would have to campaign for himself, that the best tactic to hide the lockjaw of his shrinking genius was to become the personality of our time. And here he succeeded. He went out of his way to shoot a lion or two, maybe more, he almost captured Paris with a few hundred men, he did a lot of things which very few of us could do, and I say this levelly, and not from hero worship, because for all his size, and all we've learned from him about the real importance of physical courage, he has still pretended to be ignorant of the notion that it is not enough to feel like a man, one must try to think like a man as well. Hemingway has always been afraid to think, afraid of losing even a little popularity, and so today he clowns away time worrying publicly about the feud between his good friends Leonard Lyons and Walter Winchell, and his words excite no thought in the best of my rebel generation. He's no longer

20

any help to us, he's left us marooned in the nervous boredom of a world which finally he didn't try hard enough to change.

Still, I give credit to the man, he's known the value of his own work, and he fought to make his personality enrich his books. Let any of you decide for yourselves how silly would be A Farewell to Arms or better, Death in the Afternoon, *if it had been written by a man who was five-four, had acne, wore glasses, spoke in a shrill voice, and was a physical coward. That, of course, is an impossible hypothesis—such a man would never have been able to feel the emotions of the man who wrote that early prose, but I exaggerate the point in order to stain the nuance with contrast. Suppose Hemingway had shown just a shadow of physical cowardice vis-à-vis his own heroes? That cowardice would have given a nasty joy to half the literary world, and ridicule would have followed to empty the breath of his books. Without a sense of the big man who wrote the prose, all the later work would be only skeletons of abstraction, the flesh gone.* The Old Man and The Sea *is, for my opinion, a bad piece of work if one knows nothing about the author. Only when one feels, more or less subliminally, the face of Ernest on the body of a Cuban fisherman does the fraud of the tale take on its surrealist truth.**

An author's personality can help or hurt the attention readers give to his books, and it is sometimes fatal to one's talent not to have a public with a clear public recognition of one's size. The way to save your work and reach more readers is to advertise yourself, steal your own favorite page out of Hemingway's unwritten Notes From Papa On How The Working Novelist Can Get Ahead. *Truman Capote did it bravely when he began, and my hat is off to him. James Jones did it, and did it well. Kerouac would deserve ears and tail if he weren't an Eisenhower gypsy. I, in my turn, would love to be one of the colorful old-young men of American letters, but I have a changeable personality, a sullen disposition, and a calculating*

* (*As a capsule criticism:* The Old Man and The Sea *is cheered for being an affirmative work, a triumph of the human spirit, etc., etc. But a work of affirmation must contain its moment of despair—specifically, there must be a bad moment when the old man Santiago is tempted to cut the line and let the big fish go. Hemingway avoided the problem by never letting the old man be seriously tempted. Like a giant (but not like a man) Santiago just hung onto the fish—perhaps he knew that* Life *magazine was going to provide him with all the affirmation he needed.*)

21

mind. I never have good nor accurate interviews since I always seem to get into disagreeable situations with reporters—they sense no matter how pleasant I try to be, that I do not like them—I think the psychological requirement for working on a newspaper is to be a congenital liar and a compulsive patriot. Perhaps I should hire a public relations man to grease my career, but I do not know if I can afford him (not with the size of the job he would have to do for me), and moreover I would be obliged sooner or later to spoil his work. While there would be hardly a limit to how lovable he could make me in the public eye it would be exhausting for me to pretend to be nicer than I really am. Indeed, it would be downright debilitating to the best of my creative energies. So I do not care to approach the public as a lover, nor could I succeed for that matter. I started as a generous but very spoiled boy, and I seem to have turned into a slightly punch-drunk and ugly club fighter who can fight clean and fight dirty, but likes to fight. I write this not solely out of self-pity (although self-pity is one of my vices) but also to tell the simple truth: I have not gotten nicer as I have grown older, and I suspect that what has been true for me may be true for a great many of you. I've burned away too much of my creative energy, and picked up too slowly on the hard, grim, and maybe manly knowledge that if I am to go on saying what my anger tells me it is true to say, I must get better at overriding the indifference which comes from the snobs, arbiters, managers and conforming maniacs who manipulate most of the world of letters and sense at the core of their unconscious that the ambition of a writer like myself is to become consecutively more disruptive, more dangerous, and more powerful. It will be fine if I can write so well and so strongly as to call my shot, but unfortunately I may have fatigued the earth of rich language beyond repair. I do not know, but it is possible. I've been in too many fights, I've been hit on the head by a hammer, and had my left eye gouged in a street fight—and of course I'm proud of this (I was a physical coward as a child), and so I'm proud I learned a bit about fighting even though the cost may end as waste. There may have been too many fights for me, too much sex, liquor, marijuana, benzedrine and seconal, much too much ridiculous and brain-blasting rage at the minuscule frustrations of a most loathsome literary world, necrophilic to the core—they murder their writers, and then decorate their graves.

If I put down words so final as these, it is not in any sense that

I alone have been mistreated—on the contrary I have had more good luck and conceivably more bad luck than most writers (which tends to give one the hard satisfaction of knowing a little more of what the swindle is about). No, these ill-mannered bleedings and gripes are to record a clear record: I had the luck to have a large talent and to use some of it, and if I know how very much more I could have done if new luck had come my way, well—that is not my story, but everyone's story, every last one of us could have done more, a creation or two more than we have done, and while it is our own fault, it is not all our own fault, and so I still feel rage at the cowardice of our time which has ground down all of us into the mediocre compromises of what had been once our light-filled passion to stand erect and be original.

You can see then that this collection of pieces and parts, of advertisements, short stories, articles, short novels, fragments of novels, poems and part of a play comes to be written, after all, and for the most part, on just such a sweet theme—the shits are killing us, even as they kill themselves—each day a few more lies eat into the seed with which we are born, little institutional lies from the print of newspapers, the shock waves of television, and the sentimental cheats of the movie screen. Little lies, but they pipe us toward insanity as they starve our sense of the real. We have grown up in a world more in decay than the worst of the Roman Empire, a cowardly world chasing after a good time (of which last one can approve) but chasing it without the courage to pay the hard price of full consciousness, and so losing pleasure in pips and squeaks of anxiety. We want the heats of the orgy and not its murder, the warmth of pleasure without the grip of pain, and therefore the future threatens a nightmare, and we continue to waste ourselves. We've cut a corner, tried to cheat the heart of life, tried not to face our uneasy sense that pleasure comes best to those who are brave, and now we're a nation of drug addicts (caffeine, equanil, seconal and nicotine), of homosexuals, hoodlums, fart-faced Southern governors and a President so passive in his mild old panics that women would be annoyed if one called him feminine. The heat in our juvenile delinquency is matched only by the unadmitted acceleration of our race into cancer, that disease which is other than disease, that wave of the undifferentiated function, the orgy of the lost cells.

So, yes, it may be time to say that the Republic is in real peril, and we are the cowards who must defend courage, sex, con-

sciousness, the beauty of the body, the search for love, and the cap-ture of what may be, after all, an heroic destiny. But to say these words is to show how sad we are, for those of us who believe the most have spent our years writing of fear, impotence, stupidity, ugliness, self-love, and apathy, and yet it has been our act of faith, our attempt to see—to see and to see hard, to smell, even to touch, yes to capture that nerve of Being which may include all of us, that Reality whose existence may depend on the honest life of our work, the honor of ourselves which permits us to say no better than we have seen.

PART 1 **Beginnings**

ADVERTISEMENT FOR "A CALCULUS AT HEAVEN"

Before I was seventeen I had formed the desire to be a major writer, and this desire came upon me rather suddenly in the last two months of my sixteenth year, a time I remember well because it was my first semester at Harvard. All through December 1939 and January 1940 I was discovering modern American literature. In those sixty days I read and reread Studs Lonigan, U.S.A., and The Grapes of Wrath. *Later I would add Wolfe and Hemingway and Faulkner and to a small measure, Fitzgerald; but Farrell, Dos Passos and Steinbeck were the novel for me in that sixty days before I turned seventeen.*

In my sophomore year I wrote a great many stories which were influenced by Ernest Hemingway. Although I was more excited by Dos Passos and Farrell, it was Hemingway I imitated— probably because he seemed easier. To write like Farrell or Dos Passos would have required more experience than I could possibly have had at eighteen—to sense what is real in the commonplace is not easy when one is young, shy, half in love and certainly self-beloved, sex-ridden yet still weeding out the acne—no, it is more attractive to conceive of oneself as (and so to write about) a hero who is tall, strong, and excruciatingly wounded.

"A Calculus at Heaven" is about just such a hero. It is probably the best of the ambitious pieces I tried at Harvard, and it was the next to last thing I did—I finished it for my twentieth birthday.* In the year which had gone by since the war began, I had been indoctrinated like everyone else with the superheated publicities of the mass-media. The nervous system of every American alive

---

* *The very last thing was to try to start a novel about an insane asylum. I had worked in a state hospital for a week the summer before my senior year, and twelve months later, in the summer after graduation, I began real work on the novel which was finished nine months and 600 pages later, just before I went into the Army. It was called A Transit to Narcissus, and it was based on a play I had written earlier about the same insane asylum called The Naked and The Dead.*
Yes.

was being jammed with propaganda, and it may be that "A Calculus at Heaven" is most interesting in the way it shows a young, fairly good mind throwing off large gobs of that intellectual muck at the same instant that it is creating its own special variety of the muck.

This said, I don't see how I can recommend "A Calculus at Heaven," except for those who have curiosity about my early work.* The piece does make an interesting contrast to The Naked and The Dead, *for it is an attempt of the imagination (aided and warped by books, movies, war correspondents, and the liberal mentality) to guess what war might really be like. And I think its tone gives away the peculiar megalomania of a young writer who is determined to become an important writer—I may as well confess that by December 8th or 9th of 1941, in the forty-eight hours after Pearl Harbor, while worthy young men were wondering where they could be of aid to the war effort, and practical young men were deciding which branch of service was the surest for landing a safe commission, I was worrying darkly whether it would be more likely that a great war novel would be written about Europe or the Pacific, and the longer I thought, the less doubt there was in my mind. Europe was the place.*

So if a year later, in this short novel, I chose to write about the Pacific War, it was not because I was in love with the tropics but because 1) Americans were already fighting there, 2) the Pacific war had a reactionary overtone which my young progressive-liberal nose smelled with the aid of PM *editorials, and 3) because it was and is easier to write a war novel about the Pacific—you don't have to have a feeling for the culture of Europe and the collision of America upon it. To try a major novel about the last war in Europe without a sense of the past is to fail in the worst way—as an overambitious and opportunistic slick. (Which is exactly what tainted the considerable merits of* The Young Lions *beyond repair.)*

"A Calculus at Heaven" *was printed in Edwin Seaver's* Cross-Section, *which first appeared in 1944, and Marjorie Stengel who was his reader came across it first and liked it very much. She was to help me more than once over the years, and always deftly, but she was generous in her praise then, and Edwin Seaver was most decent —I remember that I saw him for a few minutes about a month be-*

---

* Odds are the only one of these college writings worth reading today is "Maybe Next Year," a good piece of Salinger-ish prose.

fore I went into the Army, and I muttered in a small voice that "A Calculus at Heaven" had been influenced by Man's Fate.

"You admire Malraux greatly?" Seaver suggested.

"I'd like to be another Malraux," I blurted.

"Well," Seaver said, with real kindness, "maybe you will, maybe you will."

I have not come remotely close—who has?—but Seaver's generosity and Marjorie Stengel's warmth helped to keep some idea of myself alive after I went into the Army. Through most of the Great Wet Boot which was World War II for me, I kept a cold maniacal thing in my heart, sharp as a shiv. I would listen to other G.I.s beating their gums about how when they got out they were going to write a fugging book which would expose the fugging army, and I would think in my fatigue-slowed brain that if they only knew what I was going to do, they would elect me sergeant on the spot.

A CALCULUS AT HEAVEN

Father Meary, April 1942, third day

> *He will not be a part-time thing.*

Sometimes they all were running, sometimes walking running crawling. All of them, Rice the Indian, Father Meary, the captain, cursing and stumbling; thirty men, gouging, elbowing, crawling through their narrow increment in space. "Come on," the captain shouted, "Come on, come on," and Father Meary looking back at him, stumbled and fell. In the distance, he could hear the guns debating still, fiercely as if they were intolerant of each other, and the sounds were breaking and bursting in his head. He rolled over on the ground, feeling the captain tugging at his shoulder, swearing at him. "Come on, we got to get to the house." He saw men passing him, running isolated from each other, and although the panic was in him too, he felt separated from them. Not understanding, he stumbled to his feet. Jogging after the retreating men, feeling the captain by him, motivating him through space by his presence, he told himself that the man should not have sworn at him, he was an officer of God.

He did not understand, everything had suddenly mixed inside him, burbled like the running mass of men, and what had happened back in the second trench line he did not know. For two days they had been holding back the Japanese, and then suddenly the trench line had broken, had gone, and he was running with the men. "Oh, Heavenly Father," automatically he began, and then the harshness of the machine gun, the mechanical signpost to death, had sounded behind him, and feeling a hand against his back, he had prostrated himself before the earth only to hear the enemy's cry of victory, pulsing behind him, working its way up from the beach. Then they were up again, running all the time now, dropping whenever a gun sounded, stumbling up the leisurely pitted street of Tinde. His prayers lost their logical sequence, became jumbled. "Hail Mary, Pax est. . . ."

Then himself, once more a part of the struggling ill-formed matrix of men running hoarse-breathed to . . . to where? He needed assurance, his plump hands wavering uncertainly away from his body as he tripped, and caught up and tripped, trying desperately not to fall behind the men running . . . running to where? The captain was leading them, the captain must know, he thought. The captain was a military man.

Under him, he felt his thin legs bend together once more, felt himself breathing in the dirt, the city of Tinde flowing into his material self as the sounds from the arena—the Roman arena, he thought—as the sounds came closer and closer, became embodied in the intolerance of the machine gun. He didn't have to fall, he thought, he was already on the ground. But the gun had stopped, and then he felt the earth careening away from him. After a moment he realized that someone had picked him up, carrying him with his head down, his face near the man's back. He watched the cross on his shoulder, swaying from his uniform, jerkily in an unholy rhythm, and when it fell off, he found himself gazing after it, as if it were a bird disappearing in the sky. When he could see it no more, he still kept his eyes focused for it, seeing the ground twist and recede under him. He was terrified; his head upside down, felt heavy and uncomfortable, the back carrying him was not broad

—he felt an augment of his fear. The men running beside him, was there terror at their faces too? The lines had broken, he kept telling himself, but how, but when; he felt his absolute sense of time leaving him. He didn't understand such affairs, he was a godly man, he did not know of such matters, but the Japanese had come through, their faces yellow with lust. The pagan men, they would not understand, they would not respect a man of God. He had lost his cross, they would shoot him with the rest. The smoke of death was over the city.

The gun came back, hovered about him; the man carrying him made a sound, lurched and fell. Father Meary fell with him, the two tangled in the dirt. He felt blood on his face, and turning his head on the ground, realized that none of the men were running any more, that they all lay in random prostration on the ground, while the gun and then another gun spoke angrily over them. Hearing screams, he could no longer feel that men were dying, but their souls . . . it meant . . . he thought of Conditional Absolution for them. There was blood on his face but he felt no pain. . . .

Once in San Francisco an unhappiness had come to him and had remained for many months. One evening in the winter, he had been traveling through the city and, feeling hunger, had entered unthinking the first restaurant he passed. The food was not expensive, and feeling his unhappiness more pointedly, he had ordered the highest priced dinner. The meal had been excellent, the waitress attractive. She had seemed to him a little bit like a Madonna from the school of Florence, and after the meal had been over, he had given her the dollar for the meal, and happy with her face, had added half of it again for the tip. He had noted the surprise on her face, and feeling happy he had said, "If there is anything I like, it is a well-prepared meal, well served, by a pretty young waitress like yourself." Embarrassed by the effort he had made to keep his voice deep, he left before she could thank him. Outside, he had suddenly felt more unhappy than before.

. . . The machine gun came back, licking at the bodies of the men about him. Overhead, a few planes distorted the sky. "It's a death trap, it's a death trap," he heard someone muttering beside him. The terror had worked its way into his finger tips; every muscle seemed to have sprung free, quivering loosely. The fact of his probable death came to him, and it loosed a new type of fear. Already, in the road, the *tap-tap-tap* of men's souls changing existences had begun. He was afraid, he had lived his life for the moment of meeting his death, and he was afraid. He did not understand— but why? And then all thought in his mind trailed out along the ground, and he could only feel his fear. After that, only the sun, warm on his back. The machine gun, indecent, angry again; God taking His inscrutable will.

Were they all to die here, lying in a road, while a machine gun worked from body to body, seemingly never satisfying itself that the body it was striking was dead? He saw a man beside him waver to his feet, throw a hand grenade at the machine gun. Somewhere he heard a shout, and then the grenade fulfilling itself. The machine gun did not sound any more. Then the men about him, on their feet again, running. On hands and knees he saw himself counting them, guessing they were ten or twelve, until abruptly he realized that in their run down the road he was being left behind. On his feet, laboring after them, shouting, "Captain Hilliard, Captain, Captain," shouting, and then he fell. Someone had run back, was dragging him; he felt dirt forcing against his face, abrading his plump white flesh. He was trying to hold back his groan, but then the pain ceased, the rough dirt changing to mud, becoming actually wet. He remembered. They were going into the stone house by the edge of the swamp. The sounds about him seemed to be changing, perhaps he heard a cheer. The man let him go, he saw it was the Indian, Thomas Rice; he must thank him. Another machine gun ripped at them from a hill, men falling about him again. Dirt was in his eyes, he could not see; in the terrible moment, he felt a hand pulling him; half crouching, he felt himself led to the cellar window, felt its rough stone sides scraping against his flanks as he crawled through, fell suddenly for two or three feet onto a pile of sandbags. Men kept coming over him, he crawled away. Still dazed, he was able to see a little out of his eyes. Someone had kicked him angrily. Looking up, he saw it had been DaLucci, but he could feel no anger. Was the man Catholic and godless? . . . Ahh . . . these Italians.

His situation came back more clearly. He remembered now that the house had been prepared as a defense three days before. On the edge of the swamp . . . it was cool here, if only it didn't become too wet. He felt himself drifting away again . . . the cellar walls seemed sandbagged . . . that meant less splinters, he imagined, it was functional, he was certain. . . . If only his wrist weren't so painful. He must have sprained it when he fell through the window. Were they safe from a cannonading, he wondered, and then abruptly, he sat up, panic catching at him. How many men left? He counted four, counted again, there were only four besides himself—Captain Hilliard, DaLucci, Rice and a blond soldier he did not know. Did it mean he was to die after all? He could see the Indian firing the gun, the blond soldier feeding. He heard him say, "That's it, Sergeant, give it back to 'em, Sergeant, give it to those bastards." The priest noted it numbly, long conditioning having accustomed him to the sound of the profanity. He wondered how safe they were, could the brick house really shut out the Japanese? Fascinated, he watched the sunlight glancing through the window, leaving the cellar almost completely dark. . . .

For months, Sister Vittoria had been treating him with especial attention, complimenting him on his lessons when he had prepared them well; looking sad and unhappy rather than angry, when he had played ball out on the street too long the day before. He noticed, even, that she spoke of him to Sister Josette and pointed to him often, as the best student in the class. He liked it; the kids used to call him "teacher's pet," but it didn't bother him as much as it had used to, because somehow, he had always liked studying a little better than fighting the kids on the block. So that when she called him over one day and pinched his cheek, and gave him a letter to his mother, he was not surprised.

His mother had read it slowly several times; he feeling shame for her at the unease with which she read. He kept thinking of how his mother didn't smell as cool and starchy as Sister Vittoria. But then his mother had looked up at him, from her chair, and smiled at him very happily. They talked a long while. "Be a priest, be a priest, Timothy," she kept saying, "and God will always be with you." He kept feeling how uncomfortable she was with the words. "It's an honor, do you know, it's an honor." Then later . . . "God will not be a part-time thing to be shared with a woman, and sure with a paycheck, but He will stay." And he, the boy, after a long while, "But I do not want to be a priest, Mother, I do not feel a vocation." She had sighed. "You will be the most important man of all your friends, you will be more important than any rich man; do

*you know what that means for a poor man?" He had shook his head,
unhappy. "Think of it," she had said.*

*Then two weeks later, Sister Vittoria had called him into her
private little study room. She had talked to him in her beautiful soft
voice, and he had been unsure beneath it. At last when she asked,
"Do you not feel a vocation stirring within you?" he had tried, contracting his stomach forcibly to feel some inner tenseness or emotion, as he was to squeeze it in later years when he looked at religious paintings. "I think, Sister, I think I do feel a small vocation
within me." She had smiled. "You are fortunate, Timothy, you will
feel it grow and grow, there are very few men who are godly
enough to feel even the beginnings of one." As he had been about
to go out the door, he had turned to her and said, "Sister Vittoria,
I feel, I think I feel it growing a little more already."*

Light red dust was filtering across the column of sunlight in
the cellar. He saw the Indian firing every now and then, saw the
captain speaking beside him. "We're going to save the mortar until
they bring one up; just keep firing the gun. We're protected here,
we'll be able to knock their mortar out first. Now look, we've got
to hold the road out there, there's only one other way to the coastal
road, and that's being defended by a house like this one . . . only
with more men probably."

Father Meary forced himself into devotion. Oh, my God, I
am ready to meet you, he thought desperately. But a piece of plaster
broke from the ceiling, its fragments landing on his chest, and he
felt death with it. Once, he had said, in speaking to the men, "There
are no atheists in foxholes. All of you do not have the same faith I
do, but all of you believe in the supremacy of God." "But, Father
Meary," someone had interrupted him. He had stared back coldly.
"When you meet your Maker, you believe. . . . You must believe. . . ." Then why this persistent fear? His tired mind fought
against relaxing, fought against the temptings of Hell. But the words
sounded ornate to him for a moment. Almost crying, he demanded
all the resolution within him. The men must not see him crying,
they would have their faith weakened if they did. And they would
have need of him in the house when the Japanese threatened even
more. He got to his feet; he would comfort them.

In the semi-gloom of the cellar, they were crouched against
the wall or under the window, firing the machine gun irregularly,

34

being answered irregularly. They did not seem to know he was with them. He slumped, feeling his resolution ebb. Three days before, in preparing the house they had dug a slit trench against one of the side walls. It would be better if he were to remain in it, where a chance bullet could not reach him. After all, he could not do the men any good if he were dead. And then mockingly, he felt his fear disappearing, as he dropped into the greater safety of the trench. He shut his eyes. Why, why had he been afraid; it disturbed the order of things, the certainties were not so . . . well, not so certain. But he believed, he was certain he believed more than ever. For with the horrors he had seen, well of necessity God existed, for men could not bear up under the horrors they saw, if it were not for God. He kept thinking of this, trying to strengthen it in his mind.

The silence disturbed him; he realized that the guns had stopped for a moment. Crouching in the darkness, he wished for them to start again, so that he could think about it and reinforce it even more in his mind. . . .

The Captain, 1926–1930

Two tight kids on a red silk coverlet. . . .

He spent his college life with the creative clique; surrealist poetry was in vogue. He drank a lot, he would be very happy for a while, and then very unhappy, but in back of it all, he felt a certain integrity within him, a certain feeling which made him know that he would paint, that he would slap the lie of America across a thousand canvases, that he would shove beauty into a million people who had never felt it before, that he would shake people up, stamp on them, blast their smugness away, and say, "Here, here is your graft, here is your marriage morality (a picture of a businessman sleeping with a prostitute, with a little locket on the canvas entitled 'Sister') here is your democracy (a portrait of a syphilitic Negro), and finally, here is your life (which was a triptych of a motion picture, a clerk, and a plain woman to represent the clerk's wife)." Only . . . in hating all this, he was reaffirming himself, for like all college men who stop believing, he was at the particular point where he was the only person who had ever realized a slum or recognized the lie in a politician's voice.

He had come to this endowed university, wondering, already beginning to disbelieve, but he was young and enthusiastic. (Later he was to say, "You stop believing in God at seventeen, in communism at twenty-seven.") Breaking from his family, he was to paint (it was not a new situation, he had read it in several books), but his father was an army colonel, and he had been allowed to go to this university only on the agreement with his father that he, Bowen Hilliard, was to join the R.O.T.C. and to remain in it until after graduation when he would have attained a reserve commission. So that in 1926, when of the class of '30, he was one of the forty-one freshmen out of eight hundred to sport the khaki uniform with the blue lapels, it was to be to him a sign of disparity as painful and unique as the soda jerker who from some outside compulsion had been forced to grow a beard.

Bowen Hilliard, not believing, made the university's literary magazine; Bowen Hilliard, not believing, was known as the best artist in college. Bowen Hilliard went up to Boston and picketed the streets before Sacco and Vanzetti were killed, and came back to write an editorial in the magazine which was to suspend it for a half-year, "Listen, America, listen to your shame. . . ."

He defended nothing intellectually, almost everything emotionally. He said, "The only thing infinite about man is his vanity," but he liked to walk in the streets, to feel people about him. He painted a great deal, read a great many books of art criticism, so that his painting was always conscious, articulate; he was one of the few artists who could explain his work clearly, and what it made him feel. He said he believed in nothing, and he enjoyed it, for he found that believing in nothing meant believing in himself, and at that time he was capable of it. Certainly, he was growing as an artist, his line (always his weak point) was becoming more certain; he had always had an acute sense of texture, but beyond that his canvases had a measure of structural feeling, unusual for a college painter. During this time he painted a discordant abstraction in which the color did not coincide with the line area, very much like a badly printed comic in a newspaper—and he had termed this his masterpiece and called it "Society Out of Whack." . . .

He was to believe in someone else by his senior year. . . . At a party, he met a girl named Cova—there was to be a lot of drinking—and somehow at the end, he was to sleep the night with her. Eventually they were to know each other very well, but in the

36

darkness only the crudest attempts were to be made. "What color are your eyes?" she had asked, and when he had told her brown, she sighed. "I thought they were blue, somehow," she said. Then she laughed. "Of course it doesn't matter. . . ."

The intellectual's passion is ramified by its implications; the artist's is augmented. Cova became an absolute to him, and, in many ways, since she was beautiful and intense and clever, and therefore was like his image of himself (the image of the artist), he was to become an absolute for her. In the last year of college, they had their unhappinesses, but they felt them more healthy, for they came from acute realizations rather than from a doubting of themselves.

They came to a certain understanding early, for she had other lovers besides Bowen Hilliard. "I can't paint," she had said, "and I can't write music, and I don't write nearly so well as I should like to. You must see it; when I take a man, and I may take him for a lot of reasons, in back of it all is the feeling that that is when I'm making something, and that that is something I can do better than any other woman. I don't envy you your paintings, Bowen, you can't envy mine. Some women are born to have a lot of men."

In a measure he understood, and by the time they were out of college and married, it even made sense to him. For he had found that she might take a man for a variety of reasons, because (although this was not often), he attracted her, or because the situation warranted it, or because she was sorry for him. (He once said, "You like any man who is under five feet four and has acne,") or in many cases because it was necessary in the evolution of the friendship, but always she had come back to him, loving him more, taking him more fiercely, reaffirming and even re-evaluating their absolute. She said to him once after a long silence, "We're like two tight kids on a red silk coverlet," and that was what they went by. That was what they believed in. . . .

The men, April 1942, first day

There was a dame once. . . .

Heavy with morning and the tenseness of the night before, the men lay encrusted in their double line of trenches, gazing out to sea. Tight and uncomfortable with a fear of butterflies and leadenness in their bellies, gazing nervously out to sea, out between the two arms of the harbor of Tinde. All through the night, polishing the weapons, preparing themselves, cleansing themselves with furtive finalities in every motion. Anxiously, eyes at sea, waiting, who will see the first boat? Looking with dry eyes and throat, tongues licking at the backs of dry and sticky teeth. What will it be like, what will it be like, Jesus Christ . . . Jesus Christ. . . .

The major in command of the three companies at Tinde had written a dispatch for his men that morning. It read:—

THE JAPANESE ATTACKED AT OTEI 0623. THE FORCE CONSISTED OF A FLEET OF ARMORED BARGES. WE HAVE RECEIVED A REPORT THAT HALF OF THE BARGES HAVE CONTINUED ON TOWARD TINDE. ANALOW ISLAND IS SURROUNDED BY IMPASSABLE CLIFFS ON THIS SIDE. THE ONLY POSSIBLE LANDING PLACES ARE AT HANSON BEACH, OTEI, AND TINDE. SINCE THEY HAVE ALREADY ATTACKED THE OTHER TWO POINTS IT IS A CERTAINTY THAT THEY WILL PROCEED ON TO HERE.

I knew this dame once, it was back in Albany. She was saying to me I know your kind, bud, they come twenty to the dozen, so I say to her, you count a funny dozen sister, why don't you come here and play dozen with me? Funny, she says, aren't you. I wasn't going to take that from any dame, I tell her, listen, after they made me, they threw the mold away, it was cracked from laughing so hard at my line. Well, she took it a little easier after that, but . . . I dunno, it was still no deal. . . . When the hell are they gonna come? . . .

WE ARE DEFENDING ONE ISLAND IN A CHAIN OF ISLANDS. THE JAPANESE DO NOT CONSIDER THIS ISLAND IMPORTANT ENOUGH TO SEND ANY NAVAL UNITS ALONG. WE ARE GOING TO SHOW THEM THEY HAVE MADE A MISTAKE. THEIR MOTORBOAT FLEETS ARE PROGRESSING FROM ISLAND TO ISLAND. IF WE HOLD THEM HERE, THEY WILL HAVE TO REVISE THEIR PLAN OF ATTACK. CONTROL OF THE CHAIN DEPENDS ON THE CONTROL OF ANY SINGLE ISLAND. CONTROL OF THIS ISLAND DEPENDS ON CONTROL OF THE COASTAL ROAD WHICH RUNS ALONG THE NORTHERN SIDE OF THE ISLAND, FROM HANSON BEACH TO OTEI TO TINDE. OUR MAIN FORCE IS AT HANSON BEACH AND WILL HOLD THE JAPANESE UNLESS THEY ARE ABLE TO SEND REINFORCEMENTS FROM OTEI OR TINDE. WE MUST HOLD THE CITY, BUT MORE IMPORTANT, WE MUST MAINTAIN CONTROL OF THE COASTAL ROAD.

There was this movie, Jimmie Cagney, I think. Did you see it when it played in town? 'Cause I saw it you know at the Strand in New York. They had a band there . . . I can't remember the name, only the vocalist with them was all right, I can still remember her. But anyway, the movie was all about war, only it was in France; there was no little island fighting in the last one ya know, and this guy Jimmie Cagney is yellow, it gave me quite a jump 'cause you know Cagney, but then I figured that it's anybody's turn to be yella maybe when it all starts happening. Have you got any idea of the time? . . . That picture gave me quite a smack, I ain't forgetting it in a hurry. . . .

IF OUR LINES SHOULD CRACK, WE MUST STILL KEEP THEM FROM TAKING THE COASTAL ROAD WHICH IS ABOUT TWO MILES INLAND FROM THE CITY AT THIS POINT. THERE ARE TWO STREETS LEADING OUT TO IT, AND WE HAVE CONSTRUCTED FORTRESSES IN A SEPARATE HOUSE COM- MANDING EACH ROAD. FOR THE RIGHT FLANK WINDOWS COMMAND EVERY DIRECTION. THE HOUSE ON THE LEFT FLANK IS THE OLD BANKERS STONE HOUSE, SITUATED IN THE SWAMP WITH ONLY ONE SIDE ON SOLID GROUND. ALL WINDOWS HAVE BEEN SEALED WITH THE EXCEPTION OF ONE CELLAR WINDOW WHICH COMMANDS THE ROAD. IF BY ANY CHANCE YOUR LINES CRACK, YOU MUST TRY TO REACH ONE OF THE HOUSES, THAT IS ESSENTIAL.

Tamping rifle butts slowly on the ground, snapping cig- arettes nervously against thumbnails, waiting, waiting for the attack, I dunno, I never saw action before. The end of his heel delicately clicking against the other, waiting for the fall of a little clod of mud. It kinda gets ya waitin', doesn't it? I wish there was somethin' to do sort of. Fingering at a button, moving the hat back and forth. These cigarettes taste kinda good, I mean, you know, you smoke 'em all, and they taste the same, and then maybe ya find one ya like . . . I dunno, you know what I mean.

IT IS NOW APRIL, FOUR MONTHS AFTER WAR HAS STARTED, YOU ALL KNOW THAT WE ARE UNEQUIPPED, WITHOUT TANKS AND AIRCRAFT. INSTALLATIONS ARE NOT EVEN A WEEK OLD ON THE ISLAND. HOWEVER, THE JAPANESE HAVE TO MAKE A LANDING, AND THAT ADVANTAGE RESTS WITH US. YOU WILL FIGHT FOR YOUR COUNTRY, THE GREATEST IN THE WORLD. GOOD LUCK.

Just where do ya think ya're shovin' that rifle? Get it out of my face.

Take it easy bud, take it easy.

Well, I like my face, see, I don't like it ruined, there're girls back home, got to go for this face.

I said I was sorry, what the hell were ya blockin' the path?

Listen, bud, you ain't talkin' to Joe Crap, see; you watch what you say with me.

Aaaaah, save it for the Japs.

Well where are they, well when the hell are they comin'? The goddam yellow bastards, what are they, afraid to fight? . . .

The Captain: 1931–1936

Something soothing, yet jolly. . . .

The year Bowen Hilliard married Cova Reynolds was the year of the unemployment march on Washington. They were not to do very well. His art was still improving, still powerful, still better than competent in execution, but it was not the year to sell paintings. Their friends bought a few, but their friends had no money either, and Bowen, hating the talk of price, had valued his paintings low, so that when his friends bought them, they said, "I'm sorry as hell, Bowen," and he took to snarling back, "It's all right, goddam you, it's all right." Cova had a small income from her family, which she increased with her earnings as a twelve-dollar-a-week shop girl, but he hadn't seen his family since college, and there was no money in them anyway.

After a while, when the country didn't come to see his work, and he knocked no people down with it, he began to get a little tighter. Occasionally he compromised with some mantelpiece art, but even that wasn't selling very well. The galleries were closing down everywhere. Once, in one of the back galleries in the fifties, a dealer had agreed to put on a two-week exhibition of his work. . . .

For three days they sat around, Cova by him (she had lost her job), and they would not speak very much until a friend came in. Then they all started chattering very violently, becoming satirical or enthusiastic in turn over painters, screaming platitudes on Munch and Beckmann and Marin, and then abruptly going quiet. The dealer, Mr. Loestler, was taking three hours for lunch by this time. They all knew it was a mistake. Hilliard looked at his fourteen canvases, at the gray carpeting of the dealer's office, and then muttered something about the light being bad. "It's killing them," he said slowly. "It's killing them, I tell you." Cova was pacing around. She turned to his friends, who were polite, sympathetic and enthusiastic to the best degree of taste, and said, "I still can't learn anything about when they're good or not, but they are good, they are good, aren't they?"

"Cova!" he said.

He watched her coming toward him, making the most of her red dress. It fitted with the carpet he thought. "I'm sorry, Bowen," she said. He gained control of himself. "It's all right, I'm sorry, too," he said.

Their friends left. Another batch would be coming in soon, he knew. The dealer's shop was dry smelling. "They *are* good," he whispered desperately to himself. He thought of their two-room flat. If only they would let him do something for the walls he thought. A mural perhaps, "The Artist Out of Whack."

Then the terrible event occurred. A woman came in to buy something. She was forty, had dark hair, and was growing fat. She wanted a picture for her children's room. "Something soothing, yet happy-looking. In good taste, of course." How many jokes had he heard like that. How many long tedious artist's jokes. She looked about for a while. "I'd like that," she said. It was an experiment with a Barbizon Landscape. Something about the composition of the field he had been in reminded him of a bad Corot, but beyond that, the entire view had been a little too rich, a little too green, a little too much foliage, almost as if any brown cow that had strayed into the field would have had its flanks of a deep purple to maintain the color order. "What is it called?" she asked. "Whore in a Green Negligee," he said. Cova looked at him in horror, a protest of poverty in her eyes. The woman recovered, "Well, I don't have to call it that, I suppose," she said. He held his anger, "No, of course not." Afterward, she bargained with him for the painting, making the final bit of bad taste in the artist-patron breach of etiquette, he decided. She got it for thirty-five dollars. He had spent two weeks on it. After that, when he could not sell a painting right away, he gave it to somebody, be it a boy roller skating, or a shopkeeper, or a laborer in a ditch. (He once said, "I have more paintings in delicatessens than any other representative artist in America.")

For four years he held on, working with the WPA for a while, but Cova and he were losing something. People no longer thought them clever and talented; men were not so interested in making love to Cova any more. As for him, she became the last outpost. Over and over through the bad years, he took her with a terrible kind of fury, performing almost every time, it seemed, a lover's last entrance. But they were depending on each other too much, trying to draw everything, able to believe in nothing else.

Once, when his depression had lasted for months, he started to write his autobiography. As a book, it was amorphous, but since he added to it from time to time, the brunt of his thought began to fill it. He would write; "Malraux says that all that men are willing to die for tends to justify their fate by giving it a foundation in dignity. Perhaps, everywhere, this is felt. But in America, men live, work and die without even the rudest conception of a dignity. At their death . . . well then they wonder what the odds are on a heaven, and perhaps they make futile desperate bets on it, adding up their crude moral calculus, so that if the big team, heaven, comes through, and wins and therefore exists, they will be able to collect their bets that evening. . . ." And much more like that, but he felt himself weakening.

He was to surrender at last. Cova's family had been architects for several generations, and in 1936 he gave up, accepting a job with them as a draftsman. After a year, by studying on the side, he was an architect of sorts. They were living much better (they could afford to live in the Village now), but he found very little desire to paint. . . . To make up for it, he worked on his book quite steadily. . . .

DaLucci, April 1942, first, second, third days

it's cheap . . . it's cheap. . . .

After the boats had come into sight around the end of the harbor, DaLucci hadn't known what he was doing for two days. Every now and then, though, he could remember them coming nearer, coming nearer, he wishing there was a cannon around somewhere, any lousy bit of fieldpiece to keep them away, but they just kept coming. A coupla Jap planes had started fighting with an American one and they had whipped all around the sky, going out to sea and then coming back. When they started to strafe the beach and the trenches he just sort of ducked automatically, going up and down with the rest like he was a goddam jack-in-the-box, or something, but he didn't know, Jesus, they kept actin' like they was out to get him first. He wished he could shoot something, but the Jap boats were too far away, although he could see them keep coming and coming.

His sergeant, the Indian, kept bending over the machine gun, waiting for them, whistling something, lining it up this way and that, firing it short, just a little *ta-ta-ta*, to see how it was working, but all DaLucci knew was that he felt just like puking.

Holding on to his Garand, he didn't know what to do with it. After a while, with them moving in all the time, he had picked it up, and started shooting, until someone pushed him down. Then the Jap boats started beaching, and the machine guns on each side of him started going, there was more noise than he'd ever heard in his life before, he didn't know, he just kept emptying and loading his rifle, shooting at them but not taking aim. When he looked up, he could see that with all their boats coming in at once, they'd been able to sneak one up on the shore. First thing, before their men tried to come out, they started lobbing with a field mortar from the boat, but then the machine guns on each side of him and all over the place had started cutting that boat to pieces, and even a coupla of their own mortars started cracking down. It mighta been Fourth of July if it wasn't for all that black smoke.

Only during all this, the Japs got a coupla of other boats on the shore, and they were shooting for all hell from the guns they had mounted in the front part of the barge. He ducked down for a second, scared, and when he looked up again, and started shooting, he could see that there was four boats on the beach now, with their guns all going, and mortars—he heard a whistle, someone shoved him down, and then there was a guy screaming his yap off next to him, falling down, holding his face. For a second, he thought the guy's blood was his own, 'cause it was all over him, but then he knew he was standing, and there was nothing hurting him. The guy was grabbing at his feet and looking up at him. He couldn't look at the guy's face, there was so much blood, so goddam much noise. "What the hell," he said, "what the hell, whatthehell," and then another mortar came, and he had to duck again. . . .

In Terre Haute where he lived in the poor part of town, the people used to have their coalbins under the sidewalk, with big metal plates, like sewer covers, over them. When the coal trucks

43

came along, they would unscrew a plate, and dump as much coal in as they ordered. The metal covers were to keep the coal from getting wet.

When they first moved in, there was no cover for their bin. A few years before, a cover had broken, and after that, whenever a family moved out, the house without the cover would take the one that was left.

He was too young to know this when they started living there, but the first thing in his whole life that he did remember was when the family next to him moved out, and they had gotten a coal cover for their house at last. Everybody in the family was very happy, and they kept showing it to him, saying, "Here, Tony, look, look, see the cover," but he was too young and hadn't understood. Not knowing why, he had struck at the cover, and started crying. When they laughed at him for this, he had a temper fit, and Mama DaLucci had had to give him a little wine.

For two days the whole thing kept up. The Japs kept losing men, and coming in, and where they had gotten four boats in at one point, they caused a lot of trouble. Everybody was working on them (and it was hard to hit them because only the machine gunner showed, and the Japs crouched behind the steel front of the barge), and while they were trying to take care of the four boats, another two had landed on the other side of his flank, and had gone over the barbed wire with mattresses, piling into a front trench and going like mad there. They couldn't fire any mortars into the trench, because the men were fighting too close together there, and then when another part of the front trenches half emptied to send men over to where the Japs had gotten in, the first Japs, waiting in the four boats, had emptied out, and captured almost a hundred yards of front trenches. From there they set up a fire so hot that DaLucci didn't even stick his head up for five minutes. But while this was going on, all the other Jap boats, or most of them, were able to land behind the part of trench that the Japs held. All the rest of the afternoon, the Japs kept fighting in the front trenches, and along toward night, he heard a guy say that they had control of the front trenches down the whole line. After that, it got so he couldn't stick his head up without going to lose it too, and the two trenches, not seventy yards apart had kept firing up and down at each other. For two days, he had been ducking into the dugout, catching a bit of sleep that kept being interrupted, choking down a chocolate bar, and standing around under a trench, not knowing what to do, afraid to stand up and aim that gun of his, but even more afraid of the sergeant who kept yelling at him to get up and shoot. So every now and then, he just had to close his eyes almost, stand up, just fire his gun, three or four times as fast as he could, and then drop back in the trench. He never saw anyone long enough to take aim on him like they taught him at target school. The three planes that had been fighting the day it all started, had crashed, he thought, but every now and then an American or a Jap plane would come out and take shots until another plane came to fight it, and then the two of them would lace it up all over the sky, sometimes twisting all the way out to sea, or maybe getting lost on the jungle side of the island. Once, he heard that a Jap plane had crashed in the swamp, but he didn't know about that.

After two days though, it seemed as if both sides were all finished, and everything let up on the morning of the third day. The lieutenant came along, and told them that half of them could get sleep. The sergeant had picked him out as one of them, saying it looked like he wasn't any use anyway, and he might as well sleep so the sergeant could have him off his mind. He didn't like that at all, but he figured it would be awful good to get out of that goddam noise and heat.

But after he got down to the dugout, he found that he just lay on his bed going tense all over. After a while, he turned over, and that seemed to loosen him a little bit, but all the while he could feel this anger growing in him, and not knowing why, he kept murmuring, "It's cheap, it's cheap." He kept thinking of his house and his job back in Terre Haute, and somehow that made him get angrier. He kept seeing the porch with the railing in the place where it had come off, and how through the years each of the vertical sticks that held it up were pulled off to fight with, or had worked off in the rain and wind. Even when the guns sounded every now and then, he was so excited he couldn't listen to them, but kept thinking of his old man, the fat . . . and here he started cursing him, sobbing a little between the words, which he pulled out one at a time from his stomach. He remembered the old man sitting on the porch of the house that was coming apart in Terre Haute, not even a drinking Italian, goddam him, sitting there all pooped out after work . . . after working twelve hours a day, breaking a length of railroad track in, making sixteen a week, sitting on the porch in his shirt sleeves, reading a newspaper . . . turning to the sports page, and reading it slowly, talking to his friends, telling old riddles to the kids, pinching Mama's bottom, with a huh, haw, huh, not even playing cards with his friends, just sitting there on the porch, all pooped out, just a fat hunk of flesh, talking about Italy. Frig him, frig him, frig the old man, he kept saying to himself.

A shell from a mortar cracked apart ten or fifteen yards away. Some dirt came flying down the dugout steps, and all through it he heard a guy give out a bunch of yelps that died slowly, like a dog he had once heard after a car ran over it. He kept thinking that maybe some of the guy was mixed up with the earth that was blowing in the dugout, and his stomach felt like it was trying to move around.

He sat up on the bunk sweating, and for a couple of minutes he couldn't get to relax at all. He lit a cigarette, and then after the first couple of inhales, he felt the anger coming back in him, only he started crying. A guy across from him in the next bunk sat up too. "Take it easy, bud," he heard him say, "let's have a cigarette."

"Shut up, you goddam bastard," he yelled. He tossed over the pack. He felt all funny inside, he kept thinking of the lousy jobs he'd had, first blacking shoes, smelling the stink of people's feet, smelling the stink of shoe polish, he could still smell it, it made him sick even now, being laughed at in school because he had the smell on him. (His fingers came up to his nose, he sniffed at them automatically.) Then, older, another job after another; washing dishes, balancing them on his finger tips when they came out of the machine and were too hot to grab hold of, picking up two-foot piles of plates and lugging them to hell and gone, working at a gas station, best pay to start thirteen a week, he'd worked there for two years, they gave him fifteen, Mary wet against him in the park, "Why don't we get married, Tony?" he getting angry and tight, "Aaaah, go frig yourself, I play it the lone way. Whata you got that I can't get for a buck fifty?" the guys hanging out on the corner, not enough money to go to a whorehouse, sometimes enough to play pool, what I say, you bastards, is get yourselves a trade, that's the way to make dough, stay off the railroads, they bleed ya dry, looka your old man, what I say is, "Tony, for crise-sakes, whena you gonn' fix that porch railing . . . ?" He sat up again, his head was whirling. "What the hell's it all about?" he kept saying to himself softly. "What the hell . . . ?" Only very softly now.

A soldier stuck his head in. "Come on, they're starting again. Get up here." Numbly he reached for his helmet, slung the pack up, grabbed his gun, and lurched out into the sky that was like the Fourth of July only blacker. The Japs were coming over, he kept hearing, and then he began to see it a little. They were doing it the way they had with the boats, charging first at one stretch of trench, and then while all the guns were working there, setting off at another, until there weren't enough guns to cover them all. Then finally, when they did get into a trench, and waited for the reinforcements to come at them, the Japs in the second trenches really charged over with all they had wherever the reinforcements had left.

An order passed down to his platoon to march on to another section, but before they were halfway over, the Japs started racing for the part of trench he was in. Just before this, his head still whirling, he had asked of himself furiously, "What the hell am I in it for, what for, what for?" and then while the Japs came over, he kept screaming, it's cheap, it's cheap, and something musta changed in him, because when the Japs started pouring into the trench not more than forty yards away, he hadn't given a damn about the sergeant or anything, he'd just hurdled out of the trench, and started running for the city. And pretty soon it seemed to him as if the whole goddam army was running with him. . . .

The Captain, 1936–1941

"I don't know, Bowen; we're rotten."

To believe in nothing was no longer a source of comfort to him. At the architect's office, the days passed slowly. He who used to argue that to analyze the relation of line to line without considering texture was an artistic affectation, now placed line on line, inserted textures where they were necessary, only now instead of painting cement-rubble, or reinforced concrete, he sketched in the cross-sectional symbols for them. In the drafting office, the men worked with their sleeves held up by little bicep garters, bending over the long stools, their heads lower than their shoulders. Several of the draftsmen sported spats. He considered this worth a generalization, and said, "Draftsmen are not happy unless they wear spats," but since the people he told it to had never been in a drafting office, they did not consider this particularly profound.

On most mornings when he woke up, he made a grimace. For in a short while he was to spend the rest of his working day transcribing one symbol into another, but he had not invented the symbols. A day at the introverts convention, he used to say to Cova in the mornings, but she rarely smiled at it. He realized that Cova held it against him, considered that he had sold out, and for a while remembering that she had wanted him to take the job, had talked her family into it, he was angry and hurt; but later, he realized that she had felt they were at an impasse, that more money was necessary, and that the opportunity had to be made so that they could refuse it, and reaffirm each other. She had told him to take the job because that was part of the balancing factor; he was to make his decision with the scales even. He knew now that she had wanted him to say, "We'll stick it, we'll keep the WPA job, I will not sell out," which was not to say that she was not tired of living without money, for she was, but the art, he realized too late, was what kept the two tight kids on the red silk coverlet.

One evening, they were out drinking in a bar with a friend, Henry, who had several parallels with Bowen Hilliard. They had all gotten quietly drunk on sidecars, until Henry had broken the silence by chanting over and over, "We are the people of the death-urge, we are the people of the death-urge." "Shut up," Cova had said, but he kept talking. "We are the people of the death-urge. . . . Sounds like Eliot, doesn't it, Bowen?" Then Cova had done something unexpected, reaching over and slapping Henry's face.

"No don't, Cova, don't hit him," he had shouted, and then all three had become conscious of the place they were in. Cova looked at him for just a moment, and then she was crying. "Come on, let's go," he said. "I'll be late at the office tomorrow, I'll be late. I gotta put in fifteen johns on the third floor of the apartment house we're planning." Henry had started laughing. "Sounds like Eliot, doesn't it, Cova? The artist putting fifteen johns on a blueprint." He had gotten up then. "All right, Cova, let's go. . . . I'm not an artist any more, Henry." "You can't paint when you're dead, can you?" He sucked in his breath. Henry looked up. "I'm sorry," Henry said.

"Forget it."

"No, I said I'm sorry. . . . *Don't* forget it."

After that, when Cova Hilliard slept with a man it was not because it was her act of creation, but because her husband had nothing left to give her. And he, knowing that, had worked harder at the plans for the tan brick apartment house, or had found a passing woman, or even had tried to paint, feeling the rage growing in him as the paint built up on the canvas, until the moment when what he had wanted to do would not superimpose over what he had done, and he had destroyed the painting.

They were reaching a point where they would give the last hard veer away from each other. Already they had broken up several times, but every time, frightened of the step from sensualism to irrevocable cynicism, they had stopped and come together. In one of these rightings, one of the unexplainables happened, and something of the old certainty had come back. It could not remain, however. There was nothing to hold it any longer. One night, very embarrassingly, he had come home too early. Even in the pain it reminded him of the triteness of the dark-haired woman in the art gallery. When they were alone, he had tried to talk.

"What's the matter, Cova?"

"Oh, go to hell, Bowen, I don't want any sharing of our mutual troubles."

He lit a cigarette. It was very necessary to maintain whatever existed of the situation. "You're not feeling very good, Cova, are you?"

"I don't know, Bowen, we're rotten."

How many times had he asked himself that? "People like us can't afford to go in for labels."

"Listen, Bowen, I'm not afraid of them, I don't mind the words. All right I'm not creative, I'm a bitch. That's still perfectly all right. So I'm a bitch."

He let some ash drop on his pants. Abstractedly, his finger rubbed it in. "I didn't mean that, Cova. I still don't think we're rotten. Maybe we had just a little too much to buck. Maybe two people do suck each other dry."

She had worked one of her shoes off irritably. "Look, Bowen, that's been on the wall for a long time."

He stood up slowly. "And after I leave?"

"I'm sure we'll be even more pointless than ever. . . ."

He did a lot at once after that; he left his job, he moved in with Henry (feeling the symbolism of it, but he didn't have to pay Henry any rent), and he finished his book, which in one of his recurring moments of anger, he entitled *The Artist in Transit Inglorious*. It was an angry book. Published by a wildcat liberal firm, it made him very little money, but it served as meat for more than a few of the family-newspaper critics. He thought of painting some more, but it seemed a little like a dirty joke to start all over again. He spent a year working from job to job.

A good deal of his time now, he tried to re-evaluate his life. He felt that somewhere along the line he had missed not a turn so much as perhaps a flubbed traffic signal, stopping when he should have moved forward. It seemed to him that in college he had been talented, clever, and even sincere within the limits of his life that he had defined. And it seemed to him that Cova had been that, too. They had not been mismated, and yet they had broken up, because in not believing they had had to expect too much of each other. If they had believed in something outside themselves, it would have been all right, but everything they had been told for the first twenty years of their lives had become on examination a piece of disjunctivity. The form and the matter had not coincided. So that having no end for their life, they had tried to get by on style.

It seemed to him that his life could be compared to the friendly quarrel over an after-dinner check; that when for some reason two people wanted to pay a check, the battle was always fought out by jockeying, so that very rarely would two people both reach at the same time and tear the check. It was like two trucks entering a one-lane junction at the same time. Inch by inch they might try to ride the other out, but unless the stakes were very high, there was never a collision.

Since in his life he had believed in nothing external, he had never found the stakes high enough to collide. By the time he had broken with Cova this had been so ingrained in them that even then, no great wreckage had occurred. It seemed to him that he had gotten quite far away from anything direct, and that the lack of meaning in his life might be explained by that.

In early 1941 he wrote to his father that he would like to take advantage of his reserve commission to enter the army. A half-year later, he was made (after reinduction school) a captain, by virtue of his age. He thought that the United States would be at war within a short time, indeed, that was why he had entered. He told himself that he had no illusions about the war to come, that his stake was personal.

He had entered the army, because at the end of his recapitulation of himself, he had come to the conclusion that to justify his life, to find some meaning in it would be possible only when he faced death. He remembered Malraux's foundation in dignity. It might be necessary for him to die to find that dignity. Certainly, he thought, life and death and violent action were the fundamentals, and he would find no lie there. He had decided that it was time for him to clutch at the check, even if it were to tear apart in his hands. He had traveled the bridge from sensualism to mysticism, but he preferred it to cynicism. And in the meantime, he wondered like the rest what the feel and sound of actual bullets was like. . . .

Wexler, April 1942, third night

He could just see it in the Freehold papers. . . .

Jewboy, blond Jewboy Wexler perched by the cellar window, tackling Japs with machine-gun bullets, tackling them dead, for the University of Minnesota. Swearing to himself, blond Jewboy Wexler, the Farmer from Freehold, New Jersey, the big blond tackle for the Golden Gophers firing machine-gun bullets, blocking tackling the dirty yellow team from across the tracks in Trenton, doing it for the big football team. The gun bucked away from his hand. Tearing after it, he caught the elusive runner, ran his sights on the incoming interference, hit them low with machine-gun bullets for hands, and got the ball carrier. They were a little team holding off the big team he said to himself, they were a little team, and the big team couldn't get to score.

"Take it easy," Rice, the sergeant, said to him. "You're wastin' your shots."

"Listen, Sergeant, I'm firing this gun."

A grenade splattered unsuccessfully against the outside wall. He started firing again. No half-Indian sergeant was going to tell him how to fight, he was born fighting, playing football for the University of—but he had to correct himself—for the Freehold High football team.

Outside, it had become dark, and the Japs looked like bushes, or like tackling dummies in the evening when practice was over. They were the little team, they were Brooklyn College standing off the University of Minnesota, they were Minnesota standing off the world. "Come on, you Japs, come on, you yellow-shirted bastards," he muttered. "Stop holdin', come on, start tryin' to nail me."

Every now and then he could get to see them, especially when they tried to cross the flat football field in front of the house; that was when the moon coming over the house's shoulder guard played him okay, that was when he could see the faces, that was when he could see death slapping them. It was just a spray, he was holding the garden hose on them, giving feed to the hens on the farm, making butter of the Japs. The Indian next to him, feeding, fighting quiet, not talking, he didn't like the Indian, dark, whistling, doing it like it was his business. It wasn't a business, it was a game, the most it was a business was a professional football team. Come on, you Chicago Bears, this is the Philadelphia Eagles, this is the Pittsburgh Steelers, and they're holdin' you on the three-yard line. A gun behind the other goal post tried to put its fingers in his eye. He ducked down, feeling the bullets pouring through the window, smacking against the opposite wall back of him. In the distance, he could hear guns going off, this was big, this was being fought all over the island. The machine gun kept chopping at the back wall.

"I tell you not to fire so much," the Indian said. "You spot them the window."

"Don't fire, Wexler, unless they come within a hundred yards, we can't have them hitting the gun." The captain came out of the trench, wiggled over to the window. "DaLucci, you relieve at the gun in five minutes." A sound of consent came from the dugout. "I don't like the way DaLucci's actin', Captain," the Indian said, "he's too quiet." "You're quiet yourself, Sergeant," Wexler let himself say. "Me?" Rice grunted, "I'm an Indian." The captain smiled slowly. "How many do you think are out there?" he asked. "There ain't many, Cap'n, there's just a coupla platoons." "There's more, Captain," Wexler said. He must have killed thirty of them already.

The captain looked worried. "They need this road, there ought to be more." "Yessir," the Indian said. The guns outside had become quiet, the moon making divots on the field wherever a body lay. Wexler felt caught. At home he had his field, he had the hens and the butter and eggs, he had the place outside Freehold where they played football on Sunday afternoon, the biggest toughest blond Jewboy ever to play football for Freehold High. The cellar was too small, he didn't like bein' caught here. "Yessir, it's a tough war," he said to himself. The captain took out a chocolate bar, broke it in three. They chewed slowly on it. "DaLucci," the captain said, "come up here." The Italian came up slowly, bellied over. The guns of the Japs were still quiet. They were scared quiet, Wexler thought. He focused on a few broken trees at the end of the moonlit plain. He said to himself that they looked like tackling dummies too, but they didn't. He thought they were too ragged to get away with that.

"I'm afraid the other house may be taken, men," the captain said. He separated a piece of silver foil from his teeth, and dropped it to the ground. "I need the sergeant," he said. "Father Meary obviously cannot be considered. I want one of you men to make a reconnaissance over to it. If you can get in, which I doubt, tell them we need more men. If you can't, come back, and tell me how they're making out. The most important thing is that you get back. The radio here is shot out. Does one of you want to go?"

DaLucci scowled in the darkness. "Naw," he said. Wexler spat softly on his hands, "Why not?" he asked. "I'll make it, Captain." "But get back." He grinned: "You bet, Captain, that's one thing I'm gonna do." The Jewboy running broken-field, the Freehold papers carrying the story.

He was starting out the window, when the Indian held his arm. "Wait," he said. "They're quiet now, they're looking. Stay back yet." Rice fired a few random bursts. The other gun answered, crawling along the outside wall, becoming quiet after a while. "All right, now," Rice said. "Keep to the shadow of the wall as long as you can. When you come to the end, I'll start firing, then run." Jewboy inched his way through the window. The air felt looser outside, and the field seemed enormous as he crawled near the wall, his face close to the ground. He felt excited, this was tough stuff. The air of Tinde was cold suddenly, he could see the trees shivering a little. He shivered too. Hell, he didn't want to be in the papers dead.

Creeping along in the shadow, the wall seemed to go for fifty yards. It was so damn light outside, why couldn't the Japs see him,

53

he could see them. He glanced back at the house. From his angle the window was foreshortened so that he couldn't see inside. It felt very lonely out here, no interference, no tacklers, just the Japs. "This is no damn football game," he muttered to himself.

Coming to the end of the shadow, he paused, crouched into a halfback's position, waiting for the ball. If that Jap machine gunner ever saw him now, by Jesus. Jewboy Wexler alone in the dark, playing games for keeps. The machine gun sounded abruptly from the house, cutting white lines into the darkness. The Jap gun answered, both of them throwing blocks; he started running, there was forty yards in the clear, if they ever saw him, it would be like stepping on stunned bugs. He ran. The darkness of the bushes forty yards to the side of the house's shadow came toward him, whipped into his face. He sprawled in them, resting, feeling scared. To be putting eggs in crates now, that was all he asked.

The other house was a mile away, he had to keep off the road. What if all the men, including the captain, were killed back there while he was away, what then? He would be killed with them if he hadn't gone away, he thought. Was Vera making out the invoices for the eggs now, he wondered, was Vera worried about the butter?

On the other side of the bushes, the ground rose and fell in gentle slopes, with enough trees sticking out of it to make it okay for him. He had to cut in back of the town somehow, he'd be caught going through it. Running quickly, from tree to tree, he headed inland. A patrol was coming by, and he stiffened behind a branch. After they passed, he felt the tightness pulsing through his legs. He had to relax; you broke a leg taking back a kick unless you were loose. If he coulda gotten to the University of Minnesota like he'd wanted, then he'd be a captain too, sittin' on his tail sendin' out the privates to see this and to see that. He crawled through some bushes. When he poked his head out the other end, it seemed like a tree was standing with its back to him, only it was no tree, it was a sentry. He lay there waiting for the man to move, but he didn't. Slowly the Jap turned around, then showed his back again. Jewboy Wexler caught in a trap. He waited there, wondering if he should make a sudden tackle. Could he get the guy before he yelled? But he couldn't get himself to do it, the legs gave out first, every good athlete got it in the legs first. Slowly, holding his body an inch from the ground, he began to edge away on hands and toes, one foot back, one hand back, the other foot back. When he was thirty yards away, he stood up in a crouch, and backed into the shadow of a tree. He wanted a cigarette. How the hell was he expected to go over a mile like this and back? In the hills, away from the ocean, a couple of machine guns were going like all hell. That must be the jungle already, he thought. The coastal road was at his right, but he'd never make it that way, that was where the Japs were fighting.

After a while he started going again, running, crawling at times, gliding from tree to tree. He felt better; this was the longest damn run any man ever made. No Minnesota back ever did this. If only they woulda given him that football scholarship, he'd be back in the cellar now, and DaLucci would be sweatin' here. The hell with the Freehold newspaper, what the hell good would that do Vera and him? They could use that Freehold newspaper for toilet paper. And he almost started giggling. It was soft paper.

He came to the top of a hill, worked his way through the tall grass, afraid to stick his head up. From the next hill, maybe, he could see the other house. It had oughta be away from the town, like the cellar was. He heard Japs laughing, slid on his belly away from them. Something, maybe it was a snake slicked across his face. He almost yelled. When the sound of the Japs came too near, he stopped, wondering how he was to breathe. He didn't have a big Jewish nose, that was one help, and he blew his nose that was another. Minnesota hadn't given him the scholarship 'cause he was Jewish, but for crise-sakes what was in a name? He had blond hair, didn't he? He was five feet eleven, fast, and weighed one-ninety before a shower. Jewish, hell, in Freehold they said he played like a big Swede. Swede Wexler, he thought, holding his breath. The Japs were passing. Swede Wexler waited, and then ran, duckwaddling through the tall grass. At the bottom of the hill he had to cross a stream, and his shoes started squishing. After a while, he took them off, and held them in his hand, while he worked his way up the hill. A butter-and-egg farmer, what the hell kind of a life was that for Swede Wexler, he woulda been a pro footballer by now. They'd heard of him all around Freehold, Asbury, Long Branch, he bet Point Pleasant even.

When he came near the top of the other hill, he got excited, he was gonna make it after all. The road and the house oughta be on the other side, but it worried him cause there was no shooting.

At the top, he felt his way around some rocks, looked down. The Japs were marching along the road, the house seemed broken in two, he could see a little fire in places from it.

Jewboy Wexler put his shoes on, turned around, and started back. There wouldn't be anything for the papers now, they paid off on touchdowns. There wouldn't be any ads to sign and get money so the mortgage could be paid off in ten years instead of the twenty it was amortized at. It was easier going back, somehow. He kept telling himself not to get sloppy, to keep blocking, or his head'd be off, and they'd be fryin' the fat from it. He wondered what it meant now that the other house was gone. The captain'd know, he guessed, although the captain didn't look on the ball either, but he supposed it was important. He kept tellin' himself to think of Vera cause he might as well think of the best friend a man had which was no dog, you could bet your life on that, but he felt all free and easy now, not scared of being killed, and he didn't need to think of her.

Before he knew it, he was sticking his head out of the bushes, and looking at the house with its windows all filled in, and the cellar under it, where the gun still was firing. He didn't know how to get back in there, he'd have to cross the part where the moon was, and he couldn't signal them to keep the Japs' minds off him. He guessed he'd just have to wait. The guns stopped tangling with each other, and then started again. He remembered that the Japs would be busy firing. There might be a coupla them stickin' out away from the guns, and they might spot him, but he'd have to chance it. He darted across the field in the moonlight. A couple of rifles started banging at him, and then just as he hit the shadow, the machine gun changed over toward him. He scrabbled for the wall, burrowed into the right angle it made with the ground, hunching his body up, hoping they couldn't see him. He didn't have time to be scared. The damned gun kept spraying around him. They didn't know where he was. The cellar machine gun wasn't going now. They wouldn't know where the window was. He ran along the wall, dived through the window, almost knocking the gun over, and landed on the ground. The gun started going again, and he crawled up against the wall, breathing as noisy as he felt now, sort of snug against the sandbags.

"Nice goin', kid," Rice said to him. DaLucci was firing now, the captain feeding. The captain made a sign, and Rice took over the feeding. "I wonder they haven't gotten a trench mortar up yet," the captain said. Rice grunted. "They ain't many of them, they just seem to be wantin' to hold us here."

The captain kneeled beside him. "Can you talk yet?"

"Yeah," he said, trying to get control of his heaves, feeling kind of weak and tired all over.

"What happened, what's at the other house?"

"They took it, there's Japs all around, they're marchin' along the road." The captain nodded, whistling tunelessly. "That's the answer, Cap'n," Sergeant Rice said. The captain nodded again. He bent down beside him. "Oh, and say . . . Wexler, ahh . . . what was it like?"

"What?"

"Out there."

"Oh," he shrugged. "All right, I guess. Kinda tough, maybe."

It looked like the captain was going to ask him something else, but he stopped. After a while he asked, "You're sure about the house?" "Yessir," he said. He was getting control of his breath.

All of a sudden he realized that the captain had bellied over to the dugout in the middle of the floor. He was coming back with Father Meary, the two of them crawling up to the wall near the gun. "Keep firing as usual," the captain said, "there's something we have to talk over." They were all huddling around the gun emplacement. "The other house fell, and the Japs are going through on the road. They don't need this house any more. Do you all understand me?" The priest stirred a little. "Do you mean, Captain, that this is no longer an important objective?" The captain seemed to be smiling. "Yes, that's right. . . . Now, they're not going to let us stay here. They don't want any little pockets left. So sooner or later they're going to bring up some small fieldpieces and blast us out of here. There's really no point in staying. We might be fighting them on the other road, but I doubt it."

"They didn't look like they was fighting," Wexler said.

"All right. Now I . . . for personal reasons," he halted. "I'm going to stay here. But since I have no right to ask your lives, any of you that wish may surrender. There's no point in heroics in all this. I will not consider it cowardice. Now which of you wants to surrender?"

The priest spoke a little nervously. "You say there's absolutely no point in remaining."

"Too doubtful a one to demand it of any of you."

Rice made a sound of impatience. "I been in tougher spots than this." The priest made a soft sound of indecision. "There will be a lot of captured men, no doubt?" "Yes," the captain said.

"The hell with it," DaLucci said suddenly, standing up, "I'm going. You can frig this goddam war."

"You, Wexler?" the captain asked.

He didn't want to be out in the open again. If they held, maybe he'd be in the papers, maybe. . . . He didn't know what the hell to do. "I'll stay," he said slowly, before he knew it.

"All right, and you, Chaplain?"

Meary got to his feet. "The captured men will have need of me. Captured men need God perhaps . . . more." His lips were trembling. "Are any of you Catholic?" he asked. . . . "Well, God be with you anyway." DaLucci and Meary knelt by the window. "Go out with your hands up," the captain said. "Don't yell, because they won't understand you, and they may think it's a charge." The priest crossed himself. Slipping the gun to the side, Rice put his back to the wall. "So long, you bastard, DaLucci," he said. "Frig yourself," DaLucci said, his short squat form heavy with anger. They went out.

All of them watched from the window. Wexler didn't know how to figure it. He saw them pass into the light, start walking to the Japs. The moon kept catching a piece of their hands. For a moment the priest stumbled, and then went on. They had separated from each other, and walked about ten yards apart. There wasn't any sound from the Japs. They had walked across the entire field almost when the Jap gun started. DaLucci went down first, then the priest. The gun kept playing over them for a few moments.

The first thing Wexler heard was the captain saying slowly, "I never thought of that, I just didn't think of it." A yell of derision came from the Japs. Wexler grabbed the gun. "Let me at those goddam bastards, let me at them, I'll cut their goddam hides off." Rice pushed him away. "Shut up, they had it comin' to them."

"Why, you goddam Indian," Wexler said.

"Shut up, both of you!" It was the captain.

Wexler stopped. The funny thing he kept telling himself was that he didn't really feel sore, he didn't feel much at all.

A Jap soldier came crawling forward cautiously to see if any men were left. Rice bent over the gun, sighting it carefully. He pulled the trigger for just a few bursts, then ran it back and forth on the fallen soldier. He catcalled across to the Japs. "Jeez, they haven't got anything, not even flares. This ain't so bad."

The captain was silent for a few minutes. After a long while he said, "What did DaLucci do before he joined the army?"

"He was a gas-station attendant, I think," Wexler said. "I didn't get to know him very well."

"Yes, I see," the captain said.

"Huh, why sure, sir?"

"All right, start feeding the gun," the captain said to him.

The Japs were holding back now. There just wasn't anything doing. He wondered how long they had been there, maybe three hours, that was pretty long for a little team to hold off a big one. But as he thought it, there kept running something else, and he couldn't keep it back. He didn't know why it was, but he kept thinking that it was more like they were the big team and they were gettin' pushed around by the little one. He didn't know if he believed it or not, but he wasn't sure of anything. He didn't know what to think. . . .

The Captain, April 1942, fourth day 4 A.M.

. . . like men standing in line, naked, waiting to be examined. . . .

He had seen death in many forms during those three days and nights. And to the captain, waiting in the cellar now beside Wexler and the Indian, waiting for the final irrevocable attack, it seemed to him that all his life he had been waiting for his death, and now that it was approaching, there might not be any meaning extracted from it. All day and night, for three days and nights he had been seeing men fighting and dying, and perhaps it had all happened too quickly, but all he knew was that it had no emotion or meaning to him. He remembered the burnt body of a man that he had looked at for quite a time. It had seemed a terrible degradation, as if the man in burning to death had reverted to a prehistoric type. He had been blackened all over, his flesh in shriveling had given the appearance of black fur, and his features, almost burnt off, had been snubbed and shrunken, so that the man's face in death had only registered a black circle of mouth with the teeth grimacing whitely and out of place in the blackness of the ape.

59

It was not inconceivable to him that his own death could produce a similar violation of his flesh, and yet he felt no emotion from it. It seemed as if for the past three days, he had been numb, numb, not so much from fear, as from a voidity of sensation. Lying in the cellar, his back against a wall, he wondered how long it would be until morning when the Japanese would be able to see the window, and could release a fire through it that would kill any of them trying to answer it. Under that morning fire, he knew, would come Japanese, bellying forward across the plain outside. He wished for a cigarette, knowing he could not smoke one till morning when its light would no longer be dangerous. About him, the Indian and Wexler crouched on either side of the gun, only a small part of their helmets turning the angle of the window. "Stop moving around so much," he heard the sergeant say, then Wexler answering, "I feel itchy."

Now that the forces of his life were approaching this final result, he tried to imagine what his death would feel like, and whether at the very end there would be some all-encompassing sensation. Feeling the night throbbing about him in the dampness of the cellar he was trying to find some resonating quality, some bit of beauty that would have meaning before the final result enacted itself. In this darkness, he was trying, as desperately as his mind would allow, to plumb the content of it, and throw it up against the form of his life. His hand reached out tensely in the night. To achieve the ultimate in his death, to reach out and catch it and pin it up against himself in death—his arm relaxed. It would not be that way. Nor would it be, he thought, in terms of a common denominator, it would be no more and no less of one than a group of men standing in line naked, waiting to be examined.

Wexler stood up and walked away from the machine gun. In the darkness, the captain could only hear him, but it seemed as if he had felt his confinement, and wanted some sudden release. "Listen," Wexler said, "Sergeant! Did I ever tellya how I got to throw a pass in the Red Bank game one year?" A grunt came from the window. "You know I played guard, you don't even get to handle a football that way, but we had this play see? . . ." The sergeant flexed his feet, "Get away from the window. You never can tell when I can fire this gun."

The captain counted three cigarettes in his pocket. In two hours it might be light enough outside to smoke. Wexler was rang-ing the blackness with his large feet. He stumbled over something and swore indistinctly. "You see the thing was I could pass. They ain't many guards can do anything with a ball, but ya see I got these big hands. . . ." He reached the other end of the cellar, and headed back for the window, talking slowly. The captain felt a desire to make him stop. "Well, they had this play built around me, where I shift into the backfield"—he moved a few steps sideward in the dark—"making me eligible to hold the ball, see, only it don't go to me, it looks just like I'm protection for the ball carrier, like I pulled out of the line for it, so they ain't worryin' about me." His body moved tensely now—"and then after I miss a block purposely, the ball's whipped over to me, I'm eligible, see? . . ." The machine gun started suddenly from the window. "Got him," the Indian said.

"So then I pull back, hold the ball up," his arm cocked, "set to throw and . . ." The Japanese gun answered through the window. Wexler folded slowly, his arm reared back almost to the last.

The captain stood up and, then, knowing the man was dead, sat down more slowly. "I told him, the dumb bastard," the Indian muttered.

"Do you want me to feed the gun for you?" the captain asked.

"It's okay, I can handle it myself. It's kinda quiet now."

They sat there silently. By turning his head and leaning forward a little, the captain could see out the window, and he suddenly understood, now that Wexler had died, a little more what his own death would be like. He doubted if he would feel anything. It would be as casual as Wexler's, with no emotion for him. Too late, it seemed to him ridiculously clear that emotion could only come from the connotations of experience, and not from the experience itself. Things like first sex experience, if it were unexpected, violent action, death that did not come after a slow sickness, would all give no emotion when they happened. The captain, having experienced the first two, remembered that they had left him numb; the emotion was to come later in tiny quanta until a week or a year later, the remembrance of the experience would arouse a surcharge of feeling in him; at the origin, however, was only the numbness. So that his death, he knew at that moment, would come in casual form without the death orgasm, the instinct for ultimate ecstasy never to be gratified. And to anyone else, his death would be meaningless. To Cova it would be a shock, to his friends, a jar that would merely titillate them because it was expected, perhaps would mean an extra drink at some late hour. To his nation it would be a line in some newspaper, far less interesting than the line about a murdered prostitute. To anyone else . . . he couldn't think of anyone else. Perhaps someone would discover his paintings. He smiled wryly. . . .

He kept coming back to Cova. Little by little a scene was building up for him. And because he could see so much of his own shadow in it, so much of what he might have been if the war hadn't come, he let himself amplify it, not paying any attention to the scattering sounds of battle outside. . . .

He didn't know how she would find out; he supposed, he preferred to have his father call because his father would be ill-equipped for it, and because Cova listening to his stumbling would feel compelled to exhibit some emotion while listening. After she would have cradled the phone, she would go upstairs to her room and lie down to think. She would be living, he thought, in a private house, perhaps a suburb by now, sharing the rent and fornications with a woman perhaps three years older than herself.

Lying in her room, her bed would begin to feel lumpy, and in shifting her position she would begin to cry. There was so much of herself in Bowen; she would feel a little bit as if she had died too. And crying, she would begin to whisper to herself, "I feel rocky as hell, I feel rocky as hell. . . ."

There would be a ring downstairs, and she would remember that she had an appointment that night. The first impulse would be not to answer, but she didn't want to be alone; the second would be to call the date off, but that would be just too damned ostentatious. After a while, she would run downstairs, and catch the man just as he was about to go away.

"I'm sorry," she would say, "I . . . I was just sleeping a little. . . . Come in."

He would be a man of medium height with a dark sensitive face. This would be—let this be his first date with her. He would be very interested in sleeping with her. They had met at a party.

"You've . . ." but he would not say, "You've been crying." He would smile sympathetically, leaving the admission or rejection to her.

She would throw her head back as if to balance the tears on her eyeballs, preparatory to absorbing them. "Oh . . . it's too stupid," she would say. "I just found out that a man I was married to died on some damn island. I used to love him."

He would say, "You must be very unhappy." His voice would be low, in good taste, calculated to serve for emergencies such as this one. Also, he would not have declared himself by the question. He would be finding out more about this woman, and if she held her husband's death in war against his civilian's bed-courtship, he would be turning her thoughts away from himself.

She would smile a little. "Oh, I've got a bad case of nostalgics" (she had coined the word once), "but they always dissolve in cointreau."

"It's difficult to get cointreau, nowadays," he would say. "Perhaps you would prefer to remain at home; our evening can wait for a week or two." He would be thinking that for this evening she would be loving her husband again.

"Oh, no, we must go out," she would say, but the false gaiety in her voice would be misunderstood by him to mean that she wanted to be alone with her rewarmed love, whereas she had made the gaiety false so that he would be indebted to her, and if during the evening she felt a letdown, no compulsion to be witty and entertaining would exist.

The man would make his fatal error here. He would say, "I know how you feel, we would hate each other. After all, while it may be a convention to mourn and stay at home, it is also one to keep one's engagements, and since you must be conventional tonight, it would be better to do what you want, which is, I think, to stay home." He would be thinking that she would remember the kindness, but even more, the insight, so that he could enact his seduction a week later when it would have a certain logical sequence, whereas on this night it would smack too much of a perversion.

She would recognize then that all protestations would only convince him the more, and so she would acquiesce, chat for a few minutes, and then close the door to go back to the empty house. Only now, wanting perhaps a little more to cry, she would not be able to, for the moment had passed, and the situation no longer would warrant it. . . .

63

He swallowed slowly. There was a painful saltiness in his nose, and he felt a sudden hatred for himself. It was occurring to him that he was emotionally convinced of his death, and he wondered at how far he had come to feel like this, amazed that he felt no fear for it seemed to him that the fear of death must be stronger than anything else in a man's life, and that few were the men who surmounted it. Perhaps, he thought, a few that were really religious or that believed in something hard enough to clamp down on all the other feelings, but he did not know. Perhaps to die for your country, but here the captain felt a rebellion in himself. For a long time, in his moments of reaction against his fate, he had postulated, rather than believed in, he had postulated a something to rail against. And that "something" had most often been the word America; he would feel sometimes, America has cheated me, but the phrase was uncomfortable; it sounded alien to him, made up perhaps of a self-pity he was not wise enough to realize. For although it might have been true, it was too large a word to attack; it sounded awkward, and perhaps a little cheap in the language of his logic. And yet now, he hated the word America for a moment; he felt that the wreck of his life had come out of himself to a great extent, but he felt also that America had cheated him, had taught him all the wrong things, and had offered him nothing in return. He felt that it had not been strong enough to admit its faults, that when it had made a mistake or was ashamed of something, it had yelled a little louder, and had waved the flag about a little too hard. He did not know, he wanted to believe in her, but he knew that was impossible in the hour or two that remained to him. But for some little part of him, he hoped idly that others would find something there in the next few years . . . that something would come out of the country, and that it wouldn't go hard and selfish as it always had before. But he was very doubtful of this, for he had never learned anything from America to make him feel that anything worth while would come after him. He had been told to love God, but to love God beyond the mechanical emotion of the religious ritual was for very few people; he had been told of an equality, but it was only a frame; he had been told of a morality, but finally it was not of the context of its people. . . .

When his book had come out, years before, all the critics had attacked it; they had called it cynical, and cheap, filled with an undue proportion of self-pity and glory, and he, months later, had had to agree with them that in most ways it was.

But one review hurt him terribly. There had been one part in the book that he had written honestly and sincerely; centering about one sentence that had been a summation to him of the futility about him. He was thinking of the war to come when he wrote it, and he had wondered that everybody had not seen it.

Only this review noticed it. He remembered holding it in his hand for a long time. It had read:

> There have been cynics, I suppose, less witty, bitterer and less unepigrammatically epigrammatic than Bowen Hilliard. It would be very easy to dismiss Hilliard as another misanthrope, if it were not that the man advertises himself as a sage. After deciphering his key sentence . . . which is . . . "To die in terms of a subsequent humanity is a form of emotional sophistication that may be achieved only by the people of that nation which puts its philosophy in action" . . . I have been compelled to believe that Bowen Hilliard's book would have been more accurately entitled, *The Artist in Belly-Ache Inglorious.* We have had enough rot these days. . . .

Soon he could smoke a cigarette, a last futile cigarette of distaste. And yet, amused with himself, there was a hope remaining that it would taste a little better than all the thousands preceding it. He was waiting for the dawn, wanting to see a last day, hoping too that he would feel this dawn more intensely than any that had come before. He heard the Japanese outside, firing, then the Indian answering, then silence once more. The Indian with his neat efficient motions at the gun aroused his interest. For a short while he thought of the Indian and himself in terms of "they" but he could not feel it. At last he compromised by bellying over to the window, and relieving him of the gun. . . .

The Indian, April 1942, fourth day 5.30 A.M.

Some guys are born to go to whorehouses. . . .

The trouble with Rice started when he was adding up his accounts. Perched by the window, his knees bent, feeling the tight roll of his bottom against the backs of his heels, he had just picked off a Jap who was trying to sneak down the side bushes, and in relaxing had thought to himself that that made fourteen he had bagged. Rice knew what he knew, he always used to think that. He knew when he had to hit a guy, and when talking would get him out of it; he knew how to tell when a whore was tired, and if you felt like talking (which wasn't often with Rice) how to pick out the right tired whore. He also knew not to think when thinking made you crazy, which is what made his thinking now so unusual.

He'd been trading bursts with the Japs every ten minutes or so, feeling it was the slack season. Naturally, he'd been fighting so long in so many places, he had gotten to the point where if he wanted to think he could do it while he fired a gun. And he had been telling himself with pride that of the Japs that had been killed, he had knocked off thirteen out of fifteen as near as he could tell. He had to admit that he'd been firing the gun more than Wexler or DaLucci, but then they'd gotten killed which'd meant no one spelled him at the gun. And he knew that your accuracy went down when you were tired. So it all balanced out, except that he couldn't figure what percentage thirteen out of fifteen was. He tried for a while to work that out, but he quit school too early at the Indian reservation in Oklahoma ("Where whores were born," he used to say sometimes), and he didn't have much luck. He was also thinking that they'd held out for pretty long, although the Japs only had one machine gun and no flares. The thing was they hadn't gotten any more guns because the main body was probably halfway to Tinde by now, he guessed.

He was estimating about how, for an afternoon and a night, they had killed off fifteen Japs to only three of theirs, and how at the very worst the last profit-and-loss would be fifteen to five. This was where the trouble came in. He stopped. He realized he'd been figuring himself in the five. That meant they got him, the Indian. It hit him that way, he hadn't figured on being killed since . . . since, Jesus, since the first World War. He'd been eighteen, and it had been in Belleau, or wasn't it? . . . All he remembered was that he'd been sick and scared, and now although there was something in his stomach, it wasn't anything like that. He felt kinda surprised almost, he just never figured it that way. With the things he'd done, the Marines in Nicaragua, Bolivia on his own, rumrunning in New

Orleans, somehow he'd kinda forgotten that you stood a chance of dying too. . . . He kept wondering what it would be like.

He had felt like talking; it had been a tired whore that night. Except that when he'd been in the room with her, sitting on the soiled blanket, batting his eyes against the glare from the bulb naked-looking in that room, he hadn't been able to say much at all.

They smoked a couple of cigarettes. It wasn't that she was pretty, he hadn't found many pretty whores, but there was something about her that moved him back three years, or up ahead to what he would do if they gave him a grand out of nowhere one day, no strings attached.

Finally she said: "You're a funny guy" (one thing was she didn't use "dearie"), "you never talk much."

He blew his smoke out. "I'll tell ya somethin'." He paused. She nodded at him to go on. He felt queer. "I had a lot of girls in my day, for a long time, but none of them was amatures. I paid on the line every time."

She still nodded, still receptive. "I tried to think it out once. I ain't a good-lookin' guy, but I'm awright. I finally figured it out that I started too late. The first time was at twenty-two, New Orleans, I think."

She lay back on the bed. "That could be it, of course," she said, "but I dunno, darling, the way I see it is just that some guys are born to go to whorehouses."

He felt dumb for talkin'. "Yeah, that's it," he said, and left soon after.

For a while he was busy shooting the gun off, and that took his mind off his troubles, as shooting a gun always did, but there was something uncomfortable in the back of his head all this while, and the first lull there was, it popped back again to him that he was going to get his, come two three four hours. That was all right, of course, you didn't live forever, but at the same time, he had the damn craziest feeling thinking about death, because he just couldn't guess what it was like. He knew you didn't think any more, that was obvious, but, you . . . you just didn't do anything after that. It was just the end. He fired his gun viciously, ducking down as the return came back. That meant . . . no more. It was like wrestling trying to figure that out, only with your head.

He wanted suddenly to know why the hell he was gonna get his. He just wanted to know what it was all about. They called him Creepy Joe around the army camps, and said he knew all the answers 'cause he never asked questions. But he had to ask questions now, because he was buying something that cost a lot. He'd never asked what the fightin' was about; fightin' was his business, and you didn't ask questions if business was good, but now he kinda liked to know. The papers said Freedom, and he guessed maybe they were right because that was something they knew about, just like he knew about whores, but Freedom . . . ? Did it figure with a slug in the belly . . . he didn't know . . . and by now, he was damn sure he wanted to know. He wanted it put in words. He wasn't scared of dying, but he wanted it down on paper, some of the reasons anyway. Anyway, he wanted, that in the fifteen-to-five ledger, there would be a remark after his name. He'd never thought that way before, but he could see it now, a business ledger, all written in, like the mess sergeant used, with something after his name, THOMAS RICE, THE INDIAN.

He felt a hand tugging at his shoulder. It was the captain: "I'll take over the gun now." He crawled away, propping his back against the wall. For about ten minutes, he just sat there thinking. He shoulda known enough not to think when thinking didn't do any good, but he couldn't keep from it this time. After a while he crawled back to the machine gun. The captain hadn't fired in a long time. He fingered a couple of bullets in their jackets before he spoke to him. "It's getting light out, Captain." He felt funny, he was talking just for the talking. The captain turned toward him. "They've brought another machine gun up. They're not moving, so I haven't fired." He felt himself nodding, feeling more like talking than he had in a long time. The captain said, "I think they'll wait till it's light out, they only have twenty minutes, and they can take it safe." He saw the captain slap his breast pocket. "We'll be able to have a cigarette soon," he was saying. The Indian felt uncomfortable. "Of course, there's a chance," he said, "we might have knocked them back; maybe we got a patrol coming up or something." "Yeah, there's always a chance," the captain said to him. They were silent. He felt himself having to speak, and he couldn't understand it.

"Think they'll win this island?" he asked.

"I never thought we had a chance to keep them from winning here. They had more time to get ready."

He nodded. He could have answered that himself . . . but . . . "Do ya think we'll win the war?" he muttered suddenly.

The captain took so long in answering, he wished he hadn't asked it. "I think so," he said finally. "We're taking a licking now, but we've only been fighting four months." He went silent again. "Yes, I think so," he repeated. "We have more men and materials, and you know, our allies are pretty good."

"Yeah," Rice said. He felt balked somehow. Not knowing what to do he took out his pistol. "Well, what are we. . . ." but the question was too damn lousy. "We *gotta* win, don't we?" he asked. "Yes, that's the thing," the captain said, "we're fighting because we can't lose."

He felt at his buckle. "That's all?" he asked. "Just because we can't lose? Isn't there anything else?" He felt just too damn dumb, but the questions hurt him until he got them out.

"I don't know; it's too early in the war yet," the captain said.

"Well, what about us, we're goin' to have to die, because we can't lose. . . . I don't know, I want more than that."

"That's all there is," the captain shouted, his voice going hard. "Now shut up!"

It didn't matter any more whether he talked. He saw the captain's face pulsing, and he didn't want to hear him speak. The captain got control of himself. "We're dying alone, Sergeant, that's all."

"I'm sorry, sir," he said.

They could see each other's faces by now. Across from them the bushes were beginning to change from black to green. "They'll be over very soon, Captain," he said. He just felt tired, that was all. "The trouble with you, Sergeant," the captain said, his voice drawn out thin, "is that you think it is one of man's inalienable rights to have a little idealism with his death. You wouldn't mind that, would you, Sergeant?"

"No, I don't know what. I'd like a cigarette, sir."

They lit them away from the window, cupping their hands. The captain came back and felt at the gun. "The sun's starting to show," he said. "We really ought to get the trench mortar out." As he spoke, the Jap gun fired at them again, and they both ducked.

The captain peered around the side of the window. "It's going to be one hell of a sun," he said.

"Yes," the Indian answered slowly, "sometimes you want to look pretty carefully at it."

1942

ADVERTISEMENT FOR THE "GREATEST THING IN THE WORLD"

It may be interesting for some of you to take a look at "The Greatest Thing in the World," which I wrote when I was eighteen. On the advice of Robert Gorham Davis, who then was giving a writer's course at Harvard, I submitted it to Whit Burnett's Story magazine college contest in 1941, and it won first prize. Probably nothing has happened in the years I've been writing which changed my life as much. The far-away, all-powerful and fabulous world of New York publishing—which, of course, I saw through Thomas Wolfe's eyes—had said "yes" to me. All the same, I'm embarrassed to read the story today. Crude, derivative of the kind of writing which was done in the thirties, I think it stands up only in its sense of pace which is quick and nice. Perhaps that is why it won—pace is found rarely in college writers. But how little real dedication it has! At eighteen Capote was already doing work which was beautiful, whereas "The Greatest Thing in the World" reads like the early work of a young man who is going to make a fortune writing first-rate action, western, gangster, and suspense pictures.

THE GREATEST THING IN THE WORLD

Inside, out of the rain, the lunch wagon was hot and sticky. Al Groot stopped in front of the doorway, wiped his hands and wrung his hat out, and scuffed his shoes against the dirt-brown mat. He stood there, a small, old, wrinkled boy of eighteen or nineteen, with round beady eyes that seemed incapable of looking at you unless you were in back of him. He stopped at the door and waited, not sure of his reception, examining the place carefully, as if he might have need of this knowledge soon after. It was a little fancier than the ordinary lunchroom, having dark, old wood booths at the left that fronted the sharp, glittering stools and counter of well-polished chromium. A clock on the wall showed that it was after ten, which might have explained why the place was almost empty. There was no one at the counter and the few truck drivers, sprawled out on two adjoining booths to catch a late dinner, were tired, and very quiet, engrossed only in their sandwiches and hamburgers. Only one man was left behind the counter, and he was carefully cleaning the grease from the frankfurter griddle, with the slow motions of a man who has a great deal of time on his hands and is desperately afraid of finishing his work, to face the prospect of empty tables and silent people. He looked at Al, uncertain for a moment how to take him, and then he turned back to the griddle and gave it a last studious wipe. He spoke, without looking up, but his tone was friendly.

"Hi," he said.

Al said hello, watching the man scrape some crumblings off.

"It's a hell of a night, ain't it?" the counterman asked.

"Lousy."

"It sure is. Guess we needed it," he said. "The crops are hit bad when it don't rain enough."

"Sure," said Al. "Look, what does coffee and doughnuts cost?"

"Ten."

"Two doughnuts?"

"That's it."

"Uh-huh," said Al. "Could you let me have one doughnut and half a cup of coffee for five cents? I ain't got but a nickel."

"I don't know," he said. "I could, but why should I?"

"I ain't had nothing to eat today," Al pleaded. "Come on."

The man looked up. Al sucked expertly on his cheeks, just pulling them in enough to make it look good.

"I guess you could stand it. Only, pay me now."

Al reached into his pocket, and tenderly extracted a nickel

from two halves of a dollar bill. He finished over one-third of the doughnut in the first bite, and realizing how extravagant he had been, he took a small begrudging sip of the coffee.

"Nice place," he said.

"I like it," the man said.

"You own it?"

"You're damn right, buddy. I worked to get this place. It's all mine. You don't find me giving anything away on it. Every cup of coffee a guy drinks feeds me too."

"Top of the world," Al said.

"Nyahr," he answered bitterly. "Lot of good it does me. You see anybody in here? You see me clicking the cash register? The hell you do."

Al was thinking of how tough his luck was that the truck drivers should be uniformed, which was as good as a NO RIDER sign. He grinned sympathetically at the owner, trying to look as wet as he could.

"Boy," he said. "I sure am stuck."

"Been hitching, huh?"

"Yeah, walked the last three miles, ever since it started to rain."

"Must be kind of tough."

"Sure, I figure I won't be able to sleep if it don't stop raining. That was my last nickel. Say, look, you wouldn't have a job for me?" he said stupidly.

"What'll I do, watch you work?"

"Then let me sleep here tonight. It won't cost you nothing."

"I don't run a flophouse."

"Skip it, forget it," Al said. "Only let me stay here a while to dry off. When somebody comes in, maybe they'll give me a ride."

"Stay," he said. "I have such a fancy trade. New chromium, brass fixtures. Ahhhhr."

Al slipped off the stool and sat down at a table in the rear, out of sight of the counterman. He slouched down against the side of the booth and picked up a menu, supported between the salt and pepper shakers, looking at it interestedly, but past all craving or desire. He thought that it had been almost a year since he had had a steak. He tried to remember what it tasted like, but his memory failed, and to distract him from the tantalizing picture he started

72

examining the spelling on the sheet, guessing at a word first, then seeing how close he had been. Another company truck driver had come in, and Al shot a quick look back to see where the owner was. Finding him up front, almost out of sight, he quickly picked up the ketchup bottle and shook large gobs of it into his mouth as fast as he could get it out. It burned and stung inside his stomach, and he kept blowing, trying to cool his mouth. Noticing a few drops on the table, he took a paper napkin, and squeezed them over to the edge, where they hung, ready to fall. He ran his little finger along underneath, gathering them up, and catching the drops in his mouth as they dripped off.

He felt for the split dollar bill, and fingered it. This time, he thought, it was really his last. Once, three months ago, he had five dollars. He thought back and tried to remember how he had gotten it. It was very vague, and he wondered whether he had stolen it or not. The image of five separate bills, and all that he could do with them, hit him then with all its beauty and impossibility. He thought of cigarettes, and a meal, and a clean woman in a good place, and new soles to his shoes, but most of all he thought of the soft leathery feel of money, and the tight wad it made in his pants. "By God," he said thickly, "there's nothing like it. You can't beat it. If I just had five dollars again."

He withdrew his hand, taking the two pieces out, smoothing them lovely on the table. He considered breaking the bill for another doughnut, but he knew he couldn't. It was the last thing between him and . . . He stopped, realizing that he had passed the last thing —there was no "and." Still, he did not think any more of spending this last bill. Tomorrow or tonight he would be in Chicago, and he could find something to eat for a day or two. He might even pick up half a buck by mooching. In the meantime he felt hungry. He stayed in the booth, staring at the end wall, and dreaming of his one-time hoard.

Three men came in to eat. Al saw them hesitate at the door, wondering whether to eat in a booth or at the counter.

"Take a booth," one said.

Al looked at them. This might be a ride, he thought. He waited until they had started eating, and then he went over to them, hitching at his faded gray-blue dungarees.

"Hi, sports," he said.

"Hello, sweet-face," one of them said.

"They call me Al Groot."

"His father's name was Groot," said one of them turning to the others.

"I ain't asking for any dough."

They eased up a little. "Boy, you sure ain't, sweet-face," one of them said. "Sit down, sit down," he said. "My name's Cataract, account of my eye, it's no good, and this here is Pickles, and this is Cousin."

They all looked alike.

"I guess you know what I want," Al said.

"Ride?"

"Yeah, where you going?"

"Chicago."

"Start warming the seat up for me," Al said.

They grinned, and continued eating. Al watched Cataract go to work on a hamburger. He held it between thick, grease-stained fingers that dug into it, much as they might have sunk into a woman. He swallowed a large piece, slobbering a little, and slapping his tongue noisily against the roof of his mouth as he ate. Al watched him, fascinated. Wild thoughts of seizing the hamburger, and fighting the man for it, deviled him. He moved his head, in time to Cataract's jaws, and he felt madly frustrated as Cataract dropped the last bit into his mouth. Cataract lit a cigrette, and exhaled noisily, with a little belch of content.

"Jesus Christ," Al whispered.

He turned his attention to the other two, and watched them eat each piece down to the very bitter end. He hated them, and felt sick.

"Let's go," shouted Pickles. "Come on, sweet-face."

The car was an old Auburn sedan, with a short, humped-up body. Al sat in back with Cataract; Cousin was driving. Cataract took out a pack of Luckies, and passed them around. Al took the pack, and fumbled with it, acting as if he were having trouble extracting a cigarette. When he handed it back, he had a bonus of two more cuddled next to his dollar bill.

"Where you from?" Pickles asked.

"Easton," Al said. "It's in Pennsy."

Cataract rolled his tongue around. "Good town," he said, extending his arm, fist closed, twisting it in little circles at the wrist.

74

"Yeh," Al said. "One of the best. I ain't been there in four, no three, years. Been on the road since."

"Hitching?"

"Hell, no," Al exploded with contempt. "It's a sucker's game hitching. I work the trains; you know, 'Ride the rails in comfort with Pullman.'"

"Yeahr. How're the hobo camps?" Cousin asked.

It was Al's turn to extend his arm.

They all started laughing with wise, knowing, lewd laughs.

"What do you boys do?" Al asked.

They laughed again.

"We're partners in business," Cataract said.

Al looked at them, discarding one thing after another, trying to narrow down the possibilities. He decided they were sucker players of some sort.

"You guys know of any jobs in Chicago?" Al asked.

"How much you want?"

"About twenty a week. I'm in now. Got thirty-four bucks."

Pickles whistled. "What're you mooching meals for, then?"

"Who's mooching?" Al demanded. "Did I ask you guys for anything besides a ride?"

"Noooo."

"Awright, then don't go around being a wise guy."

Pickles looked out the window, grinning. "Sorry, bud."

"Well, awright then," Al said, acting sore.

"Well, awright then, dig, dig, dig, well awright," Cousin mimicked.

Cataract laughed, trying to be friendly. "They're funny boys, you know, just smart. They wish they had your thirty-four, that's all."

It worked, Al thought. He let himself grin. "It's okay," he said.

He looked out the window. They weren't in Chicago yet, but the lights shining from the houses on the side of the road were more frequent, making a steady yellow glare against the wet windows, and he knew that they must be almost at the outskirts by now. Just then, he saw a CITY LIMITS and WELCOME sign flash past. Cousin turned off the highway, and went along for a way on a dirt road that in time turned onto an old oil-stained asphalt street. They passed a few factories, and Al thought of dropping off, but he wondered if it might not pay him to stay with the men a while.

Cataract yawned. "What about a game of pool now, boys?" he asked.

So that's what they are, Al thought.

"Say," he said, "I'd like to play too. I ain't very good, but I like the game." He had played exactly three times in his life. Pickles assured him. "We're no good either, that is, I'm no good. You and me can play."

"Yeah," Al said, "it ought to be fun."

Cousin was driving up Milwaukee Avenue now. He turned left, slowing down very carefully as he did so, although there were no cars in sight.

"That Cousin drives like an old woman," Pickles commented. "I could drive faster going backwards."

Cousin jeered at him. "You couldn't drive my aunt's wheelbarrow. I'm the only guy left who hasn't lost his license," he said speaking to Al. "It's because I take it easy when I drive a car."

Al said he didn't know much about cars, but he guessed maybe Cousin was right.

The car pulled up in front of a dark gray building on the corner of a long row of old brownstone homes. It was a dark street, and the only evidence that people lived on it were the overflowing garbage and ash cans spaced at irregular intervals in front of the houses. The poolroom itself was down in the cellar, underneath a beauty parlor and a secretarial school. On the steps going down, Al could see penciled scribblings on the walls: some hasty calculation of odds, a woman's telephone number with a comment underneath it, a few bits of profanity, and one very well-drawn nude woman.

The foot of the stairs opened right onto the tables, which were strung out in one long narrow line of five. The place was almost dark, only the first table being used, and no lights were on in the back. Pickles stepped over to the counter and started talking to the boss, calling him familiarly, and for some reason annoyingly, by the name Nick. Nick was a short, very broad and sweaty Italian. He and Pickles looked up at Al at the same time, and Pickles motioned to him.

"Nick, this is a pal of mine. I want you to treat him nice if he ever comes in again. Tell thick Nick your name, sweet-face."

"Call me sweet-face," Al said.

"H'lo," Nick said. "Pleased to meet you."

"Where we play?" Al asked. He noticed that Cataract and Cousin had not come down yet.

"Take number four."

"Sweet-face and me on number four," Pickles said. "Got it."

He walked down turning on a few lights. He stopped at the cue rack, and picked one at random. Al followed him, selected one carefully, sighting along it to see if there was any warp, and sprinkling some talc over it. "Should we play a rack for table?" he asked.

"Sure," said Pickles. "You mind if we play straight? I don't know any fancy stuff."

"Me neither."

They tossed a coin, and Al had to break. He shot poorly, hit the wrong ball and scratched. Pickles overshot and splattered balls all over the table. Al sunk two, shooting as well as he could, knowing that Pickles would notice any attempts at faking. They both played sloppily and it took fifteen minutes to clear the table. Al won, eight balls to seven.

"We're pretty close," Pickles said. "What about playing for a couple of bucks this next table?"

He watched Cataract and Cousin who had just come in and were starting to play.

Al could feel the sweat starting up in the small of his back and on his thighs. I can still get out of it, he thought. At least I'll have my buck. The thought of another five dollars, however, was too strong for him. He tried to think of what would happen to him if he didn't get away with it, but he kept remembering how it felt to have money in his hands. He heard himself speaking, feeling that it was not he but someone right in back, or on top of him.

"Make it a buck," he said.

Pickles broke, again shooting too hard. Al watched him flub balls all over the table, slightly overdoing it this time. They finished the rack, Al getting a run of three at the end, to win, ten to five. Pickles handed him a dollar, and placed another on the side of the table. Al covered it with the one he had won. I wonder when he starts winning, Al thought. If I can only quit then. They played for a dollar twice more, Al winning both times. A first drop of perspiration drew together, and raced down his back. He saw Cataract watching them play, juggling two balls in his hand. They played for three dollars, Al winning, after being behind, five to two.

He straightened up, making an almost visible effort to relax. "That makes six bucks," he said.

"Sure," said Pickles. "Let's make it five this time. I want to win my dough back."

This time Pickles won. Al handed him five dollars, separating the bills with difficulty, and handing them over painfully.

"Another one for five," Pickles said.

Al looked around him desperately, wondering if he could get out. "Five," he croaked. Cataract was still juggling the balls.

It was the longest game he ever played. After every shot he stopped to wipe his hands. In the middle, he realized that this game was going to be given to him. He couldn't relax, however, because he knew the showdown would merely be delayed for another game or so.

He won, as he knew he would, but immediately the pressure was on again. They played once more for five, and he won. After it was over, he didn't trust himself to stand, and he leaned against the cue rack, trying to draw satisfaction from the money in his pocket. He dreamed of getting out, and having it all to do as he pleased, until he saw Pickles and Cataract looking at each other. Cataract threw a ball up, and closed his fingers too soon, missing it. It came down with a loud shattering crack that made Nick look up from his counter. That's the signal, Al thought.

They were the only ones in the place now.

Pickles stroked his cue, grinning. "Your luck's been too good, sweet-face. I think this is going to be my game. I got twenty bucks left. I'm laying it down."

"No," said Al. "I don't want to."

"Listen, I been losing dough. You're playing."

They all looked at him menacingly.

"I want to quit," Al said.

"I wouldn't try it," Cousin said.

Al looked about him, trapped, thoughts of fighting them mixing with mad ideas of flight.

Cataract stepped toward him, holding a cue in his hand.

"All right," Al said, "I'll play."

Pickles broke, making a very beautiful "safe," leaving Al helpless. He bent over his stick to shoot. The balls wavered in front of him, and he could see the tip of the cue shaking up and down. He wiped his face and looked around to loosen his muscles. When he tried again, it was useless. He laid his cue on the table and walked to the back.

"Where you going?" asked Pickles.

"To the can. Want to come along?" He forced a laugh from the very bottom of his throat.

He passed through a small littered room, where old soda boxes were stored. The bathroom was small and filthy; the ceiling higher than the distance from wall to wall. Once inside he bolted the door, and sank down on the floor, whimpering softly.

After a while he quieted and looked around. The only other possible exit was a window, high up on the wall facing the door. He looked at it, not realizing its significance, until a chance sound from outside made him realize where he was and what was happening to him. He got up, and looked at the wall, examining its surface for some possible boost. He saw there was none, crouched down, and jumped. His hands just grasped the edge, clung for a fraction of a second, and then scraped off. He knelt again, as close to the wall as he could possibly get, flexed himself, and leaped up. This time his palms grasped hold. He pressed his finger tips against the stone surface and chinned up enough to work his elbows over. He rested a moment, and then squeezed his stomach in and hung there on the ledge against the window, his legs dangling behind. He inched the window open noiselessly and, forgetting he was in the cellar, looked down into blackness. For a moment he was panic-stricken, until he remembered he was in the cellar, and had to look up. He shifted his position, and raised his head. There was a grating at right angles to the window, fixed above a dump heap, much like the one beneath a subway grille. It was very dark outside, but he could make out that it opened into an alley. Overjoyed, he took his money out, almost falling off in the act, kissed it, put it back, and tried to open the grating. He placed his hands under it and pushed up as hard as he could in his cramped position. The grille didn't move. He stuck one foot through the open window, and straddled the ledge, one foot in, one foot out. Bracing himself, he pushed calmly against the grating, trying to dislodge it from the grime imbedded in it. Finding his efforts useless, he pushed harder and harder until his arms were almost pushed into his chest and his back and crotch felt as if they would crack. Breathing heavily, he stopped and stared up past the grating. Suddenly, with a cry of desperation, he flung himself up, beating against it with his hands and arms, until the blood ran down them. Half crazy, he gripped the bars and shook, with impassioned groans. His fingers slipped against a little obstruction on one of the end bars. His hand felt it, caressed it, hoping to find some lever point, and discovered it to be a rivet between the foundation and the grille. He sat there, huge sobs torn from him, his eyes gazing hungrily at the sky above. After a bit, he withdrew his leg, wormed his body in again, closed the window, and dropped heavily to the floor, lying in a heap, as he had fallen, his face to the wall. I'll just wait till they come for me, he thought. He could hear someone coming toward the door. Pickles knocked. "Hey, kid," he yelled from the other side of the partition, "hurry up."

Al stood up, a mad flare of hope running through him as he thought of the money he still had. He held his hand to his throat, and struggled to control his voice. "Be right out," he said, managing to hold it through to the end. He heard Pickles walk away, and felt a little stronger. He started to wash himself, to get the blood off. His hands were still bleeding dully, the blood oozing out thickly and sluggishly, but he was able to stop the flow somewhat. He backed away, glanced out the window once more, and took his money out. He held it in his hands, and let the bills slip through his fingers. Gathering them up, he kissed them feverishly, rubbing the paper against his face and arms. He folded them tenderly, let down his pants and slipped the cash into a little secret pocket, just under the crotch. He flattened out the bump it made, and unlocked the door to go out. His heart was still pounding, but he felt calmer, and more determined.

They were waiting for him impatiently, smoking quickly and nervously.

Al took out one of Cataract's cigarettes and asked for a match. He lit it, sucking deeply and gratefully from it. They glared at him, their nerves almost as tight as his.

"Come on," said Pickles, "it's your turn to shoot."

Al picked up his cue, gripping it hard to make his hand bleed faster. He bent over, made a pretense of sighting, and then laid his cue down, exposing the place where his hand had stained it.

"What's the matter?" Cousin snapped.

"I can't hold a cue," Al said. "I cut my hand in there."

"What do you mean you can't play?" Pickles shouted. "My money's up. You got to play."

"You can't force me. I'm not going to play. It's my money,

it's mine see, and you can't make me. You guys can't pull this on me; you're just trying to work a sucker game."

It was the wrong thing to say. Cataract caught him by the shirt, and shook him. "Grab ahold of that stick," he said.

Al wrenched loose. "Go to hell," he said. "I'm quitting."

He picked up his hat, and started walking down past the tables to go out. He had to pass three tables and the counter to get to the stairs. He walked slowly, hoping to bluff his way out. He knew he had no chance if he ran. He could feel the sweat starting up much faster this time. His shoulders were twitching, and he was very conscious of the effort of forming each step, expecting something to hit him at every second. His face was wet, and he fought down an agonizing desire to turn and look at them. Behind him, they were silent. He could see Nick at the entrance, watching him walk toward him, his face expressionless. Fascinated, he hung onto Nick's eyes, pleading silently with him. A slight smile grew on Nick's face. It broke into a high unnatural laugh, squeaking off abruptly. Terrified, Al threw a quick glance back, and promptly threw himself on his face. A cue whizzed by, shattering on the far wall with a terrific smash. Before he could get up, they were on him. Cataract turned him on his back, and knelt over him. He brought the heel of his hand down hard on Al's face, knocking his head on the floor. He saw them swirl around him, the pool tables mixed in somewhere, and he shook his head furiously, to keep from going out. Cataract hit him again.

Al struck out with his foot, and hit him in the shin.

"You dirty little bastard," Cataract said. "I'll teach you."

He slammed his knee down into Al's stomach. Al choked and writhed, the fight out of him for a moment. They turned him over, and stripped his pockets, looking for his money. They shook him. "Where is it, sweet-face?" Pickles asked.

Al choked for breath.

"I lost it," he said mockingly.

"It's in his pants somewhere," Cousin said. "These rats always got a secret pocket." They tried to open his pants. He fought crazily, kicking, biting, screaming, using his elbows and knees.

"Come on," Cataract commanded, "get it off him."

Al yelled as loud as he could. Nick came over. "Get him out," he said. "The cops'll be dropping in soon. I don't want trouble."

81

"What'll we do with him?"

"Take him out on the road where no one will hear you. After that, it's your imagination." He squealed with laughter again.

They picked him up, and forced him out. He went with them peacefully, too dazed to care. They shoved him in the car, and Cousin turned it around. Al was in front, Cataract in the back heat, holding his wrist so he couldn't break loose before they started.

Al sat there silently, his head clearing, remembering how slowly Cousin drove. He looked out, watching the ground shoot by, and thought of jumping out. Hopelessly, he looked at the speed-ometer. They were going around a turn, and Cousin had slowed down to less than twenty miles an hour. He had jumped off freight trains going faster than that, but there had been no door in the way, and no one had been holding him. Discouraged, he gave up the idea.

Cousin taunted him. "See that white sign, sweet-face? We turn left there, just around it, and after that it won't be long."

Anger and rebellion surged through him. They were taking away something that he had earned dangerously, and they were going to beat him up, because they had not been as smart as he. It was not fair. He wanted the money more than they did. In a fury, he decided to jump at the turn. The sign was about a hundred yards away; it would be his last chance. He figured it would take seven seconds to reach it.

He turned around to face Cataract, his left elbow resting loosely against the door handle. He had turned the way his wrist was twisted, holding it steady, so that Cataract would not realize the pressure was slackened. One, he counted to himself. "Look," he begged Cataract, "let me off. I ain't got the money, let me off." Maybe thirty yards gone by. Cataract was talking, "Oh, you're a funny boy, sweet-face. I like you sweet-face." Another twenty. "Yeh, sure I'm funny, I'm a scream," he said. "Oh, I'm so funny." The sign, where is it? We should have reached it. Oh please God, show me the sign, you got to, it's my money, not theirs, oh please. "Goddam you, please," he shouted. "What?" Cataract yelled. Cousin slowed down. The sign slipped by. They started to turn. Al spat full in Cataract's face, and lashed out with his wrist against the thumb. His elbow kicked the door open, and he yanked his hand loose, whirled about, and leaped out, the door just missing him in its swing back.

His feet were pumping wildly as he hit the ground. He

staggered in a broken run for a few steps, before his knees crumpled under him, and he went sprawling in the dust. His face went grinding into it, the dirt mashing up into his cheeks and hands. He lay there stunned for a very long second, and then he pushed hard with his hands against the ground, forcing himself up. The car had continued around the turn, and in the confusion had gone at least a hundred feet before it stopped. Al threw a stone at the men scrambling out, and plunged off into a field. It had stopped raining, but the sky was black, and he knew they would never catch him. He heard them in the distance, yelling to each other, and he kept running, his legs dead, his head lolling sideways, his breath coming in long ripping bursts. He stumbled over a weed and fell, his body spreading out on soft wet grass. Exhausted, he lay there, his ear close to the ground, but no longer hearing them, he sat up, plucking weakly at bits of grass, saying over and over again, "Oh, those suckers, those big, dumb, suckers. Oh, those dopes, those suckers. . . ."

At two-thirty, Al Groot, his stomach full, swung off a streetcar near Madison Street, and went into a flophouse. He gave the night man a new dollar bill, and tied the eighty-five cents change in a rag that he fastened to his wrist. He stood over his bed, and lit some matches, moving them slowly over the surface of his mattress. A few bedbugs started out of their burrows, and crept across the bed. He picked them up, and squashed them methodically. The last one he held in his hand, watching it squirm. He felt uneasy for a moment, and impulsively let it escape, whirling his hand in a circle to throw it away from the bed. He stretched himself out, and looked off in the distance for a while, thinking of women, and hamburgers, and billiard balls, and ketchup bottles, and shoes and, most of all, of the thrill of breaking a five-dollar bill. Lighting the last of Cataract's cigarettes, he thought of how different things had been, when he had first palmed them. He smoked openly, not caring if someone should see him, for it was his last. Al smoked happily, tremendously excited, letting each little ache and pain well into the bed. When the cigarette was finished he tried to fall asleep. He felt wide awake, though, and after some time he propped himself on an elbow, and thought of what he would do the next day. First he would buy a pack of cigarettes, and then he would have a breakfast, and then a clean woman; he would pay a buck if he had to, and then a dinner and another woman. He stopped suddenly, unable to continue, so great was his ecstasy. He lay over his pillow and addressed it.

"By God," Al Groot said, about to say something he had never uttered before, "by God, this is the happiest moment of my life."

1940

ADVERTISEMENT FOR "MAYBE NEXT YEAR"

"A Calculus at Heaven," it may be remembered, was done when I was a senior in Robert Hillyer's English A-5; "The Greatest Thing in The World" was the writing of a sophomore; and "Maybe Next Year" was written for Theodore Morrison's English A-3 class in the year between. As was mentioned in a footnote, the prose is Salinger-ish, but the inspiration was from Faulkner. I had read The Sound and The Fury *a month or two earlier and it had a long influence on me. Its first undigested force is obvious in "Maybe Next Year," but the style, or should we say the borrowing, appears again in* Barbary Shore *with McLeod's soliloquy to Lovett (a bit of which is reprinted in this book), and is done perhaps best with Elena's letter in* The Deer Park. *I do not mean that I was deliberately thinking of Faulkner while I wrote those sections, but now looking back, it seems obvious that the influence was there. And profoundly. Faulkner's style—which is to say, his vision—was to haunt my later themes like the ghost of some undiscovered mansion in my mind.*

MAYBE NEXT YEAR

The trains used to go by, used to go by very fast in the field past the road on the other side of my house. I used to go down there and walk and walk through the fields whenever Mom and Pop were fighting, fighting about money like they always were, and after I'd listen awhile, I'd blow air into my ears so I couldn't hear them, then I'd go out in the field, across the road from my house and slide down the steep part of the grass where it was slippery like dogs had been dirty there, and then I used to climb up the other side, up the big hill on the other side, and walk and walk through the fat high grass until I would come to the railroad tracks where I'd just keep going and going and going.

Why don't we have any money, we never have any money, what kind of man did I marry, what good is he, what good is he, look at him, look at his boy there, look at your boy there, look at him, he takes after you, look at him walk away like he never hears us, look at him, no good like you, why don't you ever get any money?

The grass sticks would be rough and sharp sort of, like sharp pages in a book, and I had to walk with my hands in my pockets so I wouldn't cut my fingers. They were tall, the grasses, and sometimes they would hit me in the face, but I would hit them back, only that used to cut my fingers, and I'd start crying, but I stopped soon, because there was nobody around, and I knew that when there was nobody to hear me, I always stopped soon, although I never could figure it out, because I always could cry for a long time, and say I was going to run away and die if people were around.

I can't help it if I'm not making money, my God there's limits to what a man can do, nag, nag, nag, all the time. My God I can't help it, there's limits, there's depression, everybody's losing money, just worry about keeping the house, and don't compare the child to me, the God-damn child is splitting us up the middle, I can't help it if he's a stupid kid, he's only nine, maybe he'll get smarter yet, I can't help it if he's dumb, there's a depression going on I tell you, everybody's losing money, there just isn't any money around.

The railroad tracks made a funny kind of a mirror. I could see myself in them, one of me on each side, I was so tall in them, but I was awfully short, as short as my arm, but I was awful tall, I looked as tall as Pop, except as tall as if I was to see Pop all the way in the distance coming up the hill to our house, when he looked as tall as my arm, but I knew anyway that he was oh ten times bigger than me.

Why is the boy always disappearing, why don't you find him, you haven't a job, you just sit around, you might keep him near you, you might teach him to be like you, and sit around all day, and make it easier for me so at least I wouldn't have to look for him, but you can't even teach him that, I never saw such a man like you, they didn't make my father out of men like you.

If I walked and walked along the tracks, there was a spot where I could get to a place where all the big slow trains came into town. If I was careful I could sneak up in the grass near to where the men who jumped off the big trains camped in the fields.

They were dirty old men, they just sat around, and smoked pipes and washed their dirty old shirts in the yellow water spot where I used to go swimming before Mom started yell yell yell about the dirty old men and wouldn't let me swim there.

They're filthy old things, you'll get sick and die, they're diseased, they're diseased, why did the town let them camp and flop in a meadow like that, right on the town limits, what's the good of living out of town when our only neighbors are bums, what's the good, what's the town mean, why aren't they put in the coop where they belong, why should they be flopping so near our house in a meadow?

I didn't like the men, they used to talk and laugh to themselves all the time, sometimes they would sing songs. I knew they were dirty men 'cause Mom said they would give me diseases, but one time I came up and talked to them, when I went out Mom and Pop were shouting, and the men looked at me, one of the old ones who was sitting on his old stork bundle bag sort of, got up and looked at me, he made fun of me, he said sonny got a dime for a poor old man to have some coffee, and then all the men started laughing, haw haw haw kind of laughing. The other men came around me, one of them said he was going to take my shirt and use it for a snot-rag, and they all laughed again, the big man in the middle of them making believe he was going to throw dirt at me only I didn't know he was going to fool me until I started crying, and he laughed too, and dropped the dirt.

That boy is going to get in trouble, why don't you take care of him, keep him around you, he goes off into the meadow, and God knows what those bums are going to do to him, they're all vile, they don't live like men, they're not men I heard, they're no more men than you are, both of you are, why don't you take care of him, he'll turn out weak in everything like you, those bums will get him in trouble.

86

Pop came over, grab-me picked me up, and carried me upstairs, and licked me, and locked the door on me, and then he went downstairs, and he and Mom yelled and yelled right through my crying. I waited and waited for them to hear me, but I must have fallen asleep because the next thing it was morning, and I didn't remember stopping and rubbing my hands on my nose to wipe off the crying. They unlocked the door before I sneaked downstairs, the front door was open and Mom and Pop were sitting around front, not saying anything, I hated them, I ran out the door between them, and hid around the side of the house. Pop and Mom came running out, they ran the wrong way calling to me, they were looking for me, and they weren't smiling, but they were talking nice the way they did when they didn't mean it, just like when they wanted to catch our dog, and that made me feel sad, and oh I felt just terrible, and then when they started coming back I didn't want to get another licking so I ran away without their seeing me, and sneaked across the road further down, into the field, and up the slippery hill, run run running way off until I got to the railroad tracks. I sneaked along them to where the dirty men with the disease were, and I hid down in the grass, and hid behind some to look at them, but they were all gone, there weren't any of them, but the old man who had made fun of me the day before, and he was lying on the ground crying and yowling like he was hurt or dead.

I walked over to him, he looked at me, he started crawling to me, I could see it was his foot that was hurt 'cause it was all bloody like, and bleeding near the knee. Help me kid, help me kid, he kept yelling.

Go ahead, hit the child, hit it, hit it, it deserves it, playing with dirty old men, hit it, it's a terrible child, it never listens to us, there's something wrong with it.

The old man looked like a snake, and I stepped back to run away from him, but he kept crawling after me, yelling don't go away kid, I won't hurt you, please don't go way kid, but he looked like a snake, only bleeding. I yelled at him, I said go away, you're a dirty old man, but he wouldn't stop, and I picked up a rock, and threw it at him, it missed him, but I threw another rock, and it hit him in the head, he stopped moving to me, he was crying something terrible, there was a lot of blood all over his face.

Why kid, why kid, why kid, why hit me?

You're a dirty old man, leave me alone, I don't like you, you're a dirty old man.

Kid for God's sakes help me, I'm going crazy kid, don't leave me here, it's hot here kid, it's hot here kid.

Then I picked up a stone, and threw it at him again, only I didn't see if it hit him because I was running away. I heard him crying, screaming, and I was scared, but I kept running, and then I said I hate them, I hate them, the grass kept cutting at me, I couldn't run with my hands in my pockets, kept cutting at me and cutting at me, I fell down, and then I got up and kept running home.

I walked down the last part of the hill, and across the road, and when I got back Mom and Pop were sitting around again, and I started crying. I cried and cried, they asked me what's the matter, what's the matter with you, why are you crying, but I just kept saying the dirty old man, the dirty old man.

And Mom said I thought they all were kicked out of town, I don't know how any of them were left, you're not lying?

I'm not lying, I'm not lying.

And Pop got up, and said to Mom I told you not to do it, you get an idea in your head, and you can't stop, those men were beaten, I don't know how any were left in the dark, we had flashlights, but there might have been, it's the boy's own fault, he had no business going around there today, and anyway he wasn't hurt, he didn't start crying until he saw us, I saw him before he saw me.

And Mom said, if you were a man you'd go over there now, and finish them off, you wouldn't even go last night without any help, if I were a man I'd thrash the man that touched my boy, but you just sit there and talk talk talk that it's the boy's fault.

Pop got up, and walked around and around, and he said it isn't the boy's fault, but it isn't the man's either, and then he stood up, and said I'm not going to do anything about it, what with the boy between us, and the job ruined, and everything God-damn else, I might be one of them myself, maybe next year, and then Pop stood up and walked off down the road only farther out of town, not the way the old man was. I could see that Pop's shoulders were screwed up around his neck, and then I was happy, because all I could think of was that I'd seen two big men cry that day, and maybe that meant I was getting bigger too, and that was an awful good feeling.

1941

PART 2　**Middles**

SECOND ADVERTISEMENT FOR MYSELF:
BARBARY SHORE

Once it became obvious that The Naked and The Dead *was going to be a best seller, and I would therefore receive that small fame which comes upon any young American who makes a great deal of money in a hurry, I remember that a depression set in on me. I was twenty-five, living in Paris with my first wife, Beatrice, and I had gone through a long leaky French winter in which I discovered once again that I knew very little and had everything still to learn. So I think I probably had been hoping* The Naked and The Dead *would have a modest success, that everyone who read it would think it was extraordinary, but nonetheless the book would not change my life too much. I wished at that time to protect a modest condition. Many of my habits, even the character of my talent, depended on my humility—that word which has become part of the void in our time. I had had humility breathed into me by the war. After four serious years of taking myself seriously at Harvard, the army gave me but one lesson over and over again: when it came to taking care of myself, I had little to offer next to the practical sense of an illiterate sharecropper. Sometimes I think courage is the most exhaustible of the virtues, and I used up a share of mine in getting through the war with my lip buttoned, since it took all of me to be at best a fair rifleman. No surprise then if I was a modest young man when it was all over. I knew I was not much better and I was conceivably a little less than most of the men I had come to know. At least a large part of me felt that way, and it was the part in command while I was writing* The Naked and The Dead.

But once free of the army, I came back to some good luck. My first wife and I had saved some money during the war, and I did not have to work for a year. She believed in me and my family believed in me, and I was able to do my book. The Naked and The Dead *flowed—I used to write twenty-five pages of first draft a week, and with a few weeks lost here and there, I still was able to*

*write the novel and rewrite it in fifteen months, and I doubt if ever
again I will have a book which is so easy to write. When once in a
while I look at a page or two these days, I like its confidence—it
seems to be at dead center—"Yes," it is always saying, "this is about
the way it is."*

*Naturally, I was blasted a considerable distance away from
dead center by the size of its success, and I spent the next few years
trying to gobble up the experiences of a victorious man when I was
still no man at all, and had no real gift for enjoying life. Such a gift
usually comes from a series of small victories artfully achieved; my
experience had consisted of many small defeats, a few victories, and
one explosion. So success furnished me great energy, but I wasted
most of it in the gears of old habit, and had experience which was
overheated, brilliant, anxious, gauche, grim—even, I suspect—killing. My farewell to an average man's experience was too abrupt;
never again would I know, in the dreary way one usually knows
such things, what it was like to work at a dull job, or take orders
from a man one hated. If I had had a career of that in the army, it
now was done—there was nothing left in the first twenty-four years
of my life to write about; one way or another, my life seemed to
have been mined and melted into the long reaches of the book. And
so I was prominent and empty, and I had to begin life again; from
now on, people who knew me would never be able to react to me
as a person whom they liked or disliked in small ways, for myself
alone (the inevitable phrase of all tear-filled confessions); no, I was
a node in a new electronic landscape of celebrity, personality and
status. Other people, meeting me, could now unconsciously measure
their own status by sensing how I reacted to them. I had been moved
from the audience to the stage—I was, on the instant, a man—I
could arouse more emotion in others than they could arouse in me;
if I had once been a cool observer because some part of me knew
that I had more emotion than most and so must protect myself with
a cold eye, now I had to guard against arousing the emotions of
others, particularly since I had a strong conscience, and a strong
desire to do just that—exhaust the emotions of others. If there I was,
with two more-than-average passions going in opposed directions,
I was obviously a slave to anxiety, a slave to the fear that I could
measure my death with every evening on the town, for the town
was filled with people who were wired with shocks for the small
electrocution of oneself. It is exhausting to live in a psychic land-*

scape of assassins and victims: if once I had been a young man whom many did not notice, and so was able to take a delayed revenge—in my writing I could analyze the ones who neglected to look at me—now I came to know that I could bestow the cold tension of self-hatred, or the warmth of liking oneself again, to whichever friends, acquaintances, and strangers were weak, ambitious, vulnerable and in love with themselves—which must be of course half the horde of my talented generation.

This was experience unlike the experience I had learned from books, and from the war—this was experience without a name—at the time I used to complain that everything was unreal. It took me years to realize that it was my experience, the only one I would have to remember, that my apparently unconnected rat-scufflings and ego-gobblings could be fitted finally into a drastic vision, an introduction of the brave to the horrible, a dream, a nightmare which would belong to others and yet be my own. Willy-nilly I had had existentialism forced upon me. I was free, or at least whatever was still ready to change in my character had escaped from the social obligations which suffocate others. I could seek to become what I chose to be, and if I failed—there was the ice pick of fear! I would have nothing to excuse failure. I would fail because I had not been brave enough to succeed. So I was much too free. Success had been a lobotomy to my past, there seemed no power from the past which could help me in the present, and I had no choice but to force myself to step into the war of the enormous present, to accept the private heat and fatigue of setting out by myself to cut a track through a new wild.

Now of course this way of describing my past has a protective elegance. I could as well have described the years which followed the appearance of The Naked and The Dead *by saying that I traveled scared, excited, and nervous, ridden by the question which everyone else was ready to ask and which I was forever asking of myself: had this first published novel been all of my talent? Or would my next book be better?*

In a sense, I may have tried to evade the question by writing Barbary Shore, *but there was no real choice. If my past had become empty as a theme, was I to write about Brooklyn streets, or my mother and father, or another war novel (*The Naked and The Dead Go to Japan*) was I to do the book of the returning veteran when I had lived like a mole writing and rewriting seven hundred pages*

*in those fifteen months? No, those were not real choices. I was
drawn instead to write about an imaginary future which was formed
osmotically by the powerful intellectual influence of my friend Jean
Malaquais, and by the books I had read, and the aesthetics I considered desirable, but* Barbary Shore *was really a book to emerge from
the bombarded cellars of my unconscious, an agonized eye of a novel
which tried to find some amalgam of my new experience and the
larger horror of that world which might be preparing to destroy
itself. I was obviously trying for something which was at the very
end of my reach, and then beyond it, and toward the end the novel
collapsed into a chapter of political speech and never quite recovered. Yet, it could be that if my work is alive one hundred years
from now,* Barbary Shore *will be considered the richest of my first
three novels for it has in its high fevers a kind of insane insight into
the psychic mysteries of Stalinists, secret policemen, narcissists,
children, Lesbians, hysterics, revolutionaries—it has an air which
for me is the air of our time, authority and nihilism stalking one
another in the orgiastic hollow of this century. I suppose it is a
mistake to indulge myself, but I would like to put in some pages of
excerpts from the novel, because few people who like my work
have read it, and yet much of my later writing cannot be understood without a glimpse of the odd shadow and theme-maddened
light* Barbary Shore *casts before it.*

McLeod and Lovett

Once I mentioned a girl with whom I had recently had an
affair, and I shrugged and said, "But it didn't mean much. We got a
little bored with each other, and drifted out of it."

McLeod gave his sly grin, the side of his mouth sucking on
the imaginary candy drop. "You drifted out of it, eh?"

Irritably, I snapped, "Yes, I drifted out of it. Didn't you ever
hear of anything like that?"

"Yes, I've heard of it. I hear it all the time. People are always
drifting in and out of things." He leaned back on the bed, and

94

pressed his finger tips together. "I'll tell you the truth, Lovett, I don't know what those words mean. 'Drifted in and out, drifted in and out,'" he repeated as though the phrase were delicious. "When you have to, it's pretty convenient to think of yourself as driftwood."

"I can explain it to you."

"Oh," he said, grinning, "I know you can explain it to me. I just want to try to figure out m'self what it signified drifting out of an affair. Because in the old days when I used to cut a figure with the women, I had my share of it, and it seems to me now that when I broke up with a woman it was often somewhat nasty."

"With a sadist like you," I said in an attempt at humor. My answers were invariably dull, my temper ragged. He had a facility for wearing one down, and it was not surprising that when I swung I was wild.

McLeod nodded. "Oh, yes. When I'd examine my motives, I'd find elements which were ugly enough. I've been a bad piece of work in my time." He said this with great severity.

Almost immediately, however, he would be prodding again. "Now, I don't know about you, Lovett, but when I'd drift out of an affair I'd find if I started to think about it that the reasons were somewhat interesting. There were women I quit because I made love to them ineptly, unpleasant as that may be to admit. And then, taking the converse of the proposition, there was a woman or two in love with me and wanting to get married." He began to laugh, quietly and ferociously. "'What? Get married?' I would say to them. 'Who, me? Why I thought it was understood from the beginning that this was on a give-and-take basis.'" His mouth curled, his voice whined in a grotesque of outraged innocence. "'Girlie, you got the wrong number. I thought it was understood we were modern individuals with a modern viewpoint.'" He roared with laughter now. "Oh, my mother." And then, his mouth mocking me, McLeod said, "That's another one belongs with the driftwood."

"Now, look," I'd object, "does a man have to get married every time he starts a relation with a woman?"

"No." He lit a cigarette, amused with me. "You see, Lovett, there's a difference between you and me. You're honest. I never was. I'd start off with the lady, and we'd have a nice conversation at the beginning about how neither of us could afford to get tied up, all understood, all good clean healthy fun." His voice was steeped in ridicule. "Fine. Only you see, Lovett, I could never let it go at that. The old dependable mechanisms would start working in me. I'd begin operating. You know what I mean? I'd do everything in my power to make the girl love me—when you think of the genius I've squandered in bed. And sure enough there'd be the times when I'd talk her into being in love, when I'd worry her to death until there was never a man in the world who made love like me." He coughed. "But once she admitted that . . . finito! I was getting bored. I thought it was time we drifted apart." He laughed again, at himself and at me. "Why, when the little lady would suggest marriage you should have seen me go into my act. 'You're welshing on the bargain,' I would tell her, 'I'm disappointed in you. How could you have betrayed me so?' " Once more he roared with laughter. "Oh, there was a devilish mechanism in it. You see, she betrayed me, you get it, she betrayed me, and it was time for us to drift apart."

McLeod and Hollingsworth

I was watching McLeod. He sat back in his chair and studied what Hollingsworth had written. From time to time he chuckled without amusement. Then he passed me the pad, and I read it with my heart beating stupidly. Hollingsworth had made the following list:

> Admits to being Bolshevist.
> Admits to being Communist.
> Admits to being atheist.
> Admits to blowing up churches.
> Admits to being against free enterprise.
> Admits to encouraging violence.
> Advocates murder of President and Congress.
> Advocates destruction of the South.
> Advocates use of poison.
> Advocates rise of the colored people.
> Admits allegiance to a foreign power.
> Is Against Wall Street.

Silently, I handed the pad back to McLeod. In a flat voice, not with mockery, he said to Hollingsworth, "You made a mistake. I never advocate the use of poison."

Hollingsworth had recovered. Diffidently, but not without firmness, he shook his head. "I'm sorry, I don't like to disagree with a fellow, but you did say that. I heard you."

McLeod shrugged. "All right, leave it in." He took a long puff at his cigarette. "Tell me, old man," he drawled, "is there anything else I can do for you?"

Guinevere

A jewel. But set in brass. This morning she had sported a house dress and covered it with a bathrobe. Her red hair, with which undoubtedly she was always experimenting, had been merely blowzy and flew out in all directions from her head. Yet there had been opera pumps on her feet, her nails had been painted, her lipstick was fresh. She was a house whose lawn was landscaped and whose kitchen was on fire. I would not have been startled if she had turned around and like the half-dressed queen in the girlie show: surprise! her buttocks are exposed.

Guinevere's Movie

"I've been trying to make up my mind which stars ought to play it, but so far I'm not sure, although I suppose they decide it all in Hollywood anyway. Just to think about it gets me excited.

"Here," she offered. "It takes place in this city in New York State, and the main characters are a doctor, a real good-looking guy with a mustache, big you know, and his nurse, she looks like some

97

of those blonde stars, and then he's got a girl friend, a dark-haired girl, any feature player could do that part." Guinevere lit a cigarette. "Now, this guy, the doctor, he's a pretty good guy, good heart and so forth, and he's a wow with the women. He's got the biggest whang on him in the whole town, and maybe he don't know it. He's got dozens of girl friends, and there isn't one of them who won't surrender herself to him, you know. But he's got a favorite, the blonde star one, his nurse, and she's a good kid too, worked hard all her life, and she goes for him. You know she's really in love, but she don't show it, puts up a tough front." Guinevere sighed with content. "Now the other one is a society girl, hoity-toity, and she comes to see him about something or other, woman trouble maybe, and he seduces her in his medical chambers, and they really tie a can on. You know for weeks he just goes around with her, to night clubs and to the beach, the country club, and he can't get her out of his system, it's chemical. Only all the time, at the same time, he still keeps the nurse on the string, and they get together once in a while, and it's love with them, it's just passion with the other."

"That is," I interposed, "it's the blonde star one he's really in love with?"

"Yeah." Without missing a breath, she continued. "Well, all this time, there's been a hullabaloo with the brunette society one's parents, you know they don't like the doctor because he's also from lowly origin like the nurse. But there's nothing they can do, it's real flaming youth." She halted, and murmured in aside, "Some of this I'm drawing from my own experiences." Guinevere tapped the ash from her cigarette. "Well, this goes on for a while and there's a climax. One night just for the hell of it he has one on the house with the society gal, and she gets pregnant. Only in the meantime before she finds out, he's decided that he's really more interested in the nurse, and they're thinking of getting married. When the society girl comes in, you know, knocked up, he talks to her for a while and convinces her he's not in love, and that she ought to have an operation. And so here's the first big scene. The doctor makes an operation on this dame he's had a hot affair with, and the nurse, the woman he's in love with, assists him right at it. I mean you see how this would make a movie even though they'd have trouble with such a scene. I imagine they could work it out though. She could have a brain tumor, or something of that nature. It would be a good scene the operation, you know with him giving directions to the nurse, scalpel nurse, forceps nurse, sponge, acting cold because he's a good doctor, and he's got lots of responsibility." Guinevere stared at me blankly. "The operation turns out a failure. She isn't going to have the baby any more, but at the same time he does something, he makes a mistake, and the society girl can't make love any more. She looks perfectly okay, but she's crippled there, a beautiful girl and yet she can't do it any more. Well, when she finds out, she's mad, and she's going to expose him, but the nurse who's a wonderful character convinces him he ought to marry the society girl, and he does even though there can't be anything between them, and for a while they all keep living in the same town, and he keeps up his affair with the blonde nurse. They're still in love, and it's gotten very chemical like it used to be with the society girl, he goes down on her and everything, and she loves him. But the wife who's now turned out a bitch is going to expose him all over again, and so the nurse takes off and goes to New York, and the doctor gets richer and richer, fooling around with a lot of dames on the side, but his heart is still with the blonde nurse. Only they don't see each other for years." She stopped. "Guess what the ending's going to be?"

I was not to hear it so quickly. Guinevere went on developing wondrous detail upon detail; my attention flagged, and I listened indifferently. For Monina stood in the hall entrance performing a dance. The child was still nude, but somewhere she had picked up a coaster for a highball glass, and now in a posture of unbelievable provocation, she held it like a fig leaf, writhing her limbs sinuously through a parody of amorous advance and retreat. She would approach a few steps, her blonde head cocked to one side in sensuous repose as if she were stirred by an exotic music, and then abruptly with a tiny pout upon her lips, she would draw back, an attitude of feigned horror in the pose of her limbs. As her mother spoke she danced silently, an interpreter. The story drew to a close, and with it the dance. Monina reclined against the doorway, her arm caressing her thigh. She never looked in my direction, yet everything was done for me. Her blonde eyelashes fluttered upon her cheek, her eyes opened to gaze boldly at the wall. And all the while, Guinevere, unheeding, continued to talk.

"They meet again in New York, just about a year ago, the nurse and the doctor, and the doctor's wife is dead, and whammo do they get together. I mean drinking and making love, nothing can stop them. And the nurse doesn't tell him about that baby she had from him after she left cause she knows he won't believe her; he'll think it belongs to some other guy. And the doctor wants to get married, and she holds him off cause she doesn't know what to do with the kid. And then what do you think, she can't tell him so she murders the kid, her own child, and she's caught, and the doctor too. I forgot to say he made out the death certificate cause she brought him in on it at the end, and then in prison, which'll be the last chapter, they're brought together for a final hour by the warden who's a pretty good guy, and there in the cell behind the bars they have a last one that really makes it worth while being killed."

And Monina, resolving the chord, ran toward me on tiptoe, nude nymph, halted within the reach of my arm, and in a child's counterfeit of a leer raised the fig leaf above her head, exposed and triumphant.

For the first time she stared at me as though I were real.

In the next instant a look of confusion mounted upon her face, deepened into terror. Abruptly, her mouth crumpled, her eyebrows knotted, and she began to wail in panic. Within a minute she was hysterical.

Lannie and Hollingsworth

"I knew that if I didn't have something to drink I'd be ill, for how long may a bee live without nectar?" Lannie hugged herself, her thin arms protruding like stalks from the soiled cotton cuffs of her pajamas. And her voice suddenly hoarse, she said, "Lovett, you said you'd loan me some money."

I handed her two ten-dollar bills.

"Mikey's my banker," she said to Hollingsworth with an ironic gesture.

The sum of many small frustrations exploded for me. "I'm not your banker, and if you think I don't need that money, you're mistaken."

She danced out of her chair and over to where I sat on the sofa and pinched my cheek once. "He is a banker," she said to

Hollingsworth, "but he's a charming one, and though he suffers through investment, and the black hand of money grips his heart in the middle of the night, he cannot escape his desire to be charming, and so he must always raise bond issues for Bohemia and resent his fate." She whirled about with amusement. "Those are the worst bankers of all when they turn upon you."

I recognized without much elation that this performance was for Hollingsworth, and not a word of her speech, not a gesture in the dance of her limbs, was uninspired; she might have been a geisha tracing the ritual of the tea ceremony. And Hollingsworth sat and watched her, his buttocks seemingly suspended a millimeter above his seat, a polite look upon his face, an expression of mild curiosity in his eyes as if he would be the hick who has paid money and now watches the carnival girls strip their costumes. This is the magical evil of the big city, but he is wary of being taken in: "I come to see pussy," he says to his neighbor, "and I ain't seen pussy yet." He will smash the carnival booths if he is cheated. Perhaps he has come to be cheated.

"I would say," I offered, "that Ed Leroy here knows more about banking than I do."

The Secret Policeman Gives Advice

Hollingsworth adjusted the lamp so it shone equitably between them. In a gentle voice, he continued. "Now, unlike most people, I don't look down on such a fellow. We all have our different characters, and that's true. It's just that we mustn't be stubborn. You've been an unhappy man all your life, and you didn't want to admit it was your own fault. So you blame it on society, as you call it. That isn't necessary. You could have had a good time, you could still have a good time if you'd realize that everybody is like you, and so it's pointless to work for the future." His hand strayed over the desk. He might have been caressing the wood. "More modesty. We ain't equipped to deal with big things. If this fellow came to me and asked my advice, I would take him aside and let him know that if he gives up the pursuits of vanity, and acts like everybody else, he'd get along better. 'Cause we never know what's deep down inside us"—Hollingsworth tapped his chest—"and it plays tricks. I don't give two cents for all your papers. A good-time Charley, that's myself, and that's why I'm smarter than the lot of you." His pale face had become flushed. "You can shove theory," he said suddenly. "Respect your father and mother."

McLeod's Soliloquy

"Think of it, you've got to make the imaginative reconstruction, don't forget you're dedicated to the land across the sea, you've come to understand finally the gory unremitting task of history and the imperfect men with whom you change it, and it's a whole choice, you tell yourself, with all the good and bad of one against all the bad and good of the other, until I can tell you it's with a gloomy but nonetheless delicious satisfaction that you hear about some particularly unpleasant piece of work by the side you're on because it's a test of yourself, and you don't shrink back. It's hard is it, well then make it harder, burn out the pap and the syrup and make yourself harder because it takes that; it takes all of that." He halted in the middle of the floor, looking at me expectantly with a puckering of his mouth. If there had been a glass of water in his hand, he would have swallowed it at a gulp. "And that's only the preliminary, because soon you know that it's all renounced for yourself, all the pleasures of the plump belly, and you're burned out, burned out for the generations to come, and so you can only drive yourself. Cannot you understand, you crippled prig," he shouted at my impassive face, "why we remained so long in a situation now reactionary and stoked fuel to the counterrevolution? You have no life, and so you do not know what it means to deny what has been the meaning of your life, for if you've been wrong, mark you now, if you've been wrong, then what of the decamillion of graves, and so you're committed, you're committed wholly, do you understand? And each action you perform can only confirm you further in your political position or what I would now call the lack of one, and there's only the nightmare of yourself if you're wrong, for you see it gets turned inside out and after a while the only path to absolution is to do more of the same so that you end up religious and climb to salvation on the steps of your crimes. And in all this, in all the activity and activity, do you dare lie awake and resurrect all the old tools of surplus value and accumulation and the exploitation of one class by another, or do you sink your teeth into the meat you're permitted, no private ownership and therefore . . . therefore therefore . . . I exist, therefore I am, and so there must be socialism, except that the weirdest statements go through your head, and once I jotted it down on a piece of paper, a perfectly ridiculous remark, 'The historical function of La Sovietica is to destroy the intellectual content of Marxism.' "

Lannie to Lovett's Ear

"Have you forgotten? Do you remember how the poorest of the poor used to be driven to the room where they were given death by gas? How was it done, and with what nobility do we all die? Let me tell you. The guards were chosen from a list, so they would come from the kitchen or standing before the gate with their gun at present arms, and they would all assemble in a room and an officer would give them orders, and each of them would rate an extra cup, and they would drink it and go to collect the prisoners who had been selected already by other men. And the prisoners would march along, and if one of them weighed a hundred pounds, he was a giant to the rest, and they would shuffle and smile and try to catch the guard's eye. And the guards were drunk, and you would be amazed how happy a man may feel at such a moment. For the comedy is about to begin. They come to the antechamber, a room with gray walls and without windows, and it's men to the right and women to the left and strip your clothes, but only a moment. The clothes off, the guards are driving them into the other room, and smack their hands on skinny flesh and bony flesh, it's bag a tittie and snatch a twot, and they can smell them stinking all those naked people, while in the heart of their own pants it's sweet with brandy so slap an ass and laugh like mad while the naked go stumbling, screaming into the last room of them all. And there one might suppose they prepare to die. For, mark you, this has been a long road, and each step of the way they have been deceived.

"Yet my story is not done," she said, holding up a hand, her eyes clear, her speech distinct as though she were reciting before a mirror. "The guards have one more resource. As they are about to close the door to the last room, an announcement is made. The State in its infinite mercy will allow one of them to be saved, the strongest. The one who can beat the others will be given a reprieve. This declaration, although it is worthy of the State, is due actually to the genius of a single guard who has conceived it at the very moment. And so through a window the guards may watch while one naked pygmy tears the hair of another, and blood runs where one thought no blood was left, and half of them are dead and scream like pigs with the head down and waiting for the knife, and as they scratch and sob and bite each other's rind, the guards turn on the gas and roar like mad for the fools thought one would be saved and so ate each other.

"This is the world, Mickey. If there had been one who said, 'Let us die with dignity,' but they went choking into the gas with the blood of a friend in their mouth."

"It was too late then," I murmured.

"Listen, my friend," she said softly, "the grass waves, and we are lost again in childhood souvenir. It is too late now. Do you understand? There are no solutions . . ."

Later, same scene, Lovett speaking:

". . . what if I don't want to choose my prison?"

"You must, and gladly. That is the secret."

"No one will win," I told her. "They'll destroy each other. And that's what you really want to see."

Her expression had become remote. "Who knows what we do want? Perhaps all that is left is to love the fire."

1948–51

104

THIRD ADVERTISEMENT FOR MYSELF

For The Naked and The Dead *I had luck—it came out just at the time when everyone was ready for a long war novel.* Barbary Shore *showed its face in the worst of seasons, just a few months after the Chinese had come into the Korean War and set us off on another of our clammy national hysterias. Anybody who worked and wrote for newspapers, magazines, television, movies, and advertising was discovering (if he were still innocent) that the natural work of his pen was to hasten our return to chastity, regularity, pomposity and the worship of the lifeless, the senseless, and the safe. It would have taken a good novel to overcome that bad time—obviously* Barbary Shore *was not good enough.*

> . . . It is relatively rare to discover a novel [whose] obvious intention is to debauch as many readers as possible, mentally, morally, physically and politically. . . . I presume the success of *The Naked and The Dead* emboldened Norman Mailer to the point where he believed he could write and publish anything he wanted to in America and get away with it. . . . When one has finished reading (by way of duty) this evil-smelling novel and dropped it gingerly into the garbage can, one has an overwhelming urge to take a hot bath with very strong soap.

wrote Sterling North in his review, and that was funny, but not so funny was Time: *"paceless, tasteless, and graceless"; not funny at all was Anthony West in the* New Yorker:

> The only point in going into this confused charade at such length is that it is likely to be said that a bad press is the price Mr. Mailer has had to pay for making the courageous gesture of writing and publishing an overtly Socialist book. The truth is that it has a monolithic flawless badness, like Mussolini's play about Napoleon, that

lifts it clear out of the political arena. The essence of its defects can be seen in the uncontrolled and apparently neurotic symbolism. The choice of an orphan brought up in an institution to serve as a type figure for a generation, and the choice of sexual inadequacy and sexual defeat to symbolize the relation between the individual and the government, show something beyond disorderly or careless thinking, something close to a complete loss of emotional command.

I could go on, but what for? The reviews ran in the proportion of fifty which were bad to five which were good.

There are few insecurities like aesthetic insecurity, and when a work comes along which sets itself up in that peculiar no-man's-land between the fault of the artist and the fault of the audience, then the reviewers have a power disproportionate to their modest minds. The same people who gave up reading Barbary Shore *in fifty pages because they had heard it was bad, would instead (given good reviews) have been confessing that it was marvelous fun even if they didn't understand it all. Maybe it was right that this first of the existentialist novels in America* should have had an existentialist fate, have been torn from its expected reception and given a shrunken life which was to react on the life of the author and reduce him as well. I suppose I might have learned to take my return ticket to the minor leagues without weeping too much into the beer, except I was plagued by an odd intuition: what I sensed (to my deep depression) was that I was working my way toward saying something unforgivable, enough so that most readers were already agitated—or what is worse—bored, by their quick uneasy sense that my vision—what little I had of it—was leading toward the violent and the orgiastic. I do not mean that I was clear about where I was going, it was rather that I had a dumb dull set of intimations that the things I was drawn to write about were taboo.*

Three or four years of constipated work, lack of confidence, cowardly sweetness and bouts of churlishness were the results of these dumb dull intimations. I was obliged to work from the guts; literally; I gave up my appendix in 1952 and came down with a bad liver in 1954. But this anticipates. Immediately, I could tell the difference in the deadness of my style. I made myself work hard, I tried to start a novel too soon, a rather mechanical novel about

* *Unless one labels Faulkner correctly as an existentialist.*

Hollywood, which collapsed after a month of the worst writing I had ever done, I turned to short stories, thought dispiritedly of attempting to make some sort of interim career as a writer of short stories—a New York career, so to speak, I would get myself printed in the New Yorker, *in* Harper's Bazaar, Mademoiselle— *But enough. It is most certainly not my aim to make this a thoroughgoing auto-biography. A description in more detail of my depressions, and the episodes which went into the long year before I could start on* The Deer Park, *can be saved for that doubtful day when I sit down to write about my life. For now, what can be underlined is that the direction I took in* Barbary Shore *was a first step toward work I will probably be doing from now on. For I wish to attempt an entrance into the mysteries of murder, suicide, incest, orgy, orgasm, and Time. These themes now fill my head and make me think I have a fair chance to become the first philosopher of Hip. So the reader who is in haste to judge this possibility had best skip ahead—those interested in what I was writing soon after* Barbary Shore *have only to turn the page.*

ADVERTISEMENT FOR THREE
WAR STORIES

"The Paper House," "The Language of Men," "The Dead Gook" and "The Notebook" were all written in the same period, and they were written quickly. I used to start a story in the morning and if I didn't finish it in the same day, I would give it up, I would decide it wasn't meant to be written. In a few weeks I wrote ten stories by this method. "The Paper House" was done in a day, so was "The Language of Men." "The Dead Gook" was an exception and took two days. What I liked about writing these stories was that I had no responsibility. In a novel I push along with two pages a day, or three, on those days I work (and once in a while I have a spurt of four or five) but I always have the fear of taking a wrong turn on some easy morning full of choice only to discover six months later that I must throw one hundred and fifty pages away. Working in the cellar of a novel, in the gloom of a first draft, it is difficult to separate an exciting idea from a cheap idea, a melodramatic flip of plot from a good dramatic turn. It is easy to make a bad mistake, and I move ahead like a banker, careful not to lose the investment of my work.

In these short stories the worst I could lose was the labor of a day and I raced along. Some of the stories came out well, the ones printed here are not too bad. Yet I have no great pride in them, because they are respectable. They make no attempt to raise the house an inch or two.

In fact, I think this is the only time I took a retreat in my work. The stories go back to The Naked and The Dead—at least they try to—and likely a few readers will enjoy them more than anything else which is printed here. But I know I was not trying for more than I could do, and so I feel a sadness in the prose. My mood of those poor days was usually tied to the feeling that I had nothing important left to write about, that maybe I was not really a writer—I thought often of becoming a psychoanalyst. I even considered going into business to get material for a novel, or working

*with my hands for a year or two. Any of those choices may have
been wiser than to continue writing, but obviously I prefer to believe that I was right to go on, and so it is almost inevitable to dislike the mood of the days in which I wrote these stories, and so to
deny the stories themselves.*

*"The Paper House" is dedicated to Vance Bourjaily. He told
me the anecdote on which the story is based, and was generous
enough to let me use it when I showed interest.*

THE PAPER HOUSE

Friendship in the army is so often an accident. If Hayes and
I were friends, it was due above all else to the fact that we were
cooks on the same shift, and so saw more of one another than of
anyone else. I suppose if I really consider it seriously, I did not even
like him, but for months we went along on the tacit assumption that
we were buddies, and we did a great many things together. We got
drunk together, we visited the local geisha house together, and we
even told each other some of our troubles.

It was not a bad time. The war was over, and we were stationed with an understrength company of men in a small Japanese
city. We were the only American troops for perhaps fifty miles
around, and therefore discipline was easy, and everyone could do
pretty much what he wished. The kitchen was staffed by four cooks
and a mess sergeant, and we had as many Japanese K.P.s to assist
us. The work was seldom heavy, and duty hours passed quickly. I
never liked the army so much as I did during those months.

Hayes saw to it that we had our recreation. He was more
aggressive than me, older and stronger, much more certain of his
ideas. I had no illusions that I was anything other than the tail to
his kite. He was one of those big gregarious men who need company and an uncritical ear, and I could furnish both. It also pleased
him that I had finished two years of college before I entered the
army, and yet he knew so much more than me, at least so far as
the army was concerned. He would ride me often about that.
"You're the one who's cracked the books," he would say as he

slammed a pot around, "but it seems none of those books ever taught you how to boil water. What a cook!" His humor was heavy, small doubt about it. "Nicholson," he would yell at me, "I hear there's a correspondence course in short-arms inspections. Why don't you advance yourself? You too can earn seventy-eight bucks a month."

He was often in a savage mood. He had troubles at home, and he was bitter about them. It seems his wife had begun to live with another man a few months after he entered the army. He had now divorced her, but there were money settlements still to be arranged, and his vanity hurt him. He professed to hate women. "They're tramps, every one of them," he would announce. "They're tramps and I can tell you it's a goddam tramp's world, and don't forget that, sonny." He would shift a boiler from one stove to another with a quick jerk-and-lift of his powerful shoulders, and would call back to me, "The only honest ones are the honest-to-God pros."

I would argue with him, or at least attempt to. I used to write a letter every day to a girl I liked in my home town, and the more time went by and the more letters I wrote, the more I liked her. He used to scoff at me. "That's the kind I really go for," he would jeer. "The literary ones. How they love to keep a guy on the string by writing letters. That's the kind that always has ten men right in her own back yard."

"I know she dates other fellows," I would say, "but what is she supposed to do? And look at us, we're over at the geisha house almost every night."

"Yeah, that's a fine comparison. We're spending our money at this end, and she's coining it at the other. Is that what you're trying to say?"

I would swear at him, and he would laugh. At such moments I disliked him intensely.

There was, however, quite another side to him. Many evenings after finishing work he would spend an hour washing and dressing, trimming his black mustache, and inspecting critically the press in his best uniform. We would have a drink or two, and then walk along the narrow muddy streets to the geisha house. He would usually be in a fine mood. As we turned in the lane which led to the house, and sat in the vestibule taking off our boots, or more exactly, waiting luxuriously while a geisha or a maid removed them for us, he would begin to hum. The moment we entered the clean pretty little room where the geishas greeted the soldiers, his good mood would begin to flood him. I heard him be even poetic once as he looked at the girls in their dress kimonos, all pretty, all petite, all chirping beneath the soft lights, all treading in dress slippers upon the bright woven straw mats. "I tell you, Nicholson," he said, "it looks like a goddam Christmas tree." He loved to sing at the geisha house, and since he had a pleasant baritone voice, the geishas would crowd about him, and clap their hands. Once or twice he would attempt to sing a Japanese song, and the errors he made in pitch and in language would be so amusing that the geishas would giggle with delight. He made, altogether, an attractive picture at such times, his blue eyes and healthy red face contrasting vigorously with his black mustache and his well-set body in its clean uniform. He seemed full of strength and merriment. He would clap two geishas to him, and call across the room with loud good cheer to another soldier. "Hey, Brown," he would shout, "ain't this a rug-cutter?" And to the answer, "You never had it so good," he would chuckle. "Say that again, Jack," he might roar. He was always charming the geishas. He spoke a burlesque Japanese to their great amusement, he fondled them, his admiration for them seemed to twinkle in his eyes. He was always hearty. Like many men who hate women, he knew how to give the impression that he adored them.

After several months he settled upon a particular girl. Her name was Yuriko, and she was easily the best of the geishas in that house. She was quite appealing with her tiny cat-face, and she carried herself with considerable charm, discernible even among the collective charm all geishas seemed to possess. She was clever, she was witty, and by the use of a few English words and the dramatic facility to express complex thoughts in pantomime, she was quite capable of carrying on extended conversations. It was hardly surprising that the other girls deferred to her, and she acted as their leader.

Since I always seemed to follow in Hayes's shadow, I also had a steady girl, and I suspect that Mimiko, whom I chose, had actually been selected for me by the artifice of Yuriko. Mimiko was Yuriko's best friend, and since Hayes and I were always together, it made things cosy. Those alternate Sundays when we were not on duty in the kitchen we would pay for the girls' time, and Hayes would use his influence, established by the judicious bribes of cans of food and pounds of butter to the motor pool sergeant, to borrow a jeep. We would take the girls out into the country, drive our jeep through back roads or mountain trails, and then descend to the sea where we would wander along the beach. The terrain was beautiful. Everything seemed to be manicured, and we would pass from a small pine forest into a tiny valley, go through little villages or little fishing towns nestled on the rocks, would picnic, would talk, and then toward evening would return the girls to the house. It was very pleasant.

They had other clients besides us, but they refused to spend the night with any other soldier if they knew we were coming, and the moment we entered the place, word was sent to Yuriko or Mimiko if they were occupied. Without a long wait, they would come to join us. Mimiko would slip her hand into mine and smile politely and sweetly, and Yuriko would throw her arms about Hayes and kiss him upon the mouth in the American style of greeting. We would all go together to one of the upper rooms and talk for an hour or two while sake was drunk. Then we would separate for the night, Yuriko with Hayes, and Mimiko with me.

Mimiko was not particularly attractive, and she had the placid disposition of a draft animal. I liked her mildly, but I would hardly have continued with her if it had not been for Yuriko. I really liked Yuriko. She seemed more bright and charming with every day, and I envied Hayes for his possession of her.

I used to love to listen to her speak. Yuriko would tell long stories about her childhood and her parents, and although the subject was hardly calculated to interest Hayes, he would listen to her with his mouth open, and hug her when she was done. "This baby ought to be on the stage," he would say to me. Once, I remember, I asked her how she had become a geisha, and she told about it in detail. "Papa-san, sick sick," she began, and with her hands, created her father for us, an old Japanese peasant whose back was bent and whose labor was long. "Mama-san sad." Her mother wept for us, wept prettily, like a Japanese geisha girl, with hands together in prayer and her nose touching the tip of her fingers. There was money owed on the land, the crops were bad, and Papa-san and Mama-san had talked together, and cried, and had known that they must sell Yuriko, now fourteen, as geisha. So she had been sold and so she had been trained, and in a few moments by the aid of a montage which came instinctively to her, she showed us herself in transition from a crude fourteen-year-old peasant to a charming geisha of sixteen trained in the tea ceremony, her diction improved, her limbs taught to dance, her voice to sing. "I, first-class geisha," she told us, and went on to convey the prestige of being a geisha of the first class. She had entertained only the wealthy men of the town, she had had no lovers unless she had felt the flutterings of weakness in her heart, her hands busy fluttering at her breast, her arms going out to an imaginary lover, her eyes darting from one of us to the other to see if we comprehended. In ten years she would have saved money enough to buy her freedom and to make an impressive marriage.

But, boom-boom, the war had ended, the Americans had come, and only they had money enough for geisha girls. And they did not want geisha girls. They wanted a *joro*, a common whore. And so first-class geishas became second-class geishas and third-class geishas, and here was Yuriko, a third-class geisha, humiliated and unhappy, or at least she would be if she did not love Hayes-san and he did not love her.

She was moody when she finished. "Hayes-san love Yuriko?" she asked, her legs folded beneath her, her small firm buttocks perched upon the straw mat while she handed him a sake cup, and extended her hand to the charcoal brazier.

"Sure, I love you, baby," Hayes said.

"I, first-class geisha," she repeated a little fiercely.

"Don't I know it," Hayes boomed.

Early the next morning as we walked back to the dormitory where the company was installed, Hayes was talking about it. "She jabbered at me all night," he said. "I got a hangover. That Jap sake."

"The story Yuriko told was sad," I murmured.

He stopped in the middle of the street, and put his hands on his hips. "Listen, Nicholson, wise up," he said angrily. "It's crap, it's all crap. They'd have you bleed your eyes out for them with those stories. Poor papa-san. They're all whores, you understand? A whore's a whore, and they're whores cause they want to be whores and don't know nothing better."

"It's not true," I protested. I felt sorry for the geishas. They seemed so unlike the few prostitutes I had known in the United States. There was one girl at the house who had been sold when she was thirteen, and had entered service a virgin. After her first night of work, she had wept for three days, and even now many of the soldiers selected her shame-facedly. "What about Susiko?" I said.

"I don't believe it, it's a gag," Hayes shouted. He gripped me by the shoulder and made a speech. "I'll wise you up. I don't say I'm Superman, but I know the score. Do you understand that? I know the score. I don't say I'm any better than anybody else, but I don't kid myself that I am. And it drives me nuts when people want to make me swallow bull." He released my shoulder as suddenly as he had gripped it. His red face was very red, and I sensed what rage he had felt.

"All right," I muttered.

"All right."

In time he came to treat Yuriko the way he treated anyone with whom he was familiar. He indulged his moods. If he were surly, he did not bother to hide it; if he were aggressive, he would swear at her; if he were happy, he would sing for her or become roisteringly drunk or kiss her many times before Mimiko and myself, telling her that he loved her in a loud voice which often seemed close to choler. Once he abused her drunkenly, and I had to pull him away. The next day he brought Yuriko a present, a model of a wooden shrine which he had purchased from a Japanese cabinet maker. All the while it was evident to me that Yuriko was in love with him.

I used to think of the rooms upstairs as paper rooms. They were made of straw and light wood and parchment glued to wooden frames, and when one lay on the pallet in the center of the floor, it seemed as if all the sounds in all the adjoining rooms flowed without hindrance through the sliding doors. Mimiko and I could often hear them talking in the next cubicle, and long after Mimiko would be asleep, I would lie beside her and listen to Yuriko's voice as it floated, breathlike and soft, through the frail partitions. She would be telling him about her day and the events which had passed in the house. She had had a fight with Mama-san, the wrinkled old lady who was her madame, and Tasawa had heard from her brother whose wife had just given him a child. There was a new girl coming in two days, and Katai who had left the day before had proven to be sick. Mama-san was limiting the charcoal for the braziers, she was stingy without a doubt. So it went, a pageant of domesticity. She had resewn the buttons on his battle jacket, he looked good, he was gaining weight, she would have to buy a new kimono for the number two kimono had become shabby, and the number three was hopeless. She was worried about Henderson-san who had become drunk two nights in a row and had struck Kukoma. What should she do about him?

And Hayes listened to her, his head in her lap no doubt, and mumbled gentle answers, relaxed and tender as she caressed the bitterness from his face, drawing it out with her finger tips while her childlike laugh echoed softly through the rooms. There were other sounds: of men snoring, girls giggling, two soldiers in a quarrel, and the soft muted whisper of a geisha crying somewhere in some one of the rooms. So it washed over me in this little house with its thirty paper cells in the middle of a small Japanese city while the Japanese night cast an artist's moon over the rice paddies and the pine forests where the trees grew in aisles. I envied Hayes, envied him with the touch of Mimiko's inert body against mine, envied him Yuriko's tenderness which she gave him so warmly.

He told her one night that he loved her. He loved her so much that he would re-enlist and remain in this Japanese city for at least another year. I overheard him through the parchment walls, and I would have asked him about it next morning if he had not mentioned it himself. "I told her that, and I was lying," he said.

"Well, why did you tell her?"

"You lie to a dame. That's my advice to you. You get them in closer and closer, you feed them whatever you want, and the only trick is never to believe it yourself. Do you understand, Nicholson?"

"No, I don't."

"It's the only way to handle them. I've got Yuriko around my finger." And he insisted on giving me a detailed account of how they made love until by the sheer energy of his account, I realized what he wished to destroy. He had been sincere when he spoke to Yuriko. With her hands on his face, and the night drifting in fog against the windows, he had wanted to re-enlist for another year, had wanted to suspend her fingers upon his face, and freeze time so it could be retained. It must have all seemed possible the night before, he must have believed it and wanted it, seen himself signing the papers in the morning. Instead, he had seen me, had seen the olive-drab color of my uniform, and had known it was not possible, was not at all possible within the gamut of his nature.

He was drunk the following night when he went to see her, moody and silent, and Yuriko was without diversion to him. I think she sensed that something was wrong. She sighed frequently, she chatted in Japanese with Mimiko, and threw quick looks at him to see whether his mood was changing. Then—it must have meant so much to her—she inquired timidly, "You re-enlist one year?"

He stared back at her, was about to nod, and then laughed shortly. "I'm going home, Yuriko. I'm due to go home in one month."

"You repeat, please?"

"I'm getting out of here. In one month. I'm not re-enlisting."

She turned away and looked at the wall. When she turned around, it was to pinch his arm.

"Hayes-san, you marry me, yes?" she said in a voice sharp with its hurt.

He shoved her away. "I don't marry you. Get away. You skibby with too many men."

She drew in her breath, and her eyes were bright for a moment. "Yes. You marry skibby-girl." Yuriko threw her arms about his neck. "American soldier marry skibby-girl."

This time he pushed her away forcefully enough to hurt her. "You just go blow," he shouted at her.

She was quite angry. "American soldier marry skibby-girl," she taunted.

I had never seen him quite as furious. What frightened me was that he contained it all and did not raise his voice. "Marry you?" he asked. I have an idea what enraged him was that the thought had already occurred to him, and it seemed outrageous to hear it repeated in what was, after all, the mouth of a prostitute. Hayes picked up his bottle and drank from it. "You and me are going to skibby, that's what," he said to Yuriko.

She held her ground. "No skibby tonight."

"What do you mean, 'no skibby tonight'? You'll skibby tonight. You're nothing but a *joro*."

Yuriko turned her back. Her little head was bent forward. "I, first-class geisha," she whispered in so low a voice we almost did not hear her.

He struck her. I tried to intervene, and with a blow he knocked me away. Yuriko fled the room. Like a bull, Hayes was after her. He caught her once, just long enough to rip away half her kimono, caught her again to rip away most of what was left. The poor girl was finally trapped, screaming, and more naked than not, in the room where the geishas met the soldiers. There must

116

have been a dozen girls and at least as many soldiers for an audience. Hayes gripped her hairdress, he ripped it down, he threw her up in the air, he dropped her on the floor, he laughed drunkenly, and among the screams of the girls and the startled laughter of the soldiers, I got him out to the street. I could hear Yuriko wailing hysterically behind us.

I guided him home to his cot, and he dropped into a drunken sleep. In the morning, he was contrite. Through the dull headache of awakening, he certainly did not love her, and so he regretted his brutality. "She's a good girl, Nicholson," he said to me, "she's a good girl, and I shouldn't have treated her that way."

"You ripped her kimono," I told him.

"Yeah, I got to buy her another."

It turned out to be a bad day. At breakfast, everybody who passed on the chow line seemed to have heard what had happened, and Hayes was kidded endlessly. It developed that Yuriko had been put to bed with fever after we left, and all the girls were shocked. Almost everything had halted for the night at the geisha house.

"You dishonored her in public," said one of Hayes's buddies with a grin. "Man, how they carried on."

Hayes turned to me. "I'm going to buy her a good kimono." He spent the morning selecting articles of food to sell on the black market. He had to make enough to amass the price of a good kimono, and it worried him that the supplies might be too depleted. The afternoon was taken up with selling his goods, and at dinner we were two weary cooks.

Hayes changed in a hurry. "Come on, let's get over there." He hustled me along, did not even stop to buy a bottle. We were the first clients of the evening to appear at the geisha house. "Mama-san," he roared at the old madame, "where's Yuriko?"

Mama-san pointed upstairs. Her expression was wary. Hayes, however, did not bother to study it. He bounded up the stairs, knocked on Yuriko's door, and entered.

Yuriko was sweet and demure. She accepted his present with a deep bow, touching her forehead to the floor. She was friendly, she was polite, and she was quite distant. She poured us sake with even more ceremony than was her custom. Mimiko entered after a few minutes, and her face was troubled. Yet it was she who talked to us. Yuriko was quiet for a long time. It was only when Mimiko lapsed into silence that Yuriko began to speak.

She informed us in her mixture of English, Japanese and

pantomime that in two weeks she was going to take a trip. She was very formal about it.

"A trip?" Hayes asked.

It was to be a long trip. Yuriko smiled sadly.

Hayes fingered his hat. She was leaving the geisha house?

Yes, she was leaving it forever.

She was going perhaps to get married?

No, she was not getting married. She was dishonored and no one would have her.

Hayes began to twist the hat. She had a *musume?* She was going away with a *musume?*

No, there was no *musume.* Hayes was the only *musume* in her life.

Well, where was she going?

Yuriko sighed. She could not tell him. She hoped, however, since she would be leaving before Hayes, that he would come to see her often in the next few weeks.

"Goddammit, where are you going?" Hayes shouted.

At this point, Mimiko began to weep. She wept loudly, her hand upon her face, her head averted. Yuriko leaped up to comfort her. Yuriko patted her head, and sighed in unison with Mimiko.

"Where are you going?" Hayes asked her again.

Yuriko shrugged her shoulders.

It continued like this for an hour. Hayes badgered her, and Yuriko smiled. Hayes pleaded and Yuriko looked sad. Finally, as we were about to leave, Yuriko told us. In two weeks, at two o'clock on Sunday afternoon, she was going to her little room, and there she would commit hari-kari. She was dishonored, and there was nothing else to be done about it. Hayes-san was very kind to apologize, and the jewels of her tears were the only fit present for his kindness, but apologies could never erase dishonor and so she would be obliged to commit hari-kari.

Mimiko began to weep again.

"You mean in two weeks you're going to kill yourself?" Hayes blurted.

"Yes, Hayes-san."

He threw up his arms. "It's crap, it's all crap, you understand?"

"Yes. Crap-crap," Yuriko said.

"You're throwing the bull, Yuriko."

118

"Yes, Hayes-san. Crap-crap."

"Let's get out of here, Nicholson." He turned in the doorway and laughed. "You almost had me for a minute, Yuriko."

She bowed her head.

Hayes went to see her three times in the week which followed. Yuriko remained the same. She was quiet, she was friendly, she was quite removed. And Mimiko wept every night on my pallet. Hayes forbore as long as was possible, and then at the end of the week, he spoke about it again. "You were kidding me, weren't you, Yuriko?"

Yuriko begged Hayes-san not to speak of it again. It was rude on her part. She did not wish to cause him unnecessary pain. If she had spoken, it was only because the dearer sentiments of her heart were in liege to him, and she wished to see him often in the week which remained.

He snorted with frustration. "Now, look, you . . . cut . . . this . . . out. Do you understand?"

"Yes, Hayes-san. No more talk-talk." She would not mention it again, she told us. She realized how it offended him. Death was an unpleasant topic of conversation in a geisha house. She would attempt to be entertaining, and she begged us to forgive her if the knowledge of her own fate might cause her to be sad at certain moments.

That morning, on the walk back to the schoolhouse, Hayes was quiet. He worked all day with great rapidity, and bawled me out several times for not following his cooking directions more accurately. That night we slept in our barrack, and in the early hours of the morning, he woke me up.

"Look, Nicholson, I can't sleep. Do you think that crazy honey is really serious?"

I was wide awake. I had not been sleeping well myself. "I don't know," I said. "I don't think she means it."

"I know she doesn't mean it." He swore.

"Yeah." I started to light a cigarette, and then I put it out. "Hayes, I was just thinking though. You know the Oriental mind is different."

"The Oriental mind! Goddammit, Nicholson, a whore is a whore. They're all the same I tell you. She's kidding."

"If you say so."

"I'm not even going to mention it to her."

All through the second week, Hayes kept his promise. More than once, he would be about to ask her again, and would force himself into silence. It was very difficult. As the days passed, Mimiko wept more and more openly, and Yuriko's eyes would fill with tears as she looked at Hayes. She would kiss him tenderly, sigh, and then by an effort of will, or so it seemed, would force herself to be gay. Once she surprised us with some flowers she had found, and wove them in our hair. The week passed day by day. I kept waiting for the other men in the company to hear the news, but Hayes said not a word and the geishas did not either. Still, one could sense that the atmosphere in the house was different. The geishas were extremely respectful to Yuriko, and quite frequently would touch her garments as she passed.

By Saturday Hayes could stand it no longer. He insisted that we leave the geisha house for the night, and he made Yuriko accompany us to the boot vestibule. While she was lacing our shoes, he raised her head and said to her, "I work tomorrow. I'll see you Monday."

She smiled vaguely, and continued tying the laces.

"Yuriko, I said I'd see you Monday."

"No, Hayes-san. Better tomorrow. No here, Monday. Gone, bye-bye. You come tomorrow before two o'clock."

"Yuriko, I'm on duty tomorrow. I said I'll see you Monday."

"Say good-by now. Never see me again." She kissed us on the cheek. "Good-by, Nick-san. Good-by, Hayes-san." A single tear rolled down each cheek. She fingered Hayes's jacket and fled upstairs.

That night Hayes and I did not sleep at all. He came over to my cot, and sat there in silence. "What do you think?" he asked after a long while.

"I don't know."

"I don't know either." He began to swear. He kept drinking from a bottle, but it had no effect. He was quite sober. "I'm damned if I'm going over there tomorrow," he said.

"Do what you think is best."

He swore loudly.

The morning went on and on. Hayes worked rapidly and was left with nothing to do. The meal was ready fifteen minutes early. He called chow at eleven-thirty. By one o'clock the K.P.s were almost finished with the pots.

"Hey, Koto," Hayes asked one of the K.P.s, a middle-aged

man who had been an exporter and spoke English, "hey, Koto, what do you know about hari-kari?"

Koto grinned. He was always very polite and very colorless. "Oh, hari-kari. Japanese national custom," he said.

"Come on," Hayes said to me, "we've got till three o'clock before we put supper on." He was changing into his dress clothes by the time I followed him to the dormitory. He had neglected to hang them up the night before, and for once they were bedraggled. "What time is it?" he asked me.

"A quarter past one."

"Come on, hurry up."

He ran almost all the way to the geisha house, and I ran with him. As we approached, the house seemed quiet. There was nobody in the vestibule, and there was nobody in the receiving room. Hayes and I stood there in empty silence.

"*Yuriko!*" he bawled.

We heard her feet patter on the stairs. She was dressed in a white kimono, without ornament, and without makeup. "You do come," she whispered. She kissed him. "Bye-bye, Hayes-san. I go upstairs now."

He caught her arm. "Yuriko, you can't do it."

She attempted to free herself, and he held her with frenzy. "I won't let you go," he shouted. "Yuriko, you got to stop this. It's crap."

"Crap-crap," she said, and suddenly she began to giggle.

"Crap-crap," we heard all around. "Crap-crap, crap-crap, crap-crap."

Squealing with laughter, every geisha in the house entered the room. They encircled us, their voices going "crap-crap" like a flock of geese.

Yuriko was laughing at us, Mimiko was laughing at us, they were all laughing. Hayes shouldered his way to the door. "Let's get out of here." We pushed on to the street, but the geishas followed. As we retreated across the town, they flowed out from the geisha house and marched behind us, their kimonos brilliant with color, their black hair shining in the sunlight. While the townspeople looked and giggled, we walked home, and the geishas followed us, shouting insults in English, Japanese and pantomime. Beneath their individual voices, with the regularity of marching feet, I could hear their cadence, "Crap-crap, crap-crap."

After a week, Hayes and I went back to the house for a last

visit before we sailed for home. We were received politely, but neither Yuriko nor Mimiko would sleep with us. They suggested that we hire Susiko, the thirteen-year-old ex-virgin.

1951

THE LANGUAGE OF MEN

In the beginning, Sanford Carter was ashamed of becoming an army cook. This was not from snobbery, at least not from snobbery of the most direct sort. During the two and a half years Carter had been in the army he had come to hate cooks more and more. They existed for him as a symbol of all that was corrupt, overbearing, stupid, and privileged in army life. The image which came to mind was a fat cook with an enormous sandwich in one hand, and a bottle of beer in the other, sweat pouring down a porcine face, foot on a flour barrel, shouting at the K.P.s, "Hurry up, you men, I ain't got all day." More than once in those two and a half years, driven to exasperation, Carter had been on the verge of throwing his food into a cook's face as he passed on the serving line. His anger often derived from nothing: the set of a pair of fat lips, the casual heavy thump of the serving spoon into his plate, or the resentful conviction that the cook was not serving him enough. Since life in the army was in most aspects a marriage, this rage over apparently harmless details was not a sign of unbalance. Every soldier found some particular habit of the army spouse impossible to support.

Yet Sanford Carter became a cook and, to elaborate the irony, did better as a cook than he had done as anything else. In a few months he rose from a private to a first cook with the rank of Sergeant, Technician. After the fact, it was easy to understand. He had suffered through all his army career from an excess of eagerness. He had cared too much, he had wanted to do well, and so he had often been tense at moments when he would better have been relaxed. He was very young, twenty-one, had lived the comparatively gentle life of a middle-class boy, and needed some success in the army to prove to himself that he was not completely worthless.

In succession, he had failed as a surveyor in field artillery, a clerk in an infantry headquarters, a telephone wireman, and finally a rifleman. When the war ended, and his regiment went to Japan, Carter was still a rifleman; he had been a rifleman for eight months. What was more to the point, he had been in the platoon as long as any of its members; the skilled hard-bitten nucleus of veterans who had run his squad had gone home one by one, and it seemed to him that through seniority he was entitled to at least a corporal's rating. Through seniority he was so entitled, but on no other ground. Whenever responsibility had been handed to him, he had discharged it miserably, tensely, overconscientiously. He had always asked too many questions, he had worried the task too severely, he had conveyed his nervousness to the men he was supposed to lead. Since he was also sensitive enough and proud enough never to curry favor with the noncoms in the platoons, he was in no position to sit in on their occasional discussions about who was to succeed them. In a vacuum of ignorance, he had allowed himself to dream that he would be given a squad to lead, and his hurt was sharp when the squad was given to a replacement who had joined the platoon months after him.

The war was over, Carter had a bride in the States (he had lived with her for only two months), he was lonely, he was obsessed with going home. As one week dragged into the next, and the regiment, the company, and his own platoon continued the same sort of training which they had been doing ever since he had entered the army, he thought he would snap. There were months to wait until he would be discharged and meanwhile it was intolerable to him to be taught for the fifth time the nomenclature of the machine gun, to stand a retreat parade three evenings a week. He wanted some niche where he could lick his wounds, some army job with so many hours of work and so many hours of complete freedom, where he could be alone by himself. He hated the army, the huge army which had proved to him that he was good at no work, and incapable of succeeding at anything. He wrote long, aching letters to his wife, he talked less and less to the men around him, and he was close to violent attacks of anger during the most casual phases of training—during close-order drill or cleaning his rifle for inspection. He knew that if he did not find his niche it was possible that he would crack.

So he took an opening in the kitchen. It promised him nothing except a day of work, and a day of leisure which would be completely at his disposal. He found that he liked it. He was given at first the job of baking the bread for the company, and every other night he worked till early in the morning, kneading and shaping his fifty-pound mix of dough. At two or three he would be done, and for his work there would be the tangible reward of fifty loaves of bread, all fresh from the oven, all clean and smelling of fertile accomplished creativity. He had the rare and therefore intensely satisfying emotion of seeing at the end of an army chore the product of his labor.

A month after he became a cook the regiment was disbanded, and those men who did not have enough points to go home were sent to other outfits. Carter ended at an ordnance company in another Japanese city. He had by now given up all thought of getting a noncom's rating before he was discharged, and was merely content to work each alternate day. He took his work for granted and so he succeeded at it. He had begun as a baker in the new company kitchen; before long he was the first cook. It all happened quickly. One cook went home on points, another caught a skin disease, a third was transferred from the kitchen after contracting a venereal infection. On the shift which Carter worked there were left only himself and a man who was illiterate. Carter was put nominally in charge, and was soon actively in charge. He looked up each menu in an army recipe book, collected the items, combined them in the order indicated, and after the proper time had elapsed, took them from the stove. His product tasted neither better nor worse than the product of all other army cooks. But the mess sergeant was impressed. Carter had filled a gap. The next time ratings were given out Carter jumped at a bound from private to Sergeant T/4.

On the surface he was happy; beneath the surface he was overjoyed. It took him several weeks to realize how grateful and delighted he felt. The promotion coincided with his assignment to a detachment working in a small seaport up the coast. Carter arrived there to discover that he was in charge of cooking for thirty men, and would act as mess sergeant. There was another cook, and there were four permanent Japanese K.P.s, all of them good workers. He still cooked every other day, but there was always time between meals to take a break of at least an hour and often two; he shared a room with the other cook and lived in comparative privacy for the first time in several years; the seaport was beautiful; there was only one officer, and he left the men alone; supplies were plentiful due to a clerical error which assigned rations for forty men rather than thirty; and in general everything was fine. The niche had become a sinecure.

This was the happiest period of Carter's life in the army. He came to like his Japanese K.P.s. He studied their language, he visited their homes, he gave them gifts of food from time to time. They worshiped him because he was kind to them and generous, because he never shouted, because his good humor bubbled over into games, and made the work of the kitchen seem pleasant. All the while he grew in confidence. He was not a big man, but his body filled out from the heavy work; he was likely to sing a great deal, he cracked jokes with the men on the chow line. The kitchen became his property, it became his domain, and since it was a warm room, filled with sunlight, he came to take pleasure in the very sight of it. Before long his good humor expanded into a series of efforts to improve the food. He began to take little pains and make little extra efforts which would have been impossible if he had been obliged to cook for more than thirty men. In the morning he would serve the men fresh eggs scrambled or fried to their desire in fresh butter. Instead of cooking sixty eggs in one large pot he cooked two eggs at a time in a frying pan, turning them to the taste of each soldier. He baked like a housewife satisfying her young husband; at lunch and dinner there was pie or cake, and often both. He went to great lengths. He taught the K.P.s how to make the toast come out right. He traded excess food for spices in Japanese stores. He rubbed paprika and garlic on the chickens. He even made pastries to cover such staples as corn beef hash and meat and vegetable stew.

It all seemed to be wasted. In the beginning the men might have noticed these improvements, but after a period they took them for granted. It did not matter how he worked to satisfy them; they trudged through the chow line with their heads down, nodding coolly at him, and they ate without comment. He would hang around the tables after the meal, noticing how much they consumed, and what they discarded; he would wait for compliments, but the soldiers seemed indifferent. They seemed to eat without tasting the food. In their faces he saw mirrored the distaste with which he had once stared at cooks.

The honeymoon was ended. The pleasure he took in the kitchen and himself curdled. He became aware again of his painful desire to please people, to discharge responsibility, to be a man. When he had been a child, tears had come into his eyes at a cross word, and he had lived in an atmosphere where his smallest accomplishment was warmly praised. He was the sort of young man, he often thought bitterly, who was accustomed to the attention and the protection of women. He would have thrown away all he possessed—the love of his wife, the love of his mother, the benefits of his education, the assured financial security of entering his father's business—if he had been able just once to dig a ditch as well as the most ignorant farmer.

Instead, he was back in the painful unprotected days of his first entrance into the army. Once again the most casual actions became the most painful, the events which were most to be taken for granted grew into the most significant, and the feeding of the men at each meal turned progressively more unbearable.

So Sanford Carter came full circle. If he had once hated the cooks, he now hated the troops. At mealtimes his face soured into the belligerent scowl with which he had once believed cooks to be born. And to himself he muttered the age-old laments of the housewife; how little they appreciated what he did.

Finally there was an explosion. He was approached one day by Corporal Taylor, and he had come to hate Taylor, because Taylor was the natural leader of the detachment and kept the other men endlessly amused with his jokes. Taylor had the ability to present himself as inefficient, shiftless, and incapable, in such a manner as to convey that really the opposite was true. He had the lightest touch, he had the greatest facility, he could charm a geisha in two minutes and obtain anything he wanted from a supply sergeant in five. Carter envied him, envied his grace, his charmed indifference; then grew to hate him.

Taylor teased Carter about the cooking, and he had the knack of knowing where to put the knife. "Hey, Carter," he would shout across the mess hall while breakfast was being served, "you turned my eggs twice, and I asked for them raw." The men would shout with laughter. Somehow Taylor had succeeded in conveying all of the situation, or so it seemed to Carter, insinuating everything, how Carter worked and how it meant nothing, how Carter labored to gain their affection and earned their contempt. Carter would scowl, Carter would answer in a rough voice, "Next time I'll crack them over your head." "You crack 'em, I'll eat 'em," Taylor would pipe back, "but just don't put your fingers in 'em." And there would be another laugh. He hated the sight of Taylor.

It was Taylor who came to him to get the salad oil. About twenty of the soldiers were going to have a fish fry at the geisha house; they had bought the fish at the local market but they could not buy oil, so Taylor was sent as the deputy to Carter. He was charming to Carter, he complimented him on the meal, he clapped him on the back, he dissolved Carter to warmth, to private delight in the attention, and the thought that he had misjudged Taylor. Then Taylor asked for the oil.

Carter was sick with anger. Twenty men out of the thirty in the detachment were going on the fish fry. It meant only that Carter was considered one of the ten undesirables. It was something he had known, but the proof of knowledge is always more painful than the acquisition of it. If he had been alone his eyes would have clouded. And he was outraged at Taylor's deception. He could imagine Taylor saying ten minutes later, "You should have seen the grease job I gave to Carter. I'm dumb, but man, he's dumber."

Carter was close enough to giving him the oil. He had a sense of what it would mean to refuse Taylor, he was on the very edge of mild acquiescence. But he also had a sense of how he would despise himself afterward.

"No," he said abruptly, his teeth gritted, "you can't have it."

"What do you mean we can't have it?"

"I won't give it to you." Carter could almost feel the rage which Taylor generated at being refused.

"You won't give away a lousy five gallons of oil to a bunch of G.I.s having a party?"

"I'm sick and tired—" Carter began.

"So am I." Taylor walked away.

Carter knew he would pay for it. He left the K.P.s and went to change his sweat-soaked work shirt, and as he passed the large dormitory in which most of the detachment slept he could hear Taylor's high-pitched voice.

Carter did not bother to take off his shirt. He returned instead to the kitchen, and listened to the sound of men going back and forth through the hall and of a man shouting with rage. That was Hobbs, a Southerner, a big man with a big bellowing voice.

There was a formal knock on the kitchen door. Taylor came

in. His face was pale and his eyes showed a cold satisfaction. "Carter," he said, "the men want to see you in the big room."

Carter heard his voice answer huskily. "If they want to see me, they can come into the kitchen."

He knew he would conduct himself with more courage in his own kitchen than anywhere else. "I'll be here for a while."

Taylor closed the door, and Carter picked up a writing board to which was clamped the menu for the following day. Then he made a pretense of examining the food supplies in the pantry closet. It was his habit to check the stocks before deciding what to serve the next day, but on this night his eyes ranged thoughtlessly over the canned goods. In a corner were seven five-gallon tins of salad oil, easily enough cooking oil to last a month. Carter came out of the pantry and shut the door behind him.

He kept his head down and pretended to be writing the menu when the soldiers came in. Somehow there were even more of them than he had expected. Out of the twenty men who were going to the party, all but two or three had crowded through the door.

Carter took his time, looked up slowly. "You men want to see me?" he asked flatly.

They were angry. For the first time in his life he faced the hostile expressions of many men. It was the most painful and anxious moment he had ever known.

"Taylor says you won't give us the oil," someone burst out.

"That's right, I won't," said Carter. He tapped his pencil against the scratchboard, tapping it slowly and, he hoped, with an appearance of calm.

"What a stink deal," said Porfirio, a little Cuban whom Carter had always considered his friend.

Hobbs, the big Southerner, stared down at Carter. "Would you mind telling the men why you've decided not to give us the oil?" he asked quietly.

"Cause I'm blowed if I'm going to cater to you men. I've catered enough," Carter said. His voice was close to cracking with the outrage he had suppressed for so long, and he knew that if he continued he might cry. "I'm the acting mess sergeant," he said as coldly as he could, "and I decide what goes out of this kitchen." He stared at each one in turn, trying to stare them down, feeling mired in the rut of his own failure. They would never have dared this approach to another mess sergeant.

"What crud," someone muttered.

"You won't give a lousy five-gallon can of oil for a G.I. party," Hobbs said more loudly.

"I won't. That's definite. You men can get out of here."

"Why, you lousy little snot," Hobbs burst out, "how many five-gallon cans of oil have you sold on the black market?"

"I've never sold any." Carter might have been slapped with the flat of a sword. He told himself bitterly, numbly, that this was the reward he received for being perhaps the single honest cook in the whole United States Army. And he even had time to wonder at the obscure prejudice which had kept him from selling food for his own profit.

"Man, I've seen you take it out," Hobbs exclaimed. "I've seen you take it to the market."

"I took food to trade for spices," Carter said hotly.

There was an ugly snicker from the men.

"I don't mind if a cook sells," Hobbs said, "every man has his own deal in this army. But a cook ought to give a little food to a G.I. if he wants it."

"Tell him," someone said.

"It's bull," Taylor screeched. "I've seen Carter take butter, eggs, every damn thing to the market."

Their faces were red, they circled him.

"I never sold a thing," Carter said doggedly.

"And I'm telling you," Hobbs said, "that you're a two-bit crook. You been raiding that kitchen, and that's why you don't give to us now."

Carter knew there was only one way he could possibly answer if he hoped to live among these men again. "That's a goddam lie," Carter said to Hobbs. He laid down the scratchboard, he flipped his pencil slowly and deliberately to one corner of the room, and with his heart aching he lunged toward Hobbs. He had no hope of beating him. He merely intended to fight until he was pounded unconscious, advancing the pain and bruises he would collect as collateral for his self-respect.

To his indescribable relief Porfirio darted between them, held them apart with the pleased ferocity of a small man breaking up a fight. "Now, stop this! Now, stop this!" he cried out.

Carter allowed himself to be pushed back, and he knew that he had gained a point. He even glimpsed a solution with some honor.

He shrugged violently to free himself from Porfirio. He was in a rage, and yet it was a rage he could have ended at any instant. "All right, you men," he swore, "I'll give you the oil, but now that we're at it, I'm going to tell you a thing or two." His face red, his body perspiring, he was in the pantry and out again with a five-gallon tin. "Here," he said, "you better have a good fish fry, 'cause it's the last good meal you're going to have for quite a while. I'm sick of trying to please you. You think I have to work—" he was about to say, my fingers to the bone—"well, I don't. From now on, you'll see what chow in the army is supposed to be like." He was almost hysterical. "Take that oil. Have your fish fry." The fact that they wanted to cook for themselves was the greatest insult of all. "Tomorrow I'll give you real army cooking."

His voice was so intense that they backed away from him. "Get out of this kitchen," he said. "None of you has any business here."

They filed out quietly, and they looked a little sheepish.

Carter felt weary, he felt ashamed of himself, he knew he had not meant what he said. But half an hour later, when he left the kitchen and passed the large dormitory, he heard shouts of raucous laughter, and he heard his name mentioned and then more laughter.

He slept badly that night, he was awake at four, he was in the kitchen by five, and stood there white-faced and nervous, waiting for the K.P.s to arrive. Breakfast that morning landed on the men like a lead bomb. Carter rummaged in the back of the pantry and found a tin of dehydrated eggs covered with dust, memento of a time when fresh eggs were never on the ration list. The K.P.s looked at him in amazement as he stirred the lumpy powder into a pan of water. While it was still half-dissolved he put it on the fire. While it was still wet, he took it off. The coffee was cold, the toast was burned, the oatmeal stuck to the pot. The men dipped forks into their food, took cautious sips of their coffee, and spoke in whispers. Sullenness drifted like vapors through the kitchen.

At noontime Carter opened cans of meat-and-vegetable stew. He dumped them into a pan and heated them slightly. He served the stew with burned string beans and dehydrated potatoes which tasted like straw. For dessert the men had a single lukewarm canned peach and cold coffee.

So the meals continued. For three days Carter cooked slop,

and suffered even more than the men. When mealtime came he left the chow line to the K.P.s and sat in his room, perspiring with shame, determined not to yield and sick with the determination.

Carter won. On the fourth day a delegation of men came to see him. They told him that indeed they had appreciated his cooking in the past, they told him that they were sorry they had hurt his feelings, they listened to his remonstrances, they listened to his grievances, and with delight Carter forgave them. That night, for supper, the detachment celebrated. There was roast chicken with stuffing, lemon meringue pie and chocolate cake. The coffee burned their lips. More than half the men made it a point to compliment Carter on the meal.

In the weeks which followed the compliments diminished, but they never stopped completely. Carter became ashamed at last. He realized the men were trying to humor him, and he wished to tell them it was no longer necessary.

Harmony settled over the kitchen. Carter even became friends with Hobbs, the big Southerner. Hobbs approached him one day, and in the manner of a farmer talked obliquely for an hour. He spoke about his father, he spoke about his girl friends, he alluded indirectly to the night they had almost fought, and finally with the courtesy of a Southerner he said to Carter, "You know, I'm sorry about shooting off my mouth. You were right to want to fight me, and if you're still mad I'll fight you to give you satisfaction, although I just as soon would not."

"No, I don't want to fight with you now," Carter said warmly. They smiled at each other. They were friends.

Carter knew he had gained Hobbs' respect. Hobbs respected him because he had been willing to fight. That made sense to a man like Hobbs. Carter liked him so much at this moment that he wished the friendship to be more intimate.

"You know," he said to Hobbs, "it's a funny thing. You know I really never did sell anything on the black market. Not that I'm proud of it, but I just didn't."

Hobbs frowned. He seemed to be saying that Carter did not have to lie. "I don't hold it against a man," Hobbs said, "if he makes a little money in something that's his own proper work. Hell, I sell gas from the motor pool. It's just I also give gas if one of the G.I.s wants to take the jeep out for a joy ride, kind of."

"No, but I never did sell anything." Carter had to explain.

"If I ever had sold on the black market, I would have given the salad oil without question."

Hobbs frowned again, and Carter realized he still did not believe him. Carter did not want to lose the friendship which was forming. He thought he could save it only by some further admission. "You know," he said again, "remember when Porfirio broke up our fight? I was awful glad when I didn't have to fight you." Carter laughed, expecting Hobbs to laugh with him, but a shadow passed across Hobbs' face.

"Funny way of putting it," Hobbs said.

He was always friendly thereafter, but Carter knew that Hobbs would never consider him a friend. Carter thought about it often, and began to wonder about the things which made him different. He was no longer so worried about becoming a man; he felt that to an extent he had become one. But in his heart he wondered if he would ever learn the language of men.

1951

THE DEAD GOOK

The regiment was dispersed over an area twenty miles wide and more than ten miles deep. In the conventional sense it could hardly be called a front. Here could be found an outpost of ten men; there, one mile away, a platoon of thirty or forty men; somewhere to the rear was Hq. and Hq. company, somewhere to the flank another unit. Through all the foothills and mountains of this portion of the Philippines, a few thousand American soldiers in groups of ten and twenty and fifty faced approximately as many Japanese, established like themselves along the summits of advantageous heights or bedded in ambush in the tropical growth of the valleys and streams. There was almost no contact. If either army had wished to advance, and had added so much as another regiment, progress would have been rapid, but the fate of the campaign was being determined elsewhere. For a month and then another, as the mild winter ended and the tropical rains of spring began, the outposts and detachments of these isolated forces made long patrols against one another, tramped for miles over rice paddies, up small mountains, along narrow rivers, and through jungle forests—patrols which covered ten or fifteen or as many as twenty miles in a single day, and more often than not were entirely without incident. Instead of a front there was a mingling of isolated positions, with Japanese units between Americans, and Americans between Japanese. The patrols were as often to the rear as to the front, and small groups of men brushed one another with rotary maneuvers, each detachment sweeping its own area in a circle.

It was not the worst of situations. Casualties were very few, and supply was regular. Many of the outposts had hot food brought from the rear, and some of the detachments were stationed in Filipino villages and slept beneath a roof. Still, it was not the best of situations. There were patrols almost every day for every man, and though they were invariably uneventful, they were nonetheless hard work. A squad would leave at eight in the morning; it would be fortunate to return by the end of the afternoon. The morning sun would beat upon the men, the midday rain would drench them, mud would cake upon their boots. They went nowhere, they patrolled in circles, up mountains and down cliffs, and yet each of them was obliged to carry an assortment of gear which never weighed less than twenty-five pounds. They carried their rifles, they carried two grenades hooked to the load of their cartridge belts. Over their shoulders were slung two bandoliers of ammunition, at their hips tugged the sluggish weight of water canteens, in their breast pockets chafed the cardboard corners of a food ration. None of these items was heavy in itself; taken together they were hardly to be disregarded. It was a reasonable load for a healthy man upon a hunting trip; these were unhealthy men burdened by a chronic residue of such diseases as malaria and yellow jaundice, and such discomforts as foot ulcers, diarrhea, and fungus rot.

It was dreary. There was danger, but it was remote; there was diversion, but it was rare. For the most part it was work, and work of the most distasteful character, work which was mean and long. The men, most often, did not complain. There were better things to do, but there were certainly worse, and for those who had been overseas for several years and had participated in more than this campaign, it was certainly not the most odious way in which to serve their time. They were satisfied to let events pass in the most quiet manner possible.

On a particular spring morning, the third squad of the first platoon of B Company was preparing to go out on patrol. Because of illness and a single casualty, their numbers had been reduced in the last two months from twelve men to seven, and since two men had to be left behind on the knoll of the hill where they had dug their outpost to serve as guard and answer the telephone, only five men were left to satisfy the requirements of a patrol which counted theoretically upon a strength of ten. This fact, which in a more arduous campaign would be considered a dangerous injustice, was here accepted merely as an annoyance. There was always the possibility that something could happen where their lack of numbers might be disastrous, but inasmuch as they had been operating with five men for quite some time and nothing had as yet occurred, the main source of their grievance was that they almost never received any rest. If in one of the sudden and seemingly arbitrary disposals of replacements, they had been brought up to strength, it is likely that they would have continued to patrol with five men, and gained the advantage of an alternate day of inactivity.

This morning four Filipinos were apparently joining them. They appeared in the valley which lay beneath the knoll and strolled toward the outpost. Visible from quite a distance with their loose white shirts and bright blue pants, they advanced without caution as if expecting to be recognized. Lucas, the buck sergeant in command of the squad, had been on the phone earlier in the morning, and now he said quietly, "Well, here they are. Let's get ready." He had already named the men who were to go out, and they were strapping on their equipment. In a few minutes, he and the four other men weaved down through the grass of the hill and moved toward the Filipinos in the rice paddy.

"What's up, we got the Gooks today?" Brody, a thin hard-bitten private, asked of Lucas.

"Seems like we do." Lucas was a big relaxed man who spoke slowly and thought slowly. He was not very intelligent and did not pretend to be, but perhaps for this reason he was not a bad soldier as sergeants go. Events rarely ruffled him. He had small sensitivity to distinguish between the extraordinary and the commonplace, and so he took his orders, acted upon that portion of them he understood, and was never agitated if things turned out differently than had been expected.

Private Brody was nervous, he was high-strung, he was

134

often angry. "Well, what the hell are the Gooks here for?" he asked, pointing to the Filipinos.

"Shoot if I know," Lucas drawled. He was readjusting a grenade in his belt. "There was some kind of fuss over the telephone. The Gooks are from Panazagay, some such place. They went to headquarters this morning, and then headquarters decided to send them here."

The squad approached the Filipinos. They were small brown men with the lithe bodies of Oriental peasants, and they all smiled in unison at the soldiers.

"Sergeant Lucas, sair?" one of them inquired. By the way he stood forward from the others it was apparent that he was the only one who spoke English.

"How do," Lucas said mildly. He was courteous and bored.

The Filipino who spoke English began to talk to Lucas. He spoke at great length in a stammering mixture of what was English and of what he thought was English. The other men in the squad did not bother to listen. They squatted on their heels in the muddy turf of the rice paddy, and looked dispassionately at the Filipinos who squatted in a line, facing them, about ten yards away. From time to time one of the Filipinos would smile, and in response one of the Americans would nod. Off to one side, Lucas stood heavily, his ear inclined to catch a detail here and there in the seemingly endless story.

"Let me get this straight," he asked quietly. "The guerrillas ambushed the Japs?"

"No, sair, no don't know. Maybe Jap, maybe guerrilla, big ambush maybe. Lot of shooting. Guerrilla no come back. Now, American soldiers ambush Jap maybe."

Lucas nodded. It was obvious he knew no more than before, and as he continued to listen, it became equally obvious that he no longer bothered to distinguish the words. When the Filipino had exhausted his account, Lucas yawned.

"All right. What's your name? Miguel?"

"Yes, sair."

"Okay, Miguel, you lead us. You take us where you want. Only nice and slow, you understand? We're in no hurry, and it's a hot day."

Miguel said something to the other Filipinos in the Tagalog

language, and they answered curtly. They stood up, and began to move across the paddy at a half-trot.

"That's what I meant," Lucas said to Miguel. "Tell him to slow up."

Reluctantly, he conveyed this message to the other three Filipinos, who seemed to obey it just as reluctantly.

"Man, they're always in a hurry," Lucas drawled aloud.

The other four soldiers fell into line behind their sergeant. The Filipinos moved in a group which was bunched close together, and about thirty yards in front of the Americans, who moved in a leisurely file with some distance between them. None of the soldiers knew what the patrol was about, and they did not bother to ask. There was only so much variety to a patrol, and it had long been exhausted. There seemed no reason now to inquire. If all went well, they would find out in due time. They did not even bother to watch the direction in which they moved; they had been over these hills and paddies so often that it was almost impossible for them to get lost. They trudged along behind Lucas, their guns slung, their heads drooped forward to examine the footing before them. Not even the thought of an ambush caused them much concern. In such a large area there was small likelihood that at any given moment enemy troops might blunder into one another. To attempt to be constantly on the alert seemed a little ridiculous. Each followed the man in front of him, daydreamed a little, looked about him a little, and tried not to think too exclusively of the heat or the sores upon his legs or the familiar small distress of his chronic diarrhea.

Only Brody was an exception. Brody worried, Brody was irritable, Brody saw all kinds of possibilities. "Where are we going?" he panted as he walked behind Lucas.

"Oh, I don't know," Lucas said. "We're just following the Gooks."

Brody trotted for a few steps and caught up to the sergeant. "Well, why?"

Lucas shrugged. "I guess they sold the Old Man a bill of goods. He told me to go along with 'em."

"What did the Gooks say?" Brody persisted.

"Miguel, he said a lot, but I just can't follow that Gook talk. It's something about an ambush, and guerrillas and Japs. It's all a mess and I bet it's a false alarm. You know these Gooks, how excited they get."

"Me, I know them," Brody said with ferocity. "I hate the

Gooks." He tripped in a hole the hoof of a carabao had made and jarred his ankle. "They're always laughing at us. They're dirty, you see, they're two-faced." As abruptly as he had spoken, he lapsed into a frustrated silence.

Lucas made no answer. He had pouched a cut of tobacco in his cheek, and he moved with the long lazy pace of a big man, holding his rifle in one hand and allowing it to swing in rhythm to his steps. "Oh, there're good Gooks and bad Gooks," Lucas said after a while.

Brody cursed. "Look at them with their white shirts. They can be seen from ten miles away." His body quivered with pent emotion.

Lucas reddened. The truth was that he had not paid attention to this detail. "That don't make much difference," he muttered.

"It does to me." Lucas' dismissal of everything he had said fretted Brody. Perspiration ran into his eyes. "Hey, you," Brody shrieked at the Filipinos ahead, "hey, you Gooks, take off those shirts. You want to get us ambushed?"

They looked at him stupidly, they smiled, they tried to understand. Blindly, Brody ran toward them, his canteens, his ration, his bandolier and grenades jouncing with leaden metallic sounds as he trotted. He shoved the first Filipino in his path with force enough to send him almost to the ground. "Your shirt," Brody said apoplectically, "get it off."

They comprehended at last. They smiled again, they murmured apologies, they stripped their shirts to expose their brown chests and wrapped the white cotton about their waists like a belt.

"That's better," Brody grunted. He slowed his pace and fell into line behind Lucas who did not look at him. Lucas merely shifted the plug from one side of his mouth to the other.

Brody was in a state which all the men in the squad could recognize. It visited each of them at different times. A man's normal manner might be friendly or distant or casual, but there were periods when he seemed to consist of nothing but rage, when his outraged nerves would snap surly responses to the most insignificant questions, and everything he did expressed a generalized hatred toward the most astonishing people and objects—his best friend or a stone he might kick with his foot. Brody was experiencing such a period.

It started with a letter from his girl friend that told him

she was to marry someone else. She had waited for four years, but she was waiting no longer. In a sense the letter hardly bothered him. His girl friend had become as remote to Brody as the moon. But the letter had nonetheless served to remind Brody of how he lived, and that was unbearable. He had seen a great deal of combat, he had gone through all the stages. He had had the excitement of the untested soldier, and the competence of the veteran; he had passed from the notion that he would never be killed to the gloomy and then indifferent acceptance of the idea that he probably would be killed. He had even come to the point where it no longer mattered particularly. Like the other men, his senses diminished, his thoughts slowed, and time was a neutral vacuum in which neutral experience was spent. Life passed in a mild and colorless depression.

The letter destroyed his armor. It reminded him of a world in which people cared enough about themselves to take such actions as getting married. It awakened in him a feeling that it might not be unpleasant to live, and that feeling made much intolerable. It made death vivid to him again, and worse than that, it made him conscious of himself. It did the worst thing which could befall a soldier in combat, it made Brody wonder who he was, and what it would mean if he would die. There was no way to find out, there was no way even to think about it connectedly. The result was that every sleeping nerve in Brody's body had become alive and asked its question. The only answer, considering conditions, was a grass-fire of hatred which smoldered within him, and rasped into flame at anything which crossed his path. On this particular day it was the Filipinos. For the moment Brody considered them as directly responsible for everything which had happened to him.

Slowly, the patrol moved on. The men crossed rice paddies and swamps, they traversed trails through bamboo groves, and climbed hills with tall grass and scattered trees. The heat increased as the sun moved toward its zenith, and gnats, mosquitoes, and flies plagued the exposed surfaces of their skin. After an hour had passed they took a break and then moved on again. It was hot and the faded green fatigues of the soldiers began to turn black with their perspiration. They were thirsty. The sun beat upon their heads.

The hills were now covered with brush. Soon the brush thickened, the ground became softer, more muddy, and the trees grew higher. Their foliage met overhead and dimmed the light of the day. It was still hot, but it was dark now, it was steamy, and the air had the stagnant expectancy of a thunderstorm. The men sweated even more profusely.

The Filipinos came to a small brook which they forded. On the other side the trail split into two forks. Miguel came back to talk to Lucas.

"Sair, is very dangerous from here. Jahpanese, many Jahpanese."

Lucas nodded. "Okay, let's watch our step." He gathered his men about him, and informed them of what Miguel had said. "Seems to me," he mumbled softly, "I was over this trail a couple of weeks ago and nothing was here. But maybe the Gooks know something. Let's keep our eyes open."

This warning from Lucas changed the character of the patrol. Now, every man was alert. It was often like this. After hours of dull marching all the men in the squad would seem to awaken at once, as if the fear or readiness of one man had been communicated to all.

The trail contributed to their caution. It was very narrow, and permitted only one man to pass at a time. Moreover, it took a turn to the left or right every few yards, and each soldier had the unpleasant sensation of watching the man in front disappear around each bend. Sweat dripped from their eyes, fell from their noses, ran into their mouths. They breathed heavily, and with each step they examined the foliage on either side of them, looking for a possible sniper. Each time a man blundered over a root or made some small noise, the others winced in unison. After ten minutes of working along the trail, they were more tired than they had been at any time that day, they were hotter, they were wetter, they were more oppressed.

Lucas whistled to Miguel. "Stop your men." Miguel looked as if he wished to continue, but Lucas had sat down already. "We're taking a break. Pass it down," he whispered to the man behind him.

Quietly, each man whispered the same message to his neighbor. They all remained standing for a moment, their damp shirts collapsed wetly upon their bodies, their mouths puffing at damp cigarettes whose paper was brown where sweat had reached it. They seated themselves cautiously, each soldier facing alternately an opposite side of the trail. Although they rested their backs against tree trunks, and draped their rifles over their knees, they were not

139

exactly in repose. Their heads were turned upward, their eyes studied the foliage before them, and the muscles in their forearms were tensed to grasp their rifles if it were necessary. Nonetheless they smoked their cigarettes.

Up ahead came a dull thumping sound. Each of the men started and then relaxed. It was the blade of a machete chopping into something—a wet branch, a mass of pulpy fruit—they did not know. A minute later the sounds ceased, and each man was rewarded with an unexpected comfort. Pieces of ripe pineapple cut from a pineapple bush by the Filipinos were passed back. They ate the fruit greedily, and watched for snipers. Their legs were tired, their eyes hurt from staring into the jungle, their throats were parched and reacted with delight to the sweet tart juices, their stomachs accepted the food with lust, and their arms trembled from the tension of holding a rifle, a piece of fruit, and a cigarette. There was both the blissful satisfaction of thirst as each mouthful was gorged from a shaking hand, and the anxious heavy knowledge that to rest on a trail like this was dangerous. In the gloom of the jungle each minute seemed more ominous, and yet the deliciousness of the feast was increased by the situation.

After some minutes, Lucas sent another message down the trail. One hoarse whisper generated the next. "Let's get going. Let's get going."

As they moved on, it became evident to Lucas that the Filipinos were heading toward a particular place. Their tension increased with every step, and they proceeded with more and more caution. Now, there were halts along the trail of a minute or more, while one Filipino would work ahead, would study the trail, and then come back to wave them forward. Half an hour passed with less ground covered every moment. The pauses increased the irritation, the fatigue, and the tension. The men would stand in the narrow trail, foliage tickling the back of their necks, insects plaguing their motionless bodies. To stand still became more onerous than to move. They were able to think of nothing but the heat, the humidity, and the smart of the sores upon their feet. They could hear sounds more intensely than when they marched. They could sense danger more acutely than if they were in motion. Altogether they felt more vulnerable and it made them cranky.

Brody fretted the most. "Tell them to get a move on, Lucas," he would whisper. Or else he would wipe his chin of its sweat. "Leave it to the Gooks," he would groan.

These protests seemed to leave Lucas quite indifferent. He stood placidly at the point, watching the Filipinos dart ahead and then work their way back, nodded solemnly each time they waved for him to come ahead, and then remained still while they reconnoitered the next few hundred feet of trail. "They're taking us into a trap," Brody hissed furiously, and Lucas shrugged. "I don't think so," he whispered back.

Traveling no more than a few hundred yards every quarter of an hour, the patrol inched forward along the trail. They crossed another brook, and while they waited several of the men quietly filled their canteens and inserted one of the pills they kept to disinfect their drinking water. A little further on, they passed the corpse of a Japanese soldier who was lying near the trail, and they took pains to keep as far away from him as possible, more from their repugnance of the feeding maggots than from the novelty of seeing a dead man.

They were soon to see another. It developed that the objective of the patrol was reached before they had even learned the objective. The trail rose for a few hundred feet, and then dipped into an empty draw. In the middle of the draw, lying behind a Japanese machine gun, lay a dead Filipino. Miguel and the three peasants stood at the top of the draw, and looked sadly upon him. One by one the soldiers reached them, until a group of nine men, five in uniform, and four in blue pants and white shirts wrapped about their middle, collected on one bank of the small ravine and stared into the quiet buzzing sunlight which glinted upon the skin of the dead guerrilla and reflected the tropical yellow-green of the grass in the draw.

"Oh, sair," Miguel said softly to Lucas, "he brave mahn. He kill three Jahpanese last month. He come here every night."

"He came here alone every night?" Brody asked.

Miguel nodded. "Last night in village we hear shooting. Jahpanese grenade. Luiz no possess Jahpanese grenade. They kill him, we think, last night."

"What'd he want to set up for in the middle of the draw?" Lucas asked. "He's a sitting duck there."

"Oh," Miguel said, "Luiz only amateur soldier."

Lucas looked at him sharply, but Miguel's expression was impassive. Lucas yawned. "Let's scout around, men, there might still be Japs here."

The fragment of the squad divided into two men and three

men. Lucas and Brody circled the draw from one side, and joined the others on the continuation of the trail. The draw seemed deserted. "Cover me," Lucas said, and darted into the open grass.

He approached the dead man cautiously to make certain no wires connected him to a booby trap. After a moment he waved to Brody to join him.

"We might as well take the gun back," he said. "That's a nice Jap machine gun." He looked at it with the professional curiosity of a hobbyist. "Man, that's a funny old gun," Lucas said.

Miguel joined them at the bottom of the draw. "Sair, we go back now?"

"I guess we found what we came for." Lucas shrugged.

"Sair. Four Filipinos. We carry back body. You come with Filipinos?"

Brody shouldered his way between them. "It's going to slow us up. Let them do it on their own."

"Sair, very dangerous without American soldiers."

Lucas was working the bolt on the Japanese weapon. "This is a real light machine gun. It's sort of like our BAR," he announced. Miguel touched him tentatively on the sleeve, and Lucas looked up. "I guess we can go along with them," he said to Brody half-apologetically.

Brody felt as if an injustice were being perpetrated. "They tricked us into coming out here," he swore. "All they wanted us for was to pick up one of their lousy men. They could have done this whole patrol themselves."

"I dunno," Lucas murmured. "I mean a man deserves a funeral. We'll escort them, I suppose." He looked away from Brody, and patted the gun. "We ought to take this, too."

"What for?" Brody demanded. "It's heavy."

"Oh, just because." Lucas was thinking with pleasure of stripping the gun when he returned to the outpost. He intended to take it completely apart, and then put it back together again. The thought of this gave him a feeling of anticipation for the first time in months.

Brody was angrier than ever. Everything Lucas did seemed outrageous. Like a man who wishes to strike a woman and frustrates the impulse, Brody now effectively begged the woman to strike him. With passion he picked up the Japanese machine gun. "You want to take it back?" he asked rhetorically of Lucas. "Well, I'll carry the bugger."

"That's right, Brody, you carry it all the way back." Brody realized he had gone too far. "And I don't want to hear any griping," Lucas added.

The patrol started back. It was hotter than ever, it was wetter than ever, it began to rain again. The soldiers plodded forward through a gumbo muck, and the Filipinos staggered behind them, carrying the body of Luiz, the dead guerrilla, lashed to a pole. Now, it was the Americans who wanted to go fast, who wished to quit the contaminated area as quickly as possible, and it was the Filipinos mired in the labor of carrying a dead man on a heavy pole who time and again were forced to stop.

Brody stepped along in a rage. The Japanese machine gun must have weighed at least twenty pounds; added to the load of his own gear, it was a cruel increment. There seemed no way to hold the gun properly. No matter how he slung it, over a shoulder, upon his back, in front of his belly, the gun seemed all knobs, protuberances, points and edges. Either the stock, the muzzle, or the handle of the bolt was always pressing into his ribs, his arms, his shoulder blades. Worst of all the gun had a detestable odor. There was the smell of Japanese fish oil, and the smell of Luiz who had acquired the gun, a smell of Filipino peasant which to Brody meant carabao flop and Philippine dust and Filipino food, an amalgam not unlike stale soya sauce. Worst of all, there was the odor of Luiz' blood, a particularly sweet and intimate smell, fetid and suggesting to his nostrils that it was not completely dry. It was the smell of a man who had died, and it mingled with the fish oil and the soya sauce and the considerable stench of Brody's own body and Brody's own work-sweated clothes, until he thought he would gag. The odor was everywhere; it stuck to his lungs and eddied in his nostrils. As he perspired, his sweat touched the gun, seemed to dissolve from it newer, more unpleasant odors. Brody traveled on his anger. It was his luck, he thought incoherently, to have a man like Lucas for a sergeant; it was his luck to be in a squad so stupid that the stupidest of Filipinos and the most cunning could take them in, or more properly, could take them anywhere, take them on a five-mile hike, for what, for nothing, to serve as escort so they could bring one of their own men back, a man stupid enough to go out at night and get himself killed. Brody began to think it was a plot. It had all been calculated to make him carry the machine gun. The smell became Luiz to him, and he cursed the gun as he walked, talking to Luiz and telling him what a no-good Gook he thought him to be, spanking the gun away as it thudded upon his ribs and jabbed his sternum. Trust the Gooks, trust the Gooks, trust the blasted Gooks, he kept repeating to himself, saying it faster and faster like a talisman to protect him in his exasperation and growing exhaustion from bursting into tears of childish frenzy.

The walk back was exceptionally long. The Filipinos jogged and panted from their exertion, dropped the pole when the Americans would rest, and picked it up to run in their Oriental half-trot each time the Americans would start again. When they came out of the jungle, the patrol set across the fields toward the Filipino village, toward Panazagay. The sun broiled them, the rain wet them, the sun dried them again. Heat drenched their clothing with body moisture. Brody staggered, the Filipinos staggered, the others trudged, and the sun fried the bowl of earth over which they traveled. How the gun stank!

Brody would hardly have cared if they had been ambushed by Japanese. He would have flopped to the ground, and let the others worry about it. He did not bother to look ahead of him. He merely wavered along for thirty or forty steps, and then outraged his lungs by running for ten or fifteen yards to catch up with the last American. To the Filipinos behind him, he paid no attention. He was thinking of all kinds of things. Through the stupor of the march, he could not rid himself of the idea that he was carrying a dead man in his arms. A man who was completely dead. He had seen dead men whole and dead men in fractions and mutilations, but this was the first dead man who was completely dead to Brody, and it filled him with fright. He was not too far from delirium. It seemed almost possible that Luiz was carrying him, and he was the one who had died. What did it mean? He had seen so much death that death was the one thing absolutely without meaning to him. Except for now. It filled his pores. To the hot sweat of the sun he added the cold sweat of his thoughts. Brody's tortured nerves could have been relieved only by a scream.

"Pigs, the Gooks are pigs," he muttered aloud. "They live like pigs." And the gun hugged him, a dancing skeleton, jiggling its death's-head in his face.

The patrol came at last to Panazagay, a village of bamboo houses upon stilts with a muddy lane between the houses, and no street at all, no stores at all. The Filipino carriers brought the body of Luiz to his home. It was a small bamboo house and stood in front of the village pump. The soldiers sprawled by the pump, bathed their heads and bodies with water, and lay around heavily, too fatigued to eat.

From the house came screams. A woman's scream, then a child's wail, then the cries of several women and children. People began to emerge from all the houses of the village, they converged upon the house in front of the village pump, they climbed the bamboo ladder which led into the bamboo house. A concert of grief spread in volume from moment to moment. The soldiers lay on the ground and hardly heard these cries.

They were far too weary. The sounds of bereavement seemed as remote as Oriental music with its unfamiliar scale. Women wept, children wept, grief washed from the bamboo house with the regularity and monotony of surf. After a while the soldiers were rested enough to eat, and they plugged languidly at their hard cheese, their cardboard biscuits, and sipped indifferently at their antiseptic water.

When they had finished and their siesta was run, they were fresh enough to look with some curiosity at the tear-stained faces of the male and female peasants who left the bamboo house. Lucas decided it was time to return. The five men of the squad hooked up their cartridge belts, slung their bandoliers, grasped their rifles, and prepared to move out. Miguel intercepted them.

In his broken speech of English and its facsimile, he thanked the members of the patrol in the name of Luiz' widow, he expressed to them her gratitude for returning her husband, and conveyed her apologies for not inviting them to eat. Lucas accepted this like a courtier, and told Miguel to tell her that the American soldiers were happy to have been of aid. The two men shook hands, and Lucas slapped the stock of his rifle to cover his embarrassment.

"Say, Miguel," he said.

"Sair?"

"What made this fellow Luiz"—he pronounced it *Louise*—"go out like that?"

"Do not know, sair, very brave mahn. His son killed by Jahpanese. Luiz go out every night for month."

Lucas whistled. "Well, what do you know."

"Yes, sair."

"Yeah, I guess he was all right," Lucas said. He waved a hand at Miguel, and strolled his men out of the village.

There was a three-mile walk back to the outpost. It ran along the ridges of bare grass-covered hills, and the men climbed up, and then down, and then around the flank of endless swells of earth. Brody walked with his head down, sucking air, his chest heaving helplessly. It was one of the longest three miles he had ever walked, and he had walked some which were long indeed. When they reached the outpost, he flung himself on the ground beside the machine gun he had carried, and lay there panting. The two men who had been on guard through the day came over to examine the gun, but Brody snarled at them like an animal.

"What do you think, you own it?" one complained.

"I carried that gun, see? I get to look at it first."

While the other members of the squad were washing themselves in water which they poured from five-gallon jerricans into their helmets, or were writing letters, or were sleeping in their holes, Brody stared at the gun. He was preparing to clean it when Lucas came over to claim the prize. Brody was too tired to argue. Passively, he relinquished the gun to Lucas, and dropped into his hole to rest.

Brody fell asleep, was awakened for the evening meal which was brought up in a jeep. It consisted of hot stew in an insulated pot and heated coffee. He munched it down and fell asleep again, slumbering like a drunk drugged with his alcohol. Even when he was awakened for guard in the middle of the night, he was still tired. He sat in the machine-gun emplacement, and stared into the valley below. Illumined by a full moon, the grass rustled in swells of silver light and shadow. There was a period of fifteen minutes when he sat with his hand on the bolt of the machine gun, convinced that he could see two men standing close to one another in the field. It turned out to be a horse which had somehow wandered there, and though Brody did not even know if the guerrilla Luiz had possessed a horse, he was nonetheless certain that the horse belonged to the dead Filipino.

Luiz had waited alone in a moonlit draw, waiting for Japanese to come so he could ambush them. Luiz had carried the machine gun in darkness down the trail where they had stopped to eat the pineapple, and he had sat alone to wait on a silver night with nothing for company but the slithering of animals and the torment of insects. It seemed impossible; it seemed . . . enormous. The force of this entered Brody's recognition like an iron spike.

146

For the first time Brody really heard the weeping of the Filipino women. They had all been crying for the dead Gook. In the security of his machine-gun emplacement, Brody shivered. It made him terribly uneasy. If he were killed at this moment, the men in the squad would stand around and look at him. Eventually the news would reach the few men he knew in other squads of other platoons. They would say, "Tough, wasn't it, about Brody?" or perhaps they would say no more than, "Brody, was he the guy who . . . ?" Who did what? Brody had the uncomfortable sensation of wondering what in his life had he ever done?

He felt a million miles from anyone else on the face of the earth. He had never done a thing in his life which he could consider the least bit exceptional, he could not think of anything to do. He only felt that somehow before he died he must do something. He must be remembered.

He thought of his parents. They would cry for him, but he no longer knew what they were like. He no longer believed in them. He was isolated on a little hill beneath a vast tropic night, and no one nor nothing cared for him. The family of Luiz had wept, they had wept over a dead Gook. But who would weep for Brody?

It was unfair. He was stripped of the casual monotony, the dull work, and the saving depression which had wrapped him like a bandage. He was naked, and it was one of the most terrifying experiences in his life. When his hour of guard was over, Brody lay on his back and shuddered with dread. The sky above his head was infinite and black—like death it could absorb him.

Yet somehow, in the morning, the crisis was past. His nerves had gone to sleep. Brody took up again his anonymous place in the squad. He was just another of the seven men, one who talked no more and talked no less, who wrote his letters, and played his cards, and went out laconically for the daily patrols. It was soon the turn of another to sulk, to be moody, and to spit furious answers to well-intentioned questions.

Brody, however, did not forget completely. Out of all the patrols he had made, and out of all the patrols he was to make in the months ahead, he always remembered the patrol which had found Luiz. When the campaign ended, and the regiment went into garrison to train for the coming invasion of Japan, Brody found himself thinking of the bamboo house and the village water pump at the most extraordinary times. He would remember it when he was

147

drunk, or in the midst of a training class, and once even at the climax of a poker game when he had won a big hand. The night the war ended, he remembered the patrol in the most peculiar way of all.

He and Lucas had gone out to get drunk. They had drifted through the small Filipino city where the regiment had been garrisoned, and they had listened to the celebration of small-arms fire being shot off into the sky. They had wandered and wandered, drunk yet numb, unable to talk to one another. They each felt frozen.

At the end of town they came to a little street which had been razed in the course of the battle for the city. All the wooden and concrete homes had been destroyed, and in their place, drawn from the junkyard of war's familiar passage, were tiny shacks built from cartons and packing crates and rusted corrugated roofing. Filipinos were living in the cabins, and from several the light of a candle guttered in its holder, throwing a warm glow upon the burlap curtains which hung limply in the cool of the August evening. The shacks reminded Brody of a street of shanties at the edge of the American town where he lived, and he recalled a time when he had walked there with a girl on a warm night of summer. He kicked aside a bit of rubble, and said, "Remember the Gook with the Jap machine gun?"

"Yeah," said Lucas as if both of them had known him well, "he was a funny guy."

"Yeah."

The thaw had come. "Remember Newman, and how he got it at Aitape?" Lucas asked.

"Yeah, and Benton."

"That's right, Benton," Lucas said.

They walked, they reminisced. To Brody the two years and a fraction of harsh empty time he had spent on islands of the Pacific began to fill with the accumulation of small detail which made memory supportable. He thought it was the liquor, but he was beginning to feel very sad. He had a picture of all the men who had been killed on all the beaches, under all the coconut trees, in all the swamps and jungles and paddies of all the alien land they had traversed, and he could have wept for them if Lucas were not there. He wished that they could be present to smell the Philippine twilight on the day the war ended.

They talked, and night deepened over the rubble of a Philippine city, and they went at last to join the line of soldiers waiting to see a movie under the big tent in the tent city of the regiment. No one could sit still, and long before the movie was over, Brody and Lucas went out into the night and walked away. They bought a bottle from a Filipino dealer, and Brody drank more liquor, Brody staggered back to his cot.

As he fell asleep on the night of victory, he discovered himself weeping for Luiz, weeping as hard as the old women in the bamboo house. He wept for Luiz with all his heart because now it was no longer unbearably necessary that he find someone to weep for him.

1951

ADVERTISEMENT FOR THE NOTEBOOK

The story was published first in The Cornhill, *an English magazine, and it received some complimentary remarks in the prime editorial of the* Times Literary Supplement *that week, in fact it was given more lines of comment than any of my novels ever picked up in the short reviews of English newspapers. On the other hand, a girl came to me after I made an appearance at a writing course John Aldridge was giving in the New School a year or two ago and she said, "Mr. Mailer! How did you have the nerve to put your name on that short story?"*

Well, I don't know but what she might be right. "The Notebook" was written in an hour, and it's perfectly fair to take it seriously or decide it's a trifle. Sometimes I think it captures one of those moments which come upon people when they stare at their face too long in the mirror and realize that the face, yes, that face, is the one face they can never escape.

THE NOTEBOOK

The writer was having a fight with his young lady. They were walking toward her home, and as the argument continued, they walked with their bodies farther and farther apart.

The young lady was obviously providing the energy for the quarrel. Her voice would rise a little bit, her head and shoulders would move toward him as though to add weight to her words, and then she would turn away in disgust, her heels tapping the pavement in an even precise rhythm which was quite furious.

The writer was suffering with some dignity. He placed one leg in front of the other, he looked straight ahead, his face was sad, he would smile sadly from time to time and nod his head to every word she uttered.

"I'm sick and tired of you," the young lady exclaimed. "I'm sick and tired of you being so superior. What do you have to be superior about?"

"Nothing," the writer said in so quiet a voice, so gentle a tone that his answer might as well have been, "I have my saintliness to be superior about."

"Do you ever give me anything?" the young lady asked, and provided the response herself. "You don't even give me the time of day. You're the coldest man I've ever known."

"Oh, that's not true," the writer suggested softly.

"Isn't it? Everybody thinks you're so nice and friendly, everybody except anybody who knows you at all. Anybody who knows you, knows better."

The writer was actually not unmoved. He liked this young lady very much, and he did not want to see her unhappy. If with another part of his mind he was noticing the way she constructed her sentences, the last word of one phrase seeming to provide the impetus for the next, he was nonetheless paying attention to everything she said.

"Are you being completely fair?" he asked.

"I've finally come to understand you," she said angrily. "You don't want to be in love. You just want to say the things you're supposed to say and watch the things you're supposed to feel."

"I love you. I know you don't believe me," the writer said.

"You're a mummy. You're nothing but a . . . an Egyptian mummy."

The writer was thinking that when the young lady became angry, her imagery was at best somewhat uninspired. "All right, I'm a mummy," he said softly.

They waited for a traffic light to change. He stood at the curb, smiling sadly, and the sadness on his face was so complete, so patient and so perfect, that the young lady with a little cry darted out into the street and trotted across on her high heels. The writer was obliged to run a step or two to catch up with her.

"Your attitude is different now," she continued. "You don't care about me. Maybe you used to, but you don't care any more. When you look at me, you're not really looking at all. I don't exist for you."

"You know you do."

"You wish you were somewhere else right now. You don't like me when I'm nasty. You think I'm vulgar. Very well, then, I'm vulgar. I'm too vulgar for your refined senses. Isn't that a pity? Do you think the world begins and ends with you?"

"No."

"No, what?" she cried.

"Why are you angry? Is it because you feel I didn't pay enough attention to you tonight? I'm sorry if I didn't. I didn't realize I didn't. I do love you."

"Oh, you love me; oh, you certainly do," the young lady said in a voice so heavy with sarcasm that she was almost weeping. "Perhaps I'd like to think so, but I know better." Her figure leaned toward his as they walked. "There's one thing I will tell you," she went on bitterly. "You hurt people more than the cruelest person in the world could. And why? I'll tell you why. It's because you never feel anything and you make believe that you do." She could see he was not listening, and she asked in exasperation, "What are you thinking about now?"

"Nothing. I'm listening to you, and I wish you weren't so upset."

Actually the writer had become quite uneasy. He had just thought of an idea to put into his notebook, and it made him anxious to think that if he did not remove his notebook from his vest pocket and jot down the thought, he was likely to forget it. He tried repeating the idea to himself several times to fix it in his memory, but this procedure was never certain.

"I'm upset," the young lady said. "Of course, I'm upset. Only a mummy isn't upset, only a mummy can always be reasonable and polite because they don't feel anything." If they had not been walking so quickly she would have stamped her foot. "What are you thinking about?"

"It's not important," he said. He was thinking that if he removed the notebook from his pocket, and held it in the palm of his hand, he might be able to scribble in it while they walked. Perhaps she would not notice.

It turned out to be too difficult. He was obliged to come to a halt beneath a street light. His pencil worked rapidly in nervous elliptic script while he felt beside him the pressure of her presence. *Emotional situation deepened by notebook*, he wrote. *Young writer, girl friend. Writer accused of being observer, not partici-*

152

*pant in life by girl. Gets idea he must put in notebook. Does so, and
brings the quarrel to a head. Girl breaks relationship over this.*

"You have an idea now," the young lady murmured.

"Mmm," he answered.

"That notebook. I knew you'd pull out that notebook." She began to cry. "Why, you're nothing but a notebook," she shrieked, and ran away from him down the street, her high heels mocking her misery in their bright tattoo upon the sidewalk.

"No, wait," he called after her. "Wait, I'll explain."

It occurred to the writer that if he were to do such a vignette, the nuances could be altered. Perhaps the point of the piece should be that the young man takes out his notebook because he senses that this would be the best way to destroy what was left of the relationship. It was a nice idea.

Abruptly, it also occurred to him that maybe this was what he had done. Had he wished to end his own relationship with his own young lady? He considered this, priding himself on the fact that he would conceal no motive from himself, no matter how unpleasant.

Somehow, this did not seem to be true. He did like the young lady, he liked her very much, and he did not wish the relationship to end yet. With some surprise, he realized that she was almost a block away. Therefore, he began to run after her. "No, wait," he called out. "I'll explain it to you, I promise I will." And as he ran the notebook jiggled warmly against his side, a puppy of a playmate, always faithful, always affectionate.

1951

ADVERTISEMENT FOR "THE MAN WHO STUDIED YOGA"

My short stories didn't do too well. While they were finally taken here and there, it is difficult to sell a story which is written without a particular magazine in mind. Any agent could have told me that, but I had been looking for therapy rather than for art, I was working up my nerve to write—as I've indicated, the time after the quick disappearance of Barbary Shore *was, in a quiet way, as bad perhaps as any time I ever had. In my mind I kept having disconnected thoughts about starting a long novel, but these scattered ideas came to very little until the night some friends brought the editor of a woman's fashion magazine over to a party I was giving. I had an apartment then on Pitt Street, way over on the lower East Side beneath the Williamsburgh Bridge, a grim apartment, renovated in battleship-gray. That week "The Paper House" was being considered by this lady's magazine, and it was thought in advance that our meeting would fix the matter. It did. The woman and I were without charm to one another, and when she left, it was obvious the magazine was not going to do "The Paper House." What was worse, the woman had been condescending. I was sick with myself for having slipped into that sort of situation, for having so tricked my sense of how things work that I could believe "The Paper House" might be printed in* Mademoiselle *or* Harper's Bazaar, *or* Vogue. *One would have to win the Nobel Prize before a fashion magazine would like a heroine who was a whorehouse whore.*

That evening was the end of many dead months for me. I was done with short stories and markets and editors and agents and thoughts of making my way back as some sort of amateur literary politician, done with trying to write less than I knew, rather than getting ready for something too large. I woke up in the morning with the plan for a prologue and an eight-part novel in my mind, the prologue to be the day of a small frustrated man, a minor artist manqué. The eight novels were to be eight stages of his dream later that night, and the books would revolve around the adventures of a mythical hero, Sergius O'Shaugnessy, who would travel through many worlds, through pleasure, business, communism, church, working class, crime, homosexuality and mysticism. To thicken the scheme, I was going to twist and scatter Time, having many of the characters reappear in different books, but with their ages altered. Eitel and Elena, for example, would be forty-five and twenty-five in The Deer Park, *and Sergius would be twenty-three, but later in the working-class novel, Elena would be a girl of seventeen having her first affair with Sergius whose age would have come from twenty-three to forty. So the past for one would be the future of another.*

Not a modest novel—one would need the seat of Zola and the mind of Joyce to do it properly. But at least I was out of my depression, and I spent the best of days for many a month, fired with notes and more notes for my characters and my eight novels.

If the reader is a little surprised at the Napoleonic confidence of a man waking up one morning ready to give the next fifteen years over to so savage a journey through the art of the novel, I may as well confess that I had gone into the Army with the idea that when I came out I would write the war novel of World War II. If I had had the peculiar fortune to get into combat, if I had gone for much of a year assuming I would probably be killed and so had forgotten my desire to write a war novel (which may have been what let me have my experience) well, no matter how, I had come out at the other end, I was able to write when I finished and write better than I ever had before, and so I had a big if erratic confidence about the size of my ambition.

If you will let me have a parenthesis here, I would say that major war novels are not difficult to write—it is just difficult to find writers of sizable talent who come close to war. Particularly in the last overorganized brawl, writers usually were classified as clerks, or put in special service. Almost all the time I was overseas, I had to dodge a career as one kind of clerk or another—any man in the infantry or cavalry who has a good I.Q. is sure to have his name turned up by the personnel cards whenever a new typist is needed. But I managed to stay a rifleman, and later my pride was that I had been able to take my patrols, my combat, and my fatigue without losing the nerves of my talent. That is not so easy. If there were ten of us who wrote good war novels about combat, there must have been a hundred who lost their talent in the deadening rhythms of war, its boredom, its concussion, and—let no one count this for too little—its injustice. One of the things I found most impressive about From Here to Eternity *was that Jones had probably gone through more than I, and had at least my force—of all the novels I've read by the writers of my generation, no other book gave me as much emotion.*

But I have strayed from my eight-part novel, and a few may be wondering what happened to it. The deeper I pushed into the first draft of The Deer Park, *the more I knew that this first of the eight novels was going to die of obscurity and a tortured style unless I gave way to the simpler novel which was coming forward from my characters. The decision to forget the eight-novel scheme did not come until I finished the first draft of* The Deer Park. *That was many months later, and I had a novel to work on, and a good prologue which could stand as a short novel, and so it was not too difficult to admit I was not ready.*

But, as you will find later in this book, there are a couple of thirty-page fragments from my—will it be a thousand pages?— from that long novel which has come into my mind again, a descendant of Moby Dick which will call for such time, strength, cash and patience that I do not know if I have it all to give, and so will skip the separate parts, avoid the dream, and try a more modest ascent on the spiral of Time.

"The Man Who Studied Yoga" is the prologue to the early scheme, and I wrote it in three or four weeks of hard concentrated work, helped more than a little by praise—which I could use in those days—from Lillian Ross, from Dan Wolf (now the editor of The Village Voice), *from my sister Barbara Alson, and from Adele Morales who was later to become my second wife.*

The following Preface was printed at the beginning of the Ballantine edition.

My last novel, *The Deer Park*, was originally conceived as the first book of an enormous eight-part novel. The themes of this huge—and finally unworkable—conception are buried in "The Man Who Studied Yoga," a short novel written as a prologue to all eight novels.

Long before I finished *The Deer Park* I had given up the larger project, and that novel was finally written to stand by itself. But as I believe will be noticed by those readers who have gone through *The Deer Park*, there is a play on certain names, particularly "O'Shaugnessy," in the Prologue printed here, as well as a few parallel situations.

Since "Yoga" is not entirely functional (certain excursions and diversions remaining as part of the abandoned architecture of the large work) perhaps I should have rewritten it to be more neatly complete in itself, but for reasons which are probably sentimental, I prefer to see it printed in this, its original form.

THE MAN WHO STUDIED YOGA

1.

I would introduce myself if it were not useless. The name I had last night will not be the same as the name I have tonight. For the moment, then, let me say that I am thinking of Sam Slovoda. Obligatorily, I study him, Sam Slovoda who is neither ordinary nor extraordinary, who is not young nor yet old, not tall nor short. He is sleeping, and it is fit to describe him now, for like most humans he prefers sleeping to not sleeping. He is a mild pleasant-looking man who has just turned forty. If the crown of his head reveals a little bald spot, he has nourished in compensation the vanity of a mustache. He has generally when he is awake an agreeable manner, at least with strangers; he appears friendly, tolerant, and genial. The fact is that like most of us, he is full of envy, full of spite, a gossip, a man who is pleased to find others are as unhappy as he, and yet—this is the worst to be said—he is a decent man. He is better than most. He would prefer to see a more equitable world, he scorns prejudice and privilege, he tries to hurt no one, he wishes to be liked. I will go even further. He has one serious virtue—he is not fond of himself, he wishes he were better. He would like to free himself of envy, of the annoying necessity to talk about his friends, he would like to love people more; specifically, he would like to love his wife more, and to love his two daughters without the tormenting if nonetheless irremediable vexation that they closet his life in the dusty web of domestic responsibilities and drudging for money.

How often he tells himself with contempt that he has the cruelty of a kind weak man.

May I state that I do not dislike Sam Slovoda; it is just that I am disappointed in him. He has tried too many things and never with a whole heart. He has wanted to be a serious novelist and now merely indulges the ambition; he wished to be of consequence in the world, and has ended, temporarily perhaps, as an overworked writer of continuity for comic magazines; when he was young he tried to be a bohemian and instead acquired a wife and family. Of his appetite for a variety of new experience I may say that it is matched only by his fear of new people and novel situations.

I will give an instance. Yesterday, Sam was walking along the street and a bum approached him for money. Sam did not see the man until too late; lost in some inconsequential thought, he looked up only in time to see a huge wretch of a fellow with a red twisted face and an outstretched hand. Sam is like so many; each time a derelict asks for a dime, he feels a coward if he pays the money, and is ashamed of himself if he doesn't. This once, Sam happened to think, I will not be bullied, and hurried past. But the bum was not to be lost so easily. "Have a heart, Jack," he called after in a whisky voice, "I need a drink bad." Sam stopped, Sam began to laugh. "Just so it isn't for coffee, here's a quarter," he said, and he laughed, and the bum laughed. "You're a man's man," the bum said. Sam went away pleased with himself, thinking about such things as the community which existed between all people. It was cheap of Sam. He should know better. He should know he was merely relieved the situation had turned out so well. Although he thinks he is sorry for bums, Sam really hates them. Who knows what violence they can offer?

At this time, there is a powerful interest in Sam's life, but many would ridicule it. He is in the process of being psychoanalyzed. Myself, I do not jeer. It has created the most unusual situation between Sam and me. I could go into details but they are perhaps premature. It would be better to watch Sam awaken.

His wife, Eleanor, has been up for an hour, and she has shut the window and neglected to turn off the radiator. The room is stifling. Sam groans in a stupor which is neither sleep nor refreshment, opens one eye, yawns, groans again, and lies twisted, strangled and trussed in pajamas which are too large for him. How painful it is for him to rise. Last night there was a party, and this morning, Sunday morning, he is awakening with a hangover. Invariably, he is depressed in the morning, and it is no different today. He finds himself in the flat and familiar dispirit of nearly all days.

It is snowing outside. Sam finally lurches to the window, and opens it for air. With the oxygen of a winter morning clearing his brain, he looks down six stories into the giant quadrangle of the Queens housing development in which he lives, staring morosely at the inch of slush which covers the monotonous artificial park that separates his apartment building from an identical structure not two hundred feet away. The walks are black where the snow has melted, and in the children's playground, all but deserted, one swing oscillates back and forth, pushed by an irritable little boy who plays by himself among the empty benches, swaddled in galoshes, muffler, and overcoat. The snow falls sluggishly, a wet snow which probably will turn to rain. The little boy in the playground gives one last disgusted shove to the swing and trudges away gloomily, his overshoes leaving a small animal track behind him. Back of Sam, in the four-room apartment he knows like a blind man, there is only the sound of Eleanor making breakfast.

Well, thinks Sam, depression in the morning is a stage of his analysis, Dr. Sergius has said.

This is the way Sam often phrases his thoughts. It is not altogether his fault. Most of the people he knows think that way and talk that way, and Sam is not the strongest of men. His language is doomed to the fashion of the moment. I have heard him remark mildly, almost apologetically, about his daughters: "My relation with them still suffers because I haven't worked through all my feminine identifications." The saddest thing is that the sentence has meaning to Sam even if it will not have meaning to you. A great many ruminations, discoveries, and memories contribute their connotation to Sam. It has the significance of a cherished line of poetry to him.

Although Eleanor is not being analyzed, she talks in a similar way. I have heard her remark in company, "Oh, you know Sam, he not only thinks I'm his mother, he blames me for being born." Like most women, Eleanor can be depended upon to employ the idiom of her husband.

What amuses me is that Sam is critical of the way others speak. At the party last night he was talking to a Hollywood writer, a young man with a great deal of energy and enthusiasm. The young man spoke something like this: "You see, boychick, I can spike any script with yaks, but the thing I can't do is heartbreak. My wife says she's gonna give me heartbreak. The trouble is I've had a real solid-type life. I mean I've had my ups and downs like all of humanity, but there's never been a shriek in my life. I don't know how to write shrieks."

On the trip home, Sam had said to Eleanor, "It was disgraceful. A writer should have some respect for language."

Eleanor answered with a burlesque of Sam's indignation. "Listen, I'm a real artist-type. Culture is for comic-strip writers."

Generally, I find Eleanor attractive. In the ten years they have been married she has grown plump, and her dark hair which once was long is now cropped in a mannish cut of the prevailing mode. But, this is quibbling. She still possesses her best quality, a healthy exuberance which glows in her dark eyes and beams in her smile. She has beautiful teeth. She seems aware of her body and pleased with it. Sam tells himself he would do well to realize how much he needs her. Since he has been in analysis he has come to discover that he remains with Eleanor for more essential reasons than mere responsibility. Even if there were no children, he would probably cleave to her.

Unhappily, it is more complicated than that. She is always— to use their phrase—competing with him. At those times when I do not like Eleanor, I am irritated by her lack of honesty. She is too sharp-tongued, and she does not often give Sam what he needs most, a steady flow of uncritical encouragement to counteract the harshness with which he views himself. Like so many who are articulate on the subject, Eleanor will tell you that she resents being a woman. As Sam is disappointed in life, so is Eleanor. She feels Sam has cheated her from a proper development of her potentialities and talent, even as Sam feels cheated. I call her dishonest because she is not so ready as Sam to put the blame on herself.

Sam, of course, can say all this himself. It is just that he experiences it in a somewhat different way. Like most men who have been married for ten years, Eleanor is not quite real to him. Last night at the party, there were perhaps half a dozen people whom he met for the first time, and he talked animatedly with them, sensing their reactions, feeling their responses, aware of the life in them, as they were aware of the life in him. Eleanor, however, exists in his nerves. She is a rather vague embodiment, he thinks of her as "she" most of the time, someone to conceal things from. Invariably, he feels uneasy with her. It is too bad. No matter how inevitable, I am always sorry when love melts into that pomade of affection, resentment, boredom and occasional compassion which is the best we may expect of a man and woman who have lived together a long time. So often, it is worse, so often no more than hatred.

They are eating breakfast now, and Eleanor is chatting about the party. She is pretending to be jealous about a young girl in a strapless evening gown, and indeed, she does not have to pretend altogether. Sam, with liquor inside him, had been leaning over the girl; obviously he had coveted her. Yet, this morning, when Eleanor begins to talk about her, Sam tries to be puzzled.

"Which girl was it now?" he asks a second time.

"Oh, you know, the hysteric," Eleanor says, "the one who was parading her bazooms in your face." Eleanor has ways of impressing certain notions upon Sam. "She's Charlie's new girl."

"I didn't know that," Sam mutters. "He didn't seem to be near her all evening."

Eleanor spreads marmalade over her toast and takes a bite with evident enjoyment. "Apparently, they're all involved. Charles was funny about it. He said he's come to the conclusion that the great affairs of history are between hysterical women and detached men."

"Charles hates women," Sam says smugly. "If you notice, almost everything he says about them is a discharge of aggression." Sam has the best of reasons for not liking Charles. It takes more than ordinary character for a middle-aged husband to approve of a friend who moves easily from woman to woman.

"At least Charles discharges his aggression," Eleanor remarks. "He's almost a classic example of the Don Juan complex. You notice how masochistic his women are?"

"I know a man or two who's just as masochistic."

Sam sips his coffee. "What made you say the girl was an hysteric?"

Eleanor shrugs. "She's an actress. And I could see she was a tease."

"You can't jump to conclusions," Sam lectures. "I had the impression she was a compulsive. Don't forget you've got to distinguish between the outer defenses, and the more deeply rooted conflicts."

I must confess that this conversation bores me. As a sample it is representative of the way Sam and Eleanor talk to each other. In Sam's defense I can say nothing; he has always been too partial to jargon.

I am often struck by how eager we are to reveal all sorts of supposedly ugly secrets about ourselves. We can explain the hatred we feel for our parents, we are rather pleased with the perversions to which we are prone. We seem determinedly proud to be superior to ourselves. No motive is too terrible for our inspection. Let someone hint, however, that we have bad table manners and we fly into a rage. Sam will agree to anything you may say about him, provided it is sufficiently serious—he will be the first to agree he has fantasies of murdering his wife. But tell him that he is afraid of waiters, or imply to Eleanor that she is a nag, and they will be quite annoyed.

Sam has noticed this himself. There are times when he can hear the jargon in his voice, and it offends him. Yet, he seems powerless to change his habits.

An example: He is sitting in an armchair now, brooding upon his breakfast, while Eleanor does the dishes. The two daughters are not home; they have gone to visit their grandmother for the weekend. Sam had encouraged the visit. He had looked forward to the liberty Eleanor and himself would enjoy. For the past few weeks the children had seemed to make the most impossible demands upon his attention. Yet now they are gone and he misses them, he even misses their noise. Sam, however, cannot accept the notion that many people are dissatisfied with the present, and either dream of the past or anticipate the future. Sam must call this "ambivalence over possessions." Once he even felt obliged to ask his analyst, Dr. Sergius, if ambivalence over possessions did not characterize him almost perfectly, and Sergius whom I always picture with the flat precision of a coin's head—bald skull and horn-rimmed glasses—answered in his German accent, "But, my dear Mr. Slovoda, as I have told you, it would make me happiest if you did not include in your reading, these psychoanalytical text-works."

At such rebukes, Sam can only wince. It is so right, he tells himself, he is exactly the sort of ambitious fool who uses big words when small ones would do.

2.

While Sam sits in the armchair, gray winter light is entering the windows, snow falls outside. He sits alone in a modern seat, staring at the gray, green, and beige décor of their living room. Eleanor was a painter before they were married, and she has arranged this room. It is very pleasant, but like many husbands, Sam resents it, resents the reproductions of modern painters upon the wall, the slender coffee table, a free-form poised like a spider on wire legs, its feet set onto a straw rug. In the corner, most odious of all, is the playmate of his children, a hippopotamus of a television-radio-and-phonograph cabinet with the blind monstrous snout of the video tube.

Eleanor has set the Sunday paper near his hand. Soon, Sam intends to go to work. For a year, he has been giving a day once or twice a month to a bit of thought and a little writing on a novel he hopes to begin sometime. Last night, he told himself he would work today. But he has little enthusiasm now. He is tired, he is too depressed. Writing for the comic strips seems to exhaust his imagination.

Sam reads the paper as if he were peeling an enormous banana. Flap after flap of newsprint is stripped away and cast upon the straw rug until only the Magazine Section is left. Sam glances through it with restless irritability. A biography of a political figure runs its flatulent prose into the giant crossword puzzle at the back. An account of a picturesque corner of the city becomes lost in statistics and exhortations on juvenile delinquency, finally to emerge with photographs about the new style of living which desert architecture provides. Sam looks at a wall of windows in rotogravure with a yucca tree framing the pool.

There is an article about a workingman. His wife and his family are described, his apartment, his salary and his budget. Sam reads a description of what the worker has every evening for dinner, and how he spends each night of the week. The essay makes its point; the typical American workingman must watch his pennies, but he is nonetheless secure and serene. He would not exchange his life for another.

Sam is indignant. A year ago he had written a similar article in an attempt to earn some extra money. Subtly, or so he thought, he had suggested that the average workingman was raddled with insecurity. Naturally, the article had been rejected.

Sam throws the Magazine Section away. Moments of such anger torment him frequently. Despite himself, Sam is enraged at editorial dishonesty, at the smooth strifeless world which such articles present. How angry he is—how angry and how helpless. "It is the actions of men and not their sentiments which make history," he thinks to himself, and smiles wryly. In his living room he would go out to tilt the windmills of a vast, powerful, and hypocritical society; in his week of work he labors in an editorial cubicle to create spaceships, violent death, women with golden tresses and wanton breasts, men who act with their fists and speak with patriotic slogans.

I know what Sam feels. As he sits in the armchair, the Sunday papers are strewn around him, carrying their war news, their murders, their parleys, their entertainments, mummery of a real world which no one can grasp. It is terribly frustrating. One does not know where to begin.

Today, Sam considers himself half a fool for having been a radical. There is no longer much consolation in the thought that the majority of men who succeed in a corrupt and acquisitive society are themselves obligatorily corrupt, and one's failure is therefore the price of one's idealism. Sam cannot recapture the pleasurable bitterness which resides in the notion that one has suffered for one's principles. Sergius is too hard on him for that.

They have done a lot of work on the subject. Sergius feels that Sam's concern with world affairs has always been spurious. For example, they have uncovered in analysis that Sam wrote his article about the worker in such a way as to make certain it would be refused. Sam, after all, hates editors; to have such a piece accepted would mean he is no better than they, that he is a mediocrity. So long as he fails he is not obliged to measure himself. Sam, therefore, is being unrealistic. He rejects the world with his intellect, and this enables him not to face the more direct realities of his present life.

Sam will argue with Sergius but it is very difficult. He will say, "Perhaps you sneer at radicals because it is more comfortable to ignore such ideas. Once you became interested it might introduce certain unpleasant changes in your life."

"Why," says Sergius, "do you feel it so necessary to assume that I am a bourgeois interested only in my comfort?"

"How can I discuss these things," says Sam, "if you insist that my opinions are the expression of neurotic needs, and your opinions are merely dispassionate medical advice?"

"You are so anxious to defeat me in an argument," Sergius will reply. "Would you admit it is painful to relinquish the sense of importance which intellectual discussion provides you?"

I believe Sergius has his effect. Sam often has thoughts these days which would have been repellent to him years ago. For instance, at the moment, Sam is thinking it might be better to live the life of a worker, a simple life, to be completely absorbed with such necessities as food and money. Then one could believe that to be happy it was necessary only to have more money, more goods, less worries. It would be nice, Sam thinks wistfully, to believe that the source of one's unhappiness comes not from oneself, but from the fault of the boss, or the world, or bad luck.

Sam has these casual daydreams frequently. He likes to think about other lives he might have led, and he envies the most astonishing variety of occupations. It is easy enough to see why he should wish for the life of an executive with the power and sense of command it may offer, but virtually from the same impulse Sam will wish himself a bohemian living in an unheated loft, his life a catch-as-catch-can from day to day. Once, after reading an article, Sam even wished himself a priest. For about ten minutes it seemed beautiful to him to surrender his life to God. Such fancies are common, I know. It is just that I, far better than Sam, know how serious he really is, how fanciful, how elaborate, his imagination can be.

The phone is ringing. Sam can hear Eleanor shouting at him to answer. He picks up the receiver with a start. It is Marvin Rossman who is an old friend, and Marvin has an unusual request. They talk for several minutes, and Sam squirms a little in his seat. As he is about to hang up, he laughs. "Why, no, Marvin, it gives me a sense of adventure," he says.

Eleanor has come into the room toward the end of this conversation. "What is it all about?" she asks.

Sam is obviously a bit agitated. Whenever he attempts to be most casual, Eleanor can well suspect him. "It seems," he says slowly, "that Marvin has acquired a pornographic movie."

"From whom?" Eleanor asks.

"He said something about an old boy friend of Louise's."

Eleanor laughs. "I can't imagine Louise having an old boy friend with a dirty movie."

"Well, people are full of surprises," Sam says mildly.

"Look, here," says Eleanor suddenly. "Why did he call us?"

"It was about our projector."

"They want to use it?" Eleanor asks.

"That's right." Sam hesitates. "I invited them over."

"Did it ever occur to you I might want to spend my Sunday some other way?" Eleanor asks crossly.

"We're not doing anything," Sam mumbles. Like most men, he feels obliged to act quite nonchalantly about pornography. "I'll tell you, I am sort of curious about the film. I've never seen one, you know."

"Try anything once, is that it?"

"Something of the sort." Sam is trying to conceal his excitement. The truth is that in common with most of us, he is fascinated by pornography. It is a minor preoccupation, but more from lack of opportunity than anything else. Once or twice, Sam has bought the sets of nude photographs which are sold in marginal bookstores, and with guilty excitement has hidden them in the apartment.

"Oh, this is silly," Eleanor says. "You were going to work today."

"I'm just not in the mood."

"I'll have to feed them," Eleanor complains. "Do we have enough liquor?"

"We can get beer." Sam pauses. "Alan Sperber and his wife are coming too."

"Sam, you're a child."

"Look, Eleanor," says Sam, controlling his voice, "if it's too much trouble, I can take the projector over there."

"I ought to make you do that."

"Am I such an idiot that I must consult you before I invite friends to the house?"

Eleanor has the intuition that Sam, if he allowed himself, could well drown in pornography. She is quite annoyed at him, but she would never dream of allowing Sam to take the projector over to Marvin Rossman's where he could view the movie without her—that seems indefinably dangerous. Besides she would like to see it, too. The mother in Eleanor is certain it cannot hurt her.

"All right, Sam," she says, "but you are a child."

More exactly, an adolescent, Sam decides. Ever since Marvin phoned, Sam has felt the nervous glee of an adolescent locking himself in the bathroom. Anal fixation, Sam thinks automatically.

While Eleanor goes down to buy beer and cold cuts in a delicatessen, Sam gets out the projector and begins to clean it. He is far from methodical in this. He knows the machine is all right, he has shown movies of Eleanor and his daughters only a few weeks ago, but from the moment Eleanor left the apartment, Sam has been consumed by an anxiety that the projection bulb is burned out. Once he has examined it, he begins to fret about the motor. He wonders if it needs oiling, he blunders through a drawer of household tools looking for an oilcan. It is ridiculous. Sam knows that what he is trying to keep out of his mind are the reactions Sergius will have. Sergius will want to "work through" all of Sam's reasons for seeing the movie. Well, Sam tells himself, he knows in advance what will be discovered: detachment, not wanting to accept Eleanor as a sexual partner, evasion of responsibility, etc. etc. The devil with Sergius. Sam has never seen a dirty movie, and he certainly wants to.

He feels obliged to laugh at himself. He could not be more nervous, he knows, if he were about to make love to a woman he had never touched before. It is really disgraceful.

When Eleanor comes back, Sam hovers about her. He is uncomfortable with her silence. "I suppose they'll be here soon," Sam says.

"Probably."

Sam does not know if he is angry at Eleanor or apprehensive that she is angry at him. Much to his surprise he catches her by the waist and hears himself saying, "You know, maybe tonight when they're gone . . . I mean, we do have the apartment to ourselves." Eleanor moves neither toward him nor away from him. "Darling, it's not because of the movie," Sam goes on, "I swear. Don't you think maybe we could . . ."

"Maybe," says Eleanor.

3.

The company has arrived, and it may be well to say a word or two about them. Marvin Rossman who has brought the film is a dentist, although it might be more accurate to describe him as a frustrated doctor. Rossman is full of statistics and items of odd information about the malpractice of physicians, and he will tell these things in his habitually gloomy voice, a voice so slow, so sad, that it almost conceals the humor of his remarks. Or, perhaps, that is what creates his humor. In his spare time, he is a sculptor, and if Eleanor may be trusted, he is not without talent. I often picture him working in the studio loft he has rented, his tall bony frame the image of dejection. He will pat a piece of clay to the armature, he will rub it sadly with his thumb, he will shrug, he does not believe that anything of merit could come from him. When he talked to Sam over the phone, he was pessimistic about the film they were to see. "It can't be any good," he said in his melancholy voice. "I know

167

it'll be a disappointment." Like Sam, he has a mustache, but Rossman's will droop at the corners.

Alan Sperber who has come with Rossman is the subject of some curiosity for the Slovodas. He is not precisely womanish; in fact, he is a large plump man, but his voice is too soft, his manners too precise. He is genial, yet he is finicky; waspish, yet bland; he is fond of telling long rather affected stories, he is always prepared with a new one, but to general conversation he contributes little. As a lawyer, he seems miscast. One cannot imagine him inspiring a client to confidence. He is the sort of heavy florid man who seems boyish at forty, and the bow ties and gray flannel suits he wears do not make him appear more mature.

Roslyn Sperber, his wife, used to be a schoolteacher, and she is a quiet nervous woman who talks a great deal when she is drunk. She is normally quite pleasant, and has only one habit which is annoying to any degree. It is a little flaw, but social life is not unlike marriage in that habit determines far more than vice or virtue. This mannerism which has become so offensive to the friends of the Sperbers is Roslyn's social pretension. Perhaps I should say intellectual pretension. She entertains people as if she were conducting a salon, and in her birdlike voice is forever forcing her guests to accept still another intellectual canapé. "You must hear Sam's view of the world market," she will say, or "Has Louise told you her statistics on divorce?" It is quite pathetic for she is so eager to please. I have seen her eyes fill with tears at a sharp word from Alan.

Marvin Rossman's wife, Louise, is a touch grim and definite in her opinions. She is a social welfare worker, and will declare herself with force whenever conversation impinges on those matters where she is expert. She is quite opposed to psychoanalysis, and will say without quarter, "It's all very well for people in the upper-middle area"—she is referring to the upper middle class—"but, it takes more than a couch to solve the problems of . . ." and she will list narcotics, juvenile delinquency, psychosis, relief distribution, slum housing, and other descriptions of our period. She recites these categories with an odd anticipation. One would guess she was ordering a meal.

Sam is fond of Marvin but he cannot abide Louise. "You'd think she discovered poverty," he will complain to Eleanor.

The Slovodas do feel superior to the Rossmans and the Sperbers. If pressed, they could not offer the most convincing explanation why. I suppose what it comes down to is that Sam and Eleanor do not think of themselves as really belonging to a class, and they feel that the Sperbers and Rossmans are petit-bourgeois. I find it hard to explain their attitude. Their company feels as much discomfort and will apologize as often as the Slovodas for the money they have, and the money they hope to earn. They are all of them equally concerned with progressive education and the methods of raising children to be well adjusted—indeed, they are discussing that now—they consider themselves relatively free of sexual taboo, or put more properly, Sam and Eleanor are no less possessive than the others. The Slovodas' culture is not more profound; I should be hard put to say that Sam is more widely read, more seriously informed, than Marvin or Alan, or for that matter, Louise. Probably, it comes to this: Sam, in his heart, thinks himself a rebel, and there are few rebels who do not claim an original mind. Eleanor has been a bohemian and considers herself more sophisticated than her friends who merely went to college and got married. Louise Rossman could express it most soundly. "Artists, writers, and people of the creative layer have in their occupational ideology the belief that they are classless."

One thing I might remark about the company. They are all being the most unconscionable hypocrites. They have rushed across half the city of New York to see a pornographic film, and they are not at all interested in each other at the moment. The women are giggling like tickled children at remarks which cannot possibly be so funny. Yet, they are all determined to talk for a respectable period of time. No less, it must be serious talk. Roslyn has said once, "I feel so funny at the thought of seeing such a movie," and the others have passed her statement by.

At the moment, Sam is talking about value. I might note that Sam loves conversation and thrives when he can expound an idea.

"What are our values today?" he asks. "It's really fantastic when you stop to think of it. Take any bright talented kid who's getting out of college now."

"My kid brother, for example," Marvin interposes morosely. He passes his bony hand over his sad mustache, and somehow the remark has become amusing, much as if Marvin had said, "Oh, yes, you have reminded me of the trials, the worries, and the cares which my fabulous younger brother heaps upon me."

"All right, take him," Sam says. "What does he want to be?"

"He doesn't want to be anything," says Marvin.

"That's my point," Sam says excitedly. "Rather than work at certain occupations, the best of these kids would rather do nothing at all."

"Alan has a cousin," Roslyn says, "who swears he'll wash dishes before he becomes a businessman."

"I wish that were true," Eleanor interrupts. "It seems to me everybody is conforming more and more these days."

They argue about this. Sam and Eleanor claim the country is suffering from hysteria; Alan Sperber disagrees and says it's merely a reflection of the headlines; Louise says no adequate criteria exist to measure hysteria; Marvin says he doesn't know anything at all.

"More solid liberal gains are being made in this period," says Alan, "than you would believe. Consider the Negro—"

"Is the Negro any less maladjusted?" Eleanor shouts with passion.

Sam maneuvers the conversation back to his thesis. "The values of the young today, and by the young, I mean the cream of the kids, the ones with ideas, are a reaction of indifference to the culture crisis. It really is despair. All they know is what they don't want to do."

"That is easier," Alan says genially.

"It's not altogether unhealthy," Sam says. "It's a corrective for smugness and the false value of the past, but it has created new false value." He thinks it worth emphasizing. "False value seems always to beget further false value."

"Define your terms," says Louise, the scientist.

"No, look," Sam says, "there's no revolt, there's no acceptance. Kids today don't want to get married, and—"

Eleanor interrupts. "Why should a girl rush to get married? She loses all chance for developing herself."

Sam shrugs. They are all talking at once. "Kids don't want to get married," he repeats, "and they don't want not to get married. They merely drift."

"It's a problem we'll all have to face with our own kids in ten years," Alan says, "although I think you make too much of it, Sam."

"My daughter," Marvin states. "She's embarrassed I'm a dentist. Even more embarrassed than I am." They laugh.

170

Sam tells a story about his youngest, Carol Ann. It seems he had a fight with her, and she went to her room. Sam followed, he called through the door.

"No answer," Sam says. "I called her again, 'Carol Ann.' I was a little worried you understand, because she seemed so upset, so I said to her, 'Carol-Ann, you know I love you.' What do you think she answered?"

"What?" asks Roslyn.

"She said, 'Daddie, why are you so anxious?' "

They all laugh again. There are murmurs about what a clever thing it was to say. In the silence which follows, Roslyn leans forward and says quickly in her high voice, "You must get Alan to tell you his wonderful story about the man who studied yogi."

"Yoga," Alan corrects. "It's too long to tell."

The company prevails on him.

"Well," says Alan, in his genial courtroom voice, "it concerns a friend of mine named Cassius O'Shaugnessy."

"You don't mean Jerry O'Shaugnessy, do you?" asks Sam.

Alan does not know Jerry O'Shaugnessy. "No, no, this is Cassius O'Shaugnessy," he says. "He's really quite an extraordinary fellow." Alan sits plumply in his chair, fingering his bow tie. They are all used to his stories, which are told in a formal style and exhibit the attempt to recapture a certain note of urbanity, wit, and *élan* which Alan has probably copied from someone else. Sam and Eleanor respect his ability to tell these stories, but they resent the fact that he talks *at* them.

"You'd think we were a jury of his inferiors," Eleanor has said. "I hate being talked down to." What she resents is Alan's quiet implication that his antecedents, his social position, in total his life outside the room is superior to the life within. Eleanor now takes the promise from Alan's story by remarking, "Yes, and let's see the movie when Alan has finished."

"Sssh," Roslyn says.

"Cassius was at college a good while before me," says Alan, "but I knew him while I was an undergraduate. He would drop in and visit from time to time. An absolutely extraordinary fellow. The most amazing career. You see, he's done about everything."

"I love the way Alan tells it," Roslyn pipes nervously.

"Cassius was in France with Dos Passos and Cummings, he was even arrested with e.e. After the war, he was one of the founders of the Dadaist school, and for a while I understand he was Fitz-gerald's guide to the gold of the Côte D'Azur. He knew everybody, he did everything. Do you realize that before the twenties had ended, Cassius had managed his father's business and then entered a monastery? It is said he influenced T. S. Eliot."

"Today, we'd call Cassius a psychopath," Marvin observes.

"Cassius called himself a great dilettante," Alan answers, "although perhaps the nineteenth-century Russian conception of the great sinner would be more appropriate. What do you say if I tell you this was only the beginning of his career?"

"What's the point?" Louise asks.

"Not yet," says Alan, holding up a hand. His manner seems to say that if his audience cannot appreciate the story, he does not feel obliged to continue. "Cassius studied Marx in the monastery. He broke his vows, quit the Church, and became a Communist. All through the thirties he was a figure in the Party, going to Moscow, involved in all the Party struggles. He left only during the Moscow trials."

Alan's manner while he relates such stories is somewhat effeminate. He talks with little caresses of his hand, he mentions names and places with a lingering ease as if to suggest that his audience and he are aware, above all, of nuance. The story as Alan tells it is drawn overlong. Suffice it that the man about whom he is talking, Cassius O'Shaughnessy, becomes a Trotskyist, becomes an anarchist, is a pacifist during the second World War, and suffers it from a prison cell.

"I may say," Alan goes on, "that I worked for his defense, and was successful in getting him acquitted. Imagine my dolor when I learned that he had turned his back on his anarchist friends and was living with gangsters."

"This is weird," Eleanor says.

"Weird, it is," Alan agrees. "Cassius got into some scrape, and disappeared. What could you do with him? I learned only recently that he had gone to India and was studying yoga. In fact, I learned it from Cassius himself. I asked him of his experiences at Brahna-puth-thar, and he told me the following story."

Now Alan's voice alters, he assumes the part of Cassius and speaks in a tone weary of experience, wise and sad in its knowledge. " 'I was sitting on my haunches contemplating my navel,' Cassius said to me, 'when of a sudden I discovered my navel under a different aspect. It seemed to me that if I were to give a counter-clockwise twist, my navel would unscrew.' "

Alan looks up, he surveys his audience which is now rapt and uneasy, not certain as yet whether a joke is to come. Alan's thumb and forefinger pluck at the middle of his ample belly, his feet are crossed upon the carpet in symbolic suggestion of Cassius upon his haunches.

" 'Taking a deep breath, I turned, and the abysses of Vishtarni loomed beneath. My navel had begun to unscrew. I knew I was about to accept the reward of three years of contemplation. So,' said Cassius, 'I turned again, and my navel unscrewed a little more. I turned and I turned,' " Alan's fingers now revolving upon his belly, " 'and after a period I knew that with one more turn my navel would unscrew itself forever. At the edge of revelation, I took one sweet breath, and turned my navel free.' "

Alan looks up at his audience.

" 'Damn,' said Cassius, 'if my ass didn't fall off.' "

4.

The story has left the audience in an exasperated mood. It has been a most untypical story for Alan to tell, a little out of place, not offensive exactly, but irritating and inconsequential. Sam is the only one to laugh with more than bewildered courtesy, and his mirth seems excessive to everyone but Alan, and of course, Roslyn, who feels as if she has been the producer. I suppose what it reduces to, is a lack of taste. Perhaps that is why Alan is not the lawyer one would expect. He does not have that appreciation— as necessary in his trade as for an actor—of what is desired at any moment, of that which will encourage as opposed to that which does not encourage a stimulating but smooth progression of logic and sentiment. Only a fool would tell so long a story when everyone is awaiting the movie.

Now, they are preparing. The men shift armchairs to cor-respond with the couch, the projector is set up, the screen is un-folded. Sam attempts to talk while he is threading the film, but no one listens. They seem to realize suddenly that a frightful demand has been placed upon them. One does not study pornography in a living room with a beer glass in one's hand, and friends at the elbow. It is the most unsatisfactory of compromises; one can draw neither the benefits of solitary contemplation nor of social exchange. There

173

is, at bottom, the same exasperated fright which one experiences in turning the shower tap and receiving cold water when the flesh has been prepared for heat. Perhaps that is why they are laughing so much now that the movie is begun.

A title, *The Evil Act*, twitches on the screen, shot with scars, holes, and the dust lines of age. A man and woman are sitting on a couch, they are having coffee. They chat. What they say is conveyed by printed words upon an ornately flowered card, interjected between glimpses of their casual gestures, a cup to the mouth, a smile, a cigarette being lit. The man's name, it seems, is Frankie Idell; he is talking to his wife, Magnolia. Frankie is dark, he is sinister, he confides in Magnolia, his dark counterpart, with a grimace of his brows, black from make-up pencil.

This is what the titles read:

FRANKIE: She will be here soon.
MAGNOLIA: This time the little vixen will not escape.
FRANKIE: No, my dear, this time we are prepared.
(*He looks at his watch.*)
FRANKIE: Listen, she knocks!

There is a shot of a tall blond woman knocking on the door. She is probably over thirty, but by her short dress and ribboned hat it is suggested that she is a girl of fifteen.

FRANKIE: Come in, Eleanor.

As may be expected, the audience laughs hysterically at this. It is so wonderful a coincidence. "How I remember Frankie," says Eleanor Slovoda, and Roslyn Sperber is the only one not amused. In the midst of the others' laughter, she says in a worried tone, obviously adrift upon her own concerns, "Do you think we'll have to stop the film in the middle to let the bulb cool off?" The others hoot, they giggle, they are weak from the combination of their own remarks and the action of the plot.

Frankie and Magnolia have sat down on either side of the heroine, Eleanor. A moment passes. Suddenly, stiffly, they attack. Magnolia from her side kisses Eleanor, and Frankie commits an indecent caress.

ELEANOR: How dare you? Stop!
MAGNOLIA: Scream, my little one. It will do you no good. The walls are soundproofed.

FRANKIE: We've fixed a way to make you come across.

ELEANOR: This is hideous. I am hitherto undefiled. Do not touch me!

The captions fade away. A new title takes their place. It says, *But There Is No Escape From The Determined Pair*. On the fade-in, we discover Eleanor in the most distressing situation. Her hands are tied to loops running from the ceiling, and she can only writhe in helpless perturbation before the deliberate and progressive advances of Frankie and Magnolia. Slowly they humiliate her, with relish they probe her.

The audience laughs no longer. A hush has come upon them Eyes unblinking they devour the images upon Sam Slovoda's screen.

Eleanor is without clothing. As the last piece is pulled away, Frankie and Magnolia circle about her in a grotesque of pantomime, a leering of lips, limbs in a distortion of desire. Eleanor faints. Adroitly, Magnolia cuts her bonds. We see Frankie carrying her inert body.

Now, Eleanor is trussed to a bed, and the husband and wife are tormenting her with feathers. Bodies curl upon the bed in postures so complicated, in combinations so advanced, that the audience leans forward, Sperbers, Rossmans, and Slovodas, as if tempted to embrace the moving images. The hands trace abstract circles upon the screen, passes and recoveries upon a white background so illumined that hollows and swells, limb to belly and mouth to undescribables, tip of a nipple, orb of a navel, swim in giant magnification, flow and slide in a lurching yawing fall, blotting out the camera eye.

A little murmur, all unconscious, passes from their lips. The audience sways, each now finally lost in himself, communing hungrily with shadows, violated or violating, fantasy triumphant.

At picture's end, Eleanor the virgin whore is released from the bed. She kisses Frankie, she kisses Magnolia. "You dears," she says, "let's do it again." The projector lamp burns empty light, the machine keeps turning, the tag of film goes *slap-tap, slap-tap, slap-tap, slap-tap, slap-tap, slap-tap.*

"Sam, turn it off," says Eleanor.

But when the room lights are on, they cannot look at one another. "Can we see it again?" someone mutters. So, again, Eleanor knocks on the door, is tied, defiled, ravished, and made rapturous. They watch it soberly now, the room hot with the heat of their bodies, the darkness a balm for orgiastic vision. To the Deer Park, Sam is thinking, to the Deer Park of Louis XV were brought the most beautiful maidens of France, and there they stayed, dressed in fabulous silks, perfumed and wigged, the mole drawn upon their cheek, ladies of pleasure awaiting the pleasure of the king. So Louis had stripped an empire, bankrupt a treasury, prepared a deluge, while in his garden on summer evenings the maidens performed their pageants, eighteenth-century tableau of the evil act, beauteous instruments of one man's desire, lewd translation of a king's power. That century men sought wealth so they might use its fruits; this epoch men lusted for power in order to amass more power, a compounding of power into pyramids of abstraction whose yield are cannon and wire enclosure, pillars of statistics to the men who are the kings of this century and do no more in power's leisure time than go to church, claim to love their wives, and eat vegetables.

Is it possible, Sam wonders, that each of them here, two Rossmans, two Sperbers, two Slovodas, will cast off their clothes when the movie is done and perform the orgy which tickles at the heart of their desire? They will not, he knows, they will make jokes when the projector is put away, they will gorge the plate of delicatessen Eleanor provides, and swallow more beer, he among them. He will be the first to make jokes.

Sam is right. The movie has made him extraordinarily alive to the limits of them all. While they sit with red faces, eyes bugged, glutting sandwiches of ham, salami, and tongue, he begins the teasing.

"Roslyn," he calls out, "is the bulb cooled off yet?"

She cannot answer him. She chokes on beer, her face glazes, she is helpless with self-protecting laughter.

"Why are you so anxious, Daddie?" Eleanor says quickly.

They begin to discuss the film. As intelligent people they must dominate it. Someone wonders about the actors in the piece, and discussion begins afresh. "I fail to see," says Louise, "why they should be hard to classify. Pornography is a job to the criminal and prostitute element."

"No, you won't find an ordinary prostitute doing this," Sam insists. "It requires a particular kind of personality."

"They have to be exhibitionists," says Eleanor.

"It's all economic," Louise maintains.

176

"I wonder what those girls felt?" Roslyn asks. "I feel sorry for them."

"I'd like to be the cameraman," says Alan.

"I'd like to be Frankie," says Marvin sadly.

There is a limit to how long such a conversation may continue. The jokes lapse into silence. They are all busy eating. When they begin to talk again, it is of other things. Each dollop of food sops the agitation which the movie has spilled. They gossip about the party the night before, they discuss which single men were interested in which women, who got drunk, who got sick, who said the wrong thing, who went home with someone else's date. When this is exhausted, one of them mentions a play the others have not seen. Soon they are talking about books, a concert, a one-man show by an artist who is a friend. Dependably, conversation will voyage its orbit. While the men talk of politics, the women are discussing fashions, progressive schools, and recipes they have attempted. Sam is uncomfortable with the division; he knows Eleanor will resent it, he knows she will complain later of the insularity of men and the basic contempt they feel for women's intelligence.

"But you collaborated," Sam will argue. "No one forced you to be with the women."

"Was I to leave them alone?" Eleanor will answer.

"Well, why do the women always have to go off by themselves?"

"Because the men aren't interested in what we have to say."

Sam sighs. He has been talking with interest, but really he is bored. These are nice pleasant people, he thinks, but they are ordinary people, exactly the sort he has spent so many years with, making little jokes, little gossip, living little everyday events, a close circle where everyone mothers the other by his presence. The womb of middle-class life, Sam decides heavily. He is in a bad mood indeed. Everything is laden with dissatisfaction.

Alan has joined the women. He delights in preparing odd dishes when friends visit the Sperbers, and he is describing to Eleanor how he makes blueberry pancakes. Marvin draws closer to Sam.

"I wanted to tell you," he says, "Alan's story reminded me. I saw Jerry O'Shaugnessy the other day."

"Where was he?"

Marvin is hesitant. "It was a shock, Sam. He's on the Bowery. I guess he's become a wino."

"He always drank a lot," says Sam.

"Yeah." Marvin cracks his bony knuckles. "What a stinking time this is, Sam."

"It's probably like the years after 1905 in Russia," Sam says. "No revolutionary party will come out of this."

"No," Sam says, "nothing will come."

He is thinking of Jerry O'Shaugnessy. What did he look like? what did he say? Sam asks Marvin, and clucks his tongue at the dispiriting answer. It is a shock to him. He draws closer to Marvin, he feels a bond. They have, after all, been through some years together. In the thirties they have been in the Communist Party, they have quit together, they are both weary of politics today, still radicals out of habit, but without enthusiasm and without a cause. "Jerry was a hero to me," Sam says.

"To all of us," says Marvin.

The fabulous Jerry O'Shaugnessy, thinks Sam. In the old days, in the Party, they had made a legend of him. All of them with their middle-class origins and their desire to know a worker-hero.

I may say that I was never as fond of Jerry O'Shaugnessy as was Sam. I thought him a showman and too pleased with himself. Sam, however, with his timidity, his desire to travel, to have adventure and know many women, was obliged to adore O'Shaugnessy. At least he was enraptured with his career.

Poor Jerry who ends as a bum. He has been everything else. He has been a trapper in Alaska, a chauffeur for gangsters, an officer in the Foreign Legion, a labor organizer. His nose was broken, there were scars on his chin. When he would talk about his years at sea or his experiences in Spain, the stenographers and garment workers, the radio writers and unemployed actors would listen to his speeches as if he were the prophet of new romance, and their blood would be charged with the magic of revolutionary vision. A man with tremendous charm. In those days it had been easy to confuse his love for himself with his love for all underprivileged workingmen.

"I thought he was still in the Party," Sam says.

"No," says Marvin, "I remember they kicked him out a couple of years ago. He was supposed to have piddled some funds, that's what they say."

"I wish he'd taken the treasury," Sam remarks bitterly. "The Party used him for years."

178

Marvin shrugs. "They used each other." His mustache droops. "Let me tell you about Sonderson. You know he's still in the Party. The most progressive dentist in New York." They laugh. While Marvin tells the story, Sam is thinking of other things. Since he has quit Party work, he has studied a great deal. He can tell you about prison camps and the secret police, political murders, the Moscow trials, the exploitation of Soviet labor, the privileges of the bureaucracy; it is all painful to him. He is straddled between the loss of a country he has never seen, and his repudiation of the country in which he lives. "Doesn't the Party seem a horror now?" he bursts out.

Marvin nods. They are trying to comprehend the distance between Party members they have known, people by turn pathetic, likable, or annoying—people not unlike themselves—and in contrast the immensity of historic logic which deploys along statistics of the dead.

"It's all schizoid," Sam says. "Modern life is schizoid."

Marvin agrees. They have agreed on this many times, bored with the petulance of their small voices, yet needing the comfort of such complaints. Marvin asks Sam if he has given up his novel, and Sam says, "Temporarily." He cannot find a form, he explains. He does not want to write a realistic novel, because reality is no longer realistic. "I don't know what it is," says Sam. "To tell you the truth, I think I'm kidding myself. I'll never finish this book. I just like to entertain the idea I'll do something good some day." They sit there in friendly depression. Conversation has cooled. Alan and the women are no longer talking.

"Marvin," asks Louise, "what time is it?"

They are ready to go. Sam must say directly what he had hoped to approach by suggestion. "I was wondering," he whispers to Rossman, "would you mind if I held onto the film for a day or two?"

Marvin looks at him. "Oh, why of course, Sam," he says in his morose voice. "I know how it is." He pats Sam on the shoulder as if, symbolically, to convey the exchange of ownership. They are fellow conspirators.

"If you ever want to borrow the projector," Sam suggests.

"Nah," says Marvin, "I don't know that it would make much difference."

5.

It has been, when all is said, a most annoying day. As Sam and Eleanor tidy the apartment, emptying ash trays and washing the few dishes, they are fond neither of themselves nor each other. "What a waste today has been," Eleanor remarks, and Sam can only agree. He has done no writing, he has not been outdoors, and still it is late in the evening, and he has talked too much, eaten too much, is nervous from the movie they have seen. He knows that he will watch it again with Eleanor before they go to sleep; she has given her assent to that. But as is so often the case with Sam these days, he cannot await their embrace with any sure anticipation. Eleanor may be in the mood or Eleanor may not; there is no way he can control the issue. It is depressing; Sam knows that he circles about Eleanor at such times with the guilty maneuvers of a sad hound. Resent her as he must, be furious with himself as he will, there is not very much he can do about it. Often, after they have made love, they will lie beside each other in silence, each offended, each certain the other is to blame. At such times, memory tickles them with a cruel feather. Not always has it been like this. When they were first married, and indeed for the six months they lived together before marriage, everything was quite different. Their affair was very exciting to them; each told the other with some hyperbole but no real mistruth that no one in the past had ever been comparable as lover.

I suppose I am a romantic. I always feel that this is the best time in people's lives. There is, after all, so little we accomplish, and that short period when we are beloved and triumph as lovers is sweet with power. Rarely are we concerned then with our lack of importance; we are too important. In Sam's case, disillusion means even more. Like so many young men, he entertained the secret conceit that he was an extraordinary lover. One cannot really believe this without supporting at the same time the equally secret conviction that one is fundamentally inept. It is—no matter what Sergius would say—a more dramatic and therefore more attractive view of oneself than the sober notion which Sam now accepts with grudging wisdom, that the man as lover is dependent upon the bounty of the woman. As I say, he accepts the notion, it is one of the lineaments of maturity, but there is a part of him which, no matter how harried by analysis, cannot relinquish the antagonism he feels that

180

Eleanor has respected his private talent so poorly, and has not allowed him to confer its benefits upon more women. I mock Sam, but he would mock himself on this. It hardly matters; mockery cannot accomplish everything, and Sam seethes with that most private and tender pain: even worse than being unattractive to the world is to be unattractive to one's mate; or, what is the same and describes Sam's case more accurately, never to know in advance when he shall be undesirable to Eleanor.

I make perhaps too much of the subject, but that is only because it is so important to Sam. Relations between Eleanor and him are not really that bad—I know other couples who have much less or nothing at all. But comparisons are poor comfort to Sam; his standards are so high. So are Eleanor's. I am convinced the most unfortunate people are those who would make an art of love. It sours other effort. Of all artists, they are certainly the most wretched.

Shall I furnish a model? Sam and Eleanor are on the couch and the projector, adjusted to its slowest speed, is retracing the elaborate pantomime of the three principals. If one could allow these shadows a life . . . but indeed such life has been given them. Sam and Eleanor are no more than an itch, a smart, a threshold of satisfaction; the important share of themselves has steeped itself in Frankie-, Magnolia-, and Eleanor-of-the-film. Indeed the variations are beyond telling. It is the most outrageous orgy performed by five ghosts.

Self-critical Sam! He makes love in front of a movie, and one cannot say that it is unsatisfactory any more than one can say it is pleasant. It is dirty, downright porno dirty, it is a lewd slop-brush slapped through the middle of domestic exasperations and breakfast eggs. It is so dirty that only half of Sam—he is quite divisible into fractions—can be exercised at all. The part that is his brain worries along like a cuckolded burgher. He is taking the pulse of his anxiety. Will he last long enough to satisfy Eleanor? Will the children come back tonight? He cannot help it. In the midst of the circus, he is suddenly convinced the children will walk through the door. "Why are you so anxious, Daddie?"

So it goes. Sam the lover is conscious of exertion. One moment he is Frankie Idell, destroyer of virgins—take that! you whore!— the next, body moving, hands caressing, he is no more than some lines from a psychoanalytical text. He is thinking about the sensitivity of his scrotum. He has read that this is a portent of femininity in a male. How strong is his latent homosexuality worries Sam, thrusting stiffly, warm sweat running cold. Does he identify with Eleanor-of-the-film?

Technically, the climax is satisfactory. They lie together in the dark, the film ended, the projector humming its lonely revolutions in the quiet room. Sam gets up to turn it off; he comes back and kisses Eleanor upon the mouth. Apparently, she has enjoyed herself more than he; she is tender and fondles the tip of his nose.

"You know, Sam," she says from her space beside him, "I think I saw this picture before."

"When?"

"Oh, you know when. That time."

Sam thinks dully that women are always most loving when they can reminisce about infidelity.

"That time!" he repeats.

"I think so."

Racing forward from memory like the approaching star which begins as a point on the mind and swells to explode the eyeball with its odious image, Sam remembers, and is weak in the dark. It is ten years, eleven perhaps, before they were married, yet after they were lovers. Eleanor has told him, but she has always been vague about details. There had been two men it seemed, and another girl, and all had been drunk. They had seen movie after movie. With reluctant fascination, Sam can conceive the rest. How it had pained him, how excited him. It is years now since he has remembered, but he remembers. In the darkness he wonders at the unreasonableness of jealous pain. That night was impossible to imagine any longer—therefore it is more real; Eleanor his plump wife who presses a pigeon's shape against her housecoat, forgotten heroine of black orgies. It had been meaningless, Eleanor claimed; it was Sam she loved, and the other had been no more than a fancy of which she wished to rid herself. Would it be the same today, thinks Sam, or had Eleanor been loved by Frankie, by Frankie of the other movies, by Frankie of the two men she never saw again on that night so long ago?

The pleasure I get from this pain, Sam thinks furiously.

It is not altogether perverse. If Eleanor causes him pain, it means after all that she is alive for him. I have often observed that the reality of a person depends upon his ability to hurt us; Eleanor as the vague accusing embodiment of the wife is different, altogether different, from Eleanor who lies warmly in Sam's bed, an attractive Eleanor who may wound his flesh. Thus, brother to the pleasure of pain, is the sweeter pleasure which follows pain. Sam, tired, lies in Eleanor's arms, and they talk with the cozy trade words of old professionals, agreeing that they will not make love again before a movie, that it was exciting but also not without detachment, that all in all it has been good but not quite right, that she had loved this action he had done, and was uncertain about another. It is their old familiar critique, a sign that they are intimate and well disposed. They do not talk about the act when it has failed to fire; then they go silently to sleep. But now, Eleanor's enjoyment having mollified Sam's sense of no enjoyment, they talk with the apologetics and encomiums of familiar mates. Eleanor falls asleep, and Sam falls almost asleep, curling next to her warm body, his hand over her round belly with the satisfaction of a sculptor. He is drowsy, and he thinks drowsily that these few moments of creature-pleasure, this brief compassion he can feel for the body that trusts itself to sleep beside him, his comfort in its warmth, is perhaps all the meaning he may ask for his life. That out of disappointment, frustration, and the passage of dreary years come these few moments when he is close to her, and their years together possess a connotation more rewarding than the sum of all which has gone into them.

But then he thinks of the novel he wants to write, and he is wide-awake again. Like the sleeping pill which fails to work and leaves one warped in an exaggeration of the ills which sought the drug, Sam passes through the promise of sex-emptied sleep, and is left with nervous loins, swollen jealousy of an act ten years dead, and sweating irritable resentment of the woman's body which hinders his limbs. He has wasted the day, he tells himself, he has wasted the day as he has wasted so many days of his life, and tomorrow in the office he will be no more than his ten fingers typing plot and words for Bramba the Venusian and Lee-Lee Deeds, Hollywood Star, while that huge work with which he has cheated himself, holding it before him as a covenant of his worth, that enormous novel which would lift him at a bound from the impasse in which he stifles, whose dozens of characters would develop a vision of life in bountiful complexity, lies foundered, rotting on a beach of purposeless effort. Notes here, pages there, it sprawls through a formless wreck of incidental ideas and half-episodes, utterly without shape. He has not even a hero for it.

One could not have a hero today, Sam thinks, a man of action and contemplation, capable of sin, large enough for good, a man immense. There is only a modern hero damned by no more than the ugliness of wishes whose satisfaction he will never know. One needs a man who could walk the stage, someone who—no matter who, not himself. Someone, Sam thinks, who reasonably could not exist.

The novelist, thinks Sam, perspiring beneath blankets, must live in paranoia and seek to be one with the world; he must be terrified of experience and hungry for it; he must think himself nothing and believe he is superior to all. The feminine in his nature cries for proof he is a man; he dreams of power and is without capacity to gain it; he loves himself above all and therefore despises all that he is.

He is that, thinks Sam, he is part of the perfect prescription, and yet he is not a novelist. He lacks energy and belief. It is left for him to write an article some day about the temperament of the ideal novelist.

In the darkness, memories rise, yeast-swells of apprehension. Out of bohemian days so long ago, comes the friend of Eleanor, a girl who had been sick and was committed to an institution. They visited her, Sam and Eleanor, they took the suburban train and sat on the lawn of the asylum grounds while patients circled about intoning a private litany, or shuddering in boob-blundering fright from an insect that crossed their skin. The friend had been silent. She had smiled, she had answered their questions with the fewest words, and had returned again to her study of sunlight and blue sky. As they were about to leave, the girl had taken Sam aside. "They violate me," she said in a whisper. "Every night when the doors are locked, they come to my room and they make the movie. I am the heroine and am subjected to all variety of sexual viciousness. Tell them to leave me alone so I may enter the convent." And while she talked, in a horror of her body, one arm scrubbed the other. Poor tortured friend. They had seen her again, and she babbled, her face had coarsened into an idiot leer.

Sam sweats. There is so little he knows, and so much to know. Youth of the depression with its economic terms, what can he know of madness or religion? They are both so alien to him. He is the mongrel, Sam thinks, brought up without religion from a mother half Protestant and half Catholic, and a father half Catholic and half Jew. He is the quarter-Jew, and yet he is a Jew, or so he feels himself, knowing nothing of Gospel, tabernacle, or Mass, the Jew through accident, through state of mind. What . . . whatever did he know of penance? self-sacrifice? mortification of the flesh? the love of his fellow man? Am I concerned with my relation to God? ponders Sam, and smiles sourly in the darkness. No, that has never concerned him, he thinks, not for better nor for worse. "They are making the movie," says the girl into the ear of memory, "and so I cannot enter the convent."

How hideous was the mental hospital. A concentration camp, decides Sam. Perhaps it would be the world some day, or was that only his projection of feelings of hopelessness? "Do not try to solve the problems of the world," he hears from Sergius, and pounds a lumpy pillow.

However could he organize his novel? What form to give it? It is so complex. Too loose, thinks Sam, too scattered. Will he ever fall asleep? Wearily, limbs tense, his stomach too keen, he plays again the game of putting himself to sleep. "I do not feel my toes," Sam says to himself, "my toes are dead, my calves are asleep, my calves are sleeping . . ."

In the middle from wakefulness to slumber, in the torpor which floats beneath blankets, I give an idea to Sam. "Destroy time, and chaos may be ordered," I say to him.

"Destroy time, and chaos may be ordered," he repeats after me, and in desperation to seek his coma, mutters back, "I do not feel my nose, my nose is numb, my eyes are heavy, my eyes are heavy."

So Sam enters the universe of sleep, a man who seeks to live in such a way as to avoid pain, and succeeds merely in avoiding pleasure. What a dreary compromise is life!

1952

ADVERTISEMENT FOR SOME
POLITICAL ARTICLES

Not too much need be said about them. The first piece was part of the symposium in Partisan Review *which was called "America and the Intellectuals," and it was written about the time I was doing my short stories. The quickest comment on it came from a friend who was kind enough to say that I sounded alive. It was a compliment. The pieces submitted to the symposium were written in deadest winter of the dead years 1951-52, and few of the contributions had spirit.*

Later, and partly as a result of this piece, I was approached by Irving Howe who was then starting Dissent. *While I've not had very much to do with the magazine, and can claim no credit for its quick growth (it has tripled its circulation in five or six years), I'm still pleased to have had a little to do with it. For a few of us, it made a real difference to have a magazine for which one could write, and so discover if one's ideas were growing into more or reducing themselves to less.*

Still, I don't know that many readers will enjoy the two long pieces of political writing, "The Meaning of Western Defense" and "David Riesman Reconsidered." Their style is on the tiresome side, and I might as well confess that I have a terrible time writing political articles. Part of this, I think, comes from a reluctance to try such work—it is very bad for the reflexes of your style (like weight lifting is bad for a boxer) and only people with a gift, like George Orwell, seem able to combine the political essay with fiction.

I had examples of good polemical writing to follow—Howe's writing for Dissent *was first-rate, and Dwight Macdonald had a style one could envy—but whenever I sat down to do an article, I seemed to thicken in the throat as I worded my sentences and my rhetoric felt shaped by the bad political prose of our years, stuffed into my head by early, passionate, and injudicious reading of the worst sort of Max Lernerish liberal junk.*

Of the two pieces, the writing in "David Reisman Reconsidered" is probably less bad, because it was written later, and I was not trying for too much, and so here and there relaxed enough to say a few things well—the last few pages of section III are a good sample of this.

On the other hand, "The Meaning of Western Defense" is heavily and harshly written, and that is too bad, for the ideas are exciting if the reader can drill through to them. The piece is badly dated, and I'm wrong in a good many of my direct predictions, like many another political forecaster, but the article does point to the paradoxes of Western Defense and the logic of Russian foreign policy. For any conservative or liberal who has happened onto this book, "The Meaning of Western Defense" may be more to their serious enjoyment than anything else included, for if the insights lack the grace of Walter Lippmann's analyses, the approach is still a radical counterpart of Lippmann's nice sense of political force and contradiction.

After the piece, I've added a few remarks about Sputnik.

OUR COUNTRY AND OUR CULTURE: A SYMPOSIUM

I think I ought to declare straightaway that I am in almost total disagreement with the assumptions of this symposium. My answer, then, can hardly contribute much in an affirmative way, but perhaps it may serve the value of not allowing the question to be begged.

At any rate, one has to admit that the older American intellectuals and writers have changed their attitude toward this country and its culture. The New Criticism seems to have triumphed pretty generally, PR's view of American life is indeed partisan, and a large proportion of writers, intellectuals, critics—whatever we may care to include in the omnibus—have moved their economic luggage from the WPA to the Luce chain as a writer for *Time* or *Life* once remarked. Among the major novelists, Dos Passos, Farrell, Faulkner, Steinbeck, and Hemingway have traveled from alienation to varying degrees of acceptance, if not outright proselytizing, for the American Century. Dare one mention that their work since the Second World War has been singularly barren and flatulent? Is it entirely a coincidence that they sound now like a collective *pater familias?*

A symposium of this sort I find shocking. One expects a J. Donald Adams to initiate it, a John Chamberlain to bristle with editorials in its support, a Bernard De Voto to flex his muscles. This period smacks of healthy manifestoes. Everywhere the American writer is being dunned to become healthy, to grow up, to accept the American reality, to integrate himself, to eschew disease, to revalue institutions. Is there nothing to remind us that the writer does not need to be integrated into his society, and often works best in opposition to it? I would propose that the artist feels most alienated when he loses the sharp sense of what he is alienated from. In this context, I wonder if there has been a time in the last fifty years when the American artist has felt more alienated. He cannot enjoy the old battles against censorship; in lieu of a Comstock, or a Sumner, there is an editorial bureaucracy which uses the language of taste in the service of repression. He does not have the naïveté of the twenties with its sure pleasure of *épater le bourgeois;* he can no longer believe in the social art of the depression; he is left only with the warmed-over sentimentality of the war years. One can agree with Edmund Wilson that the last fifty years represent a revival of American arts and letters, vigorous and enthusiastic, but with almost no exceptions it is a literature of alienation and protest, disgust and rebellion. The writer had a sense of his enemy and it could nourish him.

Today, the enemy is vague, the work seems done, the audience more sophisticated than the writer. Society has been rationalized, and the expert encroaches on the artist. Belief in the efficacy of attacking his society has been lost, but nothing has replaced the need for attack. If, then, a number of important intellectuals and writers now see it as their function to interpret American society from within (the curious space relations of politics which equate right to within and left to without), must one necessarily assume that the motives are more serious than exhaustion?

Possibly. What seems never to be discussed are the alternatives. Every intellectual who is now "within" seems to regard his conversion as a result of the application of pure thought upon moral purity. The fact that there is a society outside himself which threatens, suggests, nudges, and promises is dismissed as mere mechanical leftism. It is considered the worst of bad taste to imply that the artist or intellectual who does not make his way "within" can find no community "without," and must suffer if he is first-rate the exercise of his abilities in obscurity, or if he is second-rate must incur the even more painful condition of being not at all chic.

Really, the history of the twentieth century seems made to be ignored. No one of the intellectuals who find themselves now in the American grain ever discuss—at least in print—the needs of modern war. One does not ever say that total war and the total war economy predicate a total regimentation of thought. Rather, it is suggested that society is too difficult to understand and history impossible to predict. It has become as fashionable to sneer at economics and emphasize "the human dilemma" as it was fashionable to do the reverse in the thirties. Economics is now for experts and the crisis of world capitalism is considered dull enough to be on a par with the proletarian novel. One never hears about the disappearance of the world market, nor is it polite to suggest that the prosperity of America depends upon the production of means of destruction, and it is not only the Soviet Union which is driven toward war as an answer to insoluble problems.

The symposium posed questions about mass culture and democratic society without seriously debating how much freedom there is to find the *effective* publication of one's ideas if they are dissenting ideas, without wondering whether democracy becomes more attenuated and may cease to exist when the war comes, and without considering how America may change in the future. Everything is viewed in a static way. We are democratic, we support the West, and the American artistic caravan is no longer isolated. The important work is to search out the healthy aspects of American life, and decide whether we can work with the movies.

I have said that none of the older American writers and intellectuals have produced anything of note since the war. The literary history of this last period has been made, for better or worse, by the younger writers, who seem inevitably to arrive as barbarians or decadents. Does not this, in itself, answer the question? John Aldridge in *After the Lost Generation* could come up with only one prescription—a genius is needed. If and when he arrives may I speculate that he will be more concerned with "silence, exile, and cunning," than a strapping participation in the vigors of American life. It is worth something to remind ourselves that the great artists—certainly the moderns—are almost always in opposition to their society, and that integration, acceptance, non-alienation, etc. etc., have been more conducive to propaganda than art.

1952

DAVID RIESMAN RECONSIDERED

The only review of *Individualism Reconsidered* by David Riesman (The Free Press, 1954) which I have seen up to this writing is a dithyrambic piece of Granville Hicks' in *The New Leader* of July 19, 1954. He concludes his appreciation by saying, "What I am sure of, however, is that this culture of ours, even if it should vanish from the earth, would survive in men's minds as an example of what the human race can accomplish. Among the forces which have forged that conviction must be included the writings of David Riesman."

As I say, this is the only review I have read, but I can imagine the others, and it takes no talent for prophecy to assume that Hicks' review is typical. For there is no mistaking that Riesman is the professional liberal's liberal, and while I happen to have met no particular person who has been influenced by him, I have seen his name in many references, blurbs, and occasional columns, all exceptionally laudatory, by such intellectual deacons of the liberal body as Arthur Schlesinger, Jr. and Max Lerner.

1.

After such a preface, it is little embarrassing to say that I found *Individualism Reconsidered* more boring than impressive. A book of five hundred odd pages, it is a collection of thirty essays which were published in various magazines in the last seven years, with the emphasis on those articles written from 1950 to the present; there has been a certain movement, and, from my point of view, regression in Riesman's thought since the forties; as he says himself, ". . . my later writings are less acrid and satiric; there is a somewhat more sanguine attitude toward American Culture."

The essays vary in quality and in subject matter; Riesman embarks upon such separate topics as the character of law review students, the political implications of Freud's thought, and a sociohistoric survey of the growth of football. His variety is to be praised if his treatment cannot be, yet despite the gamut of the articles, and ignoring his ideas for the moment, what is distressing in *Individualism Reconsidered* is his style, overburdened with modern sociological jargon (individuate, marginality, personality ideals, and pluralistic), and what compounds the boredom is that Riesman says so little in so many words and like so many sociologists gives little feel or sense of life itself. With the exception of his article on the legal profession which contains fascinating observations about the social character of lawyers, the life and élan of law review students, etc., I believe I can say with no conscious smugness that I learned almost nothing else in these five hundred pages. There are essays on popular culture, on individualism and its values, on minority problems, on totalitarianism, on the problems of method of the social sciences; the text of a long speech on the relationships between technical progress and social progress is reprinted; there is a condescending evaluation of Veblen with a psychoanalytical interpretation of his character added to prove why in Riesman's opinion Veblen has now become a "poor, if often amusing and provocative guide to America."

Only the essays on Freud are impressive, and this not so much for what is said (the critique will not be new to anyone familiar with Horney or Fromm), as for the considerable work which was done and the honesty of the attempt; and I should say that one can admire Riesman's honesty and his capacity for work, the number of his projects, the range of his interests. Add to his credit some remarks on what he calls "The Nerve of Failure" written in 1947, ". . . the courage to accept the possibility of defeat, of failure, without being morally crushed," and, "What kind of authority has laid down the rule that it is wrong to be critical or negative if one cannot also be constructive?"; add to that early essay his sympathetic review of *Communitas* by Percival and Paul

Goodman, which he titles "Some Observations on Community Plans and Utopia," also written in 1947, and one has gleaned almost all of Riesman's now defunct radical temper and almost all that is interesting.

I do not think I speak only from my prejudices, although in justice I must admit that I approached Riesman's work with animus. Still, even a sympathetic reader could hardly be unaware that his writings wander, his emphases shift, his articles are headed by important titles and introduce important subjects only to dissipate them, until time and again the essay comes to a close after pages of decelerated discussion, almost as if he were a verbose and needy lecturer who has lost his point, glances at his watch, discovers he is half an hour over and will be charged for continuing to use the hall and so comes to an abrupt end by reciting the final dramatic sentences he had memorized before he began. If Riesman were not considered so seriously, I doubt whether *Individualism Reconsidered* could have found an eager publisher, let alone sympathetic reviewers, let alone even the desire in himself to collect his essays and present them in a book. In his latest writings one senses, perhaps incorrectly, a certain complacency, as if Riesman has begun to regard himself as a public figure.

2.

But, after all, it is not *Individualism Reconsidered* which the reviewers are writing about. In essence they are re-reviewing *The Lonely Crowd*, which is a better book and a more important one. Indeed, since the greater part of the essays in *Individualism Reconsidered* are merely points of departure or extensions of discussion from the thesis of *The Lonely Crowd*, it is natural to relate the themes in *Individualism Reconsidered* to the structure of his thought in *The Lonely Crowd*.

Apart from his proudly eclectic approach to experience, ". . . the pluralism which is one of the glories of liberalism," which I intend to discuss later, Riesman's ideas in *The Lonely Crowd* revolve around the terminology he coined of the "tradition-directed," "the inner-directed," and "the other-directed." Briefly, and avoiding the demographic characteristics to which he connects these categories, it can be said that Riesman considers the tradition-directed person (very roughly, the peasant) to be comparatively unimportant in the study of modern American life, and *The Lonely*

Crowd is an attempt to explore the dynamics of American social movement in terms of the growing tendency of the American character to change from inner-directed to other-directed. The latter categories are explained at length. The inner-directed man—the nineteenth-century businessman would be a prototype—is essentially self-directed, "gyroscopic," production-minded, set for life from early childhood in pursuit of certain built-in goals, and therefore rigid, strong, compulsive, capable of sustaining loneliness, opposition, and strife, yet moved in his circuits by guilt. By contrast, the other-directed man is flexible, anxiety-ridden, oriented not toward such goals as success or moral probity or serious work, but toward the approval of whichever group or groups he finds congenial. His movement is "radar-controlled," his happiness acceptance, his social outlook one of consumption rather than production, his "taste" rather than his work the primary concern. He obeys "the process of paying close attention to the signals from others . . ." and he behaves by ". . . an exceptional sensitivity to the actions and wishes of others."

In the first uncritical acceptance of these categories, intellectual excitement is generated and one has the feeling that much is about to open, much sociology, much about life. But the book is reminiscent of a performance which is begun on a high note of excitement where the actor has not sufficient reserves to sustain the role. So there are lags, disappointments, rather astounding conclusions which seem constructed out of nowhere, unbelievable naïvetés, repetitions of the early excitement, and finally on an exhortative note, for Riesman is nothing if not hortatory, the curtain is lowered and one waits for the flag in the background. By the time *Individualism Reconsidered* appears, the expectation is justified: ". . . our creativity, stimulated by such conferences as this, is one element. The M.I.T. students who brought us together dreamed up the whole idea, then found the means to implement it. They exemplify the new generation of American entrepreners who engage in teamwork, are not profit-minded, and seek outlets in the world beyond our borders."

Riesman does not always sound like a *Life* editorial; but I think there is nothing in that quotation which he would not defend as it stands, and the direction of *The Lonely Crowd* was toward such remarks. For Riesman predicated the development of the other-directed personality as a response to something unique in history—an economy of abundance. Other-directed man as a social type emerges in his consumer orientation, and capitalism enters the process of becoming something other than Capitalism. Competitive strife begins to disappear and is replaced by the co-operative jockeying for position of the other-directed types who are essentially more anxious to meet approval than to succeed at any cost. The edges of conflict become rounded. The productive speed-up tends to be replaced by "mood" engineering and "feather-bedding"; management concedes more to labor than is asked, labor in turn does not demand all that it could; conspicuous spending within production (committee management, incentive systems, etc.) replaces conspicuous consumption, and in short, "In this modern atmosphere of sharing, of geniality, of muted competition and unmuted conspicuous production, who would be the Scrooge who would hoard trade secrets or hoard capital . . . or hoard time (very few top businessmen are actually as inaccessible as their secretaries like to pretend)." One feels tempted to ask Henry Luce for an appointment.

Riesman carries his conclusions to the point of declaring that there is no longer a ruling group or ruling class in America, but that power is distributed among a variety of veto groups: the Church, Jewish organizations, Protestant organizations, lobbies, consumer groups, between management and labor, between the "warring congeries of cattlemen, corn-men, dairy men, cotton men," black-belt whites, ethnic groups, "the editorializers and storytellers who help socialize the young," "the military men who control defense and in part, foreign policy," and "in the hands of the small business and professional men who control Congress, such as realtors, lawyers, car salesmen, undertakers and so on." Power in terms of control does not exist; it is "situational and mercurial." "Even those intellectuals, for instance, who feel themselves very much out of power, and are frightened of those who they think have the power, prefer to be scared by the power structures they conjure up than to face the possibility that the power structure they believe exists has largely evaporated."

There are many elements I have omitted, and Riesman, despite his infatuation with the economy of abundance, is not entirely uncritical of American life. His main objections concern the anxious joylessness of the other-directed, and in a liberal parallel to the radical dream in the thirties of a renovated super-proletariat, Riesman looks for a development of what he calls the autonomous individual, a concept very close to the analyst's norm of a "genital" member of the middle class. How the middle class legions are to move from other-direction to autonomy is left in abeyance, although Riesman finds hope in the mass-communication media. "Surely the great mass-media artists, including the directors, writers, and others behind the scenes who create and promote the artists, make an important contribution to autonomy. The entertainers . . . exert a constant pressure on the accepted peer-groups and suggest new modes of escape from them. The sharpest critics of American movies are likely to forget this too easily."

3.

What is to be said of all this? In the style of socialist polemic one could declare Riesman's structure to be sheared at a stroke because the economy of abundance is artificial, grown from a war economy, and subject either to crisis in the event of no war, or subject to war itself for continuing health. I believe that generally this is true, but since Riesman would probably argue that it is the economy of abundance which is the prime fact, and the war economy is superficial and capable of being replaced by American improvisation and the acceptance of new challenge and so forth, I would prefer to bypass these arguments which like most economic colloquies between liberals and socialists resolve themselves inevitably into a Keynes-Marx imbroglio, and try to go at the matter in another way.

There is an essay in *Individualism Reconsidered* called "Some Observations on Social Science Research" where Riesman states quite nicely that the present dichotomy in sociology between the data-collectors and the theorists is very great. The techniques and the resources of sociology permit factual research on very limited topics, and the theorists who wish to construct more elaborate syntheses of society must do so mainly on the basis of their intuitions and perceptions. In that sense, I think it can be said that any ambitious sociological work is created artistically and presents a *Weltanschauung* which is more comparable to the kind of world a novelist makes than the structures of a scientist. Naturally, I would be the last to say that the world a novelist creates is without value in helping us to understand reality (or indeed whether there is Reality) but I do want to insist on the difference. No one dreams of considering a novel, at least a good novel, as a document; we understand tacitly that its view of the world is a compound of the novelist's prejudices, instincts, and sensitivity, and we learn from the novel in degree as our own prejudices and intuitions are exercised, confirmed or confuted by the art-work.

This, then, seems to me the best way to approach *The Lonely Crowd*—as a fictional conception rather than a sociological analysis; and again I am not trying to say it has no value because its "reality" is "fictional." True, much of its material has been gathered by interviews, and other forms of sociological apparatus are used to bolster it now and again, but no one can seriously pretend (except perhaps a Ph. D. in Sociology) that the one-hour interview or the twelve-hour interview, or even a thousand interviews, are "scientific." Riesman himself would not make such claims. They are analogous to the very partial and limited encounters with "experience" which some novelists employ in finding material—and who can claim that the good sociologist with his technical jargon is *ipso facto* a better observer than the good novelist? Far more important than the data are the attitudes and preconceptions with which the artist or *equally* the sociologist begins his work. Not to mention the energy and ambition.

Viewed as a "novelist" or better as an "artist," Riesman lacks real stature in my opinion. The style of his insights is reminiscent of any number of novelists who tend to place too much emphasis upon too little, until whole systems of good and evil are elaborated out of the nuances of the drawing room. (Given sufficient genius this can of course be done, but it is obviously very difficult.) Riesman's concept of the other-directed which is recognizable in one's friends or in oneself, suffers nonetheless from our suspicion that he is extrapolating upon the vast American canvas a view of life which too closely corresponds to the generally tender and anxious world of the middle-class intellectual in or out of academic life. Moreover, one wonders how new a phenomenon is other-direction—merely think of the gallery of female characters in the Victorian novel. And in the business world where Riesman places so much emphasis on the emergence of other-directed co-operation instead of inner-directed competition, one can say that it would be surprising indeed if human relations at work were as ugly, as brutal, and as competitive now as they were let us say in the thirties. It is just as likely that Riesman has been prone to magnify the traces of other-direction which are to be found in government officials and management executives.

One may suggest similar criticisms with regard to his idea that there is no ruling group in America. Again and again there is a truly ingenuous quality to Riesman's statements. When he comes to discuss the power for influence of the advertising media, he says in effect that he, personally, has never been influenced by advertising, but merely annoyed and disgusted by it. He adds that everyone he has talked to declares the same thing, but that they make the mistake of believing that while they are not influenced by advertising, other people must be. Why assume this, asks Riesman? Why not agree that everyone is indifferent to the power of advertising and that it is all a huge hoax, perpetuated only because it is an institution?

Nowhere in his work does Riesman seem to have the faintest idea that there is an unconscious direction to society as well as to the individual, and that, just as many phenomena proceed in society at two levels, so a particular man or as easily all Americans can believe consciously that they are superior to advertising while in fact they suffer an unconscious slavery which influences them considerably. One feels almost embarrassed to remind Riesman of something so basic as this.

Riesman approaches the problem of power in America in almost the same way. One cannot keep from comparing his remarks to the apologia of the fellow-traveler who dependably will say that in the Soviet Union there is no dictatorship, but rather that the power of government is distributed among the working class, the farmers, the intelligentsia, the Communist Party, the sober industrious management executives, the esteemed public artists, etc. etc. The forms of power are taken for the content, and there is no attempt to distinguish between those who lead and those who are led.

While the problem of who has the power in America is undoubtedly more difficult to answer than it is in the Soviet Union (although certainly not astronomically so), there is no reason to assume that there is no power, or put somewhat differently, no resultant of power from its vectors. It may be true, and I would guess it is true, that no group in America nor any individuals believe consciously that they wield really important power; but it

197

is one thing to think one has no power and another for it to be so. A neurotic general overcome with work may believe he has the power to effect nothing; a drunken private on a whorehouse tear may have the illusion that all liberty in his possession and all omnipotence, but one would have to be violently antipathetic to the idea of society itself to argue that there were not social and power relations between the general and the private independent of their will or their personal conception of their state. Obviously, I do not wish to say that "Wall Street" or "General Motors" controls America or that mass-communication media determine absolutely the content of people's minds. But it is far more ridiculous to assume that "power" is distributed equitably between General Motors as an entity, and a given number of small-town lawyers who go to Congress. Riesman does not really seem to have ever considered seriously whether it is *any* small-town lawyer who can go to Congress. Again, concerning the mass-communications media, one does not need to argue that men's minds are absolutely controlled, but rather that a man's mind, and just a small part of his mind, is affected in a small way—no more is necessary for him to conform socially to the main historical trends; put another way it is men's actions which make history and not their sentiments, but the actions of a man, particularly his social and historic actions, are comparatively minute in relation to the whole man. Nonetheless it is that fraction which can be and is affected by the media, and it is that fraction which unfortunately makes history.

When one reviews the history of the last ten years and takes into account the complete about-face of American public policy toward the Soviet Union in the matter of a year or two (it will be remembered that the USSR changed neither its colors nor its stripes during all of this), I think it is a matter of small importance whether or not there is a ruling class which pulls the strings. Most responsible socialists would discard this notion for its vulgarity, its Stalinoid connotations, and its complete failure to fit more complex facts. But it is quite another thing to relinquish one's view of America as a social organism with a capitalist economy whose problems are deep and probably insoluble, and whose response to any historical situation must be a function of its need to survive as that need is reflected, warped, aided and impeded by countless smaller social organisms, traditions, and finally individuals who cancel one another out or double their force (so far as *actions* are concerned) until the result of these numerous vectors represents a statement of where the power in America rests and where the necessity. That the "power" in any important sense does not belong to nine-tenths of the "people" but rather is embedded in such massive and complementary constellations as management and labor executives, the military and the government hierarchy, the Church and mass-communication media, is more or less self-evident to radicals who would I believe agree that it is not the differences of interest in the groups I have named which are noteworthy (has there ever been a society including the Soviet Union in which there were not deep clashes of interest among the ruling elite?) but rather it is the objectives wanted in common by these powerful groups which can provide the best explanation of the virtually complete conformity in America during the Second World War and in the eight years which have followed. What characterizes all pre-socialist history and may (let us hope not) characterize a socialist history if there be one, is that the mass of men must satisfy the needs of the social organism in which they live far more than the social organism must satisfy them.

Now, I am aware that the argument I have presented is as completely a "fiction" as the world of David Riesman. There is finally no way one can try to apprehend complex reality without a "fiction." But one may choose the particular "fiction" which most satisfies the sum of one's knowledge, experience, biases, needs, desires, values, and eventually one's moral necessities. And one may even attempt to reshape reality in some small way with the "fiction" as a guide. What one can always do is to compare the "fictions" and try to see where they may lead.

4.

In *Individualism Reconsidered* another tendency becomes apparent in Riesman's ideas. He has become concerned with what he calls "reversals of emphasis," and I believe they can best be illustrated by a number of quotations:

> . . . these men act in obedience to their self-image as proper businessmen, no matter how strenuously they insist (as, depending on mood, most Americans will insist) that they act only out of self-interest.

> Wealthy students often act as if ashamed of their

wealth. I have sometimes been tempted to point out that the rich are a minority and have rights, too.

The students would be much better off if they could take a stand against taking a stand.

. . . airless conformism under the banner of non-conformity.

. . . "the tyranny of the powerless" over their group —the tyranny of beleaguered teachers, liberals, Negroes, women, Jews, intellectuals, and so on, over each other.

The current attempt to unify the country against municipal patronage and bossism seems to me dangerous, because by enforcing an ideological unity on politics we threaten with extinction a few men, soaked in gravy we can well spare, who protect our ideological pluralism.

For instance, girl students at some of our liberal universities need occasionally to be told that they are not utterly damned if they discover within themselves anti-Negro or anti-Semitic reactions—*else they may expiate their guilt by trying to solve the race question in marriage!* But even that judgment has to be made in terms of the wider social context—in this case, a judgment that the lot of Negroes, let alone Jews, in America is not always so utterly desperate as to call for the ruthless sacrifice of protective prejudices. [Italics added.]

In some colleges, professors who testify before the Velde or Jenner committees with dignity and restraint (often *educating* committee members in the process . . .) are slandered as appeasers. [Italics added.]

I recall in this connection a conversation with the energetic editor of a liberal periodical who had suggested in one of his articles that there was something to be said for the investigating committees: they were not all vicious, and after all Communist conspiracies had existed. As a result, he was bombarded by letters charging that now he, too, was betraying the cause, was giving in to hysteria, was leaving his loyal readers

in the lurch. He *did* give in to hysteria—to his readers'
—and decided to publish no more such articles.

I wonder if these "reversals of emphasis" are not essentially
intellectual tricks in which a liberal platitude is converted to its
opposite, and an illusion of insight is thereby gained. Riesman
furnishes us the altruistic businessman, the persecuted rich, "the
tyranny of the powerless," the benefits of corruption, of prejudice,
and the hysteria of the liberal, not to mention numerous others.
There is truth of course in many of these insights, but to what
degree and of what kind? Life itself viewed statically, seen as something "which-is" rather than as something "which-should-be," is
always so various in its aspects that there are a host of frozen truths.
Every man and every institution sees itself through its own eyes,
and there are probably few situations on earth whose moral judgments cannot be reversed to provide the illusion of equal truth.
Intellectual penetration of this sort can never fail, but on the other
hand it can never succeed for it is merely a flipping of switches, a
change of polarities, and the platitude turned on its head is still a
platitude.

Let me quote from *Winesburg, Ohio,* where Sherwood
Anderson says it as well as anyone could:

> The old man listed hundreds of the truths in his book.
> I will not try to tell you all of them. There was the
> truth of virginity and the truth of passion, the truth of
> wealth and of poverty, of thrift and of profligacy, of
> carelessness and abandon. Hundreds and hundreds
> were the truths and they were all beautiful.

5.

In the enormous reversal of emphasis which characterizes
Riesman's work—the absence of ruling classes, the replacement of
competition by co-operation, the change in American character
from the stereotype of the brash aggressive man to the other-
directed man, one may well wonder whether Riesman, despite his
sincere intentions to invigorate thought and to make people "see"
reality, is not really encouraging thought in circles, passive thought,
but thought which gives the illusion of making strides, emitting
energy, and approaching discovery. Is this not his basic appeal to
the liberal who wants precisely to have thought which elicits an

aura of excitement but does not force him to relinquish to his ideas any important part of his ambitions or his comforts? One feels Reisman's desire to find something justifiable, something *functional*, in all aspects of society. Ultimately, his credo seems to be that what-is must necessarily contain something good, and so an intellectual process which begins by stimulating the mind ends in eclectic monotony. At last all things are equal, are justifiable—one is drawn to quietism and acceptance. To the left liberal—for want of a better classification—who like everyone else has become progressively more exhausted by the neurotic intellectual demands of the Cold War, there is peace and an attractiveness in the endlessly varied world of what-is where finally everything can be seen inside-out or right-side-back-again if so the need arises.

One cannot emphasize enough how neurotic is the political climate of our time, and for the liberal who wishes to be active, the situation is not easy. For I would say that we live in a climate so reactionary that the normal guides to understanding contemporary American politics are reversed like the controls of a plane which bursts through the sound barrier; and to the liberal's dismay and confusion it is the Republicans who can make peace in Korea, who are obliged to fight with McCarthy no matter how reluctantly, who can accept an armistice in Indochina, who may even come to recognize Communist China with the possibility that presents of splitting China from Russia—who can in sum effect the policies which normally belong to the Democratic Party, even as it will be the Democratic Party, I would venture, which will carry out the complete reaction if and when it comes. For example, if Stevenson had been elected, could one imagine him making peace in Korea against the happy anguish and hypocritical storms of the Republicans that American lives had been lost in vain?

To the confusion of such relations in politics is added the fact that radical political life in America has become difficult, and to hold the position of a libertarian socialist is equivalent to accepting almost total intellectual alienation from America, as well as a series of pains and personal contradictions in one's work. It is difficult for us to approach the liberal, to attempt to convince him, when we can offer no place to go, no country, no cause, no movement, no thing, and are ourselves exposed to all the temptations of circular thought, of reversals of emphasis, until far from obtaining the satisfaction of thinking ourselves martyrs, we are more likely to torture ourselves with such questions as our own neurotic relation to life. Riesman speaks glibly of the airless conformity of the non-conformist, but what he ignores is that the radical temper is often turned most radically upon oneself, and he is far from the first to ask whether one is a socialist because of the easy pride non-conformity may offer. In that way, Riesman's appeal is almost as strong—if unconsciously not stronger—to radicals than to liberals, and there are probably few socialists who have not felt the temptation to substitute what-is for the more elusive what-should-be.

6.

Yet, after everything else, there remains the basic core of socialism so deep in Western culture, the idea, the moral passion, that it is truly intolerable and more than a little fantastic that men should not live in economic equality and in liberty. As serious artistic expression is the answer to the meaning of life for a few, so the passion for socialism is the only meaning I can conceive in the lives of those who are not artists; if one cannot create "works" one may dream at least of an era when humans create humans, and the satisfaction of the radical can come from the thought that he tries to keep this idea alive.

If one is to take the trend of other-direction seriously, it makes equal sense to argue that the increasing anxiety of American life comes from the covert guilt that abundance and equality remain utterly separated, and we have reached the point where socialism is not only morally demanding but unconsciously obvious—obvious enough to flood with anxiety the psyches of those millions who know and yet do nothing.

For so long as we can choose our myths, I prefer this to Riesman's essential if unstated fiction which finally revolves around the old saw that the rich are miserable and the poor lead simple happy lives. Perhaps, if one could make such statistical counts, it would be true or half-true. But, after all, the question of happiness is related not to politics, nor to action, nor to morality. As socialists we want a socialist world not because we have the conceit that men would thereby be more happy—those claims are best left to dictators—but because we feel the moral imperative in life itself to raise the human condition even if this should ultimately mean no more than that man's suffering has been lifted to a higher level, and human history has only progressed from melodrama, farce, and monstrosity, to tragedy itself.

1954

THE MEANING OF WESTERN DEFENSE

For the liberal, the problem of defending the West is perhaps even more critical a question than for the socialist, since it is the liberal who eschews Utopias and therefore finds himself without an exit. On the one side he is becoming increasingly depressed, if indeed not terrified, by the movement in America toward conformism, hysteria, and McCarthyism; as an alternative he can only see the heavy danger of "Soviet Imperialism." Before such a prospect he feels impelled in the words of Dwight Macdonald to "prefer an imperfectly living, open society to a perfectly dead, closed society."

I would argue that the mistake is precisely in so establishing the choice, and that the implement of this choice—Western Defense —has the ultimate and most abominable meaning of Western annihilation.

I must add that in support of this I will present no documentation or any research. Such a project would be not only beyond my capacities, but I see small purpose unless it were done on an heroic scale. I offer this argument therefore in all modesty. I am neither wholly convinced of it, nor confident of my political insight. Still, it is a thesis I have held for several years, and I have found it, for myself at least, a not unfruitful hypothesis by which to understand events.

1.

The nominal reason advanced for Western Defense is that it is the bulwark of civilization against the predatory and aggressive aims of the Soviet Union. If one inquires why the Soviet Union is "predatory," the answer is almost always the descriptive and circular response that it is in the nature of totalitarian regimes to be aggressive and imperialistic. Which of course answers nothing at all.

204

One finds it perfect that our third-rate imitation of Stalinist distortion of history, our government by public relations, should have coined the phrase, "Soviet Imperialism." It is a wonder the next page was never borrowed from Stalin's book which would give the USSR the credit for inventing imperialism. Whatever the Soviet's crimes and horrors and total perversions of socialism, and we know the list unbearably long, they can hardly be accused of imperialism.* The guilt for imperialism belongs to the West, that chalice of civilization, and not all the public relations from here to the millennium can word it away. Imperialism, since one is forced to go back to the ABC's of these things, is still the employment of excess surplus value to create new markets, dominate backward countries, superintend partial and specialized development of their industry, and establish spheres of influence. For a modern example, Venezuela comes to mind. What must be emphasized is that imperialism is exclusively the problem of finding investments for the collective idle profit of monopoly capitalism, and it has been the difficulty of finding such markets and backward countries which has dominated the history of Western civilization through World War I, through panics and depressions, through the loss of the world market and World War II until the only solution left since the Second War has been the war economy which marries full production to a necessarily crippled market—the Soviet Union having absorbed too many of the backward countries of the world.

This is the crisis of Monopoly Capitalism. Arthritic through most of its members, suffering from high-blood pressure in America, it can continue to function only so long as it manufactures armaments whose "ultimate consumer"—(I regret I cannot find the source for this quotation)—"is the enemy soldier." The liberal will advance the argument that "Keynesian economics" and the "welfare state" will dispose of capitalism's contradictions, but since this has

* *The Editors have raised the point that my definition of imperialism (with which they differ in varying degree) seems to give the impression that because the Soviet Union is not "imperialistic" as I define it, it is therefore less culpable than the West. We are all agreed that I do not want to give this impression. As I think will become clear in the body of my argument, the definitions which I have given to the economies of the West and the East are for analytical purposes, and are not intended to imply a moral superiority, ipso facto, to either the USSR or the United States. (This footnote was written for the original publication in* Dissent.)

proved politically impossible until now in anything approaching its intended form, the burden of proof is still upon him. In fact, one can hardly visualize the cure of capitalism's chronic agonies through a nostrum which in effect asks private financial empires to accommodate themselves to the dissipation and eventual transformation of their power. As easy to ask the state to wither away! I feel it is not too extravagant to say that if the Soviet Union were Utopia, the United States would be forced to invent a Stalinist nightmare.

2.

The economic problems of the USSR are congenitally different. Its chronic crisis has been the inability to increase production organically rather than the need to find a market for surplus profit. There is no need to recapitulate the history of its disasters, some due to Leninism, some due to capitalist encirclement, but the "great experiment" should have proved if it has proved nothing else that one cannot build socialism in an isolated bloc let alone an isolated country. When the country is backward as was Czarist Russia, everything is made worse, of course. Trotsky once said that socialism means more milk, not less milk, and the Soviet attempt to build a major economy was driven to put its emphasis upon less milk. One cannot create giant steel works and coal mines and railroads and other heavy industry at an accelerated pace without inflicting upon one's labor force a demand for longer hours of work at smaller real wages. Marx once mentioned the economic inefficiency of slavery as a productive system, and the USSR has given a further demonstration. The heart of its inability to increase the rate of its productivity vis-à-vis the United States and Western Europe has been the irremediable dilemma of being forced to demand more and more of its workers in return for less and less goods and creature comforts.

A man as well as an animal can be worked to death, and the horror which besets the Soviet bureaucrat is the recurring breakdown of economic arithmetic. To double steel production in a given sector—let us put it arbitrarily—he discovers that he must triple his labor force. Under such conditions, aggravated, repeated, and multiplied, the state of the Soviet Union can only remind one of that swelling of the joints which accompanies anemia. Far from being imperialistic, Soviet aggression bears much greater similarity to primitive capitalism. It is the need for plunder, economic plunder, which has forced its expansion since the war. With such plunder, equivalent to economic transfusions, there is the hope of breaking out of their economic trap. For plunder may be translated into consumer goods, and with more consumer goods, more efficient production can legitimately be expected of the Soviet worker. It is mainly this reason, I would argue, which has motivated the brutal and apparently irrational conduct of the Soviet bureaucracy in the Eastern satellites, rather than any theories or explanations which depend upon a mystique of totalitarianism.

Still the problem—I would call it *the* problem—of increasing the rate of production in the USSR has been alleviated only temporarily by the war gains. With the exception of Czechoslovakia and Eastern Germany, all of the nations which the Soviet Union has swallowed, as well as China, are backward countries, almost hopelessly backward, and the transfusions leeched from them have merely attenuated the problem, displaced it slightly, and created new ones. The Soviet Union is now the master of an economically emaciated empire, progressively more worthless to it (in proportion as the parts are plundered), and yet like all empires it cannot be relinquished without the danger of the center collapsing as well. Even those who plunder must pay eventually, and the Soviet is now in the position of having to offer alleviations, reforms, and what is the ultimate disaster—counter-transfusions—to its satellites.

3.

Against this background I want to place the paradox of Western Defense. The real solution, probably the only solution in these decades at least, to the contradictions of Soviet economics exists in the productive capacities and techniques of Western Europe, specifically West Germany, France, England, and to lesser degree the Scandinavian countries and Italy. The Stalinist bureaucrat must reason that if only those countries could be diverted into the Soviet orbit, the economic anemia could be solved. With an increase of consumer goods, the rate of increase of production would finally rise, and the USSR would possess at last the potentiality to overtake the United States. Given a Stalinist Europe there could be eventually a Stalinist world.

If there exists this necessity to absorb Western Europe, and I would guess that the Politburo considers it exactly a necessity, the question may well be asked why the Soviet Union has not moved to occupy all of Europe, and taken its chances on the war which would follow; particularly, why does it wait at a time when Western Defense may still become a reality? (I think we can agree that at no time since the war ended has there been a real *military* difficulty to the Soviet occupying Western Europe.) The answer, simple to the point of truism, has never even been suggested, to my knowledge, in the ten-thousand-weight of articles, "expert" analyses, and scare headlines which suffocate the question in this country. One is given two explanations, antithetical if equally distorted. The conformist press, ignoring the eight years which have passed since the Second World War, contents itself with posing the static threat of Soviet attack, and never hints there might be some alternative to immediate aggression by the Russians if we did not have armed foot soldiers to intimidate them. The microscopically smaller voice of the "progressive" press, made up in last extremity of fellow fellow-travelers, contents itself with the ingenuous (let us be kind) assumption that the Soviet wants peace, and that peace would solve its problems. (As indeed well it might if one reads "Stalinism" for the problem, and "internal revolution" for the prescription.) But it is too long and too familiar an aside to criticize the fetishistic enthusiasm of the "progressive" before the altar of nationalization of industry.

The reason the USSR does not attack is that the productive capacities of Western Europe are worthless to the Soviet economy unless they remain intact. To occupy Germany and France would be one thing; to keep them producing would be another. Without a single soldier on the soil of Europe, the United States would still be completely capable of leveling the productive plant of Western Europe. Strategic bombings, even if atomic armaments were not used, would be successful in mutilating key industries and scrambling communications. (If it would be argued that the bombing of Germany in the last war did not destroy its economy, the differences must be emphasized. Germany, after all, was fighting its own war and with some determination, which is hardly equivalent to a conquered country ordered to produce for its conquerors. I want to return to this point later.) The vista which confronts the Soviet bureaucrat is to add another graveyard to his impoverished real estate holdings. Worse. Attacking in such a way, the Soviet armies would be almost universally hated as the invaders, and to the temptations and demoralizations facing the occupation troops would be added the sabotage, inertia, and underground movements of the people of Western Europe. Under such conditions the difficulty of extracting production from a conquered Europe would be replaced by the far greater difficulty of being obliged to keep the population alive. If indeed with the disaster of such a victory the Russians would even feel themselves thus obliged. So it is not a practical solution for the USSR to invade Western Europe, it is not even a desperate solution, for desperate solutions must still have some possibility of success, and there is none here. To invade Western Europe is equivalent to destroying it (even if America should be in a position of isolation at such a time, its military necessity would be to retaliate), and the destruction of Western Europe represents the end of any chance for Soviet production to extricate itself from its crisis and its anemia.

4.

To what alternative does it look, then? I believe this is equally simple in outline. From its point of view, the Soviet must attempt to find some way of bringing Western Europe peacefully into its orbit. Indeed, the main trend of Soviet foreign policy over the last years provides numerous examples. Its aim is to alienate Western Europe ideologically and economically from the United States, open trade relations between the East and West, expand them, and finally make them central to the economies of Europe, while the Communist parties of these countries would on the surface be "liberalized" to appear more attractive. If this could be accomplished, the way would be open to plundering Western Europe by means of Soviet trade commissions. It would not even be necessary that Western Europe become formally Communist.

If this policy seems impossible to realize and more than a little fantastic, it must be placed against the background of Soviet strategy in the last few years. I would assert that Russia began the Korean War not as a blunder, but as a calculated risk to have the United States engaged in Asia at exactly that moment when its energies and the consent of Western Europe seemed to promise a quick and successful establishment of Western Defense. (In passing, one may mention other benefits for the Stalinists: a showcase demonstration of the destruction which awaited Europe, and the opportunity to keep China from being recognized by the United States, with all the eventual dangers of a Titoist deviation implicit in such recognition. But this properly is beyond my subject.) Let it suffice that the Korean War was successful for the Soviet in one way at least—the plans for Western Defense have not been fulfilled, and the prospects seem poorer today than at any time since the inception. Moreover, the contradictions in arming Western Europe have come to term; the United States is faced with the conflict of West Germany and France, the first eager to be a military power but geographically an island, and France the natural foundation of any defense, lethargic at best and antagonistic at worst. No wonder that Dulles begins to speak of the "agonizing reappraisal." It is not altogether impossible that the United States may withdraw from Europe in the next five years.

Nonetheless, I doubt it. There is a specter facing the American military, and its connotations are so frightening that a great deal will be sacrificed and a great deal more threatened before the project of Western Defense is abandoned. For if America quits Europe, and the Soviet Union succeeds in absorbing it "peacefully," there will be no good military alternative to destroying Western Europe from the air. To allow it to produce for the needs of the Soviet Union would be fatal to America's position as the dominant world power. Just as the British were forced in the last war to destroy the French fleet at Toulon, so America will be obliged to blow Western Europe into bits. Needless to say, such events will not occur without their preparation. One must foresee a major change in the ideological climate (which in fact the "withdrawal" of America would already have created), a steady deterioration of relations with Western Europe, a series of ultimatums and rejections, and a new set of attitudes in which the paranoia of American political life would be given full indulgence. The bombing attacks as finally brought off would undoubtedly be called something like Operation Liberty—its aims to destroy the taint of "Red" France's heavy commodities. One need not depend only upon Orwell. The varying prestige of the German populace in the eyes of American journalism can be a reminder. It is not so difficult after all, when one's reputation is based upon legends, to be Fascist beasts in 1945, and the heroic citizens of *West* Berlin in 1948. Nor is it any more difficult to go in reverse. After all, the portrait of Russia given to the average newspaper reader was reversed almost completely within less than a year.

5.

One cannot say in all certainty that the United States would go to war against an all-Communist Europe, but it is very likely, and what is more to the point, war or no, the situation would be intolerable to America. If it did not go to war, it would face the prospect, in a decade or more, of succumbing one way or another to Stalinism; if it did go to war and bombed Western Europe its situation would be hardly bettered. For this would be a vastly different kind of bombing than retaliatory attacks against Russian aggression. To the European nations subjected to America's Air Force, the Russian propaganda that the United States is barbaric and warlike would be given an objective demonstration, and the Third World War would become exactly what the Russians would wish it to become. All of the world would be joined in a "crusade" against America. The very aerial warfare which would succeed in making Western Europe a productive nonentity in the event of Soviet aggression, would now not succeed at all. For it is the characteristic of a crusade that economic laws can temporarily be adjourned. What is lost in factories is more than gained in the productive *esprit* of the working force, and improvisation is substituted for inertia, co-operation for sabotage, and patriotism for underground work. One needs only the example of Russia's production in the last war, where no matter the physical destruction of the economy, its rate of production, enthusiasm, and efficiency were probably never so high. (Up to a point much the same may be said of Germany.)

So the imperative facing America as the dominant world power is to keep Europe from becoming a productive annex of the Soviet Union. And since such an installation could occur only if Western Europe were first temporarily free of both Russia and the United States, it must be equally America's necessity to prevent Western Europe from becoming independent. It is here that Western Defense betrays its ambiguity. If it is on the one hand a virtually open declaration that America is determined to force European rearmament at no matter what cost to the living standard and possible political independence of the European worker, it conceals an even more sinister purpose. For what is rarely admitted, and yet is taken for granted by almost everyone, is that Western Defense

211

has no genuine capacity to defend Western Europe. It has only force enough to destroy it.

If this seems outrageous to the liberal, let him consider the conditions under which a war might now start. No matter where it would begin, and the probability is in Asia, one thing is certain. The Soviet Union would be forced to move against Germany and France. It would have failed in its cold-war strategy of gaining Western Europe peacefully, and having failed, could never allow such a productive plant to be used for the interest of the United States. Therefore, it would attack, and the limited divisions of Western Defense, never strong enough to withstand the Soviet armies, would still be strong enough to carry out an orderly retreat, a withdrawal so orderly that every factory in its path would be razed and the earth scorched clear to the Atlantic Ocean. The military destruction of Western Europe accomplished, America could face its war with the Soviet not unconfidently. All they would have lost would be the graveyard.

It may well be asked why Western Defense is not enlarged to the point where it could hold the Russians at their borders. Politically, however, this is not possible. For such a task an army of fifteen to twenty million men would be required, which is equivalent to declaring the economic bankruptcy of Europe and the most severe depression of the standard of living in the United States. From America's point of view it is not only political suicide but highly unnecessary. The key to the problem and the ugly paradox is that it is only to the Soviet Union's interest to keep the productive wealth of Western Europe intact; by military considerations America is in a far safer position with Western Europe destroyed (in the proper way of course) than to take the chance of having it become the property of the Russians. It is this paradox which the responsible liberal must face, not to mention those socialists who "choose the West." Western Defense is, at present, whether one wills it or not, the active expression of the choice, and as such it means the suppression of any opportunity for responsible socialists to prosper politically in Europe. On the one side they are uncongenial to America's need for European statesmen who must obligatorily be cynical and indifferent to the condition of the European working class; on the other is the knowledge of the European socialist that to support Western Defense is to support Western annihilation in the event of war, and it is exactly Western

Defense which brings war closer, for it destroys the hope of a Third Camp emerging.

6.

What then can one hope for? The answer is hardly easy, but I would incline to the idea that the hope of socialism and more immediately the chances for peace are best served by the collapse of the scheme for Western Defense. In the event, which would leave a vacuum, one can foresee the emergence of an independent Western Europe, neutralist and with a socialist coloration. (Hardly more than coloration, one must admit, surrounded as it would find itself by enemies, and possessing a half-moribund economy.) But still there is a hope here, provided such a Europe could maintain its independence of Soviet overtures. If it could not, the Third World War would almost certainly begin, as I have tried to argue earlier, and indeed it would hardly matter who won such a war, so disastrous would it be. But the chances for peace are equally enlarged, for if men emerge to match the occasion, it is far from impossible that such a Europe could survive, playing off the East against the West, until it grew strong in proportion to the increasing weakness and the insoluble contradictions of the Colossi. What is also possible is that an independent Europe would almost certainly revitalize the vigorous dissenting traditions of American political life. For in contrast to the present when socialist thought is splintered, and the liberal has drearily accommodated himself (I do not speak of such liberals-with-muscles as James Wechsler and Sidney Hook) to the conformity demanded by American political needs, which include the directive to keep Western Europe subservient, there would be positive aims, there would be something legitimate and tangible to support—the continuing independence of Europe—and this would provide enthusiasm with which to replace the ideological wastes and wilderness of McCarthyism, Eisenhowerism, Stevensonism, etc. On the horizon, Asia could be approaching daybreak rather than a Stalinist twilight.

But one loses oneself with images of Apocalypse. It is time to drop the habit. What remains is the argument that Western Defense, sealing Europe against the Soviet, pushes the USSR into Asian adventures which must sooner or later bring the war, and the failure of Western Defense offers the possibility of buying time, saving Europe from its cremation, and opens again the faint perspective of a socialist world.   1953

POSTSCRIPT TO "THE MEANING
OF WESTERN DEFENSE"

Just a note here. I don't want to end up writing a new article—

In "Western Defense" I was saying that the psychological and social contradictions of the Soviet Union were probably greater than those of the United States, and so the Soviet would be plagued by insoluble problems of production. But the facts don't seem to bear me out. When the Russians put Sputnik into orbit, it meant they had succeeded in extracting precise, correct, detailed and careful work from perhaps so many as a million people tied in one way or another to the chain of production which creates space-rockets. It may of course have been relatively a more wasteful and expensive use of human energy than was exhausted by our satellite projects, but we don't know that. Since the Russians have been more successful than we, the probability seems otherwise—that the kind of precise organized work necessary for us to get rockets into orbit founders in eddies of organizational feud and psychological error (everything from a top-level engineer insisting neurotically on the less satisfactory design of a major part, to the mistyping of a few figures in a key letter by a stenographer in the office pool) and so in relation to the social energy applied, we are probably less productive, relatively, than the Soviet.

If this is true, if comparatively we are wasting more productive energy (because our psychological contradictions drive us into more passivity, anxiety, hysteria and guilt than the passivity, anxiety, hysteria and wasteful obsessions of the Soviet), then the odds increase that America will face a crisis before the USSR, a crisis not only of foreign affairs, exhausted foreign loyalties, and threats of war, but an inner crisis of the social and the psychological which will show itself in some warped mirroring of the movement of millions of people toward greater sexuality. This movement has been speeded in part by the needs of a prosperous consumer goods market, and the competition for attention in the mass-media. Since this country is also churchly, antisexual and habit-ridden the acceleration of our sexual tastes has been sly, and filled with onanistic substitutes which increase our guilt and anxiety. The result may be an uneasy and subtle diminution of the national energies, less for love, less for work, and less for the Cold War, and if this is true, then the next collapse in America may come not from the center of its economy (reading one's directions by the compass of the classical Marxist) but within the superstructure of manners, morals, tastes, fashions and vogue which shape the search for love of each of us.

PART 3   **Births**

ADVERTISEMENT FOR PART THREE

This next part of the collection is put together almost entirely of writings on the fly. They are superficial, off-balance, too personal at times, not very agreeable. There would be little excuse for including such bits if I had not decided to use my personality as the armature of this book. Having made such a choice, I cannot avoid showing this worst of my work, for it was done during the two or three years when my ideas were changing character faster than my person, and I was active in a run of adventures and misadventures, feuds with publishers, self-analysis, marijuana, my private discovery of jazz, a couple of live friendships with some people in Harlem, a set of lost friendships on The Village Voice, *and a good time with my second wife, the painter Adele Morales. So these writings reflect the effort to find a style which would express what I now felt—it was all too new.*

Since I can recommend very little of these original pieces on merit, I am not unhappy to suggest that the other writings in this part, the Advertisements, particularly the long account which is here called "The Last Draft of The Deer Park," and was titled "The Mind of An Outlaw" for its publication in Esquire, *are worth reading, especially for those who are bored with a memoir until it becomes a confession.*

ADVERTISEMENT FOR ''THE HOMOSEXUAL VILLAIN''

Some time back in the early fifties, a group of young men in Los Angeles started a homosexual magazine called One. *To attract attention they sent free copies of the magazine and a personal letter out to a horde of big and little celebrities including Bishop Fulton Sheen, Eleanor Roosevelt, Tennessee Williams, Arthur Miller, and fifty-eight others including myself. It was an arresting idea. The top of the letterhead flared the legend:* One—the Homosexual Magazine, *and like a pile of chips on the left margin, we worthies had our names banked, as if we were sponsors. "Dear Norman Mailer" went my letter. "On the left you will see your name listed. You are one of those prominent Americans whom we are seeking to interest in our magazine, so that you might help us to dispel public ignorance and hostility on the subject." And the letter went on to invite us to contribute to the magazine. (I quote it from memory.) About a month later, this letter was followed by a phone call—the New York secretary of the organization called me up to say that he didn't know just what I had to do with all this, but out on the West Coast they had asked him to get in touch with me because I might be able to write for them.*

I didn't know the first thing about homosexuality I hurried to tell him.

Well, the secretary assured me (he had a high-pitched folksy voice) he could understand how I felt about the whole matter, but he could assure Mr. Mailer it was really a very simple matter, Mr. Mailer could say what he wished to say under a pseudonym.

"I told you," I said, "I don't know anything about the subject. I hardly even know any homosexuals."

"Well, Lordy-me," said the secretary, "I could introduce you to a good many of us, Mr. Mailer, and you would see what interesting problems we have."

"No . . . now look."

"Mr. Mailer, wouldn't you at least say that you're sympathetic to the aims of the magazine?"

"Well, I suppose the police laws against homosexuals are bad, and all that. I guess homosexuality is a private matter."

"Would you say that for us?"

"It's not a new idea."

"*Mr. Mailer, I can understand that a man with your name and reputation wouldn't want to get mixed up with such dangerous ideas.*"

He was right. I was ready to put my name to any radical statement, my pride was that I would say in print anything I believed, and yet I was not ready to say a word in public defense of homosexuals.

So I growled at the New York secretary of One *magazine, "If I were to write something about homosexuality, I would sign my name to it."*

"*You would, Mr. Mailer? Listen, I must tell you, by the most conservative statistics, we estimate there are ten million homosexuals in this country. We intend to get a lobby and in a few years we expect to be able to elect our own Congressman. If you write an article for us, Mr. Mailer, why then you might become our first Congressman!*"

I cannot remember the secretary's name, but he had a small knifelike talent—he knew the way to me: mate the absurd with the apocalyptic, and I was a captive. So before our conversation was over, I had promised to write an article for One *magazine.*

It is printed here. I delayed for months getting down to it, my mood would be depressed whenever I remembered my promise, I writhed at what the gossip would be—for every reader who saw my piece there would be ten or a hundred who would hear that Mailer was writing for a faggot magazine. It would be taken for granted I was homosexual—how disagreeable! I used to wish that One *magazine would fail, and be gone forever.*

Then the New York secretary had a fight with the West Coast. He wrote me a letter in which he advised me not to write the piece after all. Since he was my connection to the magazine, I was set free from my promise. Yet I took the step of writing to the editors to ask them if they still wanted an article from me. Not surprisingly, they did. I got their answer in Mexico, and in a flat dutiful mood I sat down and wrote "The Homosexual Villain." It is beyond a doubt the worst article I have ever written, conventional, empty, pious, the quintessence of the Square. Its intellectual level would place it properly in the pages of the Reader's Digest, *and if the* Reader's Digest *had a desire to be useful at their doubtfully useful level they would have scored a Square coup by reprinting it, for the article has a satisfactory dullness of thought which comes from writing in a state of dull anxiety.*

221

Now, it is easier to understand why I did this piece. The Deer Park was then in galleys at Rinehart, and I was depressed about it. Apart from its subject, I thought it a timid inhibited book. I must have known that my fear of homosexuality as a subject was stifling my creative reflexes, and given the brutal rhythms of my nature, I could kill this inhibition only by jumping into the middle of the problem without any clothes. Done gracefully this can stop the show, but I was clumsy and constipated and sick with the bravery of my will, and so "The Homosexual Villain," while honorable as a piece of work, is dressed in the gray of lugubrious caution.

Yet it was important for my particular growth. The gray prose in "The Homosexual Villain" was the end of easy radical rhetoric—I knew I had nothing interesting to say about homosexuality because the rational concepts of socialism, nicely adequate to writing about the work of David Riesman, were not related to the ills of the homosexual. No, for that one had to dig—deep into the complex and often foul pots of thought where sex and society live in their murderous dialectic. Writing "The Homosexual Villain" showed me how barren I was of new ideas, and so helped to blow up a log jam of accumulated timidities and restraints, of caution for my good name. Later when I was back in New York, my mind running wild in the first fevers of self-analysis, I came to spend some months and some years with the endless twists of habit and defeat which are latent homosexuality for so many of us, and I came to understand myself, and become maybe a little more of a man, although it's too soon to brag on it, for being a man is the continuing battle of one's life, and one loses a bit of manhood with every stale compromise to the authority of any power in which one does not believe. Which is a part of the explanation for the tenacity of organized faith, patriotism and respect for society. But that is another essay, and here is "The Homosexual Villain."

THE HOMOSEXUAL VILLAIN

Those readers of *One* who are familiar with my work may be somewhat surprised to find me writing for this magazine. After all, I have been as guilty as any contemporary novelist in attributing unpleasant, ridiculous, or sinister connotations to the homosexual (or more accurately, bisexual) characters in my novels. Part of the effectiveness of General Cummings in *The Naked and The Dead*—at least for those people who thought him well-conceived as a character—rested on the homosexuality I was obviously suggesting as the core of much of his motivation. Again, in *Barbary Shore*, the "villain" was a secret police agent named Leroy Hollingsworth whose sadism and slyness were essentially combined with his sexual deviation.

At the time I wrote those novels, I was consciously sincere. I did believe—as so many heterosexuals believe—that there was an intrinsic relation between homosexuality and "evil," and it seemed perfectly natural to me, as well as *symbolically* just, to treat the subject in such a way.

The irony is that I did not know a single homosexual during all those years. I had met homosexuals of course, I had recognized a few as homosexual, I had "suspected" others, I was to realize years later that one or two close friends were homosexual, but I had never known one in the human sense of knowing, which is to look at your friend's feelings through his eyes and not your own. I did not *know* any homosexual because obviously I did not want to. It was enough for me to recognize someone as homosexual, and I would cease to consider him seriously as a person. He might be intelligent or courageous or kind or witty or virtuous or tortured—no matter. I always saw him as at best ludicrous and at worst—the word again—sinister. (I think it is by the way significant that just as many homosexuals feel forced and are forced to throw up protective camouflage, even boasting if necessary of women they have had, not to mention the thousand smaller subtleties, so heterosexuals are often eager to be so deceived for it enables them to continue friendships which otherwise their prejudices and occasionally their fears might force them to terminate.)

Now, of course, I exaggerate to a certain degree. I was never a roaring bigot, I did not go in for homosexual-baiting, at least not face to face, and I never could stomach the relish with which soldiers would describe how they had stomped some faggot in a bar. I had, in short, the equivalent of a "gentleman's anti-Semitism."

The only thing remarkable about all this is that I was hardly living in a small town. New York, whatever its pleasures and discontents, is not the most uncivilized milieu, and while one would go too far to say that its attitude toward homosexuals bears correspondence to the pain of the liberal or radical at hearing someone utter a word like "nigger" or "kike," there is nonetheless considerable tolerance and considerable propinquity. The hard and fast separations of homosexual and heterosexual society are often quite blurred. Over the past seven or eight years I had had more than enough opportunity to learn something about homosexuals if I had wanted to, and obviously I did not.

It is a pity I do not understand the psychological roots of my change of attitude, for something valuable might be learned from it. Unfortunately, I do not. The process has seemed a rational one to me, rational in that the impetus apparently came from reading and not from any important personal experiences. The only hint of my bias mellowing was that my wife and I had gradually become friendly with a homosexual painter who lived next door. He was pleasant, he was thoughtful, he was a good neighbor, and we came to depend on him in various small ways. It was tacitly understood that he was homosexual, but we never talked about it. However, since so much of his personal life was not discussable between us, the friendship was limited. I accepted him the way a small-town banker fifty years ago might have accepted a "good" Jew.

About this time I received a free copy of *One* which was sent out by the editors to a great many writers. I remember looking at the magazine with some interest and some amusement. Parts of it impressed me unfavorably. I thought the quality of writing generally poor (most people I've talked to agree that it has since improved), and I questioned the wisdom of accepting suggestive ads in a purportedly serious magazine. (Indeed, I still feel this way no matter what the problems of revenue might be.) But there was a certain militancy and honesty to the editorial tone, and while I was not sympathetic, I think I can say that for the first time in my life I was not unsympathetic. Most important of all, my curiosity was piqued. A few weeks later I asked my painter friend if I could borrow his copy of Donald Webster Cory's *The Homosexual in America.*

Reading it was an important experience. Mr. Cory strikes me as being a modest man, and I think he would be the first to admit that while his book is very good, closely reasoned, quietly argued, it is hardly a great book. Nonetheless, I can think of few books which cut so radically at my prejudices and altered my ideas so pro-

224

foundly. I resisted it, I argued its points as I read, I was often annoyed, but what I could not overcome was my growing depression that I had been acting as a bigot in this matter, and "bigot" was one word I did not enjoy applying to myself. With that came the realization I had been closing myself off from understanding a very large part of life. This thought is always disturbing to a writer. A writer has his talent, and for all one knows, he is born with it, but whether his talent develops is to some degree responsive to his use of it. He can grow as a person or he can shrink, and by this I don't intend any facile parallels between moral and artistic growth. The writer can become a bigger hoodlum if need be, but his alertness, his curiosity, his reaction to life must not diminish. The fatal thing is to shrink, to be interested in less, sympathetic to less, desiccating to the point where life itself loses its flavor, and one's passion for human understanding changes to weariness and distaste.

So, as I read Mr. Cory's book, I found myself thinking in effect, *My God, homosexuals are people, too.* Undoubtedly, this will seem incredibly naïve to the homosexual readers of *One* who have been all too painfully aware that they are indeed people, but prejudice is wed to naïveté, and even the sloughing of prejudice, particularly when it is abrupt, partakes of the naïve. I have not tried to conceal that note. As I reread this article I find its tone ingenuous, but there is no point in trying to alter it. One does not become sophisticated overnight about a subject one has closed from oneself.

At any rate I began to face up to my homosexual bias. I had been a libertarian socialist for some years, and implicit in all my beliefs had been the idea that society must allow every individual his own road to discovering himself. Libertarian socialism (the first word is as important as the second) implies inevitably that one have respect for the varieties of human experience. Very basic to everything I had thought was that sexual relations, above everything else, demand their liberty, even if such liberty should amount to no more than compulsion or necessity. For, in the reverse, history has certainly offered enough examples of the link between sexual repression and political repression. (A fascinating thesis on this subject is *The Sexual Revolution* by Wilhelm Reich.) I suppose I can say that for the first time I understood homosexual persecution to be a political act and a reactionary act, and I was properly ashamed of myself.

On the positive side, I found over the next few months that a great deal was opening to me—to put it briefly, even crudely, I felt that I understood more about people, more about life. My life-view had been shocked and the lights and shadows were being shifted, which is equal to saying that I was learning a great deal. At a perhaps embarrassingly personal level, I discovered another benefit. There is probably no sensitive heterosexual alive who is not preoccupied at one time or another with his latent homosexuality, and while I had no conscious homosexual desires, I had wondered more than once if really there were not something suspicious in my intense dislike of homosexuals. How pleasant to discover that once one can accept homosexuals as real friends, the tension is gone with the acceptance. I found that I was no longer concerned with latent homosexuality. It seemed vastly less important, and paradoxically enabled me to realize that I am actually quite heterosexual. Close friendships with homosexuals had become possible without sexual desire or even sexual nuance—at least no more sexual nuance than is present in all human relations.

However, I had a peculiar problem at this time. I was on the way to finishing *The Deer Park*, my third novel. There was a minor character in it named Teddy Pope who is a movie star and a homosexual. Through the first and second drafts he had existed as a stereotype, a figure of fun; he was ludicrously affected and therefore ridiculous. One of the reasons I resisted Mr. Cory's book so much is that I was beginning to feel uneasy with the characterization I had drawn. In life there are any number of ridiculous people, but at bottom I was saying that Teddy Pope was ridiculous because he was homosexual. I found myself dissatisfied with the characterization even before I read *The Homosexual in America*, it had already struck me as being compounded too entirely of malice, but I think I would probably have left it that way. After Mr. Cory's book, it had become impossible. I no longer believed in Teddy Pope as I had drawn him.

Yet a novel which is almost finished is very difficult to alter. If it is at all a good book, the proportions, the meanings, and the interrelations of the characters have become integrated, and one does not violate them without injuring one's work. Moreover, I have developed an antipathy to using one's novels as direct expressions of one's latest ideas. I, therefore, had no desire to change Teddy Pope into a fine virtuous character. That would be as false, and as close to propaganda, as to keep him the way he was. Also, while a minor character, he had an important relation to the story, and it was obvious that he could not be transformed too radically without recasting much of the novel. My decision, with which I am not altogether happy, was to keep Teddy Pope more or less intact, but to try to add dimension to him. Perhaps I have succeeded. He will never be a character many readers admire, but it is possible that they will have feeling for him. At least he is no longer a simple object of ridicule, nor the butt of my malice, and I believe *The Deer Park* is a better book for the change. My hope is that some readers may possibly be stimulated to envisage the gamut of homosexual personality as parallel to the gamut of heterosexual personality even if Teddy Pope is a character from the lower half of the spectrum. However, I think it is more probable that the majority of homosexual readers who may get around to reading *The Deer Park* when it is published will be dissatisfied with him. I can only say that I am hardly satisfied myself. But this time, at least, I have discovered the edges of the rich theme of homosexuality rather than the easy symbolic equation of it to evil. And to that extent I feel richer and more confident as a writer. What I have come to realize is that much of my homosexual prejudice was a servant to my aesthetic needs. In the variety and contradiction of American life, the difficulty of finding a character who can serve as one's protagonist is matched only by the difficulty of finding one's villain, and so long as I was able to preserve my prejudices, my literary villains were at hand. Now, the problem will be more difficult, but I suspect it may be rewarding too, for deep-down I was never very happy nor proud of myself at whipping homosexual straw-boys.

A last remark. If the homosexual is ever to achieve real social equality and acceptance, he too will have to work the hard row of shedding his own prejudices. Driven into defiance, it is natural if regrettable, that many homosexuals go to the direction of assuming that there is something intrinsically superior in homosexuality, 'and carried far enough it is a viewpoint which is as stultifying, as ridiculous, and as anti-human as the heterosexual's prejudice. Finally, heterosexuals are people too, and the hope of acceptance, tolerance, and sympathy must rest on this mutual appreciation.

1954

FOURTH ADVERTISEMENT FOR MYSELF:
THE LAST DRAFT OF THE DEER PARK

In his review of The Deer Park, *Malcolm Cowley said it must have been a more difficult book to write than* The Naked and The Dead. *He was right. Most of the time, I worked on* The Deer Park *in a low mood; my liver, which had gone bad in the Philippines, exacted a hard price for forcing the effort against the tide of a long depression, and matters were not improved when nobody at Rinehart & Co. liked the first draft of the novel. The second draft, which to me was the finished book, also gave little enthusiasm to the editors, and open woe to Stanley Rinehart, the publisher. I was impatient to leave for Mexico, now that I was done, but before I could go, Rinehart asked for a week in which to decide whether he wanted to do the book. Since he had already given me a contract which allowed him no option not to accept the novel (a common arrangement for writers whose sales are more or less large) any decision to reject the manuscript would cost him a sizable advance. (I learned later he had been hoping his lawyers would find the book obscene, but they did not, at least not then in May 1954.) So he had really no choice but to agree to put the book out in February, and gloomily he consented. To cheer him a bit, I agreed to his request that he delay paying me my advance until publication, although the first half was due on delivery of the manuscript. I thought the favor might improve our relations.*

Now, if a few of you are wondering why I did not take my book back and go to another publishing house, the answer is that I was tired, I was badly tired. Only a few weeks before, a doctor had given me tests for the liver, and it had shown itself to be sick and depleted. I was hoping that a few months in Mexico would give me a chance to fill up again.

But the next months were not cheerful. The Deer Park had been done as well as I could do it, yet I thought it was probably a minor work, and I did not know if I had any real interest in starting another book. I made efforts of course; I collected notes, began to piece together a few ideas for a novel given to bullfighting, and another about a concentration camp; I wrote "David Reisman Reconsidered" during this time, and "The Homosexual Villain"; read most of the work of the other writers of my generation (I think I was looking for a level against which to measure my third novel) went over the galleys when they came, changed a line or two, sent them back. Keeping half busy I mended a bit, but it was a time of dull drifting. When we came back to New York in October, The Deer Park was already in page proof. By November, the first advertisement was given to Publishers' Weekly. Then, with less than ninety days to publication, Stanley Rinehart told me I would have to take out a small piece of the book—six not very explicit lines about the sex of an old producer and a call girl. The moment one was ready to consider losing those six lines they moved into the moral center of the novel. It would be no tonic for my liver to cut them out. But I also knew Rinehart was serious, and since I was still tired, it seemed a little unreal to try to keep the passage. Like a miser I had been storing energy to start a new book; I wanted nothing to distract me now. I gave in on a word or two, agreed to rewrite a line, and went home from that particular conference not very impressed with myself. The next morning I called up the editor in chief, Ted Amussen, to tell him I had decided the original words had to be put back.

"Well, fine," he said, "fine. I don't know why you agreed to anything in the first place."

A day later, Stanley Rinehart halted publication, stopped all ads (he was too late to catch the first run of Publishers' Weekly *which was already on its way to England with a full page for* The Deer Park) *and broke his contract to do the book. I was started on a trip to find a new publisher, and before I was done, the book had gone to Random House, Knopf, Simon and Schuster, Harper's, Scribners, and unofficially to Harcourt, Brace. Some day it would be fine to give the details, but for now little more than a few lines of dialogue and an editorial report:*

> **Bennett Cerf: This novel will set publishing back twenty years.**
>
> **Alfred Knopf to an editor: Is this your idea of the kind of book which should bear a Borzoi imprint?**

The lawyer for one publishing house complimented me on the six lines, word for word, which had excited Rinehart to break his contract. This lawyer said, "It's admirable the way you get around the problem here." Then he brought out more than a hundred objections to other parts of the book. One was the line, "She was lovely. Her back was adorable in its contours." I was told that this ought to go because "The principals are not married, and so your description puts a favorable interpretation upon a meretricious relationship."

Hiram Hayden had lunch with me some time after Random House saw the book. He told me he was responsible for their decision not to do it, and if I did not agree with his taste, I had to admire his honesty—it is rare for an editor to tell a writer the truth. Hayden went on to say that the book never came alive for him even though he had been ready to welcome it. "I can tell you that I picked the book up with anticipation. Of course I had heard from Bill, and Bill had told me that he didn't like it, but I never pay attention to what one writer says about the work of another . . ." Bill was William Styron, and Hayden was his editor. I had asked Styron to call Hayden the night I found out Rinehart had broken his contract. One reason for asking the favor of Styron was that he sent me a long letter about the novel after I had shown it to him in manuscript. He had written, "I don't like The Deer Park, *but I admire sheer hell out of it." So I thought to impose on him.*

Other parts of the account are not less dreary. The only generosity I found was from the late Jack Goodman. He sent me a photostat of his editorial report to Simon and Schuster, and because it was sympathetic, his report became the objective estimate of the situation for me. I assumed that the book when it came out would meet the kind of trouble Goodman expected, and so when I went back later to work on the page proofs I was not free of a fear or two. But that can be talked about in its place. Here is the core of his report.

> Mailer refuses to make any changes . . . [He] *will* consider suggestions, but reserves the right to make final decisions, so we must make our decision on what the book now is.
> That's not easy. It is full of vitality and power, as readable a novel as I've ever encountered. Mailer emerges as a sort of post-Kinsey F. Scott Fitzgerald. His dialogue is uninhibited and the sexuality of the book is completely interwoven with its purpose, which is to describe a seg-

ment of society whose morality is nonexistent. Locale is evidently Palm Springs. Chief characters are Charles Eitel, movie director who first defies the House Un-American Committee, then becomes a friendly witness, his mistress, a great movie star who is his ex-wife, her lover who is the narrator, the head of a great movie company, his son-in-law, a strange, tortured panderer who is Eitel's conscience and, assorted demimondaines, homosexuals, actors.

My layman's opinion is that the novel will be banned in certain quarters and that it may very well be up for an obscenity charge, but this should of course be checked by our lawyers. If it were possible to recognize this at the start, to have a united front here and treat the whole issue positively and head-on, I would be for our publishing. But I am afraid such unanimity may be impossible of attainment and if so, we should reject, in spite of the fact that I am certain it will be one of the best-selling novels of the next couple of years. It is the work of a serious artist. . . .

The eighth house was G. P. Putnam's. I didn't want to give it to them, I was planning to go next to Viking, but Walter Minton kept saying, "Give us three days. We'll give you a decision in three days." So we sent it over to Putnam, and in three days they took it without conditions, and without a request for a single change. I had a victory, I had made my point, but in fact I was not very happy. I had grown so wild on my diet of polite letters from publishing houses who didn't want me, that I had been ready to collect rejections from twenty houses, publish The Deer Park *at my own expense, and try to make a kind of publishing history. Instead I was thrown in with Walter Minton, who has since attracted some fame as the publisher of* Lolita. *He is the only publisher I ever met who would make a good general. Months after I came to Putnam, Minton told me, "I was ready to take* The Deer Park *without reading it. I knew your name would sell enough copies to pay your advance, and I figured one of these days you're going to write another book like* The Naked and The Dead," *which is the sort of sure hold of strategy you can have when you're not afraid of censorship.*

Now I've tried to water this account with a minimum of tears, but taking The Deer Park *into the nervous system of eight publishing houses was not so good for my own nervous system, nor was it good for getting to work on my new novel. In the ten weeks it took the book to travel the circuit from Rinehart to Putnam, I squandered the careful energy I had been hoarding for months; there was a hard comedy at how much of myself I would burn up in a few hours of hot telephone calls; I had never had any sense for practical affairs, but in those days, carrying* The Deer Park *from house to house, I stayed as close to it as a stage-struck mother pushing her child forward at every producer's office. I was amateur agent for it, messenger boy, editorial consultant, Macchiavelli of the luncheon table, fool of the five o'clock drinks, I was learning the publishing business in a hurry, and I made a hundred mistakes and paid for each one by wasting a new bout of energy.*

In a way there was sense to it. For the first time in years I was having the kind of experience which was likely to return some day as good work, and so I forced many little events past any practical return, even insulting a few publishers en route as if to discover the limits of each situation. I was trying to find a few new proportions to things, and I did learn a bit. But I'll never know what that novel about the concentration camp would have been like if I had gotten quietly to work when I came back to New York and The Deer Park *had been published on time. It is possible I was not serious about the book, it is also possible I lost something good, but one way or the other, that novel disappeared in the excitement, as lost as "the little object" in* Barbary Shore, *and it has not stirred since.*

The real confession is that I was making a few of my mental connections those days on marijuana. Like more than one or two of my generation, I had smoked it from time to time over the years, but it never had meant anything. In Mexico, however, down in my depression with a bad liver, pot gave me a sense of something new about the time I was convinced I had seen it all, and I liked it enough to take it now and again in New York.

Then The Deer Park *began to go like a beggar from house to house and en route Stanley Rinehart made it clear he was going to try not to pay the advance. Until then I had had sympathy for him. I thought it had taken a kind of displaced courage to be able to drop the book the way he did. An expensive moral stand, and wasteful for me; but a moral stand. When it turned out that he did not like to bear the expense of being that moral, the experience turned ugly for me. It took many months and the service of my lawyer to get the money, but long before that, the situation had become real enough to drive a spike into my cast-iron mind. I realized in some bottom of myself that for years I had been the sort of comic figure I would have cooked to a turn in one of my books, a radical who had the nineteenth-century naïveté to believe that the people with whom he did business were 1) gentlemen, 2) fond of him, and 3) respectful of his ideas even if in disagreement with them. Now, I was in the act of learning that I was not adored so very much; that my ideas were seen as nasty; and that my fine America which I had been at pains to criticize for so many years was in fact a real country which did real things and ugly things to the characters of more people than just the characters of my books. If the years since the war had not been brave or noble in the history of the country, which I certainly thought and do think, why then did it come as surprise that people in publishing were not as good as they used to be, and that the day of Maxwell Perkins was a day which was gone, really gone, gone as Greta Garbo and Scott Fitzgerald? Not easy, one could argue, for an advertising man to admit that advertising is a dishonest occupation, and no easier was it for the working novelist to see that now were left only the cliques, fashions, vogues, snobs, snots, and fools, not to mention a dozen bureaucracies of criticism; that there was no room for the old literary idea of oneself as a major writer, a figure in the landscape. One had become a set of relations and equations, most flourishing when most incorporated, for then one's literary stock was ready for merger. The day was gone when people held on to your novels no matter what others might say. Instead one's good young readers waited now for the verdict of professional young men, academics who wolfed down a modern literature with an anxiety to find your classification, your identity, your similarity, your common theme, your corporate literary earnings, each reference to yourself as individual as a carloading of homogenized words. The articles which would be written about you and a dozen others would be done by minds which were expert on the aggregate and so had senses too lumpy for the particular. There was a limit to how much appraisal could be made of a work before the critic exposed his lack of the critical faculty, and so it was naturally wiser for the mind of the expert to masticate the themes of ten writers rather than approach the difficulties of any one.*

I had begun to read my good American novels at the end of an era—I could remember people who would talk wistfully about the excitement with which they had gone to bookstores because it was publication day for the second novel of Thomas Wolfe, and in

233

college, at a Faculty tea, I had listened for an hour to a professor's
wife who was so blessed as to have known John Dos Passos. My ado-
lescent crush on the profession of the writer had been more lasting
than I could have guessed. I had even been so simple as to think that
the kind of people who went into publishing were still most con-
cerned with the few writers who made the profession not empty of
honor, and I had been taking myself seriously, I had been thinking I
was one of those writers.

Instead I caught it in the face and deserved it for not looking
at the evidence. I was out of fashion and that was the score; that was
all the score; the publishing habits of the past were going to be of
no help for my Deer Park. *And so as the language of sentiment*
would have it, something broke in me, but I do not know if it was so
much a loving heart, as a cyst of the weak, the unreal, and the needy,
and I was finally open to my anger. I turned within my psyche I can
almost believe, for I felt something shift to murder in me. I finally
had the simple sense to understand that if I wanted my work to
travel further than others, the life of my talent depended on fighting
a little more, and looking for help a little less. But I deny the se-
quence in putting it this way, for it took me years to come to this
fine point. All I felt then was that I was an outlaw, a psychic outlaw,
and I liked it, I liked it a good night better than trying to be a gen-
tleman, and with a set of emotions accelerating one on the other, I
mined down deep into the murderous message of marijuana, the
smoke of the assassins, and for the first time in my life I knew what
it was to make your kicks.

I could write about that here, but it would be a mistake. Let
the experience stay where it is, and on a given year it may be found
again in a novel. For now it is enough to say that marijuana opens
the senses and weakens the mind. In the end, you pay for what you
get. If you get something big, the cost will equal it. There is a moral
economy to one's vice, but you learn that last of all. I still had the
thought it was possible to find something which cost nothing. Thus,
The Deer Park *resting at Putnam, and new good friends found in*
Harlem, I was off on that happy ride where you discover a new
duchy of jazz every night and the drought of the past is given a rain
of new sound. What has been dull and dead in your years is now
tart to the taste, and there is sweet in the illusion of how fast you can
change. To keep up with it all, I began to log a journal, a wild set of
thoughts and outlines for huge projects—I wrote one hundred

thousand words in eight weeks, more than once twenty pages a day in a style which came willy-nilly from the cramp of the past, a lockstep jargon of sociology and psychology that sours my teeth when I look at those pages today. Yet this journal has the start of more ideas than I will have again; ideas which came so fast and so rich that sometimes I think my brain was dulled by the heat of their passage. (With all proportions kept, one can say that cocaine may have worked a similar good and ill upon Freud.)

The journal wore down by February, about the time The Deer Park had once been scheduled to appear. By then I had decided to change a few things in the novel, nothing in the way of lawyer's deletions, just a few touches for style. They were not happy about this at Putnam. Minton argued that some interest in the book would be lost if the text were not identical to Rinehart's page proofs, and Ted Purdy, my editor, told me more than once that they liked the book "just the way it is." Besides, there was thought of bringing it out in June as a summer book.

Well, I wanted to take a look. After all, I had been learning new lessons. I began to go over the page proofs, and the book read as if it had been written by someone else. I was changed from the writer who had labored on that novel, enough to be able to see it without anger or vanity or the itch to justify myself. Now, after three years of living with the book, I could at last admit the style was wrong, that it had been wrong from the time I started, that I had been strangling the life of my novel in a poetic prose which was too self-consciously attractive and formal, false to the life of my characters, especially false to the life of my narrator who was the voice of my novel and so gave the story its air. He had been a lieutenant in the Air Force, he had been cool enough and hard enough to work his way up from an orphan asylum, and to allow him to write in a style which at its best sounded like Nick Carraway in The Great Gatsby must of course blur his character and leave the book unreal. Nick was legitimate, out of fair family, the Midwest and Princeton—he would write as he did, his style was himself. But the style of Sergius O'Shaugnessy, no matter how good it became (and the Rinehart Deer Park had its moments) was a style which came out of nothing so much as my determination to prove I could muster a fine style.

If I wanted to improve my novel, yet keep the style, I would have to make my narrator fit the prose, change his past, make him an onlooker, a rich pretty boy brought up let us say by two old-maid aunts, able to have an affair with a movie star only by luck and/or the needs of the plot, which would give me a book less distracting, well written but minor. If, however, I wanted to keep that first narrator, my orphan, flier, adventurer, germ—for three years he had been the frozen germ of some new theme—well, to keep him I would need to change the style from the inside of each sentence. I could keep the structure of my book, I thought—it had been put together for such a narrator—but the style could not escape. Probably I did not see it all so clearly as I now suggest. I believe I started with the conscious thought that I would tinker just a little, try to patch a compromise, but the navigator of my unconscious must already had made the choice, because it came as no real surprise that after a few days of changing a few words I moved more and more quickly toward the eye of the problem, and in two or three weeks I was tied to the work of doing a new Deer Park. The book was edited in a way no editor could ever have time or love to find; it was searched sentence by sentence, word for word, the style of the work lost its polish, became rough, and I can say real, because there was an abrupt and muscular body back of the voice now. It had been there all the time, trapped in the porcelain of a false style, but now as I chipped away, the work for a time became exhilarating in its clarity—I never enjoyed work so much—I felt as if finally I was learning how to write, learning the joints of language and the touch of a word, felt as if I came close to the meanings of sound and could say which of two close words was more female or more forward. I even had a glimpse of what Flaubert might have felt, for as I went on tuning the book, often five or six words would pile above one another in the margin at some small crisis of choice. (Since the Rinehart page proof was the usable copy, I had little space to write between the lines.) As I worked in this fine mood, I kept sending pages to the typist, yet so soon as I had exhausted the old galley pages, I could not keep away from the new typewritten copy—it would be close to say the book had come alive, and was invading my brain.

Soon the early pleasure of the work turned restless; the consequences of what I was doing were beginning to seep into my stamina. It was as if I were the captive of an illness whose first symptoms had been excitement, prodigies of quick work, and a confidence *that one could go on forever, but that I was by now close to a second stage where what had been quick would be more like fever, a first wind of fatigue upon me, a knowledge that at the end of the drunken night a junkie cold was waiting. I was going to move at a pace deadly to myself, loading and overloading whatever little centers of the mind are forced to make the hard decisions. In ripping up the silk of the original syntax, I was tearing into any number of careful habits as well as whatever subtle fleshing of the nerves and the chemicals had gone to support them.*

For six years I had been writing novels in the first person; it was the only way I could begin a book, even though the third person was more to my taste. Worse, I seemed unable to create a narrator in the first person who was not overdelicate, oversensitive, and painfully tender, which was an odd portrait to give, because I was not delicate, not physically; when it was a matter of strength I had as much as the next man. In those days I would spend time reminding myself that I had been a bit of an athlete (house football at Harvard, years of skiing) that I had not quit in combat, and once when a gang broke up a party in my loft, I had taken two cracks on the head with a hammer and had still been able to fight. Yet the first person seemed to paralyze me, as if I had a horror of creating a voice which could be in any way bigger than myself. So I had become mired in a false style for every narrator I tried. If now I had been in a fight, had found out that no matter how weak I could be in certain ways, I was also steady enough to hang on to six important lines, that may have given me new respect for myself, I don't know, but for the first time I was able to use the first person in a way where I could suggest some of the stubbornness and belligerence I also might have, I was able to color the empty reality of that first person with some real feeling of how I had always felt, which was to be outside, for Brooklyn where I grew up is not the center of anything. I was able, then, to create an adventurer whom I believed in, and as he came alive for me, the other parts of the book which had been stagnant for a year and more also came to life, and new things began to happen to Eitel my director and to Elena his mistress and their characters changed. It was a phenomenon. I learned how real a novel is. Before, the story of Eitel had been told by O'Shaugnessy of the weak voice; now by a confident young man: when the new narrator would remark that Eitel was his best friend and so he tried not to find

Elena too attractive, the man and woman he was talking about were larger than they had once been. I was no longer telling of two nice people who fail at love because the world is too large and too cruel for them; the new O'Shaugnessy had moved me by degrees to the more painful story of two people who are strong as well as weak, corrupt as much as pure, and fail to grow despite their bravery in a poor world, because they are finally not brave enough, and so do more damage to one another than to the unjust world outside them. Which for me was exciting, for here and there The Deer Park now had the rare tenderness of tragedy. The most powerful leverage in fiction comes from point of view, and giving O'Shaugnessy courage gave passion to the others.

But the punishment was commencing for me. I was now creating a man who was braver and stronger than me, and the more my new style succeeded, the more was I writing an implicit portrait of myself as well. There is a shame about advertising yourself that way, a shame which became so strong that it was a psychological violation to go on. Yet I could not afford the time to digest the self-criticisms backing up in me, I was forced to drive myself, and so more and more I worked by tricks, taking marijuana the night before and then drugging myself into sleep with an overload of seconal. In the morning I would be lithe with new perception, could read new words into the words I had already, and so could go on in the pace of my work, the most scrupulous part of my brain too sluggish to interfere. My powers of logic became weaker each day, but the book had its own logic, and so I did not need close reason. What I wanted and what the drugs gave me was the quick flesh of associations, and there I was often oversensitive, could discover new experience in the lines of my text like a hermit savoring the revelation of Scripture; I saw so much in some sentences that more than once I dropped into the pit of the amateur: since I was receiving such emotion from my words, I assumed everyone else would be stimulated as well, and on many a line I twisted the phrase in such a way that it could read well only when read slowly, about as slowly as it would take for an actor to read it aloud. Once you write that way, the quick reader (who is nearly all your audience) will stumble and fall against the vocal shifts of your prose. Then you had best have the cartel of a Hemingway, because in such a case it is critical whether the reader thinks it is your fault, or is so in awe of your reputation that he returns on the words, throttles his pace, and tries to discover why he is so stupid as not to swing on the off-bop of your style.

An example: In the Rinehart Deer Park *I had this:*

> "They make Sugar sound so good in the newspapers," she declared one night to some people in a bar, "that I'll really try him. I really will, Sugar." And she gave me a sisterly kiss.

I happened to change that very little, I put in "said" instead of "declared" and later added "older sister," so that it now read:

> And she gave me a sisterly kiss. Older sister.

Just two words, but I felt as if I had revealed some divine law of nature, had laid down an invaluable clue—the kiss of an older sister was a worldly universe away from the kiss of a younger sister —and I thought to give myself the Nobel Prize for having brought such illumination and division to the cliché of the sisterly kiss.

Well, as an addition it wasn't bad fun, and for two words it did a bit to give a sense of what was working back and forth between Sergius and Lulu, it was another small example of Sergius' hard eye for the world, and his cool sense of his place in it, and all this was to the good, or would have been for a reader who went slowly, and stopped, and thought. But if anyone was in a hurry, the little sentence "Older sister" was like a finger in the eye, it jabbed the unconscious, and gave an uncomfortable nip of rhythm to the mind.

I had five hundred changes of this kind. I started with the first paragraph of the book, on the third sentence which pokes the reader with its backed-up rhythm, "Some time ago," and I did that with intent, to slow my readers from the start, like a fighter who throws his right two seconds after the bell and so gives the other man no chance to decide on the pace.

There was a real question, however, whether I could slow the reader down, and so as I worked on further, at some point beginning to write paragraphs and pages to add to the new Putnam galleys, the attrition of the drugs and the possibility of failure began to depress me, and Benzedrine entered the balance, and I was on the way to wearing badly. Because, determined or no that they would read me slowly, praying my readers would read me slowly, there was no likelihood they would do anything of the sort if the reviews were

239

bad. *As I started to worry this it grew worse, because I knew in advance that three or four of my major reviews had to be bad*—Time *magazine for one, because Max Gissen was the book review editor, and I had insulted him in public once by suggesting that the kind of man who worked for a mind so exquisitely and subtly totalitarian as Henry Luce was not likely to have any ideas of his own. The New York Daily* Times *would be bad because Orville Prescott was well known for his distaste of books too forthrightly sexual; and* Saturday Review *would be bad. That is, they would probably be bad; the mentality of their reviewers would not be above the level of their dean of reviewers, Mr. Maxwell Geismar, and Geismar didn't seem to know that my second novel was titled* Barbary Shore *rather than* Barbary Coast. *I could spin this out, but what is more to the point is that I had begun to think of the reviews before finishing the book, and this doubtful occupation came out of the kind of inner knowledge I had of myself in those days. I knew what was good for my energy and what was poor, and so I knew that for the vitality of my work in the future, and yes even the quantity of my work, I needed a success and I needed it badly if I was to shed the fatigue I had been carrying since* Barbary Shore. *Some writers receive not enough attention for years, and so learn early to accommodate the habits of their work to little recognition. I think I could have done that when I was twenty-five. With* The Naked and The Dead *a new life had begun, however; as I have written earlier in this book, I had gone through the psychic labor of changing a good many modest habits in order to let me live a little more happily as a man with a name which could arouse quick reactions in strangers. If that started as an overlarge work, because I started as a decent but scared boy, well I had come to live with the new life, I had learned to like success—in fact I had probably come to depend on it, or at least my new habits did.*

When Barbary Shore *was ambushed in the alley, the damage to my nervous system was slow but thorough. My status dropped immediately—America is a quick country—but my ego did not permit me to understand that, and I went through tiring years of subtle social defeats because I did not know that I was no longer as large to others as I had been. I was always overmatching myself. To put it crudely, I would think I was dropping people when they were dropping me. And of course my unconscious knew better. There was all the waste of ferocious if unheard discussion between the* armies of ego and id; I would get up in the morning with less snap in me than I had taken to sleep. Six or seven years of breathing that literary air taught me a writer stayed alive in the circuits of such hatred only if he were unappreciated enough to be adored by a clique, or was so overbought by the public that he excited some defenseless nerve in the snob. I knew if The Deer Park was a powerful best seller (the magical figure had become one hundred thousand copies for me) that I would then have won. I would be the first serious writer of my generation to have a best seller twice, and so it would not matter what was said about the book. Half of publishing might call it cheap, dirty, sensational, second-rate, and so forth and so forth, but it would be weak rage and could not hurt, for the literary world suffers a spot of the national taint—a serious writer is certain to be considered major if he is also a best seller; in fact, most readers are never convinced of his value until his books do well. Steinbeck is better known than Dos Passos, John O'Hara is taken seriously by people who dismiss Farrell, and indeed it took three decades and a Nobel Prize before Faulkner was placed on a level with Hemingway. For that reason, it would have done no good if someone had told me at the time that the financial success of a writer with major talent was probably due more to what was meretricious in his work than what was central. The argument would have meant nothing to me—all I knew was that seven publishing houses had been willing to dismiss my future, and so if the book did poorly, a good many people were going to congratulate themselves on their foresight and be concerned with me even less. I could see that if I wanted to keep on writing the kind of book I liked to write, I needed the energy of new success, I needed blood. Through every bit of me, I knew The Deer Park had damn well better make it or I was close to some serious illness, a real apathy of the will.

Every now and again I would have the nightmare of wondering what would happen if all the reviews were bad, as bad as Barbary Shore. I would try to tell myself that could not happen, but I was not certain, and I knew that if the book received a unanimously bad press and still showed signs of selling well, it was likely to be brought up for prosecution as obscene. As a delayed convulsion from the McCarthy years, the fear of censorship was strong in publishing, in England it was critically bad, and so I also knew that the book could lose such a suit—there might be no one of reputation to say it was serious. If it were banned, it could sink from sight. With the reserves I was throwing into the work, I no longer knew if I was ready to take another beating—for the first time in my life I had worn down to the edge, I could see through to the other side of my fear, I knew a time could come when I would be no longer my own man, that I might lose what I had liked to think was the incorruptible center of my strength (which of course I had had money and freedom to cultivate). Already the signs were there—I was beginning to avoid new lines in the Putnam Deer Park which were legally doubtful, and once in a while, like a gambler hedging a bet, I toned down individual sentences from the Rinehart Deer Park, nothing much, always a matter of the new O'Shaugnessy character, a change from "at last I was able to penetrate into the mysterious and magical belly of a movie star," to what was more in character for him: "I was led to discover the mysterious brain of a movie star." Which "brain" in context was fun for it was accurate, and "discover" was a word of more life than the legality of "penetrate," but I could not be sure if I were chasing my new aesthetic or afraid of the cops. The problem was that The Deer Park had become more sexual in the new version, the characters had more force, the air had more heat, and I had gone through the kind of galloping self-analysis which makes one very sensitive to the sexual nuance of every gesture, word and object—the book now seemed overcharged to me, even a terror of a novel, a cold chisel into all the dull mortar of our guilty society. In my mind it became a more dangerous book than it really was, and my drug-hipped paranoia saw long consequences in every easy line of dialogue. I kept the panic in its place, but by an effort of course, and once in a while I would weaken enough to take out a line because I could not see myself able to defend it happily in a court of law. But it was a mistake to nibble at the edges of censoring myself, for it gave no life to my old pride that I was the boldest writer to have come out of my flabby time, and I think it helped to kill the small chance of finding my way into what could have been a novel as important as The Sun Also Rises.

But let me spell it out a bit: originally The Deer Park had been about a movie director and a girl with whom he had a bad affair, and it was told by a sensitive but faceless young man. In changing the young man, I saved the book from being minor, but put a disproportion upon it because my narrator became too interesting, and not enough happened to him in the second half of the book,

242

and so it was to be expected that readers would be disappointed by this part of the novel.

Before I was finished, I saw a way to write another book altogether. In what I had so far done, Sergius O'Shaugnessy was given an opportunity by a movie studio to sell the rights to his life and get a contract as an actor. After more than one complication, he finally refused the offer, lost the love of his movie star Lulu, and went off wandering by himself, off to become a writer. This episode had never been an important part of the book, but I could see that the new Sergius was capable of accepting the offer, and if he went to Hollywood and became a movie star himself, the possibilities were good, for in O'Shaugnessy I had a character who was ambitious, yet in his own way, moral, and with such a character one could travel deep into the paradoxes of the time.

Well, I was not in shape to consider that book. With each week of work, bombed and sapped and charged and stoned with lush, with pot, with benny, saggy, Milltown, coffee, and two packs a day, I was working live, and overalert, and tiring into what felt like death, afraid all the way because I had achieved the worst of vicious circles in myself, I had gotten too tired, I was more tired than I had ever been in combat, and so as the weeks went on, and publication was delayed from June to August and then to October, there was only a worn-out part of me to keep protesting into the pillows of one drug and the pinch of the other that I ought to have the guts to stop the machine, to call back the galleys, to cease—to rest, to give myself another two years and write a book which would go a little further to the end of my particular night.

But I had passed the point where I could stop. My anxiety had become too great. I did not know anything any more, I did not have that clear sense of the way things work which is what you need for the natural proportions of a long novel, and it is likely I would not have been writing a new book so much as arguing with the law. Of course another man might have had the stamina to write the new book and manage to be indifferent to everything else, but it was too much to ask of me. By then I was like a lover in a bad, but uncontrollable affair; my woman was publication, and it would have cost too much to give her up before we were done. My imagination had been committed—to stop would leave half the psyche in limbo.

Knowing, however, what I had failed to do, shame added

243

momentum to the punishment of the drugs. By the last week or two, I had worn down so badly that with a dozen pieces still to be fixed, I was reduced to working hardly more than an hour a day. Like an old man, I would come up out of a seconal stupor with four or five times the normal dose in my veins, and drop into a chair to sit for hours. It was July, the heat was grim in New York, the last of the book had to be in by August 1. Putnam had been more than accommodating, but the vehicle of publication was on its way, and the book could not be postponed beyond the middle of October or it would miss all chance for a large fall sale. I would sit in a chair and watch a baseball game on television, or get up and go out in the heat to a drugstore for sandwich and malted—it was my outing for the day: the walk would feel like a patrol in a tropical sun, and it was two blocks, no more. When I came back, I would lie down, my head would lose the outer wrappings of sedation, and with a crumb of benzedrine, the first snake or two of thought would wind through my brain. I would go for some coffee—it was a trip to the kitchen, but when I came back I would have a scratch-board and pencil in hand. Watching some afternoon horror on television, the boredom of the performers coming through their tense hilarities with a bleakness to match my own, I would pick up the board, wait for the first sentence—like all working addicts I had come to an old man's fine sense of inner timing—and then slowly, but picking up speed, the actions of the drugs hovering into collaboration like two ships passing in view of one another, I would work for an hour, not well but not badly either. (Pages 195 to 200 of the Putnam edition were written this way.) Then my mind would wear out, and new work was done for the day. I would sit around, watch more television and try to rest my dulled mind, but by evening a riot of bad nerves was on me again, and at two in the morning I'd be having the manly debate of whether to try sleep with two double capsules, or settle again for my need of three.

Somehow I got the book done for the last deadline. Not perfectly—doing just the kind of editing and small rewriting I was doing, I could have used another two or three days, but I got it almost the way I wanted, and then I took my car up to the Cape and lay around in Provincetown with my wife, trying to mend, and indeed doing a fair job because I came off sleeping pills and the marijuana and came part of the way back into that world which has the proportions of the ego. I picked up on The Magic Mountain, *took it slowly, and lowered* The Deer Park *down to modest size in my brain. Which events proved was just as well.*

A few weeks later we came back to the city, and I took some mescaline. Maybe one dies a little with the poison of mescaline in the blood. At the end of a long and private trip which no quick remark should try to describe, the book of The Deer Park *floated into mind, and I sat up, reached through a pleasure garden of velveted light to find the tree of a pencil and the bed of a notebook and brought them to union together. Then, out of some flesh in myself I had not yet known, with the words coming one by one, in separate steeps and falls, hip in their turnings, all cool with their flights, like the touch of being coming into other being, so the last six lines of my bloody book came to me, and I was done. And it was the only good writing I ever did directly from a drug, even if I paid for it with a hangover beyond measure.*

That way the novel received its last sentence, and if I had waited one more day it would have been too late, for in the next twenty-four hours, the printers began their cutting and binding. The book was out of my hands.

Six weeks later, when The Deer Park *came out, I was no longer feeling eighty years old, but a vigorous hysterical sixty-three, and I laughed like an old pirate at the indignation I had breezed into being with the equation of sex and time. The important reviews broke about seven good and eleven bad, and the out-of-town reports were almost three-to-one bad to good, but I was not unhappy because the good reviews were lively and the bad reviews were full of factual error, indeed so much so that it would be monotonous to give more than a good couple.*

Hollis Alpert in the Saturday Review *called the book "garish and gauche." In reference to Sergius O'Shaugnessy, Alpert wrote: "He has been offered $50,000 by Teppis to sell the rights to his rather dull life story . . ." As a matter of detail, the sum was $20,000, and it must have been mentioned a half dozen times in the pages of the book. Paul Pickrel in* Harper's *was blistering about how terrible was my style and then quoted the following sentence as an example of how I was often incomprehensible:*

> **"(he) could talk opening about his personal life while remaining a dream of espionage in his business operations."**

I happened to see Pickrel's review in Harper's *galleys, and so was able to point out to them that Pickrel had misquoted the sentence. The fourth word was not "opening" but "openly." Harper's corrected his incorrect version, but of course left his remark about my style.*

More interesting is the way reviews divided in the New York magazines and newspapers. Time, *for example, was bad,* Newsweek *was good;* Harper's *was terrible but* The Atlantic *was adequate; the* New York Daily Times *was very bad, the* Sunday Times *was good; the* Daily Herald Tribune *gave a mark of zero, the* Sunday Herald Tribune *was better than good;* Commentary *was careful but complimentary, the* Reporter *was frantic; the* Saturday Review *was a scold and Brendan Gill writing for the* New Yorker *put together a series of slaps and superlatives which went partially like this:*

> . . . a big, vigorous, rowdy, ill-shaped, and repellent book, so strong and so weak, so adroit and so fumbling, that only a writer of the greatest and most reckless talent could have flung it between covers.

It's one of the three or four lines I've thought perceptive in all the reviews of my books. That Malcolm Cowley used one of the same words in saying The Deer Park *was "serious and reckless" is also, I think, interesting, for reckless the book was—and two critics, anyway, had the instinct to feel it.*

One note appeared in many reviews. The strongest statement of it was by John Hutchens in The New York Daily Herald Tribune:

> . . . the original version reputedly was more or less rewritten and certain materials eliminated that were deemed too erotic for public consumption. And, with that, a book that might at least have made a certain reputation as a large shocker wound up as a cipher . . .

I was bothered to the point of writing a letter to the twenty-odd newspapers which reflected this idea. What bothered me was that I could never really prove I had not "eliminated" the book. Over the years all too many readers would have some hazy impression that I had disemboweled large pieces of the best meat, perspiring in a coward's sweat, a publisher's directive in my ear. (For that matter, I still get an occasional letter which asks if it is possible to see the unbowdlerized Deer Park.) *Part of the cost of touching the*

Rinehart galleys was to start those rumors, and in fact I was not altogether free of the accusation, as I have tried to show. Even the six lines which so displeased Rinehart had been altered a bit; I had shown them once to a friend whose opinion I respected, and he remarked that while it was impossible to accept the sort of order Rinehart had laid down, still a phrase like the "fount of power" had a Victorian heaviness about it. Well, that was true, it was out of character for O'Shaugnessy's new style and so I altered it to the "thumb of power" and then other changes became desirable, and the curious are invited to compare the two versions of this particular passage in this collection, but the mistake I made was to take a small aesthetic gain on those six lines and lose a larger clarity about a principle.

What more is there to say? The book moved fairly well, it climbed to seven and then to six on The New York Times *best-seller list, stayed there for a week or two, and then slipped down. By Christmas, the tone of the* Park *and the Christmas spirit being not all that congenial, it was just about off the lists forever. It did well, however; it would have reached as high as three or two or even to number one if it had come out in June and then been measured against the low sales of summer, for it sold over fifty thousand copies after returns which surprised a good many in publishing, as well as disappointing a few, including myself. I discovered that I had been poised for an enormous sale or a failure—a middling success was cruel to take. Week after week I kept waiting for the book to erupt into some dramatic change of pace which would send it up in sales instead of down, but that never happened. I was left with a draw, not busted, not made, and since I was empty at the time, worn-out with work, waiting for the quick transfusions of a generous success, the steady sales of the book left me deeply depressed. Having reshaped my words with an intensity of feeling I had not known before, I could not understand why others were not overcome with my sense of life, of sex, and of sadness. Like a starved revolutionary in a garret, I had compounded out of need and fever and vision and fear nothing less than a madman's confidence in the identity of my being and the wants of all others, and it was a new dull load to lift and to bear, this knowledge that I had no magic so great as to hasten the time of the apocalypse, but that instead I would be open like all others to the attritions of half-success and small failure. Something God-like in my confidence began to leave, and I was reduced in dimension if now less a boy. I knew I had failed to bid on the biggest hand I ever held.*

Now a few years have gone by, more years than I thought, and I have begun to work up another hand, a new book which will be the proper book of an outlaw, and so not publishable in any easy or legal way. Two excerpts from this novel come later in this collection, and therefore I'll say here only that O'Shaugnessy will be one of the three heroes, and that if I'm to go all the way this time, the odds are that my beat senses will have to do the work without the fires and the wastes of the minor drugs.

But that is for later, and the proper end to this account is the advertisement I took in The Village Voice. *It was bought in November 1955, a month after publication, it was put together by me and paid for by me, and it was my way I now suppose of saying good-by to the pleasure of a quick triumph, of making my apologies for the bad flaws in the bravest effort I had yet pulled out of myself, and certainly for declaring to the world (in a small way, mean pity) that I no longer gave a sick dog's drop for the wisdom, the reliability, and the authority of the public's literary mind, those creeps and old ladies of vested reviewing.*

Besides, I had the tender notion—believe it if you will—that the ad might after all do its work and excite some people to buy the book.

But here it is:

In the cactus wastes of Southern California, a distance of two hundred miles from the capital of cinema, is the town of Desert D'Or. There I went from the Air Force to look for a good time.

Whether or not it is enough of an explanation, I can only say that I arrived at the resort with fourteen thousand dollars, a particular sum I picked up in a poker game while waiting with other fliers in Tokyo for our plane home. The irony is that I was never a gambler. I did not even like the game, and perhaps for such a reason I accepted the luck of my cards. Let me leave it at that. I came out of the Air Force with no place to go, no family to visit, and I wandered down to Desert D'Or.

Built since the Second World War, it is the only place I know which is altogether new. Desert D'Or, one is told, was called originally Desert Door by the prospectors who assembled their shanties at the edge of its oasis, and from there went into the mountains overhanging the desert to look for gold. There is nothing left, however, of such men; when the site of Desert D'Or was chosen, not enough of the abandoned shacks remained to create even one of those many California museums the size of a two-car garage.

No, everything is of the present, and in the months I stayed at the resort, I came to know its developed and cultivated real estate in a way given us to know few places. I can still see the straight paved roads and the curved roads, each laid out by the cross hair of the surveyor's transit. The hotels with their pastel colors are visible again in the subtle camouflage which dominated all style in Desert D'Or. It was a place built out of no other need than commercial profit and therefore no sign of commerce was allowed to appear. Desert D'Or was without a main street, and its shops, where nothing but a variety of luxuries could be bought, looked like anything but stores. In those buildings which sold clothing, no clothing was displayed, and one waited in a modern living room while salesmen opened panels in the wall to exhibit summer slacks, or displayed between their hands the lush blooms of a tropical scarf. There was a jewelry store built like a cabin cruiser; on the street one peered through no more than a porthole to see a necklace hung upon the silver antlers of a piece of driftwood transported across the desert from Pacific waters. None of the hotels I remember so well—not the Yacht Club, nor the Debonair, not the Yucca

In the cactus wild of Southern California, a distance of two hundred miles from the capital of cinema as I choose to call it, is the town of Desert D'Or. There I went from the Air Force to look for a good time. Some time ago.

Almost everybody I knew in Desert D'Or had had an unusual career, and it was the same for me. I grew up in a home for orphans. Still intact at the age of twenty-three, wearing my flying wings and a first lieutenant's uniform, I arrived at the resort with fourteen thousand dollars, a sum I picked up via a poker game in a Tokyo hotel room while waiting with other fliers for our plane home. The curiosity is that I was never a gambler, I did not even like the game, but I had nothing to lose that night, and maybe for such a reason I accepted the luck of my cards. Let me leave it at that. I came out of the Air Force with no place to go, no family to visit, and I wandered down to Desert D'Or.

Built since the Second World War, it is the only place I know which is all new. A long time ago, Desert D'Or was called Desert Door by the prospectors who put up their shanties at the edge of its oasis and went into the mountains above the desert to look for gold. But there is nothing left of those men; when the site of Desert D'Or was chosen, none of the old shacks remained.

No, everything is in the present tense, and during the months I stayed at the resort, I came to know it in a way we can know few places. It was a town built out of no other obvious motive than commercial profit and so no sign of commerce was allowed to appear. Desert D'Or was without a main street, and its stores looked like anything but stores. In those places which sold clothing, no clothing was laid out, and you waited in a modern living room while salesmen opened panels in the wall to exhibit summer suits, or held between their hands the blooms and sprays of a tropical scarf. There was a jewelry store built like a cabin cruiser; from the street one peeped through a porthole to see a thirty-thousand-dollar necklace hung on the silver antlers of a piece of driftwood. None of the hotels—not the Yacht Club, nor the Debonair, not the Yucca Plaza, the Sandpiper, the Creedmor, nor the Desert D'Or Arms—could even be seen from outside. Put behind cement-brick fences or wooden palings, one hardly came across a building which was not green, yellow, rose, orange, or pink, and the approach was hidden by a shrubbery of bright flowers. You passed through the gate to

Plaza, the Sandpiper, the Creedmor, nor the Desert D'Or Arms—could even be seen from outside. Concealed behind cement-brick fences or wooden palings painted in the prevalent palette of Desert D'Or, one rarely saw a building which was not green, yellow, rose, orange, or pink, and the approach on a twisting sandy road was obscured by a shrubbery of bright flowers. As an instance, one passed through the gate to the Yacht Club, the most important hotel in the resort, and followed its private road, expecting a mansion at the end, but came to no more than a carport, a swimming pool in the shape of a free-form coffee table with curved-wall cabanas and canasta tables, and a set of lawn-tennis courts, unique through all that region of Southern California. From there, along yellow sidewalks which crossed and crossed again a meandering artificial creek by way of trellised footbridges, illumined at night with paper lanterns suspended from the tropical trees, one passed the guest bungalows dispersed through the grounds, their anonymous pastel-colored doors serving to emphasize the intimacy of the arrangement.

(Pages 134-8)

We soon developed another dispute. I had discovered that to make love to Lulu was to make myself an accessory to the telephone. It was always ringing, and no moment was rare enough to hinder her from answering. Her delight was to ignore the first few rings. "Don't be so nervous, Sugar," she would say, but before the phone had pealed five times, she would have picked it up. Invariably, it was business. She would be talking to Herman Teppis, or Munshin who was back in the capital, or a writer, or her director for the next picture, or once even her hairdresser—Lulu was interested in a coiffure she had seen. The conversation could not go on for long before she was fondling me again; to make love and talk business possessed a special attraction for her.

"Of course I'm being a good girl, Mr. Teppis," she would say, giving me a lewd wink. "How can you think these things of me?" As the ultimate in virtuosity, she succeeded one time in weeping through a phone call with Teppis while entertaining a passage with me.

I would try to get her to visit my place but she had developed a sudden aversion. "It depresses me, Sugar, it's in such bland taste. Do you know you're a bland boy?" For a while everything would the Yacht Club, the biggest and therefore the most exclusive hotel in the resort, and followed its private road which twisted through the grounds for several hundred yards, expecting a mansion at the end, but came instead to no more than a carport, a swimming pool in the shape of a free-form coffee table with curved-wall cabanas and canasta tables, and a set of lawn-tennis courts, the only lawn in all that part of Southern California. At night, along yellow sidewalks which crossed a winding artificial creek, lit up with Japanese lanterns strung to the tropical trees, you could wander by the guest bungalows scattered along the route, their flush pastel-colored doors another part of the maze of the arrangement.

(Pages 134-9)

We soon found something new to fight about. I discovered that to make love to Lulu was to make myself a scratch-pad to the telephone. It was always ringing, and no moment was long enough to keep her from answering. Her delight was to pass the first few rings. "Don't be so nervous, Sugar," she would say, "let the switchboard suffer," but before the phone had screamed five times, she would pick it up. Almost always, it was business. She would be talking to Herman Teppis, or Munshin who was back in the capital, or a writer, or her director for the next picture, or an old boy friend, or once her hairdresser—Lulu was interested in a hair-do she had seen. The conversation could not go on for two minutes before she was teasing me again; to make love and talk business was a double-feature to her.

"Of course I'm being a good girl, Mr. Teppis," she would say, giving me the wink. "How can you think these things of me?" As the end in virtuosity, she succeeded one time in weeping through a phone call with Teppis while rendering a passage with me.

I would try to get her to visit my place but she had grown an aversion. "It depresses me, Sugar, it's in such bland taste." For a while everything would be bland. Her own place was now spoiled be bland. Her own place was now spoiled by that word. To my amazement at her prodigality, she insisted one day upon having her room suite redecorated. Between morning and evening its beige walls were transformed to a delicate blue, which Lulu claimed was her most flattering color. So, too, were the sheets. Now she lay with her gold head on pale-blue linen, ordering from that telephone, as essential as any limb or organ, pink roses and red roses; the florist at the Yacht Club must arrange them himself. She would buy a dress and give it to her maid before she had even worn it, she would complain she had not a thing to wear. Her convertible she traded in one afternoon for another car almost its duplicate, and yet the exchange must have cost her a thousand dollars. When she remembered she must drive the new car slowly until it had accumulated the necessary mileage, she hired a chauffeur to trundle it through the desert and spare her the bother. Her first phone bill was five hundred dollars for the month.

Yet when it came to making money she was not without talent. While I knew her, negotiations were in progress for a three-picture contract. She would phone her lawyers, they would call her agent, the agent would speak to Teppis, Teppis would speak to her. She asked an outrageous price and received more than three-quarters of it. "I can't stand my father," she explained to me, "but he's a gambler at business. He's wonderful that way." It developed that when she was thirteen and going to a school for professional children in the capital, Magnum Pictures had wanted to sign her to a seven-year contract. "I'd be making a stinking seven hundred and fifty a week now like all those poor exploited schnooks, but Father wouldn't let me. 'Free-lance,' he said, he talks that way, 'this country was built on free-lancing.' He's just a chiropodist with holdings in real estate, but he knew what to do for me." Her toes nibbled and twisted at the telephone cord. "I've noticed that about men. There's a kind of man who never can make money for himself. Only for others. That's my father."

Of her father and mother, Lulu's opinion changed by the clock. One time it would be her father who was marvelous. "What a bitch my mother is. She just squeezed all the manhood out of him. Poor Daddy." Her mother had ruined her life, Lulu explained. "I never wanted to be an actress. She made me one. It's her ambition. She's just an . . . octopus." Several phone calls later, Lulu would be chatting with her mother. "Yes, I think it gives me hives," she would say of some food, "glycerine, will that do, Mommie? . . .

by that word, and one day she told the management to have her room suite redecorated. Between morning and evening its beige walls were painted to a special blue, which Lulu claimed was her best color. Now she lay with her gold head on pale-blue linen, ordering pink roses and red roses from the telephone; the florist at the Yacht Club promised to arrange them himself. She would buy a dress and give it to her maid before she had even worn it, she would complain she had not a thing to wear. Her new convertible she traded in one afternoon for the same model in another color, and yet the exchange cost her close to a thousand dollars. When I reminded her that she had to drive the new car slowly until it accumulated the early mileage, she hired a chauffeur to trundle it through the desert and spare her the bother. Her first phone bill from the Yacht Club was five hundred dollars.

Yet when it came to making money she was also a talent. While I knew her, negotiations were on for a three-picture contract. She would phone her lawyers, they would call her agent, the agent would speak to Teppis, Teppis would speak to her. She asked a big price and got more than three-quarters of it. "I can't stand my father," she explained to me, "but he's a gambler at business. He's wonderful that way." It came out that when she was thirteen and going to a school for professional children in the capital, Magnum Pictures wanted to sign her to a seven-year contract. "I'd be making a stinking seven hundred and fifty a week now like all those poor exploited schnooks, but Daddy wouldn't let me. 'Free-lance,' he said, he talks that way, 'this country was built on free-lance.' He's just a chiropodist with holdings in real estate, but he knew what to do for me." Her toes nibbled at the telephone cord. "I've noticed that about men. There's a kind of man who never can make money for himself. Only for others. That's my father."

Of her father and mother, Lulu's opinion changed by the clock. One round it would be her father who was marvelous. "What a bitch my mother is. She just squeezed all the manhood out of him. Poor Daddy." Her mother had ruined her life, Lulu explained. "I never wanted to be an actress. She made me one. It's her ambition. She's just an . . . octopus." Several phone calls later, Lulu would be chatting with her mother. "Yes, I think it gives me hives," she would say of some food, "glycerine, will that do, Mommie? . . . He's what? . . . He's acting up again. . . . Well, you tell him to leave you alone. I wouldn't put up with it if I were you. I would have divorced him long ago. I certainly would. . . .

He's what? . . . He's acting up again. . . . Well, you tell him to leave you alone. I wouldn't put up with it if I were you. I would have divorced him long ago. I certainly would.

"I don't know what I'd do without her," Lulu would say on hanging up the phone, "men are terrible," and she would have nothing to do with me for the next half hour.

It took me longer than it need have taken to realize that the heart of her pleasure was to display herself. She abhorred concealing an impulse. If Lulu felt like burping, she would burp; if it came to her mind that she wished to put cold cream on her face, she would do it while entertaining half a dozen people. So it went with her acting. She could say without embarrassment to the most casual acquaintance that she wished to be the greatest actress in the world. Once, talking to a stage director, she was close to tears because the studio never gave her a part in a serious picture. "They ruin me," she complained. "People don't want glamour, they want acting. I'd take the smallest role if it was something I could get my teeth into." Still, she quarreled for three days running, and how many hours of telephone calls I could not guess, because Munshin who was producing her next picture would not enlarge her part. Publicity, she announced, was idiotic, but with her instinct for what was pleasing to an adolescent, she did more than co-operate with photographers. The best ideas always came from Lulu. One occasion when she was photographed sipping a soda she shaped the second straw into a heart, and the picture as it was printed in many hundreds of newspapers showed Lulu peeping through the heart, at once coy, chaste, hoydenish and lovable. On those few times I would be allowed to sleep the night with her, I might awaken to see Lulu writing an idea for publicity in the notebook she kept by her bed table, and I had a picture of her marriage to Eitel, each of them with his own notebook and own bed table. With pleasure, she would expound to me the subtleties of being well photographed. I learned that the core of her dislike for Teddy Pope was that each of them was photographed best from the left side of the face, and when they played a scene together Teddy was as determined as Lulu not to expose his bad side to the camera. "I hate to play with queers," she complained. "Teddy pulled seniority and they gave him his way. I thought I had mumps when I saw myself. Boy, I threw a scene." Lulu acted it out for me. "You've ruined me, Mr. Teppis," she shrieked to my private ear. "There's no chivalry left."

"I don't know what I'd do without her," Lulu would say on hanging up the phone, "men are terrible," and she would have nothing to do with me for the next half hour.

It took me longer than it need have taken to realize that the heart of her pleasure was to show herself. She hated holding something in. If Lulu felt like burping, she would burp; if it came up that she wanted to put cold cream on her face, she would do it while entertaining half a dozen people. So it went with her acting. She could say to a stranger that she was going to be the greatest actress in the world. Once, talking to a stage director, she was close to tears because the studio never gave her a part in a serious picture. "They ruin me," she complained. "People don't want glamour, they want acting. I'd take the smallest role if it was something I could get my teeth into." Still, she quarreled for three days running, and how many hours on the telephone I could never guess, because Munshin who was producing her next picture would not enlarge her part. Publicity, she announced, was idiotic, but with her instinct for what was good to an adolescent, she did better than co-operate with photographers. The best ideas always came from Lulu. One sortie when she was photographed sipping a soda she shaped the second straw into a heart, and the picture as it was printed in the newspapers showed Lulu peeping through the heart, coy and cool. On the few times I would be allowed to spend the night with her, I would wake up to see Lulu writing an idea for publicity in the notebook she kept on her bed table, and I had a picture of her marriage to Eitel, each of them with his own notebook and own bed table. With pleasure, she would expound the subtleties of being well photographed. I learned that the core of her dislike for Teddy Pope was that each of them photographed best from the left side of the face, and when they played a scene together Teddy was as quick as Lulu not to expose his bad side to the camera. "I hate to play with queers," she complained. "They're too smart. I thought I had mumps when I saw myself. Boy, I threw a scene." Lulu acted it for my private ear. "You've ruined me, Mr. Teppis," she shrieked. "There's no chivalry left."

For odd hours, during those interludes she called at her caprice, things had come around a bit. To my idea of an interlude which must have left her exhausted, she coached me by degrees to something different. Which was all right with me. Lulu's taste was for games, and if she lay like a cinder under the speed of my sprints,

In bed, in those interludes she permitted me at her caprice, matters had altered considerably. To my idea of sport which must have left her exhausted, she directed me by degrees to something quite different. Lulu's taste was for games, and if she lay beneath me like a captive, pallid before the fury she aroused, her spirits improved with a play. In my innocence, there seemed a fabulous lewdness to her imagination, and I thought I had managed at a coup to reach the heart of sexual delights. I was convinced no two people ever had shared such excesses, nor even conceived of them. We were extraordinary lovers I felt in my pride; I had pity for those hordes who could know none of this. Yet, like the Oriental monarch who feels a subtle malaise on seeing the beggars of his kingdom, I was at a pitch of greediness to prove everyone else a beggar. For that, Lulu was the sweetest of mistresses. She would never allow comparisons. This was completely the best. I was superb. She was superb. We were beyond all. Unlike Eitel who now could not bear a word of Elena's former lovers, I was more than charitable to all of Lulu's. Why should I not be? She had sworn they were poor sticks to her Sugar. I was even so charitable that I argued in Eitel's defense. She had marked him impossible as a lover, and in a breach of friendship my heart had quickened with spite. I overcame that quickly enough, I wished to set Eitel at the place nearest my feet, vizier to the potentate, and it charmed me that in my first big affair I should be so proficient.

We played our games. I was the iceman and she was the housewife; she was the movie star and I was the bellhop; she the queen, I the slave; or in reverse of those situations she adored so well, Lulu mimed the prostitute to my client. We even met in equality. The game she cherished was to play the bobby-soxer who petted with a date in the living room and was finally seduced, always for the first time naturally enough. She was never so happy as when we acted at theater and fornicated on clouds of myth. I was exactly young enough to wish nothing else ever than to be alone with her. It was not even possible to be sated. Each time she gave herself, and I could never know, not five minutes in advance, when it would happen, my appetite was sharp, dressed by the animus of what I had suffered in public.

To eat a meal with her in a restaurant became a torture. It never mattered with what friends she found herself nor with what her spirits improved with a play. I was sure no two people ever had done such things nor even thought of them. We were great lovers I felt in my pride; I had pity for the hordes who could know none of this. Yes, Lulu was sweet. She would never allow comparison. This was the best. I was superb. She was superb. We were beyond all. Unlike Eitel who now could not bear to hear a word of Elena's old lovers, I was charitable to all of Lulu's. Why should I not be? She had sworn they were poor sticks to her Sugar. I was even so charitable that I argued in Eitel's defense. Lulu had marked him low as a lover, and in a twist of friendship my heart beat with spite. I stopped that quickly enough, I had an occasional idea by now of when Lulu was lying, and I wanted to set Eitel at my feet, second to the champion. It pleased me in my big affair that I had such a feel for the ring.

We played our games. I was the photographer and she was the model; she was the movie star and I was the bellhop; she did the queen, I the slave. We even met even to even. The game she loved was to play the bobby-soxer who sat with a date in the living room and was finally convinced, always for the first time naturally enough. She was never so happy as when we acted at theater and did the mime on clouds of myth. I was just young enough to want nothing but to be alone with her. It was not even possible to be tired. Each time she gave the signal, and I could never know, not five minutes in advance, when it would happen, my appetite was sharp, dressed by the sting of what I suffered in public.

To eat a meal with her in a restaurant became the new torture. It didn't matter with what friends she found herself nor with what enemies, her attention would go, her eye would flee. It always seemed to her as if the conversation at another table was more interesting than what she heard at her own. She had the worry that she was missing a word of gossip, a tip, a role in a picture, a financial transaction, a . . . it did not matter; something was happening somewhere else, something of importance, something she could not afford to miss. Therefore, eating with her was like sleeping with her; if one was cut by the telephone, the other was rubbed by her itch to visit from table to table, sometimes dragging me, sometimes parking me, until I had to wonder what mathematical possibility there was for Lulu to eat a meal in sequence since she was always having a bit of soup here and a piece of pastry there, joining me strangers, her attention would flee, her eye would wander with impatience. It always seemed to her as if the conversation at another table was more interesting and more provocative than what she heard at her own. She suffered the intolerable anxiety that she was missing a word of gossip, a tip, a role in a picture, a financial transaction, a . . . it did not matter; something was happening somewhere else, something of importance, something she could not afford to miss. Therefore, eating with her was like sleeping with her; if one was interrupted by the telephone, the other was broken by her need to visit from table to table, sometimes dragging me, sometimes parking me, until I often wondered what mathematical possibility there was for Lulu to eat a meal in sequence since she was always having a bit of soup here and a piece of pastry there, joining myself and her friends for breast of squab, and departing to greet new arrivals whose crabmeat cocktail she nibbled. There was no end, no beginning, no certainty that one would even see her during a meal. I remember a dinner when we went out with Dorothea O'Faye and Martin Pelley. They had just been married and Lulu treasured them. Dorothea was an old friend, a dear friend, Lulu assured me, and before ten minutes she disappeared. When at last Lulu returned, she perched on my lap and said in a whisper the others could hear, "Sugar, I tried, and I couldn't make doo-doo. Isn't that awful? What should I eat?"

Five minutes later she insisted upon picking up the check.

(Page 277)

Tentatively, she reached out a hand to caress his hair, and at that moment Herman Teppis opened his legs and let Bobby slip to the floor. At the expression of surprise on her face, he began to laugh. "Just like this, sweetie," he said, and down he looked at that frightened female mouth, facsimile of all those smiling lips he had seen so ready to be nourished at the fount of power and with a shudder he started to talk. "That's a good girlie, that's a good girlie, that's a good girlie," he said in a mild lost little voice, "you're just an angel darling, and I like you, and you understand, you're my darling darling, oh that's the ticket," said Teppis.

1952-4

Putnam (cont'd.)

for breast of squab, and taking off to greet new arrivals whose crab-meat cocktail she nibbled on. There was no end, no beginning, no surety that one would even see her during a meal. I remember a dinner when we went out with Dorothea O'Faye and Martin Pelley. They had just been married and Lulu treasured them. Dorothea was an old friend, a dear friend, Lulu promised me, and before ten minutes she was gone. When Lulu finally came back, she perched on my lap and said in a whisper the others could hear, "Sugar, I tried, and I couldn't make doo-doo. Isn't that awful? What should I eat?"

Five minutes later she outmaneuvered Pelley to pick up the check.

(Page 284)

Tentatively, she reached out a hand to finger his hair, and at that moment Herman Teppis opened his legs and let Bobby fall to the floor. At the expression of surprise on her face, he began to laugh. "Don't you worry, sweetie," he said, and down he looked at that frightened female mouth, facsimile of all those smiling lips he had seen so ready to serve at the thumb of power, and with a cough, he started to talk. "That's a good girlie, that's a good girlie, that's a good girlie," he said in a mild little voice, "you're an angel darling, and I like you, you're my darling darling, oh that's the ticket," said Teppis.

1955

TWO REVIEWS

TIME *Magazine, October 17, 1955*

Love Among the Love-Buckets

"Please do not understand me too quickly," warns Author Mailer by way of a tag (from André Gide). There is not much to understand in this narrative about the life of the West Coast's film fauna: the prose and the sex are as thick as ever. This seemed forgivable in *The Naked and The Dead;* the boys in a jungle combat platoon ("Kinsey's Army," as one British reviewer called it) were not supposed to talk like lady members of a book club. But in *The Deer Park* (the title is taken from a huge private sex resort maintained by Louis XV of France), the ladies talk just like the boys in the jungle as well as act like the animals in it.

Peering like a wrestling referee among the writhing limbs of this melee, the reader can detect one hero: a blond, blue-eyed orphan with a medical discharge from the Air Force, named Sergius O'Shaugnessy. Dropping napalm on Korean villages has upset him deeply (he has, in fact, become temporarily impotent), so naturally he Wants to Write. His methods are interesting. He takes a $14,000 stake to a desert gambling resort called Desert D'Or, 200 miles from Hollywood—a suburb in the literary country of tough-guy nihilism mapped by James M. Cain, Dashiell Hammett and Raymond Chandler. O'Shaugnessy does not get around to writing but he meets 1) a real lulu named Lulu who helps him over his embarrassing bedroom block; 2) a misunderstood film genius called Charles Francis Eitel (symbolically pronounced "eye-TELL"), who is trying to decide whether to tell all before a congressional committee. While skulking in Desert D'Or, Eitel dreams about the great film he hopes to make some day—a story about an M.C. of a *This-Is-Your-Life*-like TV program who decides to become a saint. That idea is a vulgarized Mailer version of a book called *Miss Lonelyhearts* by Nathanael West—who also wrote a little satirical tale of Hollywood (*The Day of the Locust*), which in one page shows more style, wit and distinction than could be combed from all *The Deer Park*.

All *The Deer Park's* problems are solved in a predictable way, but not before the contents of a madame's memory for sexual oddities has spilled all over the book. (Incidental intelligence, which will cause lifted eyebrows in Europe: after an illicit night, it is the gentleman who makes breakfast.) There is some good recorded speech, and readers of *Confidential* magazine can brush up their vocabularies. Sample: "Don't panic, love-bucket . . . Get me a small martin."

One piece of Hollywood argot not to be found in *The Deer Park* is "subpoena envy," which may be defined as the state of mind of the Hollywood liberal who never got called before a committee investigating anything. Author Mailer seems to have a bad case of it. His account of the interrogation by a pair of foul-mouthed goons in the hire of the "Subversive Committee" is calculated to frighten little children. It is bad enough for Mailer to paw every bed on the coast without finding Senator McCarthy underneath it.

NEWSWEEK *Magazine, October 17, 1955*

Norman Mailer's Despair

This big new novel by the author of the long war tale, "The Naked and the Dead," is a study of moral confusion and despair among a number of modern Americans. Their locus is Hollywood, widely chronicled as a center of moral confusion and despair, and a luxury resort, Desert D'Or, in the nearby badlands. There is no need, however, to feel that such personal disasters are confined to movieland or to café society. It is the peculiar insight and power of the novel that it does not present its unhappy conditions sensationally, but as though they were common enough, which they are, and as though people succeeded in living with them for years, which they do.

Mailer takes his title from Mouffle D'Angerville's "Private Life of Louis XV": ". . . The Deer Park, that gorge of innocence and virtue in which were engulfed so many victims who when they returned to society brought with them . . . all the vices they naturally acquired from the infamous officials of such a place." The leading male figure is a movie director, Charles Francis Eitel, an acid but magnanimous study of a man who suggests any sensitive, aspiring person lured into slick compromises and sensual follies. Having divorced a glowing, egomaniacal young star, Lulu Meyers, he takes up with Elena Esposito, the castoff mistress of the producer, Munshin, who is the son-in-law of the studio chief, Teppis. Munshin and Teppis are comic-horrible characters on a fairly grand scale. Together, in effect, they manage to get control of Eitel. Meanwhile—as they say—the radiant Miss Meyers slips into a love affair with the narrator of the story, an intelligent Air Force veteran who is spending heavy poker winnings and wondering what else to do with himself in Desert D'Or.

In describing these worldlings, Mailer shows a particular mastery of two areas of experience: The multiple colors of disillusionment, and the morbidity of expecting sexual fascination to do duty for more all-embracing affections. Mailer's second epigraph in his book is a quotation from André Gide: "Please do not understand me too quickly." Mailer has the fine novelist's strength of presenting his characters in depth.

Western Views: As a Hollywood novel, the book ranks well up with such impressive rivals as F. Scott Fitzgerald's "The Last Tycoon" and Nathanael West's "The Day of the Locust."

There are innumerable nuggets of comment: "Munshin, like many people from [Hollywood], could talk openly about his personal life while remaining a dream of espionage in his business operations." Eitel, after his capitulation to the movie bosses, tells the narrator: "After a while, I knew they had me on my knees, and that if I wasn't ready to take an overdose of sleeping pills, I would have to let myself slide through the experience, and not try to resist it. So for the first time in my life I had the sensation of being a complete and total whore . . . and I accepted every blow, every kick, and every gratuitous kindness with the inner gratitude that it could have been a good deal worse."

Such states of mind are hardly monopolized by Hollywood. Mailer's novel speaks for promising, gifted people anywhere, who have succumbed to their appetites and lost their spirit among the singularly intricate temptations of the modern world.

Summing Up: The fully dressed and the desolate.

POSTSCRIPT TO THE FOURTH
ADVERTISEMENT FOR MYSELF

Rewriting The Deer Park *I had come to recognize by the time I was done that willy-nilly, in admiration for Hemingway's strength and with distaste for his weaknesses, I was one of the few writers of my generation who was concerned with living in Hemingway's discipline, by which I do not mean I was interested in trying for some second-rate imitation of the style, but rather that I shared with Papa the notion, arrived at slowly in my case, that even if one dulled one's talent in the punishment of becoming a man, it was more important to be a man than a very good writer, that probably I could not become a very good writer unless I learned first how to keep my nerve, and what is more difficult, learned how to find more of it.*

Filled with this hard new knowledge that the secret to everything was never to cheat life, I set out immediately to try to cheat life. The Deer Park *was done, it would be out in six weeks; I could not keep myself from thinking that twenty good words from Ernest Hemingway would make the difference between half-success and a breakthrough. He would like the book, he would have to—it would be impossible for him not to see how much there was in it. So I cracked the shell of my pride, got his address from a reliable source, and sent him an inscribed copy. But because I was furious with myself for stealing a trick from that Hollywood I knew so well, I turned on my intent, and put the following words on Father Ernest's copy:*

> To ERNEST HEMINGWAY
>
> —because finally after all these
> years I am deeply curious to know
> what you think of this.

—but if you do not answer, or if you
answer with the kind of crap you
use to answer unprofessional writers,
sycophants, brown-nosers, etc., then
fuck you, and I will never attempt
to communicate with you again.

—and since I suspect that you're even
more vain than I am, I might as well
warn you that there is a reference to
you on page 353 which you may or may
not like.

NORMAN MAILER

*About ten days later, the book came back in the mail, same
wrapper and maybe the same string enclosing the package. Stamped
all over it was the Spanish equivalent of* Address Unknown—Return
to Sender. *So I had the following possibilities to choose from:*

*1. The address was not correct, and the mail clerk in the
Havana post office had never heard of Ernest Hemingway.*

*2. By Standard-Operating-Procedure, all unsolicited books
received by Mr. and Mrs. Hemingway were returned unreceived to
insure the minimum of bile for the sender.*

*3. Good wife Mary saw the inscription first, thought it best
to leave the husband to his work, and made a lady's executive
decision.*

4. Hemingway looked at The Deer Park, *decided he wasn't
ready to say yes or no, called up his good friend Colonel C. ——
in the Cuban postal service, had the island searched for shipping
paper similar to mine (the original wrapper having been torn by a
Latin houseboy on reception), had the best Havana forger copy the
handwriting, gave a* mordida *to the proper authorities for this
breach of postal etiquette, and broke a bottle of champagne over the
book just before it was stamped by some of the best bureaucratic
hands in Havana and sent on its way back to Putnam where Walter
Minton put it in his desk, figuring the copy might be worth half a
grand to the grandchildren.*

*Or, 5. The inscription was read, and that carried the day.
"If you want to come on that hard, Buster, don't write words like
'deeply curious,'" Papa said, had the original wrapper put back on,
stamped it with his private Address Unknown stamp (purchased at*

Abercrombie and Fitch) and started to drink fifteen minutes early that day.

This is all fine in its way, but once on television in the eighth round, as I remember, I saw Carmen Basilio take one of Paddy De Marco's best punches, go out on his feet, start to sit down on the canvas, and then with his butt three inches from the ground, Basilio did a one-legged knee stand, pushed up, avoided the knockdown (he had never been knocked down in a fight before or since) and went on to knock out De Marco in a few rounds. The story in the newspapers the next day which I would like to think is true, was that Basilio, when asked why he didn't take an eight-count and get some rest, answered, "I didn't want to start any bad habits."

I could have followed that advice. Moderation is the last virtue I'll capture, and a day or two after the book went off to Hemingway, the broken shell of my pride collapsed into powder, and I sent off inscribed copies to Graham Greene, Cyril Connolly, Philip Rahv, and a dozen others whom I no longer remember, probably from shame. The only one who answered was Moravia, but then we knew each other, and I had told him I didn't want his comment for advertising copy, so that particular effort to promote myself ended in fiasco, and I hope I'm not so hungry again as to send off novels of which I'm not ashamed to the narrow attention of established novelists and critics.

This confession off my liver forever, it occurs to me now that I must have carried the memory as a silent shame which helped to push me further and deeper into the next half year of bold assertions, half-done work, unbalanced heroics, and an odd notoriety of my own choice. I was on the edge of many things and I had more than a bit of violence in me.

ADVERTISEMENT FOR SIXTY-NINE QUESTIONS AND ANSWERS

Not very much need be claimed for this interview. Those who like a dialogue of questions and answers between a newspaper and an author may find it interesting. Lyle Stuart, an old friend and the editor of The Independent *(then called* Exposé*) set me a list of 69 questions after I had agreed to do an interview with him. I glanced at the questions once during the day, and then later that night answered them more or less consecutively, a friend taking down my words. The only merit of the interview is that it was published in this spontaneous form. Literary dialogues of the sort one sees in* The Paris Review *are invariably reworked by the author, who often spends years polishing his remarks. There is nothing wrong with that; in fact it can produce good writing. Hemingway's interview in* The Paris Review, Issue 18, *is perhaps the best piece of writing he has done since the war; his prose has never been better.*

But here, for this interview, for what it is worth, we have a document of the way our most unsatisfactory hero was talking a month after The Deer Park *had come out—at least the way he was talking with his brain full of marijuana—he had turned on a half-hour before he started to answer the questions.*

One apology: Early in the interview there is a fatuous remark about Henry Miller.

One anticipation: The confidence of these remarks (at a time when it was still expected that The Deer Park *would become an enormous best-seller) will turn later in the columns for* The Village Voice *into an intricate and less forthright narcissism.*

SIXTY-NINE QUESTIONS
AND ANSWERS

Q. What is the literary situation in America now?

A. I think my attitude will come out as I answer the questions.

Q. Why?

A. Because that is the way I answer questions.

Q. If you were giving advice to a young writer on the brink of fame, what would you say?

A. Try to keep the rebel artist in you alive, no matter how attractive or exhausting the temptations.

Q. Why do you write?

A. I suppose I write because I want to reach people and by reaching them, influence the history of my time a little bit.

Q. Do you believe anybody listens to writers?

A. Yes. But most readers listen with the unconscious ear.

Q. Philip Rodman once remarked that if a writer were very successful, he might reach six people who really understand what he is trying to say. Are you reaching your six?

A. In a certain sense no one can "really understand" what another person is trying to say, not if we take into account the enormous complexity of experience and the greater complexity, if not total uniqueness, of every human alive. But as a practical matter, depending on the artistry of the writer, and in inverse proportion to the difficulty of his style, a sizable number of people can usually "understand" most of what the writer is saying.

Q. What are you trying to say in *The Deer Park*?

A. Everything I know about life at the age of thirty-two.

Q. How do you feel about book reviewers in general? (Would you classify them as eunuchs or whores?)

A. Depends on their prose.

Q. Why didn't Rinehart publish *The Deer Park*?

A. Because he was afraid to.

Q. It is really, as some critics charge, a book about sex?

A. Yes, it is totally about sex. And it is also totally about morality. A writer who grows up in this country can hardly write about one without invoking the other. Henry Miller is the only exception I know. And I smell a moralist in him somewhere.

Q. How do you feel about sex?

A. How I feel about it personally is none of your business. How I feel about it as a literary subject is something else. I believe it is perhaps the last remaining frontier of the novel which has not been exhausted by the nineteenth and early twentieth century novelists.

Q. Isn't *The Deer Park* really every young man's dream of paradise?

A. I'm beginning to wonder.

Q. Did you have any censorship problems with your publisher?

A. I had none with G. P. Putnam. The other six houses *The Deer Park* was sent to tried to exercise censorship directly and by the indirect excuse of saying they did not like the book sufficiently.

Q. What is the function of a censor?

A. To retard whatever movement is in the air.

Q. Do you think the current censorship wave will make us a nation of mental eunuchs?

A. The situation is exceptionally complicated. There is not only a wave of censorship but there are counterwaves which are opposed to censorship. I feel more optimistic about the general situation than I have in years. But this may conceivably be no more than a reflection of my present mood.

Q. Is *The Deer Park* autobiographical in that its narrator speaks for you?

A. *The Deer Park* is not autobiographical. No one in it speaks directly for me. I've been writing too long to make that kind of mistake any more.

Q. Do you know if *The Deer Park* is selling well in Hollywood?

A. I understand that it is.

Q. Isn't this book really a love sonnet directed at the film industry?

A. Let's say a sonnet of love and hate.

Q. If you could be any other living writer but Norman Mailer, whom would you choose to be?

270

A. I can't imagine. Since I have only my own life, I might just as well put the bet on myself.

Q. Do you write to eat or eat to write?

A. Anyone who asks a question like that knows nothing about writers. Every serious novelist in the world obviously does both. If he ate only to write, he would be merely a poet, a dilettante or a deadly small critic who is kept in a cage until his editor lets him out to devour a new book.

Q. Do you write better before or after sexual activity, or during the periods you deny yourself such activity?

A. I've thought about this a lot, but I don't know that I have any definite feeling about the answer.

Q. How has your social ken changed since you wrote *The Naked and The Dead*?

A. I was an anarchist then, and I'm an anarchist today. In between I belonged to the Progressive Party during the Wallace campaign, and then broke off rather abruptly at the time of the Waldorf Peace Conference in 1949. What followed was a period of political wandering in the small circle of libertarian socialism. I was at the same time very radical and yet half-hearted about it. I've also been a contributing editor on *Dissent*. Still am, of course. This is all very sketchy, but I'm trying to put seven years into a capsule. Let me put it that today I'm a Marxian anarchist, which is a contradiction in terms, but a not unprofitable contradiction for trying to do some original thinking. I suppose part of the change in my "social ken" is that politics as politics interests me less today than politics as a part of everything else in life.

Q. If you were forced to do something other than writing to earn your living, what would you choose?

A. One hundred different things. Just so long as I didn't do any one of them for the rest of my life.

Q. Whom do you hate?

A. People who have power and no compassion, that is, no simple human understanding.

Q. Do you believe socialism or nationalism will ever come to America?

A. Not in the way the words are understood today. Possibly in some vastly complex mutant of one or another of those words.

Q. If you could send a ten word message to every man and woman in America, what would you say?

A. Please don't understand anybody too quickly.

Q. What is your opinion of the current crop of artistic aspirants in Greenwich Village?

A. I have a sincere feeling—perhaps it is no more than a hunch—that more than a few really exciting novels are going to come from there in the next ten years. Provided of course we don't dip back into the cold war again. A cold war is obviously equal to greater censorship, greater censorship is equal to greater fear, especially in serious writers, more anxiety, and hence poorer work generally.

Q. Do you believe that there are good writers unable to find publication in America today?

A. If good writers write novels which are conventionally obscene or exceptionally radical, you can be sure that they would have one hell of a time getting their books published. However there are some good people scattered through the publishing houses, and considering that no two publishing houses are even remotely the same, there is always a kind of chance to get a good but difficult book in bound covers.

Q. Will television put an end to novel reading?

A. It certainly seems to be cutting down on it.

Q. Is there a future for the hard-bound novel?

A. A most doubtful future, I think.

Q. Do you have political ambitions?

A. You can't grow up in America without thinking once in a while of becoming president. But since I'm an anarchist, I try not to think about that too much.

Q. What does religion mean to you?

A. Organized religion has never meant much to me. I do believe in God, but it is a very personal faith and I find in myself, as of this year, no detectable desire to join any church. Too many churches seem like prisons of the spirit to me.

Q. What social problem seems most important to you?

A. That more people do more things their inner nature dreams of doing. In other words that there be less anguish and less depression in the world, for all authoritarian social horrors are ultimately no more than a mirror of the quantity of despair in the world.

Q. Do you believe in life after death?

A. I would have to write a book to answer.

Q. If Jesus Christ were alive today, do you think they would permit him to enter the church?

A. I think I will retire behind the answer Dostoyevski gave in the chapter of *The Grand Inquisitor*.

Q. Who is your favorite writer?

A. I have favorites, but they vary.

Q. Are you a Freudian?

A. I believe Freud was a genius, an incredible mighty discoverer of secrets, mysteries, and new questions. But the answers he gave were doctrinaire, deathlike, and philosophically most dreary. Of the world's geniuses he strikes me as being unique. He had so little optimism and it is rare to find a genius who does not have even angry optimism. Or, at the very worst—an apocalyptic view of the final disaster.

Q. Are blacklists necessary?

A. They are necessary for propaganda.

Q. Why?

A. Because they give people the idea that an impotent conspiracy is actually potent, and therefore dangerous to fatherland, flag and family.

Q. Have you ever been blacklisted?

A. I think I have been, but of course I could never prove it.

Q. Are people afraid of you because they can't understand you or because they do understand you?

A. I'm surprised that people are afraid of me. What can I possibly do to them? It's a nice question to be asked though.

Q. Was the character of Charles Eitel in *The Deer Park* in any way modeled after Charles Chaplin?

A. Not at all. Chaplin is a genius and I wouldn't presume to write about a genius. Not yet.

Q. Eitel finally did tell. Do you feel that this is the only way the commercial artist can survive—by telling the things Congressional committees want to hear?

A. An artist follows his own nature. A commercial man follows the nature that society exacts from him. So my answer is: of course commercial talents do what they are obliged to do, and say what they are obliged to say.

Q. You precede your story with Gide's "Do not understand me too quickly." Have the reviews indicated that you are understood at all by reviewers?

A. One or two had a vague idea of what I was trying to do. Malcolm Cowley was right on the nose when he wrote that *The Deer Park* was a far more difficult book to write than *The Naked and The Dead*.

Q. Do you think communism will ever again become an American fad?

A. It may, if some sort of co-existence is settled with the USSR. But it's not the sort of thing I lose sleep over. If it does happen it's likely to attract a new type. The gray-flannel-suit contingent perhaps.

Q. What quality do you most prefer in a woman?

A. Love, infused with rich sexuality.

Q. G. Legman once remarked that a man is either a sheep or a goat. Which are you?

A. I try to be a man. Why should I take Legman's word for the varieties of human nature?

Q. Is rebellion healthy?

A. As healthy as the sense of life.

Q. Do you find the greatest pleasure in desire or in fulfillment?

A. Both are beautiful. Like most people I've had enough luck to know the advantages and satisfaction of each from time to time.

Q. Ben Hecht and a number of other onetime literary lights have seen the candle of conformity and swallowed it. Do you feel that age will mold you into a high-priced please-the-public author?

A. I doubt it, but I also know that exhaustion of the will can come to anyone.

Q. Do you have advice for your enemies?

A. Yes. In all modesty let them beware just a little of me.

Q. How do you feel about money?

A. I think having money is probably a little better than not having it. Money is one of the things which gives energy to people and I believe that's why most people scramble so cruelly to get it.

Q. About clothes?

A. It's one of the few things I haven't been deeply interested in at one time or another. I probably dress a little better than the average man, at least when I get dressed up. Or is that every ex-rifleman's idea of himself?

Q. How do you feel about Ernest Hemingway?

A. I said what my character, Sergius O'Shaugnessy thought of him in one sentence in *The Deer Park*. If one is going to make a statement about Hemingway it can be done either by posing a riddle or else one has to write at least ten thousand words to say something new in the critical literature. Obviously if I've said this much, it's evident that I think he's been very important as an influence on all American writers, even if like Faulkner they were stimulated to writing in the opposite and possibly greater direction. But just how I rate Hemingway is impossible to answer because each time I think of him—which is not that often—I find that my estimate of him goes up or down a little on the basis of the new thing I've thought. I suppose at the very least it's a sign of some kind of greatness and I would guess right now that Hemingway is going to last for quite some time.

Q. What is happening to the union movement?

A. I don't know, and I don't know that anything much is happening.

Q. Do you think Hitler still lives?

A. No. I don't believe he could ever find a place to hide.

Q. Your General Cummings in *The Naked and The Dead* appears to symbolize the triumph of fascism. Can fascism ever triumph?

A. Fascism is a very vague word. One variant or another of "fascism" may very conceivably triumph. It's one of the possible alternatives, isn't it? If it ever comes to America, it will be a very sophisticated and loose fascism. Or is "loose" spelled Luce?

Q. The lonely mountain in *The Naked and The Dead* seemed to represent the conquest men strive for but never make. Can man ever conquer loneliness?

A. I believe that is at the heart of man's goal.

Q. What can a man believe in?

A. Better to believe in his feelings than in the advice of others.

Q. What is your major ambition?

A. To be a really great writer.

Q. Do you think psychiatry will solve the problems that beset us?

A. It will solve some problems and inevitably create new ones. Whether it is generally a cultural current for good or for bad remains to be learned by the history of this century.

Q. Who will analyze the psychiatrists?

A. The novelists.

Q. Do you believe man will survive the H-bomb?

A. Yes. I really don't believe we're going to destroy ourselves. But we may come very close time and again.

Q. What papers do you read? What magazines?

A. A little bit of everything. The *Scientific American*, *Cue* Magazine, and the *Commonweal* ought to give a small idea of what I mean.

Q. If you were to be exiled to a desert island and could take only five books with you, what would they be?

A. I wrote two unpublished novels before "Naked," so in my life I've written five novels. I would take those five novels to a desert island with me because if one is left alone on a desert island it's hardly feasible to learn very much more from books. One can only contemplate nature, become mystic and seek to penetrate more deeply into one's own primitive nature. So, I would take my five novels not because they are so very good, but because they are the best documents I would have about myself with which to take that self-exploratory journey back to the questions of self.

Q. If you could leave a message to a young man who will be your age one hundred years from today, what would you say?

A. I would say: please use your science to discover the secrets of communicating with the dead, because I, for one, would like to know what has happened since I died. That is if I don't really know "out there," and am not really laughing at you.

Q. Are you happy?

A. Every man and every woman has his or her own idea of happiness. Let people decide for themselves on the basis of my answers how happy or unhappy I am.

Q. How do you feel about Marilyn Monroe?

A. She must be very brave because she has come such a long way. She is one of the few actresses I still have some real curiosity about.

Q. Are you at work on a new novel?

A. Yes.

Q. What is the role of the artist in our society?

A. I think it is to be as disturbing, as adventurous, as penetrating, as his energy and courage make possible.

1955

FIFTH ADVERTISEMENT FOR MYSELF:
General Marijuana

The Village Voice *was started by Daniel Wolf, Edwin Fancher and myself, the idea for such a newspaper coming from Wolf, and the money to start it from Fancher and me (and later from Howard Bennett). All through the spring and summer of 1955, Fancher and Wolf were alone in the labor of educating themselves to the thousand and more details which go into starting a weekly newspaper. Busy at first with the work of finishing* The Deer Park, *later dredged by the effort, I did not much more than contribute a few bits of amateur advice and the name:* The Village Voice. *When a first issue of the paper appeared in late September, I was able to read it with the detachment of someone who had paid a nickel at a newsstand.*

Two weeks later my novel came out. By another month the small excitements of The Deer Park's *appearance not growing into any swell which could hint of more excitement, I was beginning to feel the empty winds of a post-partum gloom. There were odds that it would take months, or even years to get back what I had given to the book, and I did not have the heart to sit in idleness and wait to mend. In fact, it was probably not possible. My self-analysis was still going at locomotive speed, and since I was anxious above all else to change a hundred self-defeating habits which locked my character into space too narrow for what I wanted to become, I was at the time like an actor looking for a rare role. It was not the season then to pick up again on the private habits of a novel. At heart, I wanted a war, and the Village was already glimpsed as the field for battle.*

Besides, the paper was losing a thousand dollars a week. I could give myself the excuse that I was needed. I began to work on The Voice, *playing at one job and then another, too charged with impatience to plug at chores, too doubtful in stamina to see the end of a project through from its beginning. For weeks I lost face in a drift of bold programs and dull resolutions, and all the while my partners and I were coming to see that there were different ideas of how the paper should develop. They wanted it to be successful; I wanted it to be outrageous. They wanted a newspaper which could satisfy the conservative community—church news, meeting of political organizations, so forth. Before the paper could be provocative, went their argument, it must be established. I believed we could grow only if we tried to reach an audience in which no newspaper had yet been interested. I had the feeling of an underground revolution on its way, and I do not know that I was wrong. Beat, the Christmas tree of Hip, arrived with Kerouac, and because it is sweet and oddball, a cross between folklore and fairy tale, Madison Avenue took it up, they had to, this was the first phenomenon in years to come out of the Great Unwashed which Madison Avenue hadn't rigged, manipulated or foreseen. I was ready too early but I still wonder if the kind of newspaper I wanted might not have managed to give a little speed to that moral and sexual revolution which is yet to come upon us. That however is moot. What is for fact is that in the fourth month of the uncertain early life of the newspaper, with nothing else working particularly well, Fancher, Wolf, and I came to the agreement that the novelist Norman Mailer might just as well become a newspaper columnist. What they did not know was that the column began as the declaration of my private war on American journalism, mass communications, and the totalitarianism of totally pleasant personality.*

Like all generals in command of an army of one, I started in the confidence of a secret weapon. I had marijuana. Mary-Jane, at least for me, in that first life of smoking it, was the door back to sex, which had become again all I had and all I wanted. Once again there was sanction to gallop on self-love—God's gift to women, wife, letters and history, marijuana my horse. So soon as I recovered from one bust-out, I was waiting to kiss off another; sex was the sword of history to this uncommissioned General, for only when sex triumphed could the mind seize the hip of new experience. Drawing upon hash, lush, Harlem, Spanish wife, Marxist culture, three novels, victory, disaster, and draw, the General looked over his terrain and found it a fair one, the Village a seed-ground for the opinions of America, a crossroads between the small town and the mass-media. Since the General was nothing if not Hip (in the self-estimation of his brain) he was of course aware that the mind of the Village was a tight

278

sphincter, ringed with snobbery, failure, hatred and spleen. The way to charge attention was to dare that hatred. The General calculated to stick his ideas up the ego of the Village, and in the middle of January, 1956, he wrote his first column as a declaration of war.
This is the way it went:

QUICKLY: A Column for Slow Readers

Column One

Many years ago I remember reading a piece in the newspapers by Ernest Hemingway and thinking: "What windy writing." That is the penalty for having a reputation as a writer. Any signed paragraph which appears in print is examined by the usual sadistic literary standards, rather than with the easy tolerance of a newspaper reader pleased to get an added fillip for his nickel.

But this is a fact of life which any professional writer soon learns to put up with, and I know that I will have to put up with it since I doubt very much if this column is going to be particularly well-written. That would take too much time, and it would be time spent in what is certainly a lost cause. Greenwich Village is one of the bitter provinces—it abounds in snobs and critics. That many of you are frustrated in your ambitions, and undernourished in your pleasures, only makes you more venomous. Quite rightly. If I found myself in your position, I would not be charitable either. Nevertheless, given your general animus to those more talented than yourselves, the only way I see myself becoming one of the cherished traditions of the Village is to be actively disliked each week.

At this point it can fairly be asked: "Is this your only reason for writing a column?" And the next best answer I suppose is: "Egotism. My search to discover in public how much of me is sheer egotism." I find a desire to inflict my casual opinions on a half-captive audience. If I did not, there would always be the danger of putting these casual opinions into a new novel, and we all know what a terrible thing that is to do.

I also feel tempted to say that novelists are the only group of people who should write a column. Their interests are large, if shallow, their habits are sufficiently unreliable for them to find something new to say quite often, and in most other respects they are more columnistic than the columnists. Most of us novelists who are any good are invariably half-educated; inaccurate, albeit brilliant upon occasion; insufferably vain of course; and—the indispensable requirement for a good newspaperman—as eager to tell a lie as the truth. (Saying the truth makes us burn with the desire to convince our audience, whereas telling a lie affords ample leisure to study the result.)

We good novelists also have the most unnewspaperly virtue of never praising fatherland and flag unless we are sick, tired, generally defeated, and want to turn a quick dishonest buck. Nobody but novelists would be asked to write columns if it were not for the sad fact that newspaper editors are professionally and obligatorily patriotic, and so never care to meet us. Indeed, even *The Village Voice*, which is remarkably conservative for so young a paper, and deeply patriotic about all community affairs, etc., etc., would not want me either if they were not so financially eager for free writing, and a successful name to go along with it, that they are ready to put up with almost anything. And I, as a minority stockholder in the *Voice* corporation, must agree that this paper does need something added to its general languor and whimsy.

At any rate, dear reader, we begin a collaboration which may go on for three weeks, three months, or, the Lord forbid, for three-and-thirty years. I have only one prayer—that I weary of you before you tire of me. And therefore, so soon as I learn to write columnese in a quarter of an hour instead of the unprofitable fifty-two minutes this has taken, we will all know better if our trifling business is going to continue. If it does, there is one chance in a hundred—make it a hundred-thousand—that I will become an habitual assassin-and-lover columnist who will have something superficial or vicious or inaccurate to say about many of the things under the sun, and who knows but what some of the night.

It was blitzkrieg. The column opened the hatred of more than a few, and the General had his attention. Now one had only to divert the hatred from oneself to more deserving subjects.

The second column was, however, a disaster. The General

*thought to follow the first column with an armored demonstration
of philosophical powers, but the result was not altogether impressive. Just before the column went to the printer, the publisher suggested that it might be a little demanding on many of the readers.
Abruptly, the General agreed. In a few minutes he wrote a short
Preface to be set in italics.*

The Preface went:

A WARNING: The column this week is difficult.
True to my commitment to the *Voice*, I wrote it quickly.
Because I do not want to lose all my readers at once, I
suggest that all but the slowest readers pass me by this
time. If you are not in a mood to think, or if you have no
interest in thinking, then let us ignore each other until the
next column. And if you do go on from here, please have
the courtesy to concentrate. The art of careful writing is
beginning to disappear before the mental impotence of
such lazy audiences as the present one. Thought, after all,
is one of the two prime pleasures available (at least theoretically) in a rational democracy, the other being sensual
love, politely called the pursuit of happiness.

*The quick paragraph was to sap the column for the next
sixteen weeks. In answer to the* WARNING, *a bombardment of letters
fell upon* The Voice.

Outside of getting yourself a "reputation" by gut-
lessly imitating (prim term for thievery) Dos Passos in
your ONE & ONLY book, and now *again* imitating by sten-
cilling yourself upon the very overworked, tired, boring,
creaky, mimeographed Henry Miller in your column, well,
why you consider yourself anything but an adequate jour-
neyman writer is a serious inner disturbance you ought to
take up with an analyst. The very obvious trouble with you
is you really suffer from illusion of grandeur: sometimes
you must think you're the indisputably great Norman
Mailer. It's a cinch your romance with yourself will be
recorded as one of the most magnificent love stories in
history.

Curiously, will you have the *Voice* run this letter,
too? I doubt it. Kiddo, you're not *that* contemptuous of
public criticism. When the chips are down, you play it too
safe and shrewd and crafty behind your manufactured
scornful façade.

—Joe Jensen
Bank Street

When the following week brought more letters, some now in defense of the column, the General greeted them with the calm of a Douglas MacArthur receiving news of a favorable turn at the front. In command of his first major war, the General was slow to dig there was a difference between a battle which was turning and a battle which had turned. He thought the home front was already with him, and rushed reserves of wit into the third column. Prematurely. Nine-tenths of the Village was still digging itself out from the blitz, and so the populace was nowhere in evidence as he mounted this new attack in an opposite direction, on the following strong points of the American Establishment: Mr. Ed Sullivan, Mr. Leonard Lyons, Mr. Max Lerner, Miss Dorothy Kilgallen, Mr. Walter Winchell, Miss Hedda Hopper, the Columbia Broadcasting System, the New York Post, *The New York* Daily News, *The N. Y.* Journal American, *The New York* Daily Mirror, *as well as Poets, Liberals, Reactionaries, Mr. Adlai Stevenson, and the optimistic heart.*

When the reaction to the third column produced no more than a parody of his second column by a gentleman-ranker named Schmidt which was at least as good as the General's parody, and was enjoyed outrageously more by the Village, the General began to realize the campaign might not necessarily be won in six weeks, and that there seemed to be some charge after all to the military maxim that one does well to avoid a war on two fronts. He sent more wit to the near front, but the wit ran out over the next month. Solemn sluggish movements of muddy words now slogged to the trenches and went to sleep there. By Column Eight, barbed wire was up everywhere, and the campaign wore its way into the spring. The General and his colleagues were not always speaking, and the war ended, as you shall see, by internecine battle between armor and supply.

It is humor today, but it was not cool then. At a time in my life when I was feeling more than I ever had before, when my experience was close to giving an answer to more than one of my notions, and my senses were still electric, at exactly that time when the smallest action of an indifferent day was still a clue that one was growing into something new or relapsing into the defeat of familiar

282

*habit, in precisely those months of the year (for good or bad)
which were most decisive for me, in the heart of those columns I
did for* The Village Voice, *the column came to suffer from the one
fault I had not expected—it was badly written.*

*Self-expression has become one of the icons of our time,
almost as revered by the Republic as the Community Chest, but it
is ignored too easily that self-expression usually ends as therapy.
What is detestable about a bad style is that the author is cleaning
his own nervous system at the expense of mucking our own in the
psychic sediments of his taste. All too often in these columns, the
language was to become arch and pious, self-righteous and pompous,
overambitious and imprecise. With marijuana for analyst, there were
weeks when the need of the psyche must have been to free itself
of habits of style which had bedded themselves in the mind like
geological strata. The drug had acted as an explosive charge—the
debris of mediocre ore seemed to have collected at every exit of the
brain, and there was little to do but mine it out. So my readers suffered through more than one week, while the column served as
therapy for me: I was eliminating some of the sludge of the past.
My style then came into being out of no necessity finer than a
purgative to bad habit, but my emotions, warlike and dictatorial,
came from rage. It was rage for what had been wasted in me, and
conceivably there was equal rage for what had been wasted in others.
If I had one noble emotion it was rage against that national conformity which smothered creativity, for it delayed the self-creation
of the race, a most desperate delay, since man might no longer have
all the Time of eternity to discover himself—this rage, first for my
own loss, and as well I think for what had been lost by others, came
into the heat of newspaper prose through no delicate balances of
the higher senses. Good style is the record of such powerful emotion reaching the surface of the page through fine conscious nets of
restraint, caution, tact, elegance, taste, even inhibition—if the inhibition is not without honor. But my consciousness was a war
landscape, burned out, blasted to rubble, the reasonable habits of
my head groaning like half-wrecked buildings in the small wind of
every encounter. I had not wanted to enter the depressing work
of counting my losses and estimating where and how to build a new
city of the brain; now my will was a dictator; like all tyrants it felt
the urgency of the present as unendurable. This was not the time
for peace: there was a generation which was ready to be awakened, a*

task for whose heroic proportions some part of me seemed to consider myself divinely suited. Good enough. The time cried then and begs today for a journalist and a newspaper whose words would cut the smog of apathy, gluttony, dim hatred, glum joy, and the general victory of all that is smug, security-ridden and mindless in the American mind.

But obviously I never found a tone for my column and so I was not able to learn how much or how little was possible. The involutions of marijuana were disgorging all that was most unattractive in me, and my style was in liege to the heavy unhappy prose of three generations of great radicals, and radicals not so great (let us not mention the brick walls and plumbers' waddings of the psychologists and sociologists I also studied), and so there were veins of lead through which the blood of the emotion had to pass.

It is of course the devil's-own-wit more complicated than that. For I sensed little of this at the time; most of the columns seemed marvelous to me (what is a General without his morale?) and I went so far at times as to believe every friend my enemy if they had doubtful words for the column. I had, after all, so much to lose. Since I had seen the column as the first lick of fire in a new American consciousness, since I would lose nothing less if the column failed than my rediscovered desire, so implacable, to be a hero of my time, I was gambling all I had; it was in truth worse than that. For after the devastations of creative reserve which the forced last draft of The Deer Park had burned across my brain, I was, as I have indicated, in need of a fallow year; instead I had pushed myself into the center of an ugly and ridiculous situation. Trying to do too much with too little, the simple act of getting out a weekly column destroyed resources which might better have been used for ten weeks of good work on a new novel a year later.

After such advertisement, the writing may seem relatively quiet to the disinterested eye. Many of the columns will read like the sort of mild work which a writer commits at a poor time, not too well done, not altogether hopeless, diverting here, and best forgotten there. But by their inner history, these columns are a debacle, because never before had I done so little where I committed so much. If I do not finish the novel I have now in my mind it is likely that the better part was lost in that drug-ridden gutting of my possibilities which has become for me the real if muted theme of these columns for The Village Voice.

284

Column Two

A WARNING: The column this week is difficult. True to my commitment to the *Voice*, I wrote it quickly. Because I do not want to lose all my readers at once, I suggest that all but the slowest readers pass me by this time. If you are not in a mood to think, or if you have no interest in thinking, then let us ignore each other until the next column. And if you do go on from here, please have the courtesy to concentrate. The art of careful writing is beginning to disappear before the mental impotence of such lazy audiences as the present one. Thought, after all, is one of the two prime pleasures available (at least theoretically) in a rational democracy, the other being sensual love, politely called the pursuit of happiness.

Since a newspaper column is supposed to be concerned with communication, it would not be the worst idea to attempt to trace what communication might be.

Thought begins somewhere deep in the unconscious—an unconscious which conceivably is divine—or if finite may still be vast enough in its complexity to bear comparison to an ocean. Out of each human being's vast and mighty unconscious, perhaps from the depths of our life itself, up over all the forbiddingly powerful and subterranean mental mountain ranges which forbid expression, rises from the mysterious source of our knowledge, the small self-fertilization of thought, conscious thought.

But for a thought to live (and so give us dignity) before it disappears, unexpressed and perhaps never to be thought again, it must be told to someone else—to one's mate, to a good friend, or occasionally to a stranger. It is in the act of telling a thought that the thought—no matter how unlikely—may be convincing to another, and inspiring* him or her to some small action. Needless to

---

* *'inspiring' was 'inspire' in my copy—the first of a series of typographical errors. I have corrected the others.*

say that small action is not likely to be the one we have suggested, but it is an action to which we have been the tangential father. We have at least, no matter how crudely or ineptly, succeeded in communicating something, and the actions of others, as well as our own, are the result. In this rigorous sense there is no communication unless action has resulted, be it immediately or in the unknown and indefinite future. Communication which does not lead to new action is not communication—it is merely the abortive presentation of new social ideas or the monotonous transportation of old ones.

LIES

But an old social idea is a lie. Where it is not sheer premeditated falsity (four-fifths of gossip-columnists' spew, for example) it is at best a description of something which no longer exists. Society at any moment is the stubborn retarded expression of mankind's previous and partially collected experience. Yet our previous experience is the past, it is our knowledge of death, and theologians to the side (for I frankly am all but ignorant of theology) I would argue most seriously that growth is a greater mystery than death. All of us can understand failure, we all contain failure and death within us, but not even the successful man can begin to describe the impalpable elations and apprehensions of growth. When we can all agree, including odd dialectical idealists like myself, that history is not foreseeable and the future is unknown, we must also agree that although society is a machine, it does not determine man's fate, but merely processes nine-tenths of his possibilities on the basis of what society has learned from the past. Since we are all in the process of changing, since we are already in the privacy of our minds far ahead of the life we see around us (for civilized man has always been outraged by what he sees, or else there would be no civilization)—since we are all advanced in our dreams beyond the practical social possibilities open to our immediate time, that present *living* time which is all but strangled by the slow mechanical determinations of society, we know and feel that whatever happens to us will happen as the reaction between our urgent desires to express ourselves, to discover the passionate attachment of our lives, and the resistant mechanical network of past social ideas, platitudes, and lies.

POWER

Only it is difficult to express oneself. The act of writing something (which one expects or hopes will be published) is a social act; it becomes—even at its best—all but a lie. To communicate socially (as opposed to communicating personally or humanly) means that one must accept the sluggish fictions of society for at least nine-tenths of one's expression in order to present deceptively the remaining tenth which may be new. Social communication is the doom of every truly felt thought. (Naturally, all men who wish to communicate seek social communication nonetheless, for it is the only way to influence great numbers of people in a relatively short time.)

To communicate socially is to communicate by way of the mass-media—movies, radio, television, advertising, newspapers, best-selling novels, etc.—which is to communicate by way of the largest and most debased common denominator—which in turn is equivalent to communicating very little, for procedurally one becomes part of a machine which is antithetical to one's individual existence. Antithetical, I say, because this machine attempts to direct the fortunes of men by the obsolete and hence impractical results of the past. As one writes, one enters an external network of expectations, consequences, fears, cupidities, social fashions: in short, reward or punishment turns the language and alters the thought. This is true even of the most serious attempts to communicate, by artists let us say, or the occasional creative scholar. Once one enters the land of massive social communication, of network communication, once one becomes attached to the machine belt of the mass-media—specifically, in our case, the assembly line of the columnist—there is no desire to retain even the father's ghost of a thought. There is only power for the sake of power, and it is cowardly power for it masquerades in coy and winsome forms. On the surface there is only the attempt to entertain in a conventional way. (Obviously, to entertain and yet say nothing new is quite a difficult game, which is why perhaps columnists, commercial writers, and so forth, are paid so well.)

Therefore, I propose to try something I do not believe I can accomplish. I will try to write for you (this column to the contrary) as if I were talking in my living room, or in yours. So my opinions will be half-formed, if not totally inarticulate, but at least they can be awkwardly close to the questions I am really thinking about.

OBSCENITY

Even so, I promise very very little. For example I will be able to use no obscenities, and obscenities communicate a great deal in the living room and indeed in other places as well. For what are obscenities finally but our poor debased gutturals for the magical parts of the human body, and so they are basic communication, for they awake, no matter how uneasily, many of the questions, riddles, aches, and pleasures which surround the enigma of life.

No, I will not be able to use obscenities—what a pity!—because a little social fact which is too often forgotten is that obscene language which is used at least once in awhile by 95 per cent of the people living in this country would forbid the passage of this newspaper through the mails. And there are other restrictions, stories I cannot tell about unpleasant people in the daily news, people who are pusillanimous, or archly vicious, or hypocritical, or worse, or simply no good, stories I cannot tell because this paper would be sued for libel. (Ah, well, perhaps we will find a way yet.)

So these restrictions and all others sadden me, because I would like to express myself properly, and the true communication of soul to soul is speeded on its way, as every soldier and ex-soldier knows, by the foul language God gave our tongues, along with everything else He gave us including malicious stories, women, society, pain, pleasure, lights and darks, and all the other mysterious dualities of our mysterious universe.

Therefore, brethren, let me close this sermon, by asking the grace for us to be aware, if only once in a while, that beyond the mechanical communication of all of society's obvious and subtle networks, there remains the sense of life, the sense of creative spirit (we are all creative if it is for no less than to create new life itself) and therefore the sense no matter how dimly felt of some expanding and not necessarily ignoble human growth.

With this worthy homilectic come to a close, I promise next week to provide some diversion. Perhaps even a dialogue or two. If I say so myself, I am pretty good at that.

LETTERS TO THE VOICE

Dear Sir:

This guy Mailer. He's a hostile, narcissistic pest. Lose him. He reminds me of a character who moves into a nice neighborhood and can't stand the warmth and harmony, so he does all in his power to disrupt it. You have such a nice paper. Don't spoil it. The only thing Mailer has to communicate is his own self-glorification.

—Phyllis Lynd
West 87th Street

Dear Sir:

Why does Norman Mailer insist that he is a philosopher? It has already marred two of his novels and killed the middle one altogether. A less capable writer would not have survived at all. It's an obsession like that of Congreve, who yearned to be regarded as a man of fashion rather than a man of letters. And now, at long last, in a paper which he partly owns, he has a heaven of space for it. If he continues as he has started, he bids fair to do the job on himself that Lillian Ross once did on Hemingway. On the other hand, if he gets it out of his system and eliminates it from his future novels, the *Voice* will have done literature a real service. But can the *Voice* itself survive the operation? Can it survive the insufferable coyness of Mr. Mailer's condescension to his readers, his hypocritical warnings "not to read me today," his silly insistence that he be read slowly and carefully? And then when he finally turns to fling us a bone ("All right, then, if you insist, but just one!"), he drops his little mask, and with the pomposity of T. S. Eliot, the verbosity of Maxwell Anderson, and the wit of Lloyd Douglas, proceeds to intone his homily for the day: that communication is difficult, that some people tell lies, that communication is facilitated by obscenities. I am sure that Mr. Mailer's philosophy is facilitated by obscenities. I wonder if they don't constitute the only readable part of it.

—Sheridan Dale
Broad Street

Dear Sir:

Lookit that self-conscious Norman Mailer. He begins by patronizing his readers (would-be's and failures and Bohemians, he calls us) and indicates that this having to write a column bores him. And he ends by telling us that we probably won't understand him but he is going to give the thing a manful try anyway.

What is all this whining that communication is so difficult because you have to address whole lots of people in society and not just some old pal in your living room who will patiently put up with your obscenity and your inarticulate gasps about the profundity and sensuality of life?

Mr. Mailer feels the cause of his difficulty in communicating his thoughts lies in society. "Social communication," he says, "is the doom of every truly felt thought."

Society, Mr. Mailer, is people, and in this country most of us speak English, and I venture to say that most of us have much the same sort of feelings and some of the same sort of thoughts that you do. I venture to say that we can understand you, if you make yourself plain. If we don't it is still a question in my mind whether that is our fault or yours.

—Lu Burke
Bleecker Street

REPLY
I'm tempted to call my column "TONIC—A Charge for the Sluggish." Since the criticisms about my most indefensible personality have almost nothing to do with what I wrote last week, I suggest my correspondents read last week's column over again. Mailer, poor chap, does suffer from megalomania, but it is more or less true of all his work that it improves on second reading.

N.M.

Column Three

Here is the diversion I promised.

COMMUNIQUES FROM THE MARSH MEDIA

ED SULLEN-VAIN on C's of B. S.

Tonight, I want you to meet a great American, a clean cut boy. . . . One of our up and coming champions in the next uh Olympics. . . . A fellow who has overcome the heartbreaking and crippling handicap of early success, I mean a great fellow. . . . A very well-neat. . . . That is a very well-knit prince of an American-type who has promised in the international sports and athletic competitions. . . . Which we all call the Olympic Games. . . . That is, he has promised to bring us back the Bongo Board Championship from the Iron curtains. . . .

I am happy and privileged to introduce Mr. Lightning on the Bongo Board . . . that pride to our flag. . . . *Norman Mailer? ? ? ?*

CHEDDAR CHOPPER in the N. Y. Daily Nose

I wish some of the uninformed and downright sinister elements which still exist in our cleaned-up and happy movie colony would realize that they don't have to keep on buying all those novels by novelists with dirty fingernails. Those fancy New York publishers have been giving snow-jobs to the weaker element out here. Why there's enough talent in this town to write "The Caine Mystery" fifty times a year.

WAX BURNER in the N. Y. Homely

On my recent exclusive lecture trip for this newspaper, I had the opportunity to talk to hundreds of stimulating young faces in the latest college generation. To generalize too quickly on what I learned, and I have learned so much, would be inadequate and would tend to blur the lights and shadows of the psychological and sociological nuances and shadings I have been exploring. However, briefly, crudely, despite all the contradictions and fascinating cross-currents, I would say that the new American college generation is not rebellious, iconoclastic, cynical, and destructive, but rather shows an encouraging health, maturity, and intrinsic integration. . . . The young people I met on my talks are Anti-Fascist, Anti-Marxist, Anti-Republican, Anti-Nihilist and Anti-Pacifist. Yet they await the war with no calm equanimity. They show an informed interest in getting married. They are frank in their lack of fear or sex. On the other hand they are *not* not-afraid of sex. They realize it can be abused. I have been encouraged by all the signs I have seen of the continuing earnest, serious, liberal, and essential individuation of the people's spirit which was refracted, no matter how imperfectly, everywhere I traveled. So, modestly, tentatively, I await the future with informed confidence.

LEARNED LIONS in the N. Y. Homely

I was walking through Central Park with my family when we saw the Hon. Prime Minister Emeritus of England feeding a sparrow at the Tavern-on-the-Green. "How do you do again, Mr. Churchill," I said, and he answered with his famous smile: "Nonsense, Learned, call me Winnie. Why I remember when we were boys together, and you used to borrow puffs on my old cigar."

VOLTAIRE VEIN-CHILL in the N. Y. Daily Rimmer

Jail to you, Mr. and Mrs. Erotica and all the flips on Tea. . . . Several solovisions down in Greenwich Village where they put two holes in the doughnuts for the perverts are putting out a monthly rag called "Village Vices." Playwright Norman Miller— he scripted "Naked to the Death"—now Svengaling those hammy hermits into Poverty Row where there are NO holes in the doughnuts!!!

DOROTHY KILL-TALENT in the N. Y. Churlish-American

If the real sordid story behind the dangerous growth of that new Greenwich, Conn., weekly, the Village "VOICES," were ever to be told, it would put me in jail for libel!!

NICHE TOUCHEE in the Village Void

Smash the television sets! Beat the brains out of conformity, beat them into the beauty of little birds' wings. Yet show all honor to those who refuse to pose with their fingers in their nose forever. So I will make the humble hesitating gesture of joining Humbly Ad's campaign train where the beautiful speeches are beautified, and let us start Poets-for-Stevenson!

LETTERS TO THE VOICE

Dear Sir:

It's a shame that Norman Mailer is being curtailed in your paper. Without being free to express the *raw* facts of life in his exuberant way, certainly ulcers will result! Take care of him, please.

We, in the country, are reading "Deer Park" in a nice sneaky fashion—behind the *Farm Journal*.

—Ruth McGray
Glastonbury, Conn.

Dear Sir:

To Norman Mailer:

What intrigues me is the distance you have traveled (from a point in innocence, many years back) for you to arrive at the position you are now in of having to cloak your precious little portion of truth in pretended insincerity, sarcasm, paradox, and id-ism.

One of the first things I get from reading you is a sense of your having been hurt and misunderstood too many times. You have been pushed by a listless and untender reading public beyond the point of polite intellectual rebuttal. Now you must use your pen like a hammer.

It is a very delicate matter, trying to build an opinion about what you are doing and whether it's worth it. One of the reasons this letter wasn't written three weeks ago is that I was afraid of responding too immediately. I wanted to be relatively sure, first, what parts of what you said you didn't (and couldn't possibly) believe yourself and what parts you did. It is, of course, intellectually and otherwise unsafe to take all of what you say at face value. Half of what you say is pure pointless talk (of course you know this) and not all of the half of you that remains is valid or worth holding. The task of understanding you was made even more arduous by the snobbish attitude you felt compelled to assume.

Now, it is not easy to assume snobbery if it did not grow up with you (I guess you are finding this out). I am half-sure (total surety about anything being detrimental to awareness) that you consciously and conscientiously assume snobbery in order to more effectively convey to your readers that small nugget of sincerity you have hidden somewhere in your words. Snobbery (as you know) isn't always offensive or oppressive; it has its uses, and it is possible, in certain situations, to accept it. Ortega wrote "Revolt of the Masses" and a lot of sensitive people didn't call him a bastard for it. You would have people think that you would be willing to unwrite Ortega's book and call it "The Masses are Revolting," but privately I think you have, still, even in your battered state, some feeling for them. If you didn't, I don't think you'd be writing. A lot of good writing comes from being impatient with humanity, but I don't think it is possible for any good writing to come from being heartlessly cruel to it.

The quickest first feeling to have after reading your column is: Mailer has become a tiger; he claws now and shows fierce naked teeth. If you feel more slowly however you understand that the tiger isn't real. It is a desperate (and even somewhat pathetic) device of yours enabling you to move from the defensive to the offensive, and to violently say quiet things that have taken you (most probably) much suffering and anguish to learn.

It is, admittedly, hard at times to ignore the audacious, megalomaniacal, and generally unpretty mask you usually insist on wearing and objectively attempt to evaluate and understand the man behind it. (I have a suspicion that the man behind the mask is basically an abnormally tender and sensitive person; it's too bad the world isn't nicer to sensitive people.)

It is very easy, I suppose, to hate you. My own initial reaction was to sympathize with you. And I guess the ideal reaction (for you) is to have people attempt quite simply to understand. I don't suppose, however, that the majority of them will take the time to do this so I guess I am back where I started from, sympathizing with you.

—Robert A. Perlongo
West 12th Street

Dear Sir:
Observations in the Metre of Tamburlaine on the Norman Mailer Turbulence and Its Relations: with the Presence of Byron, Dostoievsky, Bodenheim, and Everyone.

—But Norman Mailer's turbulence is still
The deep, deep turbulence a man can have—
Compelled to see himself: a moving world,
Impinging, hitting, charming—at one time,
The selfsame moment, by the selfsame mind.
Complacency at least is fought by him
Who asks what flesh can do to formal thought—
And keeps on asking, in the smoke and sun.
We must see lusciousness in thought—
The pale madonna in the hot desire.
The need is sterner now than ever; now
Our self-respect demands, demands, demands
We place the viscera with logic, time.
The turbulence of Norman Mailer helps.

The ostentation of this writer makes
Us ask: The nature of true modesty—
Is what? Assertion, can it go with us
Who always question what we truly are?
How good we are, how strong, how weak, how real?
Then show off in your torturous way, O mind!
Abase yourself in swirling smoke of hours.
The blue flame of the factory within
May be resplendent yet in sun without.
But work is needed; Norman Mailer's work:
A novelist confronting smugness more—
And fakery within, even when it's his.
The way to glory is the way of show:
The show of fall and rise, of murk and light—
The show of self as drama all the day.
So Mailer has a bit of Byron, yes—
Of Dostoievsky and of Bodenheim—
And Lord knows what—each artist has and is
A world of love and anger by himself.
We can but wish that love and scorn so merge
In him, they stand for form in everyone
Of *us*. These lines of now are a salute,
A criticism and—a friendly Oh!

—Eli Siegel
Jane Street

Columns One, Two and Three were printed intact, and a few of the letters which were set in the paper during those weeks were also included. For the remainder, I have cut or trimmed all the columns but the fourth, the fifth and the seventeenth, and have omitted nearly all the letters. To an extent, this defeats the purpose of the Advertisement *to this section, for much of the bad writing has been removed, and what is left will seem less unsuccessful than I have described it. But it occurred to me that I have given fair attention to much bad writing in this book, and I do not know that it is necessary to work through any more of the mediocre.*

Still, I did go on about the psychological roots of bad style, and it may be frustrating to offer no thoroughgoing specimens now. The prime exhibit is Column Two—rarely have ideas which were worth a clean show been given such a muscle-bound presentation, but to satisfy the curiosity of a few. I add here a few cuttings which are typical of what was deleted. Needless to say, there are similar nuggets still left in the body of edited columns which follow.

FROM COLUMN SIX

Because if everyone were to express the greatest number of actions possible for them, allowing only the inhibitions of time and energy for their restraints, and if man should prove to be more good-than-bad, then ultimately the state and society would prove superfluous, and humankind, whatever its continuing and newly discovered ills, would have the desire and the possibility to create a world of truly individual liberty.

FROM COLUMN EIGHT

For the analyst—let us say, for most analysts—his own condition, his own emotions, are seen as the product of parental and social conditions beyond his control, and so in his turn the analyst is not likely to ascribe the same dignity to emotion, nor to believe it is very relatively free to choose its desired action. On the contrary, each man is virtually determined in his fate, and his emotions, his subjective state, are a private counterfeit with which he conceals from himself the nature of congealed, unconscious, and unreasonable needs which dominate his movements. Far from granting emotion its general human validity, the analyst is likely rather to argue that there is an individual misapprehension of reality present in almost every emotion.

Column Four

This week the first half of Quickly has been considerately supplied by Kenneth J. Schmidt of the Village, who has written what I believe is a most amusing parody of my second column. So let us go into:

Burp: A Column for People Who Can Read by Normal Failure

A WARNING: The column this week is easy. I wrote it slowly because that's the way I think. If you don't have a strong stomach and a weak mind I suggest you pass me by. But if you do concentrate on this, please have the decency not to pass it along. Bear in mind the pursuit of happiness and let it go at that.

THOUGHT

Like when you see someone on the subway with a shoe on his ear. You think: "How strange, the shoe-strings aren't tied." You tell the stranger and he ties the shoestrings. Your original thought spurred the stranger to action. This can be called communication.

LIES

Like when I write something and expect people not to believe it. (Even though it's true they shouldn't believe it, because when I wrote it I thought it was a lie.) This is my favorite type of communication. One where truth and un-truth are indistinguishable.

POWER

Like when I write a truly great book and feel like a crumb because the only ones who can read it are people. Why do I write? Because I want to influence a great number of people in a relatively short time. Social communication. Ugh! What I wouldn't give for one really smart monkey. I'll bet he could grasp my awkward, half-formed, or even totally inarticulate opinions. This can be called tele-communication.

OBSCENITY

Like when you're at a gay party in a cozy Village apartment and the hostess asks do you find it "stuffy"? You want to communicate freely, soul to soul, as it were, and bounce a few four-lettered words off her low-slung brow. Instead you say politely: "Gosh no, it's delightful. Like one huge armpit." This is called tactful communication.

With this worthless epistle come to a close, I promise next week to offer some diversion. Perhaps even an eructation or two. If I say so myself, I am rather good at that.

Thank you, Kenneth. You're a friendly sort.

Now, to pick up my column again:

LIVING ROOM TALK—for very slow readers

When a columnist with his ever-sensitive teeth on the public pulse begins to realize he is just a touch don't you know disliked, why then if he is really a columnist and has his eye on the main chance, he sits down and writes a column about his family, preferably about his children.

Since the situation may conceivably apply to your most Humble Hostile Servant, m'self, I am obliged to take the side of prudence, and so present the following sentimental dialogue between my tough two-fisted little daughter Susan, age 6, and your beloved Narcissist.

(*SCENE: Living room at the Norman Mailers. Susan is, as always, watching television. I hover in the background, reading a copy of the* Voice. *As is my habit, I read from bottom to top. The tension mounts.*)

"Susie," I say inquiringly, "why do people go to war?"

"Because, Daddy-O," she pipes at me, "*they get tired of staying at home.*"

At this point my daughter furrowed her brow, as if to declare cease to all the retcheries of man, and in her childlike voice which has the cold thrumming tones of the hippest hipster on the psychopath side, she said: "And while we're at it, you were most uncool to point out so cruel to the paying gentry about how they are mentally nopotent and under-ushered in their pleasures."

"Yes," I said sadly, "no one forgives you for reminding them of that."

"Illimate horror, indeed they don't." And in the tones of sternest grandmotherly scorn, she lashed me with: "Man, play it cool with those squares in the Village, because they are most unhip" —and here Susan came out of her murderous gloom, and with the brightest tinkling merry old child's laugh, she repeated: "Because they are most unhip, and you, *mon chou,* was a pint over on the uncool side."

SO—NEXT WEEK—FOLLOWING HIS DAUGHTER'S ADVICE, THE VILLAGE VILLAIN WILL BE BACK WITH A FEW COOL INSULTS, AND A COLUMN OR TWO FROM

HIS LATEST TOME: "THE NIHILISTIC IDEALISM OF A DIALECTICAL EXISTENTIALIST." AND IF HE IS IN THE MOOD, HE WILL DEMONSTRATE, CONTRARY TO HERR DOKTOR KENNETH J. SCHMIDT, THAT LIES AND TRUTH ARE PERHAPS IMPOSSIBLE TO SEPARATE, AFTER ALL, AND THEREFORE MUST BE CONSIDERED PROVISIONALLY, IN THE WORLD OF EVENTS, AS BEING THE SAME THING.

Column Five

A parody is a return to common sense, and its appeal is due precisely to its common sense—it attracts the common denominator in everyone, it is horizontally vulgar, it flattens all spurs of thought. The meaty satisfaction of a parody is that it rouses in a reader the satisfying emotion of "How ridiculous, how perfectly ridiculous."

Still, the fear of being ridiculous stifles more thought than the act of being ridiculous, and common sense is notoriously uncreative. What distinguishes Kenneth J. Schmidt's parody of last week is that he is unwittingly if happily profound. I quote:

> Like when I write something and expect people not
> to believe it. (Even though it's true they shouldn't
> believe it, because when I wrote it I thought it was
> a lie.) This is my favorite type of communication.
> One where truth and un-truth are indistinguishable.

With poetic concentration, Schmidt has succeeded in capturing the essence of social communication. To the people who work in the mass-media, truth and untruth are indeed the same thing, and as a practical matter are usually indistinguishable to them.

For once, I am going to take a most definite example. The item concerns myself, and I quote it to satisfy my profound egotism, and incidentally to avoid any larger arguments about "facts."

The following bit appeared in Hedda Hopper's syndicated column in the N. Y. Daily News a few weeks ago:

The British are gloating over "The Big Knife"; they love the way the film takes a swing at practically everybody in Hollywood. In light of this, I can't understand a major studio paying $200,000 for Norman Mailer's story "Deer Park," which takes an even more sadistic look at our industry.

Hedda Hopper is a human being, and so probably has a virtue or two tucked away somewhere. But her accuracy is not what will bring her to heaven. The item I quoted is untrue. Not only did no major studio pay $200,000 for "The Deer Park," but indeed I have not yet put the book up for sale, as every story editor in Hollywood knows by now.

Yet Hedda's untruth produces very real if small reactions. People who have read the item in Hopper's column, and are impressed by money, were bound to have raised me a little in their unconscious estimation. People who dislike wealthy authors doubtless put me down a bit. Years from now it is quite likely I will meet someone who will act toward me in a very real way on the basis of a very unreal story. An "untruth" begets a "truth."

I am taking of course a very special definition of the word "truth." Still, in the world of events, I do not see how social truth can be defined as anything other than that which happens, that which makes history. Long after it is impossible to determine the truth or falsity of a given "fact," people continue to act on the basis of what they believe has happened, and their actions in turn create further actions. History, finally, is the sum not of people's sentiments, but of people's actions. (And, please, no letters that sentiments lead to action. Obviously, not all sentiments do, and a sentiment which remains just a sentiment never enters the network of human actions whose overt result is change, is human history.)

Yet if social truth is to be defined as that which happens, then for the mass-media a lie, a half-truth, or a whole truth (whatever that is) must all be considered in the same way, and can be measured only by their social effect. At a guess 10,000,000 people read Hedda Hopper; 20,000 read this column. For whatever tiny social significance it has, the un-truth of Hopper has more social reality, hence more social truth than my refutation, and five years from now, let us say, when my next novel comes out, some reviewer in some literary purlieu like Kansas City will think unconsciously: "That rich dastard, Mailer, I hate his guts," and his review—a modest social reality—will be partially a reflection of the $200,000 I never saw.

It will be remembered that this column is called "Quickly." I have made my points in great haste and most sketchily. Yet what I have tried to present more or less formally is taken for granted by all columnists, reporters, publicity men, editors, advertisers, moviemen, etc., etc., etc., and they always proceed on the unself-conscious rule-of-thumb that personal truth and untruth become, through the alchemy of the mass-media, equal social realities. So I would suggest that the only way to guess what might possibly be happening in any historical event big or small is not to accept what you read as that which is actually happening, but rather to attempt to divine what public personages A, B, C, D, and E and their mass-media midwives a, b, c, d, e, wish you to believe about event X. And in a small way this is as true of The Village Voice as it is of Life Magazine, the N. Y. Post, the Journal American, and for that matter, the New York Times.

Even though it's true, they shouldn't believe it, because when I wrote it, I thought it was a lie.

Column Eight

I see an interesting contest. No doubt a large portion of the readers of The Voice have been psychoanalyzed, or are reasonably familiar with the subject—at the very least there must be hardly a reader of this paper who does not use psychoanalytical jargon in one way or another. In turn, I would like to write about some aspects of the subject. (To keep the record from the beginning, I will say that I have never been analyzed, but that I have spent the last year in analyzing myself, and not in ways which have much to do with Karen Horney. As a hint. I will add that if I were ever to look for an analyst I would be inclined to get me to a Reichian.)

At any rate, I issue a challenge—call it an invitation—to have a debate back and forth in this column with any young or old analyst in or out of the Village who is willing to step forth out of confidence, frustrated polemical vigor, or the open desire to teach and to learn in public argument. And the subject may be anything we agree might be mutually stimulating.

The offer is open. I doubt, frankly, if any analyst will come forward. Legitimately, work occupies much of their energy, and less openly—and from my point of view, less honorably—there is a certain tendency among all too many of them to avoid psycho-analytical discussion with laymen on the theory that the mysteries of the new religion might suffer, not to mention the snobbery of medical decorum.

But if we do not have the debate, what a shame! For it is a natural contest. The novelist, like the analyst, spends his life absorbed with the nuances of human nature—yet each approach their vocation diametrically opposed.

The novelist trusts his "vision," the analyst distrusts it; the novelist, romantically, is more concerned with what a man or a woman might become in a situation which would bring out the extreme of his or her character (an idea expressed by Georges Simenon); the analyst, realistically, must be concerned with what is the most likely and practical choice available to his patient. Intellectively, the analyst must usually ascribe more power to society than to man, and though he works with individuals, he thinks socially, he is always aware of the world which surrounds his patient, while the novelist, who begins by addressing the world with some part of the world as his subject, becomes truly interesting only if he can present some solitary human possibility of choice which goes a little further, a little deeper, into the mysteries of the self than the last writer before him. Concerned with the same subject the analyst and the novelist are antithetical in their view, their method, and conceivably in their aims, for despite the vast confusion of contradictory declarations by artist and analyst alike, I wonder if their ends are not essentially different, the artist a rebel concerned with Becoming, the analyst a regulator concerned with Being.

Can we have this debate? I invite those readers of The Voice who are in analysis to bring my proposed literary joust to the attention of their analyst. If for once a novelist finds himself in a mood of genial public service, the psychoanalysts, who are, after all, at the mercy of the public service, should be able to respond.

Column Nine

One of my few really good friends died last week at the age of 41. He was Robert Lindner, the psychoanalyst, and he had been suffering from a heart ailment for many years.

Perhaps some of the readers of this column are familiar with his work for he was a prolific author, and wrote "Rebel Without a Cause" (not to be confused with the movie), "Stone Walls and Men," "Prescription for Rebellion," "The Fifty-Minute Hour," and "Must You Conform?," which was published last month.

Bob Lindner was so good a friend that I simply have no heart to write about him now. I should go on at length about his charm, his generosity, his intellectual curiosity, his foibles, his weaknesses, his kindnesses, his ambitions, his achievements, his failures, and his great warmth (he was truly one of the warmest people I have known), but to write immediately about a man so complex, so individual, and yet so much part of our generation would be to do him a disservice, for Bob Lindner was nothing if not alive, and he would have loathed a facile eulogy.

So, rather, let me give the rest of this column over to a few passages from his books. These passages are undoubtedly not the best which could be found in his work, nor the most exciting, but they are representative of the main themes which preoccupied him. In addition to his early work on the criminal psycopath, Lindner was almost alone among analysts in his sustained argument that the healthy man was a rebel, and that it was crippling for psychoanalysis to try to adjust a patient to the warpings of an unjust world.

From "The Fifty-Minute Hour," Rinehart and Company, Jan. '55:

Around psychoanalysis there has been built a fence of mystery and something resembling awe. Its practitioners, if not the objects yet of veneration and fear, are well on their way to elevation as priests of a certain kind; and the initiates—those who have

303

lain on couches, that is—threaten to become a confraternity of the saved, a latter-day community of saints whose cancelled checks comprise a passport to heavens denied those less (or more?) favored by fortune.

A psychoanalyst is . . . an artist at understanding, the product of an intensive course of study and training which has—if it has been successful—rendered him unusually sensitive to his fellow men. And it is this sensitivity—in short, the analyst's own person—which is the single instrument, the only tool, with which he performs. Only on himself, and on nothing else, does he depend.

From "Must You Conform," Rinehart and Company, Jan. '56:

This is the day of the psychological mountebank. Everyone with access to print apparently conceives of himself as a psychologist, and few hesitate to pontificate about man, his nature, his mind, and his future.

One of the effects of this widespread psychologizing is a loss of precision in many of the key concepts important for the study of human behavior. Somewhere in the process of verbal mauling, words and ideas that have been arrived at laboriously in science or philosophy become vague and essentially meaningless. They acquire new semantic alliances which, in time, so distort them that they are rendered completely useless for the further pursuit of knowledge.

Such a word is *maturity*, and such a fate seems to be in store for it. . . .

I am of the opinion that the definitions of maturity which assail us in such profusion currently are uniformly founded on the tacit hypothesis that human development is linked to human passivity. All that I have encountered assume that adjustment and conformity are the desirable modes of life, and that the closer one comes to a condition of domestication, the more mature one is. None of them, to my knowledge, takes account of man's nature and spirit, of his innate rebelliousness, of his intrinsic values, or of his individuality. With monotonous regularity, these definitions predicate themselves upon, and defend, a society that is everyday and everywhere becoming more and more oppressive. Hence, the standards for mature behavior they advise are those standards that may apply to mature cattle or mature puppets—but not to mature men.

The simple truth, stark and severe in its simplicity, is that *we cannot conform;* for it seems there is an ingredient in the composition of our cells, a chemistry in our blood, and a substance in our bones that will not suffer man to submit forever.

Built into man, the foundation of his consciousness, the source of his humanity and the vehicle of his evolution up from the muck of a steaming primeval swamp, is an instinct. I have chosen to call it the "instinct of rebellion," since it reveals itself as a drive or urge toward mastery over every obstacle, natural or man-made, that stands as a barrier between man and his distant, perhaps never-to-be-achieved but always-striven-after goals. It is this instinct that underwrites his survival, this instinct from which he derives his nature: a great and powerful dynamic that makes him what he is—restless, seeking, curious, forever unsatisfied, eternally struggling and eventually victorious. . . . Because of the instinct of rebellion man has never been content with the limits of his mind: it has led him to inquire its secrets of the universe, to gather and learn and manipulate the fabulous inventory of the cosmos, to seek the very mysteries of creation. Because of the instinct of rebellion, man has never been content, finally, with the limits of his life: it has caused him to deny death and to war with mortality.

Man is a rebel. He is commited by his biology *not* to conform, and herein lies the paramount reason for the awful tension he experiences today in relation to Society. . . .

Column Ten

Robert Lindner's death has left me in an ugly mood.

I feel a touch edgy as I sit down to write this, and I know from experience that when one feels modestly murderous it is good to vent it for the health of one's nervous system.

You see, I was hoping for a letter from an analyst which would prove promising, but this has not been the case. The only functional letter I have received so far in answer to my challenge is from an analyst who strikes me as being almost hopelessly minor league. So I will not try to answer him too seriously, but instead will break up his work, sentence by sentence, omitting nothing and obeying his sequence of argument, in order to note my separate replies in a mock-dialogue. Since this is taking a considerable liberty with his letter, I will not print his name unless he requests it after seeing this column. Until such time I will call him Doctor Y. (Incidentally, this gentleman practices in the Village, or at least his address is in Greenwich Village, and so by studying his letter I have come to understand a little better why some of you are the way you are.)

Now, for some off-couch theatre:

Dr. Y.: (His letter indeed began this way.) If you were a true artist, you would not be threatened by psychoanalysts and would not stoop to challenge them.

Norman Mailer: The sad reality, I'm afraid, is that an artist must step up in class these days to challenge an analyst, for the greater part of the public listens far more carefully to a third-rate practitioner than a first-rate novelist.

Dr. Y.: We psychoanalysts derive a good deal of our sustenance from authors and are not in competition with them.

N. M.: It has been my experience that when you derive your sustenance from someone, you are invariably in competition with him.

Dr. Y.: The clue to your dilemma is your stated boredom.

N. M.: As an analyst you should be more cautious about taking remarks at their face value. Just because I stated I was bored by writing this column does not make it so. I refer you to my first column where I indicated that a good newspaperman is as ready to tell a lie as the truth.

Dr. Y.: A true artist is never bored.

N. M.: Freud was more cautious than you in his remarks about artists.

Dr. Y.: I feel sorry for anyone who would be bored with the stimulating challenge of turning out a weekly column at this early stage.

N. M.: Isn't it being a self-righteous bully to think in such formulas as "stimulating challenge?" Like everything else in life, the intrinsic challenge of this column varies by turns to be amusing, irritating, boring, or stimulating.

Dr. Y.: Boredom is suffering.

N. M.: You said it, doc.

Dr. Y.: It's a serious business, boredom, because behind it lies felt emptiness, a condescending attitude toward everyone, and enormous self-dissatisfaction.

N. M.: Yes, it must be painful to feel like that.

Dr. Y.: You cannot break through this with self-analysis.

N. M.: I wonder if you have the imagination to begin to guess what my self-analysis is like.

Dr. Y.: Freud could do this (analyze himself) only partially after decades of work, but he was a genius and an expert in helping people, and you are not.

N. M.: Not yet, not yet at all. Still, what would Freud have done if he had had your attitude?

Dr. Y.: Dozens of our greatest literary figures have kept on leading most unhappy personal lives despite their keen introspective talents simply because intellectual insight is not enough.

N. M.: No, it is indeed not enough for self-analysis. But surely your authoritarian bent is not so severe that you would banish all intellectual inquiry which does not take place between analysts. Or would talented but unhappy analysts—of whom there are more than a few—be disqualified as well?

Dr. Y.: Your boredom with your column shields your fear that you could not sustain reader interest in what for you should be a casual and enjoyable experience.

N. M.: You bring out my disappearing modesty. I assure you, doctor, as a practical matter it is relatively easy for a weathered charlatan like myself to sustain interest in so small a carnival as this.

Dr. Y.: Your knowledge of psychoanalysis is faulty.

N. M.: Very faulty. As is everyone else's, including—one must whisper it—the analysts. Psychoanalysis, after all, is the exploration of a most mysterious part of nature—a human being.

Dr. Y.: I would disagree most emphatically with your assertions that the analyst distrusts his "vision," is concerned only with practical reality, that he ascribes more power to society than to man, that he thinks only socially, and that he is only a regulator concerned with being.

N. M.: Unless you are interested in dulling the minds of the public, and in presenting yourself precisely as a Regulator, you would exhibit more intellectual grace by trying to disprove what I wrote, rather than declaring it null and void.

Dr. Y.: But if the purpose of your column was to provoke, you certainly succeeded: there your talent is undeniable.

N. M.: I? Provoke? Why I'm never rude to anyone.

Dr. Y.: I would rather not play along further with your challenge.

N. M.: Sleep is wisdom for gladiators like yourself.

Dr. Y.: It could only further serve your narcissism. . . .

N. M.: Which you will admit is self-confessed. I'm more honest than most, you know.

Dr. Y.: (over-riding the interruption): . . . with the dice too heavily loaded in your favor according to your prescribed conditions.

N. M.: I wonder if you read very carefully. These were my "prescribed conditions:" *As a possible mode of procedure, I propose —although I am not in the least rigid about this—that one of us open the discussion and the other prepare a rebuttal for the same issue, and that we take it from there. But virtually any other ground rules are agreeable to me.*

Dr. Y.: You'll have to write your own column anyhow—eventually.

N. M.: Is this supposed to be a last pointed thrust?

Since it is true that I have the unfair privilege of the final word, I think I will repay the doctor's kindness for giving me a free session of psychiatric advice by returning the duty-call. Doctor Y. impresses me as being only mildly neurotic, and in ways which most people consider socially constructive. He suffers from small compulsions and expulsions of guilt, undoubtedly anal-retentive in their seat, but so relatively harmless, given his successful sublimation of sadism, that his conditioned conservatism allocates powerful super-ego energies to control the mildly paranoid element revealed today by his literary style and his obvious (to any clinician) projections upon me of his own conflicts. One may add that Dr. Y. is ambitious beyond his means, but is covertly aware that his power-drives are unrealistic. This expresses itself beneath his general depression by ambivalence and intermittent timidity. However, he does impress me as a steady worker, perhaps due to the psychic equilibrium maintained exactly by his general depression. He would be suitable for treating weak unfortunate patients whose dependencies he would buttress by his authoritarian nature. Psychopathic, aggressive, or unusual cases would cause him anxiety, however, for they would be ego-threatening, and so the prognosis for such analyses would be poor, since they would be in danger of terminating abruptly with some damage to both parties.

Column Eleven

The news-box which appeared on page 1 of The Voice last week went: *Who's Norman Mailer's candidate for President? Those readers who turn to page 5 and read "Quickly" slowly, might find some clue. In any case there's a $10 prize for the first correct solution received at this office. (His choice, by the way, is in a sealed envelope pasted on to the center of the Village Voice window. You can see it there from the street.)*

Now this was a trifle misleading, since there were no portentous clues in last week's column. I had said to the gentleman who wrote the news-box that there might be a few hints in all my columns taken together, but this was unfortunately garbled a bit in transmission. So, as an apology for neglecting to look at the news-box in galleys, I will double the ante to $20, and give a few more pointed suggestions.

The greatest clues of course are buried in those parts of my character which have been revealed week by week. What it comes down to, is who, by God, would that megalomaniac Mailer nominate besides himself? And of course the wise man—if there is one among you—would answer: "Why, even a bigger megalomaniac."

Clue #2. Last week I had a line in answer to Dr. Y. which went: "Sleep is wisdom for gladiators like yourself." So your columnist demonstrated indirectly that in his cold bitter soul, he has respect for gladiators who are on their feet. Therefore, Candidate X must fulfill this condition as well.

Clue #3. Candidate X would approve of slow readers.

Clue #4. Candidate X must of course be Hip, and yet not display himself unduly as a hipster. Perhaps we can assume that he was one of the germinal influences in the birth of the hipster.

Clue #5. (And this should be enough.) My passion, as a few slow readers may have realized by now, is to destroy stereotypes, categories, and labels. So Candidate X who has never been considered (to my knowledge) as a political candidate for anything, by either party—as indeed was once true of Eisenhower—is nonetheless an important figure in American life. To a degree he has affected the style of American manners. If he were drafted as a candidate, the emanations of his personality might loosen the lugubrious rhetorical daisy-chains of liberal argument which so deaden the air about all these Demo-bureaucratic candidates.

The rest of this column I wish to give over to a little talk about politics, most of which will be, as usual, in the first person. I have not voted since 1948, and I doubt if I will vote in 1956 even if by some fantastic mischance, Candidate X would be drafted. (My sole motive in all this is to look for a good time. I want the next Presidential campaign to be an interesting circus, rather than the dreary set of opposed commercials it now promises to be.)

Still, most of you will be taking your vote seriously, and to go on like this is only to offend you further. Most people, given their massage by propaganda, believe that a man who doesn't vote is a little lower than a man who beats his mother, or to be more psychically exact, a son who strikes his father. And perhaps even the Mailer would come off his mountain long enough to vote, if he felt any confidence that the Republican or Democratic party was relatively the least bit more effective—for a given year—at going in historical directions one might think to be encouraging. But the curious contradictions of power and party politics are such, that if I were to vote on this principle, I would be forced ever so slightly toward the Republicans. Not because I like them, mind you—I rather dislike them, they are such unconscionable hypocrites. Yet the disagreeable fact of power in these politically depressed years—like it or leave it—is that the Republican Party is a little more free to act, precisely because it does not have to be afraid of the Republicans, whereas the Democrats do.

I know this is unpleasant to all of you who believe that truth and un-truth are separate, but then I have no particular desire to bring you pleasure. The antitheses of power are such today that I believe the party in power must adopt the opposite in office of what it announced as its desires when it was out of power. It is metaphorically similar to the change in personality which you may have noticed in some of your friends who came to marriage after living together for years.

Column Twelve

Yes, it may seem a trifle fantastic at the first approach, but the man I think the Democrats ought to draft for their Presidential candidate in 1956 is Ernest Hemingway.

To begin with, the Democratic Party has the poorest of chances against Eisenhower, and whether it be Stevenson, Kefauver, or some other political half-worthy, the candidate's personality would suffer from his unfortunate resemblance to a prosperous undertaker. There is no getting around it—the American people tend to vote for the candidate who gives off the impression of having experienced some pleasure in his life, and Eisenhower, whatever his passive vicissitudes, looks like he has had a good time now and again.

Hemingway, I would guess, possesses exactly that kind of charm, possesses it in greater degree than Eisenhower, and so he would have some outside chance to win.

Another of Hemingway's political virtues is that he has an interesting war record, and that he succeeded in becoming a man of more physical courage than most—and this is no easy nor unexhausting attainment for a major writer. Whether the Village will like it or not, most Americans like warriors, indeed so much that they have been ready to swallow the bitter pill of an Army General in office. Yet I think they are not so far submerged into the hopeless conformity which plagues us, as to ignore the independent initiative of a General-at-liberty like Hemingway, who came so close to taking Paris in the last war with only a few hundred men.

Again, Hemingway might be inclined to speak simply, and so far as politics goes, freshly, and the energy this would arouse in the minds of the electorate, benumbed at present by the turgid Latinisms of the Kefauvers, the Stevensons, and the Eisenhowers, is something one should not underestimate, for almost never has the electorate been given the opportunity to have their minds stimulated.

Finally, Hemingway's lack of a previous political life is an asset, I would argue, rather than a vice. Politics has become static in America, and Americans have always distrusted politicians. (Which distrust indeed accounts for a great deal of Eisenhower's original appeal.) The glimmer of hope on all our murky horizons is that civilization may be coming to the point where we will return to voting for individual men (or individual women) rather than for political ideas, those political ideas which eventually are cemented into the social network of life as a betrayal of the individual desires which gave birth to them—for society, I will argue, on the day I get the wit, is the assassin of us all.

The above is for people who like a point-by-point discussion. What it comes down to by rebel rule-of-Hip is that Hemingway is probably a good bit more human than Eisenhower or the others, and so there might be a touch more color in our Roman Empire. More than that is unfair to expect of any President.

Now, for those who believe that a nominating speech must have a little warmth, and even—I tighten my stomach for this—a little sentimentality, I suppose I ought to go on to say that Hemingway is one of the few people in our national life who has tried to live with a certain passion for capturing what he desired, and I believe he indeed succeeded in earning a degree of the self-respect for which he has always searched, and yet at the same time he was able, with what writing pains only another serious writer (good or not) can know, to write his novels as well; and so no matter what his faults of character, and they must be many, I have the feeling that he probably has achieved a considerable part of his dream—which was to be more man than most—and this country could stand a man for President, since for all too many years our lives have been guided by men who were essentially women, which indeed is good for neither men nor women. So, to me, Ernest Hemingway looks like the best practical possibility in sight, because with all his sad and silly vanities, and some of his intellectual cowardices, I suspect that he's still more real than most, you know?

P. S. Since my endorsement can only cause Hemingway various small harms, I promise to any Democratic Party leader who hears of this, and is wise enough to see the political sex appeal of drafting Ernest Hemingway, that I will devote my political time to attacking old Hemingway for whatever small number of voters I will influence by reverse English to vote for him. You see, friends and constituents of this paper, one advantage of being a village villain is that one is always certain of influencing events by arguing the opposite of what one really wants.

Column Thirteen

LETTER TO THE VOICE

I do not admire your column. But I shall in a constructive spirit offer a few words of criticism.

You take up 98 per cent of the column talking about yourself. Very wrong.

The pronoun "I" occurs 26 times, "me" 5 times, "my" 8 times, "I'm" 3 times, "I'll" one time. Total times of reference to yourself: 43. Anyone who did not know what a swell guy you are might think you were in love with yourself . . .

[Why don't you have] a little favorable review of some one of the multitude who never get their names in print—but without having recourse to that patronizing air of a great man condescending to say something nice about one of the "common herd." These "common" men and women feel very deeply about such things and can be made lifelong friends. If you do not think you need friends, there is no sense in talking to you at all. Yours,

—Karl L. Ekstrand
Queens Village, New York

REPLY
Dear Mr. Ekstrand: I really do have a poor character. Wouldn't it be dishonest and a fraud on the public, as well as deeply un-American, to present myself as better than I am? Let others profit by my unseemly self-absorption, and so look to improve their own characters.

N.M.

Column Sixteen: The Hip and the Square

To a Square, a rapist is a rapist. Punish the rapist, imprison him, be horrified by him and/or disinterested in him, and that is the end of the matter. But a hipster knows that the act of rape is a part of life too, and that even in the most brutal and unforgivable rape, there is artistry or the lack of it, real desire or cold compulsion, and so no two rapists nor no two rapes are ever the same.

Hip is an exploration into the nature of man, and its emphasis is on the Self rather than Society. As one of the neo-Medieval philosophies which the agony of the twentieth century is bringing to birth, the ultimate tendency of Hip is to return man to the center of the universe rather than to continue his reduction into less and less of a biochemical mechanism placed in some insignificant corner of the rational and material universe which we have inherited from the nineteenth century. Moreover, Hip is an American existentialism, profoundly different from French existentialism because Hip is based on a mysticism of the flesh, and its origins can be traced back into all the undercurrents and underworlds of American life, back into the instinctive apprehension and appreciation of existence which one finds in the Negro and the soldier, in the criminal psychopath and the dope addict and jazz musician, in the prostitute, in the actor, in the—if one can visualize such a possibility—in the marriage of the call-girl and the psychoanalyst. Unlike the rationality of French existentialism, which has its point of inauguration in the work of Sartre, Hip is an American phenomenon, and it has come into being without an intellectual mentor. It is a language to describe states of being which is as yet without its philosophical dictionary.

Yet, Hip as a philosophy is still metaphorically at the back of the body, it is passive, it is the all-but-despairing philosophy of all the sensitive congeries of the defeated, the isolated, the violent, the tortured, and the warped, and so it is still a vast human and historical distance from the philosophy which may follow it, a philosophy which may be imbedded some day in a four-letter word so famous and infamous that this newspaper would be destroyed if I were to put it into print.

So, passive, despairing, a philosophical yeast which has arisen almost spontaneously out of the very conditions of existence of so many of the alienated in America, Hip with its special and intense awareness of the present tense in life, is I believe one of the philosophies of the future—assuming we have a future—and because Hip is not totally negative, and has a view of life which is predicated on growth and the nuisances of growth, I intend to continue writing about it for at least the next few weeks.

Column Seventeen

I have not seen "Waiting for Godot" nor read the text, but of course I have come across a good many reviews of it, and heard more than a little in its favor and disfavor. What amuses me is the deference with which everyone is approaching Beckett, and the fault of course, the part which is sad, is that none of the celebrators of Beckett have learned anything from Joyce (for whom Beckett worked as a secretary). By this I do not mean that one has to read all of Joyce to understand the style of Joyce's mind and the dialectical beauties of his spirit. But so far, it has been mainly the academicians who have attempted to grapple with the Hip intricacies of Joyce's mysticism of the flesh as it suffered and was mutilated and elaborated against the social anvil of Christianity.

Nor do I mean that I am an expert on Joyce—like many of you who will read this, I have read perhaps half of "Ulysses" and fragments from "Finnegan's Wake"—but then it is not necessary to read all of Joyce in order to feel or not feel the meaning of his language and the reach of his genius. He is after all the only genius of the twentieth century who has written in the English language.

But at the very least, the critics could have done a little rudimentary investigation into the meaning of the title of "Waiting for Godot," and the best they have been able to come up with so far is that Godot has something to do with God. My congratulations. But Godot also means 'ot Dog, or the dog who is hot, and it means God-O, God as the female principle, just as Daddy-O in Hip means the father who has failed, the man who has become an O, a vagina. Two obvious dialectical transpositions on "Waiting for Godot" are To Dog The Coming, and God Hot for Waiting, but anyone who has the Joycean habit of thought could add a hundred subsidiary themes. As for example on Go, Dough! (Go, Life!)

Nonetheless, I like To Dog The Coming as the best, because what I smell in all of this is that "Waiting for Godot" is a poem to impotence, and I suspect (again out of the ignorance of not having seen it) that Beckett sees man as hopelessly impotent, and the human condition as equally impotent. Given the caliber of the people who have applauded "Waiting for Godot," I further suspect that the complex structures of the play and its view of life are most attractive to those who are most impotent. So I doubt if I will like it, because finally not everyone is impotent, nor is our final fate, our human condition, necessarily doomed to impotence, as old Joyce knew, and Beckett I suspect does not. When it comes to calling a work great one must first live with the incommensurable nuance of the potent major key and the impotent minor key.

Now, to make a most brutal transition, nearly all of the rest of this column is deeply depressing for me to write:

THE NUISANCES OF GROWTH

Errors in type-setting and proof-reading fall into two categories—those which are obvious mis-spellings, and those (more serious and more interesting psychologically) where a word is left out or changed into another, and the meaning of the sentence thereby becomes altered. Yet the reader never knows that an error was made.

Last week a classic of this sort occurred. Writing about Hip, part of my final sentence was supposed to read:

> . . . because Hip is not totally negative, and has a view of life which is predicated on growth and the nuances of growth, I intend to continue writing about it. . . .

As it appeared in The Voice, it read:

> . . . because Hip is not totally negative, and has a
> view of life which is predicated on growth and the
> nuisances of growth, I intend to continue writing
> about it. . . .

In the four months I have been writing this column, similar
(for me) grievous errors have cropped up in all but two of the
pieces I have written, and these errors have made for steadily increasing friction between the Editor, an Associate Editor, and myself. Since no cliché is more true than that there are two sides to
every story, the Editor and Associate Editor, who are hard-working
gentlemen, claimed that the fault was due to the fact that I am in
the habit of turning in my column at the last minute, which undeniably increases their difficulties.

At any rate, we all had some words, some fairly sharp words,
certain things were said which can hardly be unsaid, and the result
is that this is to be my last column for The Voice—at least under
its present policy.

Now, the quarrel was actually trivial, and I can take most of
the blame for the way it went, but as happens so often, we were all
of us at bottom arguing about something else—a much more serious
difference of opinion which I have had with the Editor and Publisher.

They wish this newspaper to be more conservative, more
Square—I wish it to be more Hip. We have compromised our
differences for many weeks as best we could, and The Voice has
perhaps suffered from the compromise. But, at present, since I am
a minority stockholder and have no real voice in the control of
anything except my column, I have decided that this contradictory
association can go on no longer. If the paper is to become anything
at all, it is necessary that I step out, for too many energies are being
wasted in internal disputes. (Let me add that these disputes were
not about my column. Although the Editor and Publisher agreed
with very little in it, they allowed or submitted to a most rare
freedom of the press.)

For those of you who are Hip and wish The Voice to be a
Hip newspaper (which would make it the first in New York) I
think I ought to add that the Editor and Publisher are very
responsive to their readers' opinions, and if you make yourself
heard, this newspaper will reflect your influence. If you do not,
then the Editor and Publisher will prove to have been right—to

317

have made a better objective estimate of the situation and of what interests readers—and so the fortunes of this newspaper will prosper more without me than with me. Perhaps there is room in Greenwich Village for two community newspapers—which has been their contention all along.

At any rate, this is a farewell column, and I for one am sorry it had to come to an end so abruptly. We may not have had the most pleasant of relationships, but it has been stimulating for me, and perhaps stimulating for some of you. I regret only that it became impossible to go on writing about the nature of The Hip and the Square, for that was fascinating to me, and I had finally found the subject (yes, after all these columns) which I wished to explore. So, regretfully, good-bye for awhile. I wonder in which form some of us will swing into communication again.

ENCORE

As a last fillip, I would like to print here the only poem I have ever written, a poem about potency and impotence (as well as other things), which is called "The Drunk's Bebop and Chowder," and appeared in my novel, "The Deer Park." Let us see how many typos there are in this. If there aren't too many, try reading it aloud.

Shirred athe inlechercent felloine namelled Shash
Head tea lechnocerous hero calmed Asshy

Befwen hes prunt cuddlenot riles fora lash
Whenfr hir cunck woodled lyars affordelay?

"Yi munt seech tyt und speets tytsh"
"I-uh wost tease toty ant tweeks tlotty"

"And/or atuftit n pladease slit,"
"N ranty off itty indisplacent,"

"Frince Yrhome washt balostilted ina laydy."
"Sinfor her romesnot was lowbilt inarouter dayly."

ADVERTISEMENT FOR THE END OF A COLUMN AND A PUBLIC NOTICE

Two days after I quit the paper I read Waiting For Godot. *I did not like it on the first reading, but I was uneasy, so I went to see the play. It was not a happy production, yet something of Beckett's art could still be glimpsed through the warp of a Broadway mounting, and I was sick in all depression on the way home. "Baby," said my wife not so softly, "you fucked up."*

The general read the play again. It was, at the least, very good. He could not quit the paper without one last raid on the mind of the Village. Calling on some forced assembly of the whipped energies, finally putting together what had been learned in seventeen weeks, the general spoke from his self-conceived island of exile, a farewell address to his disenchanted troops—the hero finally allowed himself the freedom from calculation of a writer's white heat, and he wrote a three-thousand-word advertisement in a day and a half, and he paid his cash for it.

The piece was sloppy, marred by heavy language, elliptic in its jumps, and open to error—one even called the Montgomery bus strike the Birmingham bus strike—but toward the end, the writing broke into the free, and in the last five paragraphs of the last piece I did for The Voice, *from the place where I begin, "For I believe Beckett is also saying . . . that God's destiny is flesh and blood with ours," I finally found what I had been trying to write about. A most elevated moment for the undeserving. It gave a hint not everything need end in defeat, and through the months which followed, the hint was sometimes ready to remind one that the career was not necessarily dead, that one was still perhaps a novelist, and if the cost had been not cheap, there had been offered in exchange a fine novelistic education in such subjects as ambition, failure, office politics, the economics of small business, loss, disorder, and how it feels to be a club fighter in an off-year.*

A PUBLIC NOTICE ON WAITING FOR GODOT

It is never particularly pleasant for me to apologize, and in the present circumstances I loathe doing so. To announce a farewell appearance and then be on the scene again the following week is to ooze all the ebbing charm and reeking sweat of the desperate old actor or the failing middle-aged bullfighter who simply cannot let go, cannot disappear, even if it is for no more than to hear some new catcalls, and conceivably get gored.

Since I have my pride, I would have preferred to keep my word and not appear again in this newspaper unless and until its general policy would change. But I have a duty to my honesty as well, and I did something of which I am ashamed, and so must apologize in the hardest but most meaningful way:—by public advertisement.

I am referring of course to what I wrote about "Waiting for Godot" in my last column. Some of you may remember that I said Beckett's play was a poem to impotence and appealed precisely to those who were most impotent. Since then I have read the play, seen the present Broadway production, read the play again, have thought about it, wrestled with its obscurities (and my conscience), and have had to come up reluctantly with the conviction that I was most unfair to Beckett. Because "Waiting for Godot" is a play about impotence rather than an ode to it, and while its view of life is indeed hopeless, it is an art work, and therefore, I believe, a good. While I still think it is essentially the work of a minor artist because its range of life-experience is narrow if deep, it is all the same, whether major or minor, the work of a man who has conscientiously and with great purity made the uncompromising effort to abstract his view of life into an art work, no matter how unbearable that view of life may be. It is bad enough and sad enough when the critics of any given time attack an artist and fail to understand him, but then this is virtually to be taken for granted. For one artist to attack another, however, and to do it on impulse, is a crime, and for the first time in months I have been walking around with a very clear sense of guilt.

320

Oddly enough, in superficial ways, and without reading "Godot," I was on the target in what I wrote last week. As I type this now—it is Sunday—there is an interview with Samuel Beckett in the Times drama section written by Israel Shenker, and I wish to quote from it. Beckett says at one point:

"The kind of work I do is one in which I'm not master of my material. The more Joyce knew the more he could. He's tending toward omniscience and omnipotence as an artist. I'm working with impotence, ignorance. I don't think impotence has been exploited in the past. There seems to be a kind of aesthetic axiom that expression is an achievement—must be an achievement. My little exploration is that whole zone of being that has always been set aside by artists as something unuseable—as something by definition incompatible with art.

"I think anyone nowadays who pays the slightest attention to his own experience finds it the experience of a non-knower, a non-can-er (somebody who cannot). The other type of artist—the Apollonian—is absolutely foreign to me."

Fair enough and honest enough—it elicits one's respect. What still distresses me and distresses Beckett as well, I would guess, is that "Godot" has become the latest touchstone in social chi-chi, and people who don't have the faintest idea of what he is talking about, and who as they watch the play, scream and gurgle and expire with a kind of militant exacerbated snobbery, are exactly the majority of people who have promoted "Godot" here. Because not to like "Waiting for Godot" is to suffer damnation—one is no longer chic.

> (As a long parenthesis, I must add that it is impossible to understand the play without reading it, because the present production is in my opinion abominable: insensitive, hammy, sentimental, and pretentious in every wrong way—the acting is equally misleading. Only Alvin Epstein who plays Lucky gives an exciting and illuminating performance—the other actors merely flatten characterization into caricature.)

Most of the present admirers of "Godot" are, I believe, snobs, intellectual snobs of undue ambition and impotent imagination, the worst sort of literary type, invariably more interested in being part of some intellectual elite than in the creative act itself. This combination almost always coincides with a sex-hater, for if one is ashamed of sex or is unhappy with sex, then the next best thing is to rise in the social world. But since people with poor sexual range seldom have the energy and the courage to rise imaginatively or defiantly, they obligatorily give themselves to the escalator of the snob which is slow but ultimately sure of some limited social ascension.

And for these reasons I assumed in advance that "Godot" was essentially and deeply anti-sexual, and I was wrong. It has almost no sexual hope within it, but that is its lament, that is Beckett's grief, and the comic tenderness of the story comes from the resignation of that grief. So far as it is a story, it is a sad little story, but told purely.

Two men, two vagabonds, named Vladimir and Estragon (Didi and Gogo), a male and female homosexual, old and exhausted, have come to rest temporarily on a timeless plain, presided over by a withered cross-like tree, marooned in the purgatory of their failing powers. Their memories have become uncertain as vapors, their spirits are broken, they cannot even make love to each other any longer, they can only bicker and weep and nag and sulk and sleep, they are beyond sex, really neither old men nor old women but debilitated children looking for God, looking for the Life-Giver. They are so desperate they even speak wanly of hanging themselves, because this at least will give them one last erection. But they have not the power to commit suicide, they are exhausted and addled by the frustration of their failures to the point where they cannot even commit a despairing action. They can only wait for Godot, and they speculate feebly about his nature, for Godot is a mystery to them, and after all they desire not only sex and rebirth into life, but worldly power as well. They are looking for the potency of the phallus and the testes. Vladimir speaks of the Saviour and the Two Thieves, and how one of the thieves was saved. The implication is that since he and Gogo are withered puff-balls, balls blown passively through life, opportunistic and aimless as small thieves, perhaps one of them and only one may be saved, and he is tempted: perhaps he is the one. Which would be of course at the expense of his life-mate Gogo. So in the religious sense he is not even pure in his despair, but is already tempted into Sin.

Enter Pozzo and Lucky: Pozzo the fat gentleman with the whip and the rope around the neck of Lucky his slave, his wretch, the being at the mercy of his will. Pozzo dominates Lucky, abuses him, commands him about like a cruel brain abusing its own body.

And Vladimir has his opportunity for action, he can rescue Lucky, indeed he protests at the treatment of Lucky. But Vladimir, like Gogo, is seduced by the worldly power of Pozzo, and finally the two vagabonds collaborate in torturing Lucky, or at the very least in aiding Pozzo to beat Lucky into unconsciousness at the end of his single impassioned speech.

Thereafter, the action (what there is of it) descends, and when Pozzo and Lucky reappear, Pozzo is blind and Lucky is dumb —we will hear his wisdom no longer. Their condition is even more debased than Gogo's and Didi's. But for some will remain the echo of Lucky's speech.

It is the one strangled cry of active meaning in the whole play, a desperate retching pellmell of broken thoughts and intuitive lunges into the nature of man, sex, God, and time, it comes from a slave, a wretch, who is closer to the divine than any of the other characters, it is a cry across the abyss from impotence to Apollo (Dionysus is indeed quite beyond the horizon) and Pozzo, Gogo and Didi answer the cry by beating Lucky into unconsciousness. Thereafter, Lucky—the voice, the midwife, to the rebirth of the others—is stricken dumb, for he too suffers from failing powers, he too is overcome by the succession of his defeats and so brought closer to death. Later, much later, at the end of the play, Vladimir talks to the boy who brings the message that Godot will not come that day, and as Vladimir questions him about Godot, the boy says that Godot has a white beard. But Lucky, who has a head of white hair, had begun his speech (which again is the intellectual lock and key of the play) by talking of "a personal God quaquaquaqua with white beard . . ." exactly the speech which the others had destroyed. So Vladimir has a moment of agony: "Christ have mercy on us!" he says to the boy. Through vanity, through cupidity, through indifference, through snobbery itself, Vladimir and Gogo have lost the opportunity to find Godot —they have abused the link which is Lucky. (I must say that I am not altogether unconvinced that Lucky himself may be Godot—it is, at the least, a possibility.) At any rate, Vladimir and Gogo have failed still again, their condition is even more desperate, and so the play ends. "Yes, let's go," says Gogo in the final line, but Beckett follows with the stage direction: "They do not move. Curtain."

It is possible that consciously or unconsciously Beckett is restating the moral and sexual basis of Christianity which was lost with Christ—that one finds life by kissing the feet of the poor, by giving of oneself to the most debased corners of the most degraded, that as the human condition in the world is to strive, no matter how cruelly, to rise to the top, so life and strength come from adoring the bottom for that is where God conceals himself.

Yet, there is another and richer possibility. For I believe Beckett is also saying, again consciously or unconsciously, that God's destiny is flesh and blood with ours, and so, far from conceiving of a God who sits in judgment and allows souls, lost souls, to leave purgatory and be reborn again, there is the greater agony of God at the mercy of man's fate, God determined by man's efforts, man who has free will and can no longer exercise it and God therefore in bondage to the result of man's efforts. At the end, Vladimir and Gogo having failed again, there is the hint, the murmur, that God's condition is also worse, and he too has come closer to failure—when Vladimir asks the boy in the closing minutes of the play what Godot does, the boy answers: "He does nothing, Sir." Godot, by implication, lives in the same condition, the same spiritual insomnia, agony, limbo, the same despair of one's fading powers which has hung over the play.

As a description of the nadir of the twentieth century, the play whether destined to be prophetic or a curiosity is at least the pure end of a tendency—its total lack of hope is salutory if one demands that art works be salutory, for like the notorious black canvas of Clifford Styll which was hung at the Museum of Modern Art in the 15 Modern Americans show a few years ago, the end of a particular road has been reached, indeed the tendency has been accelerated by the artist, and so once again time has been accelerated by the artist (for perhaps the most intense and dedicated of the artist's purposes is to accelerate historical time itself). The velocity of history is made by the rate of increase of human consciousness, *provided* that consciousness can express itself in action and so alter society. (For where consciousness cannot be supported by the courage to make one's action, then consciousness lapses into despair and death.)

Beckett's work brings our despair to the surface, it nourishes it with air, and therefore alters it, for the despair of the 20th century is that man's consciousness has increased at an incredible rate and yet his capacity to alter history, to make change, has never been more impotent. So the last ten years have been part of the vast cramp of our history, that cramp which will reduce us all to angry impotence (otherwise known as false sweetness) or cowardly passivity (the passivity of the creep who absorbs and does not give back) that cramp which will finally destroy Will and Consciousness and Courage and leave us in the fog of failing memory, expiring desire, and the vocation for death.

But I wonder if we have not passed through the bottom of the nadir already. I know that for myself, after years of the most intense pessimism, I feel the hints, the clues, the whispers of a new time coming. There is a universal rebellion in the air, and the power of the two colossal super-states may be, yes, may just be ebbing, may be failing in energy even more rapidly than we are failing in energy, and if that is so, then the destructive, the liberating, the creative nihilism of the Hip, the frantic search for potent Change may break into the open with all its violence, its confusion, its ugliness and horror, and yet like all Change, the violence is better without than within, better as individual actions than as the collective murders of society, and if we have courage enough, there is beauty beneath, for the only revolution which will be meaningful and natural for the 20th Century will be the sexual revolution one senses everywhere, everywhere from the cheapest television comedian straining at his dirty leash to the mysterious and exciting phenomenon of the White South terrified of the Birmingham bus strike and the growing power of the Negro,—everywhere, including the comic feminization of what had been once the iron commissars of the Soviet superstate.

Man's nature, man's dignity, is that he acts, lives, loves, and finally destroys himself seeking to penetrate the mystery of existence, and unless we partake in some way, as some part of this human exploration (and war) then we are no more than the pimps of society and the betrayers of our Self.

1956

LETTERS TO THE VOICE

Dear Sir:
Without Norman Mailer there is no Village Voice.
—Penny Funt
East 10th Street

325

VOTER

This to to say that I am for a more Hip newspaper.

—Ben Newman
Washington Place

SMALL TOWN

Dear Sir:

Man you goofed—but really goofcd. You will feature articles written by Yahoo the Yak and newsy items concerning the Schmidlapps' daughter Sophronia spending a week's vacation home from Schlepp State Teachers College. But The Village Voice without Mailer is merely a smalltown newspaper with amusing pretensions.

—Joan Lorraine Smith
Bedford Street

RICHER

Dear Sir:

The Voice is richer for the loss of the castrated bellow of N. Mailer. That the author of "Naked and the Dead" deteriorated to a point where he wrote such undisciplined gibberish is pitiful.

Once I was a Mailer admirer. Now I feel like putting a quarter in his tin cup and saying a prayer over his departed literary genius.

—A. Kent MacDougall
West 112th Street

INDICATIVE

Dear Sir:

The typo, "nuisances of growth," was fairly indicative of what happened. It *is* one of the nuisances of growth that would lead you to question the value of his column. You are in danger of becoming a success, so you panic at the thought of not being another stale formula. You would be well advised to ask yourself: Why is the paper becoming successful?

Rest assured, the predictableness of your other pages more than balance anything fresh or stimulating that Mr. Mailer or Mr. Tucci may dream up. If you don't like that kind of thought and writing, why don't you give *them* the paper and take a job on

Madison Avenue, where you would probably feel more at home and make as much money, too?

—Maxwell Kenton
West 23rd Street

WHEN THE CHIPS WERE DOWN

Dear Sir:
To Mr. Mailer:

Let me say I am extremely sorry your May 2 column is your final one. In all your columns, while some were so damned aggravating (and why shouldn't they have been), what you did say, in essence, when the decorations were dismissed, and when the chips were down, was true and truly strong and original to read. Sincerely,

—Joe Jensen,
Bank Street

POSTSCRIPT TO A PUBLIC NOTICE

The Voice has had an interesting history since I left it, and has settled by now into a literate, civilized, liberal and occasionally unpredictable paper. I doubt if there is a weekly sheet in the country which is as good to read, for there must be several hundred people in the Village who are capable of a thousand or less words of first-rate prose every now and again. It has also been the first paper to use the considerable talents of Jules Feiffer whose cartoon Sick, Sick, Sick gave a focus to The Voice.

Still, the paper is not yet the voice of anything larger than a cultivated and politely rebellious sense of new taste. Where it will go now is still as much a question as it was the day I ended my column. What can be suspected is that Hip continues to grow as an underground force, The Voice will go with it, for the paper inhabits part of the foreground.

PART 4 Hipsters

SIXTH ADVERTISEMENT FOR MYSELF:

After I left The Voice, *I knew it was time to clean myself up. I had a novel in me, the novel which I have talked about in these prefaces, but if I were ever to do it, I had to start the slow and not encouraging work of learning how to work all over again.*

We had been in Paris for a while, and I had stripped a few of my habits, seconal and benzedrine at any rate, but I was also tense and brain-deadened from ten weeks of withdrawal. When we returned to New York, the city was not alive for me. I was on edge. My wife was pregnant. It seemed abruptly too punishing to live at the pace we had been going for several years. So we found a house in the country. Before it lost novelty and New York became attractive again, we each did fair work there. In those two years I worked slowly, but I did write "The White Negro," sixty pages of my novel, some of the new writing in this book, and I made a play out of The Deer Park. *Talk of such work, however, can come later. I have been leading toward an exchange of letters I had with William Faulkner through a friend.*

When I first went to the country, I decided to cut out cigarettes. I had made an attempt or two in New York, yet always went back after a few weeks—when one smokes forty cigarettes a day, it is not much easier to quit nicotine than heroin. But I was doing some boxing now. My father-in-law had been a professional; he was always putting on the gloves with me. I thought it might not be so bad to get into condition. So I fought with ambition, greed, tension, new violence, new passivity, and did without cigarettes for four months. In that time, I blew up to one hundred and seventy-five pounds, but I was in nice shape, and my senses were alert, I was liking a hundred things I had not liked before; it was the first time in the two years I had been traveling on marijuana that I could feel as if I might be gathering force instead of dissipating it. Everything was good, exctpt that I could not write; my mind would have fine moments, but its powers of connection were dim; my brain seemed stuffed in cotton.

It was the first pause I had had in years, and it seemed to me that I was punch-drunk. In company I felt stupid; when my mind would try to work, there were gaps in the link of my associations. I thought I might now be paying for the years I had twisted my nerves with benzedrine and seconal. At times it would come over me that I could not keep away from writing much longer, and I began to live with the conviction that I had burned out my talent.

It was on this scene that I had Lyle Stuart for a weekend visit. We were arguing one night about how much freedom there was in the mass-media. Stuart was more optimistic than me, and said in passing that there was no idea he would not print in his monthly newspaper, The Independent. *I countered by saying that if I were to work up half a page about what I thought of integration in the schools, he might print it, but no large newspaper would ever pick it up.*

"Write it, and we'll find out," Stuart answered.

I wrote a few words before I went to bed that night. They were brutal with undressed assertion. I felt I had to say what I knew to say in language so ugly it could not be ignored. Staggering for each word with the thick tongue of a nicotine addict deprived of his drug, I came up with this:

> Can't we have some honesty about what's going on now in the South? Everybody who knows the South knows that the white man fears the sexual potency of the Negro. And in turn the Negro has been storing his hatred and yet growing stronger, carrying with him the painful wound that he was usually powerless to keep from being cuckolded.
>
> For the white, symbolically and materially, has possessed Negro womanhood for two centuries. Which is what all the literary critics mean when they talk about the blood guilt of the South.
>
> The comedy is that the white loathes the idea of the Negro attaining equality in the classroom because the white feels that the Negro already enjoys sensual superiority. So the white unconsciously feels that the balance has been kept, that the old arrangement was fair. The Negro had his sexual supremacy and the white had his white supremacy.
>
> By this logic, the unconscious logic of the Southern white, it is fatal to give the Negro equality because that is the same as to give him victory. And like all poor winners and small losers the Southern whites are unwilling to accept the reversals of history, even though the flower-

ing of the Negro and the temporary but nonetheless certain spiritual enslavement of the Southern white ought to be nourishing for both races—not to mention the moral justice of it.

Stuart was pleased. He was sure the news services would do something with it. We made our bet, and Lyle Stuart took my presidential message home with him.

Stuart is first-rate as a journalist, and before he went further, he had the instinct to send my words to Faulkner who chose to answer briefly. Faulkner wrote:

> I have heard this idea expressed several times during the last twenty years, though not before by a man.
> The others were ladies, northern or middle western ladies, usually around 40 or 45 years of age. I don't know what a psychiatrist would find in this.

I did not laugh so very much when I read this. My words may have been badly chosen, but they were not that easy to put into print. I wrote an answer:

> Like many novelists who have created an extraordinary body of work, Mr. Faulkner is a timid man who has led a sheltered life. So I would not be surprised if he has had his best and most intense conversations with sensitive middle-aged ladies.

If I had left it there, it would have been all right, but of course I was rusty with no writing, and scuffled on to take the showboat. Still, I might as well stand by it—I'm not so certain it doesn't have a bit of truth in it.

> I think it is interesting and attractive that they hold such ideas because I heard "my" ideas expressed in one form or another by a most intelligent Negro car-washer in Queens, a mulatto sneak-thief and pimp who was a friend of some friends of mine, and lastly by a rather remarkable woman who had been the madam of a whorehouse in South Carolina, had sold dope in Harlem to keep afloat, and somehow succeeded in raising her family and passing into a life-loving middle age.
> She was no saint, this woman, she was even downright treacherous upon one occasion, but I would tend to trust her sense of Negro-White relations in the South sooner than Mr. Faulkner's.
> I'm a bit surprised that William Faulkner should think a psychiatrist could ever understand a writer.

Armed with this exchange, Stuart sent copies of our letters to a number of people, and received replies from Eleanor Roosevelt, Dr. W. E. B. DuBois, William Bradford Huie, George Sylvester Viereck, Murray Kempton, and a few others. An unidentified "prominent Negro leader" (I quote from Stuart's piece in The Independent, *March 1957*) *"explained that he could not comment publicly but felt that 'Of course Mailer is one-hundred per cent correct.'"*

Eleanor Roosevelt sent in this line:

I think Mr. Mailer's statement is horrible and unnecessary.

It occurred to me that this may have been the first time Mrs. Roosevelt had used the word "horrible" in print.

William Bradford Huie wrote a long reply to the general effect that I was a commercial novelist and sex was good for my business so of course I would think the way I did.

Most of the others were dismayed, critical, moderate, and/or liberal—Kempton, a columnist for the N.Y. Post *was certain sex was not the center of the Southern dilemma and almost drew a reply when he said in passing, "I don't think Mailer has anything more than a reading knowledge of the South." I was tempted to remind him that I served in the Pacific with a Texas outfit, the 112th Cavalry, composed by the time I joined it of Texans, Southerners, and a few others. (Indeed, anyone looking for a fairly close portrait of that outfit is invited to read* The Day the Century Ended *—in pocketbook called* Between Heaven and Hell *—by an Arkansawyer who has been a good friend, Francis Irby Gwaltney.)*

Stuart sent the various comments to the editors of six Southern newspapers, and they did not say a word, nor print a line. No news-service picked up the story. The only reference to it was a diatribe in some Mississippi paper which neglected to mention what I had said, it merely indicated that it had been awful.

All the same, I was feeling uneasy about my motives. My statement had been incendiary but unilluminating. I would have to do better, I would have to do a good deal better, because if I did not, I might lose one emotion and gain another, an exchange I was in fever to avoid, since the first emotion included no less than my faith that I was serious, that I was right, that my work would give more to others than it took from them.

As for the other emotion—the one I might be in danger of

acquiring—it was worse. It came down to no more than that I had been dismissed by a novelist who was to me a great writer, and in reflection from the ice of his few lines had been cast the light of how I would properly be seen if I could not flesh the bold loud air of my pronouncements with writing better than I had so far done. Like a latent image in the mirror of my ego was the other character Faulkner must have seen: a noisy pushy middling ape who had been tolerated too long by his literary betters. So I owe Faulkner the Biblical act of banishing me. Fearful of consequence, I had at last no choice but to begin the trip into the psychic wild of "The White Negro."

Before I wrote the piece, however, I happened to have a week in Mexico, a week as good as a good short novel for me, and I came out not altogether bad in my eyes. But I will not try to give even a hint of that time. Whatever proves to be alive for one's writing—love, violence, drugs, sex, loss, family, work, death, defeat, victory or something unimportant to anyone else—comes from those few moments which reach the psychic crossroads of the mind and there become a nucleus of new imagination. It is costly to strip such memory of its detail, for one loses the power to project the best of one's imagination out into a creative space larger than the items of one's life.

For whatever reason then, proper caution or incapacity, I must pass over that week in Mexico and the good weeks which followed, and mention only in passing the next month of depression and desperation in which I went back to smoking cigarettes and wrote "The White Negro." No more need be said of how it was done except that I wrote in the fear that I was no longer a writer. Since I have taken space in many of these Advertisements to talk of the faults of my pieces, it may be tonic here to say that "The White Negro" is one of the best things I have done, and if it is difficult to read, it is also I think worth attention. In "The White Negro," in "The Time of Her Time," and in "Advertisements For Myself on the Way Out" can be found the real end of this muted autobiography of the near-beat adventurer who was myself. With these three seeds, let us say the book has its end. Seed is an end, it is the end of the potentialities seen for oneself, and every organism creates its seed out of the experience of its past and its unspoken vision or curse upon the future. So a hint of the best and the worst of what really happened over the years of these advertisements may live in this last part which has nothing and everything to do with me.

Here, and with this, I find myself forced to bring to an end whatever trace of an autobiography has slipped into these advertisements. The writing which comes after "The White Negro" has been written too close to the present to permit any style in the telling of a personal memoir. The confession is over—I sense that to give any more of what happened to me in the last few years might make for five thousand good words, but could also strip me of fifty thousand better ones.

THE WHITE NEGRO

Superficial Reflections on the Hipster

Our search for the rebels of the generation led us to the hipster. The hipster is an *enfant terrible* turned inside out. In character with his time, he is trying to get back at the conformists by lying low . . . You can't interview a hipster because his main goal is to keep out of a society which, he thinks, is trying to make everyone over in its own image. He takes marijuana because it supplies him with experiences that can't be shared with "squares." He may affect a broad-brimmed hat or a zoot suit, but usually he prefers to skulk unmarked. The hipster may be a jazz musician; he is rarely an artist, almost never a writer. He may earn his living as a petty criminal, a hobo, a carnival roustabout or a free-lance moving man in Greenwich Village, but some hipsters have found a safe refuge in the upper income brackets as television comics or movie actors. (The late James Dean, for one, was a hipster hero.) . . . It is tempting to describe the hipster in psychiatric terms as infantile, but the style of his infantilism is a sign of the times. He does not try to enforce his will on others, Napoleon-fashion, but contents himself with a magical omnipotence never disproved because never tested. . . . As the only extreme nonconformist of his generation, he exercises a powerful if underground appeal for conformists, through newspaper accounts of his delinquencies, his structureless jazz, and his emotive grunt words.

—*"Born 1930: The Unlost Generation"*
by Caroline Bird
Harper's Bazaar, *Feb. 1957*

Probably, we will never be able to determine the psychic havoc of the concentration camps and the atom bomb upon the unconscious mind of almost everyone alive in these years. For the first time in civilized history, perhaps for the first time in all of history, we have been forced to live with the suppressed knowledge that the smallest facets of our personality or the most minor projection of our ideas, or indeed the absence of ideas and the absence of personality could mean equally well that we might still be doomed to die as a cipher in some vast statistical operation in which our teeth would be counted, and our hair would be saved, but our death itself would be unknown, unhonored, and unremarked, a death which could not follow with dignity as a possible consequence to serious actions we had chosen, but rather a death by *deus ex machina* in a gas chamber or a radioactive city; and so if in the midst of civilization—that civilization founded upon the Faustian urge to dominate nature by mastering time, mastering the links of social cause and effect—in the middle of an economic civilization founded upon the confidence that time could indeed be subjected to our will, our psyche was subjected itself to the intolerable anxiety that death being causeless, life was causeless as well, and time deprived of cause and effect had come to a stop.

The Second World War presented a mirror to the human condition which blinded anyone who looked into it. For if tens of millions were killed in concentration camps out of the inexorable agonies and contractions of super-states founded upon the always insoluble contradictions of injustice, one was then obliged also to see that no matter how crippled and perverted an image of man was the society he had created, it was nonetheless his creation, his collective creation (at least his collective creation from the past) and if society was so murderous, then who could ignore the most hideous of questions about his own nature?

Worse. One could hardly maintain the courage to be individual, to speak with one's own voice, for the years in which one could complacently accept oneself as part of an elite by being a radical were forever gone. A man knew that when he dissented, he gave a note upon his life which could be called in any year of overt crisis. No wonder then that these have been the years of conformity and depression. A stench of fear has come out of every pore of American life, and we suffer from a collective failure of nerve. The only courage, with rare exceptions, that we have been witness to, has been the isolated courage of isolated people.

2.

It is on this bleak scene that a phenomenon has appeared: the American existentialist—the hipster, the man who knows that if our collective condition is to live with instant death by atomic war, relatively quick death by the State as *l'univers concentrationnaire*, or with a slow death by conformity with every creative and rebellious instinct stifled (at what damage to the mind and the heart and the liver and the nerves no research foundation for cancer will discover in a hurry), if the fate of twentieth-century man is to live with death from adolescence to premature senescence, why then the only life-giving answer is to accept the terms of death, to live with death as immediate danger, to divorce oneself from society, to exist without roots, to set out on that uncharted journey into the rebellious imperatives of the self. In short, whether the life is criminal or not, the decision is to encourage the psychopath in oneself, to explore that domain of experience where security is boredom and therefore sickness, and one exists in the present, in that enormous present which is without past or future, memory or planned intention, the life where a man must go until he is beat, where he must gamble with his energies through all those small or large crises of courage and unforeseen situations which beset his day, where he must be with it or doomed not to swing. The unstated essence of Hip, its psychopathic brilliance, quivers with the knowledge that new kinds of victories increase one's power for new kinds of perception; and defeats, the wrong kind of defeats, attack the body and imprison one's energy until one is jailed in the prison air of other people's habits, other people's defeats, boredom, quiet desperation, and muted icy self-destroying rage. One is Hip or one is Square (the alternative which each new generation coming into American life is beginning to feel), one is a rebel or one conforms, one is a frontiersman in the Wild West of American night life, or else a Square cell, trapped in the totalitarian tissues of American society, doomed willy-nilly to conform if one is to succeed.

A totalitarian society makes enormous demands on the courage of men, and a partially totalitarian society makes even greater demands, for the general anxiety is greater. Indeed if one is to be a man, almost any kind of unconventional action often takes disproportionate courage. So it is no accident that the source of Hip is the Negro for he has been living on the margin between totalitarianism and democracy for two centuries. But the presence of Hip as a working philosophy in the sub-worlds of American life is probably due to jazz, and its knifelike entrance into culture, its subtle but so penetrating influence on an avant-garde generation—that postwar generation of adventurers who (some consciously, some by osmosis) had absorbed the lessons of disillusionment and disgust of the twenties, the depression, and the war. Sharing a collective disbelief in the words of men who had too much money and controlled too many things, they knew almost as powerful a disbelief in the socially monolithic ideas of the single mate, the solid family and the respectable love life. If the intellectual antecedents of this generation can be traced to such separate influences as D. H. Lawrence, Henry Miller, and Wilhelm Reich, the viable philosophy of Hemingway fit most of their facts: in a bad world, as he was to say over and over again (while taking time out from his parvenu snobbery and dedicated gourmandize), in a bad world there is no love nor mercy nor charity nor justice unless a man can keep his courage, and this indeed fitted some of the facts. What fitted the need of the adventurer even more precisely was Hemingway's categorical imperative that what made him feel good became therefore The Good.

So no wonder that in certain cities of America, in New York of course, and New Orleans, in Chicago and San Francisco and Los Angeles, in such American cities as Paris and Mexico, D.F., this particular part of a generation was attracted to what the Negro had to offer. In such places as Greenwich Village, a ménage-à-trois was completed—the bohemian and the juvenile delinquent came face-to-face with the Negro, and the hipster was a fact in American life. If marijuana was the wedding ring, the child was the language of Hip for its argot gave expression to abstract states of feeling which all could share, at least all who were Hip. And in this wedding of the white and the black it was the Negro who brought the cultural dowry. Any Negro who wishes to live must live with danger from his first day, and no experience can ever be casual to him, no Negro can saunter down a street with any real certainty that violence will not visit him on his walk. The cameos of security for the average white: mother and the home, job and the family, are not even a mockery to millions of Negroes; they are impossible. The Negro has the simplest of alternatives: live a life of constant humility or ever-threatening danger. In such a pass where paranoia is as vital to survival as blood, the Negro had stayed alive and begun to grow by following the need of his body where he could. Knowing in the cells of his existence that life was war, nothing but war, the Negro (all exceptions admitted) could rarely afford the sophisticated inhibitions of civilization, and so he kept for his survival the art of the primitive, he lived in the enormous present, he subsisted for his Saturday night kicks, relinquishing the pleasures of the mind for the more obligatory pleasures of the body, and in his music he gave voice to the character and quality of his existence, to his rage and the infinite variations of joy, lust, languor, growl, cramp, pinch, scream and despair of his orgasm. For jazz is orgasm, it is the music of orgasm, good orgasm and bad, and so it spoke across a nation, it had the communication of art even where it was watered, perverted, corrupted, and almost killed, it spoke in no matter what laundered popular way of instantaneous existential states to which some whites could respond, it was indeed a communication by art because it said, "I feel this, and now you do too."

So there was a new breed of adventurers, urban adventurers who drifted out at night looking for action with a black man's code to fit their facts. The hipster had absorbed the existentialist synapses of the Negro, and for practical purposes could be considered a white Negro.

To be an existentialist, one must be able to feel oneself— one must know one's desires, one's rages, one's anguish, one must be aware of the character of one's frustration and know what would satisfy it. The overcivilized man can be an existentialist only if it is chic, and deserts it quickly for the next chic. To be a real existentialist (Sartre admittedly to the contrary) one must be religious, one must have one's sense of the "purpose"—whatever the purpose may be—but a life which is directed by one's faith in the necessity of action is a life committed to the notion that the substratum of existence is the search, the end meaningful but mysterious; it is impossible to live such a life unless one's emotions provide their profound conviction. Only the French, alienated beyond alienation from their unconscious could welcome an existential philosophy without ever feeling it at all; indeed only a Frenchman by declaring that the unconscious did not exist could then proceed to explore the delicate involutions of consciousness, the microscopically sensuous and all but ineffable *frissons* of mental becoming, in order finally to create the theology of atheism and so submit that in a world of absurdities the existential absurdity is most coherent.

In the dialogue between the atheist and the mystic, the atheist is on the side of life, rational life, undialectical life—since he conceives of death as emptiness, he can, no matter how weary or despairing, wish for nothing but more life; his pride is that he does not transpose his weakness and spiritual fatigue into a romantic longing for death, for such appreciation of death is then all too capable of being elaborated by his imagination into a universe of meaningful structure and moral orchestration.

Yet this masculine argument can mean very little for the mystic. The mystic can accept the atheist's description of his weakness, he can agree that his mysticism was a response to despair. And yet . . . and yet his argument is that he, the mystic, is the one finally who has chosen to live with death, and so death is his experience and not the atheist's, and the atheist by eschewing the limitless dimensions of profound despair has rendered himself incapable to judge the experience. The real argument which the mystic must always advance is the very intensity of his private vision—his argument depends from the vision precisely because what was felt in the vision is so extraordinary that no rational argument, no hypotheses of "oceanic feelings" and certainly no skeptical reductions can explain away what has become for him the reality more real than the reality of closely reasoned logic. His inner experience of the possibilities within death is his logic. So, too, for the existentialist. And the psychopath. And the saint and the bullfighter and the lover. The common denominator for all of them is their burning consciousness of the present, exactly that incandescent consciousness which the possibilities within death has opened for them. There is a depth of desperation to the condition which enables one to remain in life only by engaging death, but the reward is their knowledge that what is happening at each instant of the electric present is good or bad for them, good or bad for their cause, their love, their action, their need.

It is this knowledge which provides the curious community of feeling in the world of the hipster, a muted cool religious revival to be sure, but the element which is exciting, disturbing, nightmarish perhaps, is that incompatibles have come to bed, the inner life and the violent life, the orgy and the dream of love, the desire to murder and the desire to create, a dialectical conception of existence with a lust for power, a dark, romantic, and yet undeniably dynamic view of existence for it sees every man and woman as moving individually through each moment of life forward into growth or backward into death.

3.

It may be fruitful to consider the hipster a philosophical psychopath, a man interested not only in the dangerous imperatives of his psychopathy but in codifying, at least for himself, the suppositions on which his inner universe is constructed. By this premise the hipster is a psychopath, and yet not a psychopath but the negation of the psychopath, for he possesses the narcissistic detachment of the philosopher, that absorption in the recessive nuances of one's own motive which is so alien to the unreasoning drive of the psychopath. In this country where new millions of psychopaths are developed each year, stamped with the mint of our contradictory popular culture (where sex is sin and yet sex is paradise), it is as if there has been room already for the development of the antithetical psychopath who extrapolates from his own condition, from the inner certainty that his rebellion is just, a radical vision of the universe which thus separates him from the general ignorance, reactionary prejudice, and self-doubt of the more conventional psychopath. Having converted his unconscious experience into much conscious knowledge, the hipster has shifted the focus of his desire from immediate gratification toward that wider passion for future power which is the mark of civilized man. Yet with an irreducible difference. For Hip is the sophistication of the wise primitive in a giant jungle, and so its appeal is still beyond the civilized man. If there are ten million Americans who are more or less psychopathic (and the figure is most modest), there are probably not more than one hundred thousand men and women who consciously see themselves as hipsters, but their importance is that they are an elite with the potential ruthlessness of an elite, and a language most adolescents can understand instinctively, for the hipster's intense view of existence matches their experience and their desire to rebel.

Before one can say more about the hipster, there is obviously much to be said about the psychic state of the psychopath—or, clinically, the psychopathic personality. Now, for reasons which may be more curious than the similarity of the words, even many people with a psychoanalytical orientation often confuse the psychopath with the psychotic. Yet the terms are polar. The psychotic is legally insane, the psychopath is not; the psychotic is almost always incapable of discharging in physical acts the rage of his frustration, while the psychopath at his extreme is virtually as incapable of restraining his violence. The psychotic lives in so misty a world that what is happening at each moment of his life is not very real to him whereas the psychopath seldom knows any reality greater than the face, the voice, the being of the particular people among whom he may find himself at any moment. Sheldon and Eleanor Glueck describe him as follows:

> The psychopath . . . can be distinguished from the person sliding into or clambering out of a "true psychotic" state by the long tough persistence of his anti-social attitude and behaviour and the absence of hallucinations, delusions, manic flight of ideas, confusion, disorientation, and other dramatic signs of psychosis.

The late Robert Lindner, one of the few experts on the subject, in his book *Rebel Without a Cause—The Hypnoanalysis of a Criminal Psychopath* presented part of his definition in this way:

> . . . the psychopath is a rebel without a cause, an agitator without a slogan, a revolutionary without a program: in other words, his rebelliousness is aimed to achieve goals satisfactory to himself alone; he is incapable of exertions for the sake of others. All his efforts, hidden under no matter what disguise, represent investments designed to satisfy his immediate wishes and desires. . . . The psychopath, like the child, cannot delay the pleasures of gratification; and this trait is one of his underlying, universal characteristics. He cannot wait upon erotic gratification which convention demands should be preceded by the chase before the kill: he must rape. He cannot wait upon the development of prestige in society: his egoistic ambitions lead him to leap into headlines by daring performances. Like a red thread the predominance of this mechanism for immediate satisfaction runs through the history of every psychopath. It explains not only his behaviour but also the violent nature of his acts.

Yet even Lindner who was the most imaginative and most sympathetic of the psychoanalysts who have studied the psychopathic personality was not ready to project himself into the essential sympathy—which is that the psychopath may indeed be the perverted and dangerous front-runner of a new kind of personality which could become the central expression of human nature before the twentieth century is over. For the psychopath is better adapted to dominate those mutually contradictory inhibitions upon violence and love which civilization has exacted of us, and if it be remembered that not every psychopath is an extreme case, and that the condition of psychopathy is present in a host of people including many politicians, professional soldiers, newspaper columnists, entertainers, artists, jazz musicians, call-girls, promiscuous homosexuals and half the executives of Hollywood, television, and advertising, it can be seen that there are aspects of psychopathy which already exert considerable cultural influence.

What characterizes almost every psychopath and part-psychopath is that they are trying to create a new nervous system for themselves. Generally we are obliged to act with a nervous system which has been formed from infancy, and which carries in the style of its circuits the very contradictions of our parents and our early milieu. Therefore, we are obliged, most of us, to meet the tempo of the present and the future with reflexes and rhythms which come from the past. It is not only the "dead weight of the institutions of the past" but indeed the inefficient and often antiquated nervous circuits of the past which strangle our potentiality for responding to new possibilities which might be exciting for our individual growth.

Through most of modern history, "sublimation" was possible: at the expense of expressing only a small portion of oneself, that small portion could be expressed intensely. But sublimation depends on a reasonable tempo to history. If the collective life of a generation has moved too quickly, the "past" by which particular men and women of that generation may function is not, let us say, thirty years old, but relatively a hundred or two hundred years old. And so the nervous system is overstressed beyond the possibility of such compromises as sublimation, especially since the stable middle-class values so prerequisite to sublimation have been virtually destroyed in our time, at least as nourishing values free of confusion or doubt. In such a crisis of accelerated historical tempo and deteriorated values, neurosis tends to be replaced by psychopathy, and

345

the success of psychoanalysis (which even ten years ago gave promise of becoming a direct major force) diminishes because of its inbuilt and characteristic incapacity to handle patients more complex, more experienced, or more adventurous than the analyst himself. In practice, psychoanalysis has by now become all too often no more than a psychic blood-letting. The patient is not so much changed as aged, and the infantile fantasies which he is encouraged to express are condemned to exhaust themselves against the analyst's nonresponsive reactions. The result for all too many patients is a diminution, a "tranquilizing" of their most interesting qualities and vices. The patient is indeed not so much altered as worn out—less bad, less good, less bright, less willful, less destructive, less creative. He is thus able to conform to that contradictory and unbearable society which first created his neurosis. He can conform to what he loathes because he no longer has the passion to feel loathing so intensely.

The psychopath is notoriously difficult to analyze because the fundamental decision of his nature is to try to live the infantile fantasy, and in this decision (given the dreary alternative of psychoanalysis) there may be a certain instinctive wisdom. For there is a dialectic to changing one's nature, the dialectic which underlies all psychoanalytic method: it is the knowledge that if one is to change one's habits, one must go back to the source of their creation, and so the psychopath exploring backward along the road of the homosexual, the orgiast, the drug-addict, the rapist, the robber and the murderer seeks to find those violent parallels to the violent and often hopeless contradictions he knew as an infant and as a child. For if he has the courage to meet the parallel situation at the moment when he is ready, then he has a chance to act as he has never acted before, and in satisfying the frustration—if he can succeed—he may then pass by symbolic substitute through the locks of incest. In thus giving expression to the buried infant in himself, he can lessen the tension of those infantile desires and so free himself to remake a bit of his nervous system. Like the neurotic he is looking for the opportunity to grow up a second time, but the psychopath knows instinctively that to express a forbidden impulse actively is far more beneficial to him than merely to confess the desire in the safety of a doctor's room. The psychopath is ordinately ambitious, too ambitious ever to trade his warped brilliant conception of his possible victories in life for the grim if peaceful attrition of the analyst's couch. So his associational journey into the past is lived out in the theatre of the present, and he exists for those charged situations where his senses are so alive that he can be aware actively (as the analysand is aware passively) of what his habits are, and how he can change them. The strength of the psychopath is that he knows (where most of us can only guess) what is good for him and what is bad for him at exactly those instants when an old crippling habit has become so attacked by experience that the potentiality exists to change it, to replace a negative and empty fear with an outward action, even if—and here I obey the logic of the extreme psychopath—even if the fear is of himself, and the action is to murder. The psychopath murders—if he has the courage—out of the necessity to purge his violence, for if he cannot empty his hatred then he cannot love, his being is frozen with implacable self-hatred for his cowardice. (It can of course be suggested that it take little courage for two strong eighteen-year-old hoodlums, let us say, to beat in the brains of a candy-store keeper, and indeed the act—even by the logic of the psychopath—is not likely to prove very therapeutic, for the victim is not an immediate equal. Still, courage of a sort is necessary, for one murders not only a weak fifty-year-old man but an institution as well, one violates private property, one enters into a new relation with the police and introduces a dangerous element into one's life. The hoodlum is therefore daring the unknown, and so no matter how brutal the act, it is not altogether cowardly.)

At bottom, the drama of the psychopath is that he seeks love. Not love as the search for a mate, but love as the search for an orgasm more apocalyptic than the one which preceded it. Orgasm is his therapy—he knows at the seed of his being that good orgasm opens his possibilities and bad orgasm imprisons him. But in this search, the psychopath becomes an embodiment of the extreme contradictions of the society which formed his character, and the apocalyptic orgasm often remains as remote as the Holy Grail, for there are clusters and nests and ambushes of violence in his own necessities and in the imperatives and retaliations of the men and women among whom he lives his life, so that even as he drains his hatred in one act or another, so the conditions of his life create it anew in him until the drama of his movements bears a sardonic resemblance to the frog who climbed a few feet in the well only to drop back again.

Yet there is this to be said for the search after the good

orgasm: when one lives in a civilized world, and still can enjoy none of the cultural nectar of such a world because the paradoxes on which civilization is built demand that there remain a cultureless and alienated bottom of exploitable human material, then the logic of becoming a sexual outlaw (if one's psychological roots are bedded in the bottom) is that one has at least a running competitive chance to be physically healthy so long as one stays alive. It is therefore no accident that psychopathy is most prevalent with the Negro. Hated from outside and therefore hating himself, the Negro was forced into the position of exploring all those moral wildernesses of civilized life which the Square automatically condemns as delinquent or evil or immature or morbid or self-destructive or corrupt. (Actually the terms have equal weight. Depending on the telescope of the cultural clique from which the Square surveys the universe, "evil" or "immature" are equally strong terms of condemnation.) But the Negro, not being privileged to gratify his self-esteem with the heady satisfactions of categorical condemnation, chose to move instead in that other direction where all situations are equally valid, and in the worst of perversion, promiscuity, pimpery, drug addiction, rape, razor-slash, bottle-break, what-have-you, the Negro discovered and elaborated a morality of the bottom, an ethical differentiation between the good and the bad in every human activity from the go-getter pimp (as opposed to the lazy one) to the relatively dependable pusher or prostitute. Add to this, the cunning of their language, the abstract ambiguous alternatives in which from the danger of their oppression they learned to speak ("Well, now, man, like I'm looking for a cat to turn me on . . ."), add even more the profound sensitivity of the Negro jazzman who was the cultural mentor of a people, and it is not too difficult to believe that the language of Hip which evolved was an artful language, tested and shaped by an intense experience and therefore different in kind from white slang, as different as the special obscenity of the soldier, which in its emphasis upon "ass" as the soul and "shit" as circumstance, was able to express the existential states of the enlisted man. What makes Hip a special language is that it cannot really be taught —if one shares none of the experiences of elation and exhaustion which it is equipped to describe, then it seems merely arch or vulgar or irritating. It is a pictorial language, but pictorial like nonobjective art, imbued with the dialectic of small but intense change, a language for the microcosm, in this case, man, for it takes the immediate experiences of any passing man and magnifies the dynamic of his movements, not specifically but abstractly so that he is seen more as a vector in a network of forces than as a static character in a crystallized field. (Which latter is the practical view of the snob.) For example, there is real difficulty in trying to find a Hip substitute for "stubborn." The best possibility I can come up with is: "That cat will never come off his groove, dad." But groove implies movement, narrow movement but motion nonetheless. There is really no way to describe someone who does not move at all. Even a creep does move—if at a pace exasperatingly more slow than the pace of the cool cats.

4.

Like children, hipsters are fighting for the sweet, and their language is a set of subtle indications of their success or failure in the competition for pleasure. Unstated but obvious is the social sense that there is not nearly enough sweet for everyone. And so the sweet goes only to the victor, the best, the most, the man who knows the most about how to find his energy and how not to lose it. The emphasis is on energy because the psychopath and the hipster are nothing without it since they do not have the protection of a position or a class to rely on when they have overextended themselves. So the language of Hip is a language of energy, how it is found, how it is lost.

But let us see. I have jotted down perhaps a dozen words, the Hip perhaps most in use and most likely to last with the minimum of variation. The words are man, go, put down, make, beat, cool, swing, with it, crazy, dig, flip, creep, hip, square. They serve a variety of purposes and the nuance of the voice uses the nuance of the situation to convey the subtle contextual difference. If the hipster moves through his life on a constant search with glimpses of Mecca in many a turn of his experience (Mecca being the apocalyptic orgasm) and if everyone in the civilized world is at least in some small degree a sexual cripple, the hipster lives with the knowledge of how he is sexually crippled and where he is sexually alive, and the faces of experience which life presents to him each day are engaged, dismissed or avoided as his need directs and his lifemanship makes possible. For life is a contest between people in which the victor generally recuperates quickly and the loser takes long to mend, a perpetual competition of colliding explorers in which one must grow or else pay more for remaining the same (pay in sickness, or depression, or anguish for the lost opportunity), but pay or grow.

Therefore one finds words like go, and make it, and with it, and swing: "Go" with its sense that after hours or days or months or years of monotony, boredom, and depression one has finally had one's chance, one has amassed enough energy to meet an exciting opportunity with all one's present talents for the flip (up or down) and so one is ready to go, ready to gamble. Movement is always to be preferred to inaction. In motion a man has a chance, his body is warm, his instincts are quick, and when the crisis comes, whether of love or violence, he can make it, he can win, he can release a little more energy for himself since he hates himself a little less, he can make a little better nervous system, make it a little more possible to go again, to go faster next time and so make more and thus find more people with whom he can swing. For to swing is to communicate, is to convey the rhythms of one's own being to a lover, a friend, or an audience, and—equally necessary—be able to feel the rhythms of their response. To swing with the rhythms of another is to enrich oneself—the conception of the learning process as dug by Hip is that one cannot really learn until one contains within oneself the implicit rhythm of the subject or the person. As an example, I remember once hearing a Negro friend have an intellectual discussion at a party for half an hour with a white girl who was a few years out of college. The Negro literally could not read or write, but he had an extraordinary ear and a fine sense of mimicry. So as the girl spoke, he would detect the particular formal uncertainties in her argument, and in a pleasant (if slightly Southern) English accent, he would respond to one or another facet of her doubts. When she would finish what she felt was a particularly well-articulated idea, he would smile privately and say, "Other-direction . . . do you really believe in that?"

"Well . . . No," the girl would stammer, "now that you get down to it, there is something disgusting about it to me," and she would be off again for five more minutes.

Of course the Negro was not learning anything about the merits and demerits of the argument, but he was learning a great deal about a type of girl he had never met before, and that was what he wanted. Being unable to read or write, he could hardly be interested in ideas nearly as much as in lifemanship, and so he eschewed any attempt to obey the precision or lack of precision in the girl's language, and instead sensed her character (and the values of her social type) by swinging with the nuances of her voice.

So to swing is to be able to learn, and by learning take a step toward making it, toward creating. What is to be created is not nearly so important as the hipster's belief that when he really makes it, he will be able to turn his hand to anything, even to self-discipline. What he must do before that is find his courage at the moment of violence, or equally make it in the act of love, find a little more between his woman and himself, or indeed between his mate and himself (since many hipsters are bisexual), but paramount, imperative, is the necessity to make it because in making it, one is making the new habit, unearthing the new talent which the old frustration denied.

Whereas if you goof (the ugliest word in Hip), if you lapse back into being a frightened stupid child, or if you flip, if you lose your control, reveal the buried weaker more feminine part of your nature, then it is more difficult to swing the next time, your ear is less alive, your bad and energy-wasting habits are further confirmed, you are farther away from being with it. But to be with it is to have grace, is to be closer to the secrets of that inner unconscious life which will nourish you if you can hear it, for you are then nearer to that God which every hipster believes is located in the senses of his body, that trapped, mutilated and nonetheless megalomaniacal God who is It, who is energy, life, sex, force, the Yoga's *prana*, the Reichian's orgone, Lawrence's "blood," Hemingway's "good," the Shavian life-force; "It"; God; not the God of the churches but the unachievable whisper of mystery within the sex, the paradise of limitless energy and perception just beyond the next wave of the next orgasm.

To which a cool cat might reply, "Crazy, man!"

Because, after all, what I have offered above is an hypothesis, no more, and there is not the hipster alive who is not absorbed in his own tumultuous hypotheses. Mine is interesting, mine is way out (on the avenue of the mystery along the road to "It") but still I am just one cat in a world of cool cats, and everything interesting is crazy, or at least so the Squares who do not know how to swing would say.

(And yet crazy is also the self-protective irony of the hipster. Living with questions and not with answers, he is so different in his isolation and in the far reach of his imagination from almost everyone with whom he deals in the outer world of the Square, and meets generally so much enmity, competition, and hatred in the world of Hip, that his isolation is always in danger of turning upon itself, and leaving him indeed just that, crazy.)

If, however, you agree with my hypothesis, if you as a cat are way out too, and we are in the same groove (the universe now being glimpsed as a series of ever-extending radii from the center), why then you say simply, "I dig," because neither knowledge nor imagination comes easily, it is buried in the pain of one's forgotten experience, and so one must work to find it, one must occasionally exhaust oneself by digging into the self in order to perceive the outside. And indeed it is essential to dig the most, for if you do not dig you lose your superiority over the Square, and so you are less likely to be cool (to be in control of a situation because you have swung where the Square has not, or because you have allowed to come to consciousness a pain, a guilt, a shame or a desire which the other has not had the courage to face). To be cool is to be equipped, and if you are equipped it is more difficult for the next cat who comes along to put you down. And of course one can hardly afford to be put down too often, or one is beat, one has lost one's confidence, one has lost one's will, one is impotent in the world of action and so closer to the demeaning flip of becoming a queer, or indeed closer to dying, and therefore it is even more difficult to re-cover enough energy to try to make it again, because once a cat is beat he has nothing to give, and no one is interested any longer in making it with him. This is the terror of the hipster—to be beat—because once the sweet of sex has deserted him, he still cannot give up the search. It is not granted to the hipster to grow old gracefully —he has been captured too early by the oldest dream of power, the gold fountain of Ponce de León, the fountain of youth where the gold is in the orgasm.

To be beat is therefore a flip, it is a situation beyond one's experience, impossible to anticipate—which indeed in the circular vocabulary of Hip is still another meaning for flip, but then I have given just a few of the connotations of these words. Like most primitive vocabularies each word is a prime symbol and serves a dozen or a hundred functions of communication in the instinctive dialectic through which the hipster perceives his experience, that dialectic of the instantaneous differentials of existence in which one is forever moving forward into more or retreating into less.

5.

It is impossible to conceive a new philosophy until one creates a new language, but a new popular language (while it must implicitly contain a new philosophy) does not necessarily present its philosophy overtly. It can be asked then what really is unique in the life-view of Hip which raises its argot above the passing verbal whimsies of the bohemian or the lumpenproletariat.

The answer would be in the psychopathic element of Hip which has almost no interest in viewing human nature, or better, in judging human nature, from a set of standards conceived a priori to the experience, standards inherited from the past. Since Hip sees every answer as posing immediately a new alternative, a new question, its emphasis is on complexity rather than simplicity (such complexity that its language without the illumination of the voice and the articulation of the face and body remains hopelessly incommunicative). Given its emphasis on complexity, Hip abdicates from any conventional moral responsibility because it would argue that the result of our actions are unforeseeable, and so we cannot know if we do good or bad, we cannot even know (in the Joycean sense of the good and the bad) whether we have given energy to another, and indeed if we could, there would still be no idea of what ultimately the other would do with it.

Therefore, men are not seen as good or bad (that they are good-and-bad is taken for granted) but rather each man is glimpsed as a collection of possibilities, some more possible than others (the view of character implicit in Hip) and some humans are considered more capable than others of reaching more possibilities within themselves in less time, provided, and this is the dynamic, provided the particular character can swing at the right time. And here arises the sense of context which differentiates Hip from a Square view of character. Hip sees the context as generally dominating the man, dominating him because his character is less significant than the context in which he must function. Since it is arbitrarily five times more demanding of one's energy to accomplish even an inconsequential action in an unfavorable context than a favorable one, man is then not only his character but his context, since the success or failure of an action in a given context reacts upon the character and therefore affects what the character will be in the next context. What dominates both character and context is the energy available at the moment of intense context.

Character being thus seen as perpetually ambivalent and dynamic enters then into an absolute relativity where there are no truths other than the isolated truths of what each observer feels at each instant of his existence. To take a perhaps unjustified meta-physical extrapolation, it is as if the universe which has usually existed conceptually as a Fact (even if the Fact were Berkeley's God) but a Fact which it was the aim of all science and philosophy to reveal, becomes instead a changing reality whose laws are remade at each instant by everything living, but most particularly man, man raised to a neo-medieval summit where the truth is not what one has felt yesterday or what one expects to feel tomorrow but rather truth is no more nor less than what one feels at each instant in the perpetual climax of the present.

What is consequent therefore is the divorce of man from his values, the liberation of the self from the Super-Ego of society. The only Hip morality (but of course it is an ever-present morality) is to do what one feels whenever and wherever it is possible, and—this is how the war of the Hip and the Square begins—to be en-gaged in one primal battle: to open the limits of the possible for oneself, for oneself alone, because that is one's need. Yet in widening the arena of the possible, one widens it reciprocally for others as well, so that the nihilistic fulfillment of each man's desire contains its antithesis of human co-operation.

If the ethic reduces to Know Thyself and Be Thyself, what makes it radically different from Socratic moderation with its stern conservative respect for the experience of the past is that the Hip ethic is immoderation, childlike in its adoration of the present (and indeed to respect the past means that one must also respect such ugly consequences of the past as the collective murders of the State). It is this adoration of the present which contains the affirma-tion of Hip, because its ultimate logic surpasses even the unfor-gettable solution of the Marquis de Sade to sex, private property, and the family, that all men and women have absolute but tem-porary rights over the bodies of all other men and women—the nihilism of Hip proposes as its final tendency that every social restraint and category be removed, and the affirmation implicit in the proposal is that man would then prove to be more creative than murderous and so would not destroy himself. Which is exactly what separates Hip from the authoritarian philosophies which now appeal to the conservative and liberal temper—what haunts the middle of the twentieth century is that faith in man has been lost, and the appeal of authority has been that it would restrain us from ourselves. Hip, which would return us to ourselves, at no matter what price in individual violence, is the affirmation of the barbarian, for it requires a primitive passion about human nature to believe that individual acts of violence are always to be preferred to the collective violence of the State; it takes literal faith in the creative possibilities of the human being to envisage acts of violence as the catharsis which prepares growth.

Whether the hipster's desire for absolute sexual freedom contains any genuinely radical conception of a different world is of course another matter, and it is possible, since the hipster lives with his hatred, that many of them are the material for an elite of storm troopers ready to follow the first truly magnetic leader whose view of mass murder is phrased in a language which reaches their emotions. But given the desperation of his condition as a psychic outlaw, the hipster is equally a candidate for the most reactionary and most radical of movements, and so it is just as possible that many hipsters will come—if the crisis deepens—to a radical comprehension of the horror of society, for even as the radical has had his incommunicable dissent confirmed in his experience by precisely the frustration, the denied opportunities, and the bitter years which his ideas have cost him, so the sexual adventurer deflected from his goal by the implacable animosity of a society constructed to deny the sexual radical as well, may yet come to an equally bitter comprehension of the slow relentless inhumanity of the conservative power which controls him from without and from within. And in being so controlled, denied, and starved into the attrition of conformity, indeed the hipster may come to see that his condition is no more than an exaggeration of the human condition, and if he would be free, then everyone must be free. Yes, this is possible too, for the heart of Hip is its emphasis upon courage at the moment of crisis, and it is pleasant to think that courage contains within itself (as the explanation of its existence) some glimpse of the necessity of life to become more than it has been.

It is obviously not very possible to speculate with sharp focus on the future of the hipster. Certain possibilities must be evident, however, and the most central is that the organic growth of Hip depends on whether the Negro emerges as a dominating force in American life. Since the Negro knows more about the ugliness and danger of life than the white, it is probable that if the Negro can win his equality, he will possess a potential superiority, a superiority so feared that the fear itself has become the underground drama of domestic politics. Like all conservative political fear it is the fear of unforeseeable consequences, for the Negro's equality would tear a profound shift into the psychology, the sexuality, and the moral imagination of every white alive.

With this possible emergence of the Negro, Hip may erupt as a psychically armed rebellion whose sexual impetus may rebound against the antisexual foundation of every organized power in America, and bring into the air such animosities, antipathies, and new conflicts of interest that the mean empty hypocrisies of mass conformity will no longer work. A time of violence, new hysteria, confusion and rebellion will then be likely to replace the time of conformity. At that time, if the liberal should prove realistic in his belief that there is peaceful room for every tendency in American life, then Hip would end by being absorbed as a colorful figure in the tapestry. But if this is not the reality, and the economic, the social, the psychological, and finally the moral crises accompanying the rise of the Negro should prove insupportable, then a time is coming when every political guidepost will be gone, and millions of liberals will be faced with political dilemmas they have so far succeeded in evading, and with a view of human nature they do not wish to accept. To take the desegregation of the schools in the South as an example, it is quite likely that the reactionary sees the reality more closely than the liberal when he argues that the deeper issue is not desegregation but miscegenation. (As a radical I am of course facing in the opposite direction from the White Citizen's Councils—obviously I believe it is the absolute human right of the Negro to mate with the white, and matings there will undoubtedly be, for there will be Negro high school boys brave enough to chance their lives.) But for the average liberal whose mind has been dulled by the committee-ish cant of the professional liberal, miscegenation is not an issue because he has been told that the Negro does not desire it. So, when it comes, miscegenation will be a terror, comparable perhaps to the derangement of the American Communists when the icons to Stalin came tumbling down. The average American Communist held to the myth of Stalin for reasons which had little to do with the political evidence and everything to do with their psychic necessities. In this sense it is equally a psychic necessity for the liberal to believe that the Negro and even the reactionary Southern white are eventually and fundamentally people like himself, capable of becoming good liberals too if only they can be reached by good liberal reason. What the liberal cannot bear to admit is the hatred beneath the skin of a society so unjust that the amount of collective violence buried in the people is perhaps incapable of being contained, and therefore if one wants a better world one does well to hold one's breath, for a worse world is bound to come first, and the dilemma may well be this: given such hatred, it must either vent itself nihilistically or become turned into the cold murderous liquidations of the totalitarian state.

6.

No matter what its horrors the twentieth century is a vastly exciting century for its tendency is to reduce all of life to its ultimate alternatives. One can well wonder if the last war of them all will be between the blacks and the whites, or between the women and the men, or between the beautiful and ugly, the pillagers and managers, or the rebels and the regulators. Which of course is carrying speculation beyond the point where speculation is still serious, and yet despair at the monotony and bleakness of the future have become so engrained in the radical temper that the radical is in danger of abdicating from all imagination. What a man feels is the impulse for his creative effort, and if an alien but nonetheless passionate instinct about the meaning of life has come so unexpectedly from a virtually illiterate people, come out of the most intense conditions of exploitation, cruelty, violence, frustration, and lust, and yet has succeeded as an instinct in keeping this tortured people alive, then it is perhaps possible that the Negro holds more of the tail of the expanding elephant of truth than the radical, and if this is so, the radical humanist could do worse than to brood upon the phenomenon. For if a revolutionary time should come again, there would be a crucial difference if someone had already delineated a neo-Marxian calculus aimed at comprehending every circuit and process of society from ukase to kiss as the communications of human energy—a calculus capable of translating the economic relations of man into his psychological relations and then back again, his productive relations thereby embracing his sexual

357

relations as well, until the crises of capitalism in the twentieth century would yet be understood as the unconscious adaptations of a society to solve its economic imbalance at the expense of a new mass psychological imbalance. It is almost beyond the imagination to conceive of a work in which the drama of human energy is engaged, and a theory of its social currents and dissipations, its imprisonments, expressions, and tragic wastes are fitted into some gigantic synthesis of human action where the body of Marxist thought, and particularly the epic grandeur of *Das Kapital* (that first of the major *psychologies* to approach the mystery of social cruelty so simply and practically as to say that we are a collective body of humans whose life-energy is wasted, displaced, and procedurally stolen as it passes from one of us to another)—where particularly the epic grandeur of *Das Kapital* would find its place in an even more God-like view of human justice and injustice, in some more excruciating vision of those intimate and institutional processes which lead to our creations and disasters, our growth, our attrition, and our rebellion.

1957

NOTE TO "REFLECTIONS ON HIP"

A prime virtue of The White Negro *may be in the number of heresies it commits. Here, on this exchange with Jean Malaquais and Ned Polsky two such heresies are engaged: that a modern revolution can arise out of some other condition than an organized militant movement of the proletariat, and that there are other cures to neurosis than the couch of the analyst. For readers who are indifferent to these subjects, the exchange will be of doubtful interest; for those who would like a little more of* The White Negro, *the matter may be worth the difficulty.*

I have taken one liberty. The exchange was called "Reflections on Hipsterism," when it appeared in Dissent. I did not choose the title, and so I have altered the name of the piece.

REFLECTIONS ON HIP
1) Jean Malaquais

Once upon a time there was a myth named *le prolétariat.* Though obviously a male, the myth was believed to be pregnant with child—a well conformed socialistic baby true to the Scriptures. Baby being long overdue, the congregation of the faithful first became skeptical, then frankly disgusted. Feeling cheated, never allowing that they may have misread the Book, they repudiated *le prolétariat,* sued for divorce, and being an idealistically inclined flock, started to shop around for a better, less sterile myth. Great schisms followed, yet few of flock turned cynical. Quite the contrary. Prompted by their thirst for eternal values, many made dangerous inroads into heretofore uncharted lands. There, as in a secret Eden happily rediscovered, amazingly new and refreshing reasons to live awaited the bold myth hunter: Liberalism, Democracy, Free World, Peace, Stop-the-AH-Experiments, etc., and— honor to whom honor is due—the long neglected bastard-brother of *le prolétariat:* marijuana soaked Hip.

That Hip found in Norman Mailer its most outstanding and original theologist (I don't say apologist), seems quite clear in the light of his essay [DISSENT, Summer 1957]. He may be correct in stating that Hip and psychopathology follow two parallel paths, but he has still to persuade this reader that the American Negro bohemian and his white imitator embody a special brand of the human species. Starting with the fact that the Negro's status within the American community is a marginal one, Mailer is not content to allow him his particular or characteristic psychological bent; he bestows upon him a Messianic mission.

He seems to forget that the American hipster has his counterparts and equivalents in countries with no Negro population: Sweden, England, Russia, Poland, France, to name only a few places. The Swedish youth runs properly amok. The British Teddy, the Russian *besprizornyé*, the Polish hooligans, the French pseudo-existentialist fauna, don't behave differently toward life than the hipster. All are the product of an identical social phenomenon prevailing in highly industrialized and more or less paternalistically ruled countries: extreme inner insecurity dipped in a State-sponsored "welfare" at the price of a terrific loss to the individual's self. That's one reason why, as a rule, they react on the level of a purely personal idea of "recovery"—but from what and toward what none of them really knows.

When Mailer says of the hipster that he has "converted his unconscious experience into much conscious knowledge," he may speak of the hipster's knowledge in a very narrow practical way, as for instance knowledge on how to survive momentarily in a back alley; but he is mistaken if he takes it for more than it is: an instinctive and empirical know-how. The remarkable thing about hipsters of all kinds and variety (and they vary indeed in many aspects) is that, except for a case or two in a generation, as a body they are sooner or later swallowed up by the most conforming routine ever.

Hip is but another name for lumpen, and lumpen make excellent conformists and the best of potential hangmen for "order's" sake. Even before they fall into rank and file, rather than raping and murdering they blabber of rape and murder; they dream of rape and murder in idiotic clichés, vicariously, with a hand from the tabloids and other such literature. Yet if a handful among the tens of thousands, as Mailer numbers them, do go through rape and murder, it is mostly by accident, by a tragic mistake, almost never by deliberate clear choice, and then only once, for they are ambushed as soon as they have zipped up their pants.

One other reason why lumpen of all kind are but a myth in terms of social action, except possibly a small home-made pogrom with the implicit or explicit blessing of State and municipality, is that they do not form any coherent social body. Negro shopkeepers and white shopkeepers, should their shops be endangered, would dismiss all color lines and slaughter hand in hand Negro and white lumpen. There is more real solidarity (class solidarity) between white and Negro "law abiding citizens" than between people of "Caucasian" or "African" complexion.

Moreover, there is hardly a hipster alive who doesn't long to conform (like his extreme representative, the psycopath, he is always a case of a frustrated conformist), and there is hardly a conformist alive, white or Negro, who doesn't long to rape and murder (like his extreme representative, the pulpit moralist, he is always a case of a frustrated rebel). The difference is that the conformist hardly ever becomes a lumpen, that the lumpen almost always becomes a conformist (all exceptions granted). In turn, the difference is due to the only real relationship in modern society: property relationship. For the conformist to become a lumpen means to give up his actual or virtual property, which he cannot do by free choice; for the lumpen to become a conformist means to acquire property, which he always wills by free choice—however strong his overt denial. (As a matter of fact, lumpen *is* a way of making a living.)

On the other hand, the rebel who outgrew the romantic stage of his rebellion, who knows himself to be a grown up rebel—which is quite different from being a "radical," for after all a McCarthy too was a "radical"—knows also that *he conforms*, that he moves within the bonds of social and cultural institutions whose weight he cannot shake off in his private way, but who keeps within his conformity a lucid mind and a clear heart as to what conforming and what rebellion means in terms not of his subjective immediate I, but in terms of man as such, of man as a social creature. To make an image: the lumpen yells sh . . to the cop on the street-corner and feels purged, the conformist lifts his cap to the same cop and feels reassured in his pants, the grown up rebel ignores the cop (though he may summon his help in an emergency) and applies his energy to fell the tree that breeds cops, conformists and lumpen.

The amusing thing is that one can read into Mailer's essay precisely the proposition that the hipster is nothing but a conformist in reverse. "If," says Hip in Mailer's words, "if the fate of 20th century man is to live with death . . . why then the only life-giving answer is to accept the terms of death, to live with death as immediate danger, to divorce oneself from society," etc. Now if man's fate is to live with death, how does the hipster manage to divorce himself from society since he does accept "the terms of death"? If the terms are death, and if he accepts the terms—nay, if he so to speak naturalizes the terms generally prevailing for his private use, why he conforms nice and clean, he is at the avant-garde of conformity.

"Death you want?" says Hip to society. "Good, death there'll be!" And there he goes, the small entrepreneur in death competing with industrial death. One Mr. Verdoux once made a superb parody of our death-bent hipster. But no. Hip, says Mailer truly, Hip wants love, wants peace in a nice kitchenette with a white apron around his girl's waist. All the "mysticism," all the "dialectical conception of existence" Mailer so generously bestows upon Hip is, as far as I am concerned, a gorgeous flower of Mailer's romantic idealism.

Paris   September 4, 1957

Mailer's Reply

In his search for a sexual life which will suit his orgiastic needs, the hipster willy-nilly attacks conventional sexual morality, and to some degree succeeds in disturbing the balance. If capitalist society is grounded upon property relations, these relations are wed to monogamy, family, and the sexual strictures which maintain them. It is yet to be established that sexual life can be promiscuously altered without affecting the psychic real estate of capitalism. Since Malaquais seems to be indirectly arguing the affirmative, I would suggest that there are obstructions to his proof which the poetic excellences of his style cannot storm by metaphor.

Man is a flux of possibilities and energies long before and perhaps long after he is a manipulator of land, properties, and productions. A civilization from now, the vast chapter of Western expansion which was built on property and such inhuman abstractions of human energy as money, credit, and surplus value, may be seen as an ice-age of cruel and brutally slow liberations of productive, purposive, creative and sexual energies which the contradictions of inequity and exploitation congealed not only into the working habits of men, elaborated not only into the institutional hypocrisies of society, but indeed drove as cancerous ambivalences and frustrations into the texture of being itself.

The growth of human consciousness in this century demanded—for its expanding vitality—that a revolution be made, that a mankind be liberated, and since the attempt failed in its frontal revolutionary attack, failed precisely to change the exploitative character of our productive relations, it may well be that the rise of the hipster represents the first wind of a second revolution in this century, moving not forward toward action and more rational equitable distribution, but backward toward being and the secrets of human energy, not forward to the collectivity which was totalitarian in the proof but backward to the nihilism of creative adventurers, a revolution admittedly impossible to conceive even in its outlines, for unlike that first revolution which was conscious, Faustian, and vain, enacted in the name of the proletariat but more likely an expression of the scientific narcissism we inherited from the nineteenth century, a revolution motivated by the rational mania that consciousness could stifle instinct and marshal it into productive formations, the second revolution, if it is to come, would come indeed as antithesis to the "Great Experiment":—its desire would be to turn materialism on its head, have consciousness subjugated to instinct. The hipster, rebel cell in our social body, lives out, acts out, follows the close call of his instinct as far as he dares, and so points to possibilities and consequences in what have hitherto been chartless jungles of moral nihilism. The essence of his expression, his faith if you will, is that the real desire to make a better world exists at the heart of our instinct (that instinctual vision of a human epic which gave birth to consciousness itself), that man is therefore roughly more good than evil, that beneath his violence there is finally love and the nuances of justice, and that the removal therefore of all social restraints while it would open us to an era of incomparable individual violence would still spare us the collective violence of rational totalitarian liquidations (which we must accept was grossly a psychic index of the buried, voiceless, and ineradicable violences of whole nations of people), and would—and here is the difference—by expending the violence directly, open the possibility of working with that human creativity which is violence's opposite.

But of course this may be no more than the sword dance of my "romantic idealism." Immediately, the charge by Malaquais is that the hipster is our old black sheep, our discontented nephew of the proletariat, the impotent lumpen no more than a thousand dollars away from kissing the penny-calloused hands of the petit-bourgeoisie. I wonder. Is it so very lumpen to be able to influence American culture? The mass audience may turn in for the night to the chest-out, stomach-in, pinch-buttocks of the Star-Spangled Banner, with perhaps a five-minute sermonette to speed them to churchly sleep, but their waking hours were vibrated by that now déclassé (so fast does it change) Holy Shaker, that ex-apostle of small-town Southern orgasm, Elvis Presley.

Malaquais says the hipster has his opposite number in the British Teddy, the *besprizornyé* (still untamed?—how unlumpen!), the Polish hooligans, the French existentialists, all Hip, and not a drop of Negro blood in a thousand of their black masses. But Malajquais would be hard-put to find the taint of Hip without the blood of jazz. The Negro's experience appears to be the most universal communication of the West, and the authority of their tortured senses may indeed be passing by the musical states of their artistic expression, *without language, without conscious communication*, into the no doubt equally tortured senses of the wild sensitive spawn of two vast wars. But to Malaquais the lumpen is the lumpen. If Marx did not find it necessary to take them seriously, how dare we?

I wonder, however, if it would not be more "Marxist" to recognize that the superstructure of society has attained vast autonomies outside productive relations, psychological undercurrents which often clash with material economic realities—as, for example, the swoop of the stockmarket in response to the Sputnik. There may even be ineradicable conflicts of interest between the superstructure and the base of productive relations. At the least, is it not reasonable to assume that society has reached a point of such complexity, such "organismishness," that it is capable of adapting itself to avoid economic crisis by unwillingly (owing to the contradictions of mass manipulation) communicating mass psychological crises via the mass communications?

The contemporary contradictions from which America has been suffering (given the virtually self-regulating economic valves of war finance) have been almost insupportable psychological contradictions, virtually perfect Orwellian ambivalences—(War is Peace, Love is Hate, Ignorance is Knowledge); if these psychic contradictions should eventually introduce an apathy sufficient to turn our country back into economic contradictions and economic depression, which is indeed far from impossible, it will not mean that the process was a simple dialectic whose breath moved only through the circuits of productive relations. What one may fumble toward is a dialectic which can bridge the material and the ideal—which can infuse material notions of energy into that philosophical country of the ideal (read: the individual unconscious) which psychoanalysis now occupies with a middle-class mechanistic *weltanschauung*. If we socialists, radicals, anarchists, rebels, nihilists, and dissenters are to become more than the dried twigs of an old family tree, the shabby genteel clerks who end the line of a warrior family, it can at least be recognized that until the radical bridge from Marx to Freud is built, and our view of man embraces more facts, contradictions, and illuminations than any conservative view, and stares into such terrifying alternatives as totalitarianism or barbarism, we are doing no more than scolding ourselves, and ignoring that revolutionary indictment which every human alive can respond to in some part of himself: that an unjust society wreaks cruel if subtle imprisonments and destructions of personal energy, wreaks them not only upon an individual class or race, but upon the being of each of us. For, ultimately, unjust societies must, out of the nature of their contradictions, stifle the best part of each creativity, and so starve into neglect and atrophy that future we hear raging to be born.

2) Ned Polsky

Although Norman Mailer, in "The White Negro," shows ample awareness of some drawbacks of hipster life, others he romanticizes away or ignores. Mailer is right in seeing the hipsters as the only significant new group of rebels in America. He is also right to recognize the new Bohemia, extend it his "essential sympathy," and where he cannot find much of merit, perhaps yet encourage it by praising with faint damns. But it is equally legitimate and desirable to recognize that there are qualitative differences among Bohemias and that the current Bohemia is greatly inferior to its predecessors of at least the past four decades.

1.

The new Bohemia's inferiority shows up clearly in its lack of intellectual content. Most hipsters scarcely read at all, not because they can't (nearly all of them have finished high school, and a surprising number of the whites have attended our better universities) but because they won't. The closest thing to an intellectual discussion is their chatter about the pseudo-profundities of contemporary jazz; they don't even know—worse, don't want to know —that the things they praise were achieved by art-music composers years ago. As for the few who can be said to read with any regularity: they turn their backs not only on the horrors but the grandeurs of the past, restrict their horizon to contemporary literature, and from this area select what is in large part tripe—a compound of Rexroth and Rimbaud, Henry Miller and *Mad Comics*, Sartre and science fiction, jazz magazines and jerkoff magazines.

Their own literary productions are few, and what there are of them—with the exception of some poems by Robert Duncan and parts of his unpublished play, *Faust Foutu*—have almost no literary merit whatever. (Buy *Evergreen Review No. 2* and back issues of *Origin* and see for yourself.) The reason is not far to seek: even if we grant Mailer's dubious claim that the American existentialists feel their existentialism more than the French do, it is still true that for art something more is required than the raw recital of raw emotion. Thus the American hipsters' writings cannot begin to compare with the work of the arch-hipsters of modern European literature, Celine and Genet, to say nothing of any number of non-hipsters.

2.

Hipster hedonism takes many forms. Some hipster groups, for example, have everything to do with motorcycles, whereas others have nothing to do with them. But not significant in any of these groups, Mailer to the contrary, is a sexual revolution. Of course hipsters are willing to try a variety of partners and positions, have no objection to interracial intercourse, etc.—but this is merely to say that they are "liberated" in the superficial ways that many "liberals" are. For all its probings of hipster pathology, Mailer's rhetoric covers up the fact that hipsters are not only more "psychologically" crippled than most people but sexually likewise— that they are not sexually free and have no chance to become so, and that this means they are not actual or potential sexual revolutionaries in the profound sense that Mailer is talking about. Two examples: many male hipsters (if I am to believe the testimony of several Hip men and women) are extremely sadistic in their sexual relationships, and many others are so narcissistic that inevitably their orgasms are premature and puny. No amount of plain or fancy screwing is going to change this. When Mailer glamorizes the hipsters' "search after the good orgasm" he is simply accepting at face value their rationalization for what is in truth a pathetic, driven sex life in which the same failures are repeated again and again. On this matter as on others, Mailer confuses the life of action with the life of acting out.

I imagine that Mailer really knows all this but that he cannot state it baldly because it would then be obvious that "bad orgasm" is one habit the hipster will never kick without the "dreary alternative" of psychoanalysis. Of course now that psychoanalysis has become a respectable part of psychiatry and the old-style European analysis, who were mostly rebels by definition, are being rapidly replaced by bourgeois young American M.D.'s, it is undeniable that the patient runs a much greater risk of encountering the analyst for whom "cure" necessarily includes "adjustment" to the present social structure. And not a few pioneer analysts now devote all their energies to making rich men's children content with their lot in life. But it is equally undeniable that psychoanalysis—whatever the brand—still provides greater sexual benefits than does the dreary alternative that Mailer glorifies. Psychoanalysis has been domesticated but not castrated.

3.

The world of the hipster is commonly held to break down racial barriers, and indeed it does. If we accept the usual ultimate test (and Mailer's)—whether whites and Negroes sleep together— hipsters undoubtedly meet it much more often than squares do. Nevertheless there is a built-in barrier to full acceptance of black hipsters by white ones (and to a lesser extent vice versa), which stems from the fact that hipsters are marginal in a very special way.

The white Negro, as Mailer aptly calls him, is of course a marginal man. He puts down the white world from which he came. And he can never fully make it in, or be accepted by, the Negro world; so with rare exceptions (notably Mezz Mezzrow) he doesn't even try to live within the Negro community, and if he does he is put down by Negroes a lot. He exists, then, between the two worlds, where he meets his obverse: the Negro hipster, who puts down the Negro community at large (one reason, though not the main one, being that most Negroes are also squares, Mailer's stereotype of the Negro notwithstanding) and can never fully make it in the white world.

The first thing to notice about these marginal men—white or black—is that they are not the utterly isolated, atomized individuals whom sociologists assume all marginal men to be. They come together and create a little world of their own which elaborates its own worldview, code of behavior, institutions, argot, and so on. They create what to sociologists is a contradiction in terms: a subculture of marginal men.*

Now, the inner tragedy of the hipster subculture is this: the white member is attracted to the Negro member because of the latter's Negro-ness, whereas the Negro—and this Mailer ignores—is attracted to the white precisely because of his whiteness. Although the interracial groups which constitute the hipster subculture are "primary" groups in sociological terms, since in them whites and Negroes meet in "intimate, face-to-face relationships," this does not automatically imply the deepest kind of social bond; sociological theory is too gross at this point because it neglects the fact that "face to face" occasionally means, among other things, "looking in opposite directions." Many a time I have heard white hipsters, when no Negro members were present, put down one of the absent Negroes with "The trouble with X is that he's too fay-oriented," or "Y is a drag; all he's interested in is laying white chicks." And I'd bet my bottom dollar that Negro hipsters, among

* *A good index of the subculture's strength is provided by that most pervasive of hipster activities, marijuana-smoking and its attendant exploration of exotic states of consciousness, for the reactions of one under the influence of marijuana are determined not nearly so much by his individual psychology or physiology as by subcultural norms. For a related point of view, and much concrete evidence, cf. Howard S. Becker, "On Becoming a Marihuana Smoker,"* American Journal of Sociology, LIX (*November 1953*), *pp. 235-242.*

themselves, often put down the whites with something like "Man, those fay cats are pretty cool and don't want us to be Uncle Toms, but they still want us to be spooks. They don't really dig us as people; they just dig us for our music and our pot." Which is true. Even in the world of the hipster the Negro remains essentially what Ralph Ellison called him—an invisible man. The white Negro accepts the real Negro not as a human being in his totality, but as the bringer of a highly specified and restricted "cultural dowry," to use Mailer's phrase. In so doing he creates an inverted form of keeping the nigger in his place.

Mailer's Reply

As a cool critical view of the affectations, vanities, and hypocrisies of the hipster, I have little quarrel with Ned Polsky's remarks. They were written with a keen eye. But I believe he overrides a most complex question when he declares that many male hipsters have orgasms premature and puny. Since he can hardly have had the requisite personal experience—"Uncle," said a bisexual Negro to me once, "I couldn't have more charge for that chick if I'd gone down on a platoon of Marines"—I wonder if Polsky isn't really just passing on a tyrannical assumption which is one of the cement blocks of the Square throne of psychoanalysis.

In the Western sexual literature with which I am familiar, classical, technical, and pornographic, I can remember—with the harsh radical exception of Wilhelm Reich—almost no incisive discussion of male orgasm. The very notion of "good orgasm" (which indeed I used superficially in "The White Negro," DISSENT, Summer '57) betrays the lack of examination we bring to it, for it assumes there are two domains, good orgasm and bad, each clearly set apart by a defense line of psychic dragon teeth. But the Hip argument, if one is to dredge it forth, would claim that even in an orgasm which is *the most* there is always the vision of an outer wider wilder orgasm which is even more *with it*. The nature of orgasm is a spectrum, perhaps an infinite spectrum, perhaps intimately dialectical: in the worst of orgasm there are nips of pleasure, in the best of orgasms some mannered containments denying pleasure beyond high pleasure, restraining the rarer liberations of energy for the next day.

I am sure that the average psychoanalyst would now say, "The fact that the advocate of this thesis wants more of orgasm, is an indication of dissatisfaction with his narcissistic involvements. The adjusted social person knows better than to worry about his orgasm. It has been improved by psychoanalytical therapy." Of course one could walk through a mile of analysand-type persons to find one who really believed that his orgasm had been sexually improved.

But to argue this way is to stalk one's opponent about a circle, each a safe diameter apart. Finally, one cannot enter another being's orgasm and measure its scope (especially since many people's frustrated theatrical talents are brought resolutely to bed), one can only guess from the spectrum of one's own what the possibilities may be for others. And the line I would prefer to engage is to call into account the psychoanalyst's self-interest in believing that almost all sexual rebels are sick sexually. Indeed, he is right. But almost everyone is sick sexually in more or less degree, and so the indictment by the psychoanalyst should come forth no more maternally than to claim: better you should be sick as a Square than sick as a Hip.

Still the impolite question remains to be asked: does the direct experience of the analyst's own life prepare him to judge the inner states of Hip? Sedentary, middle-class, in fief to fifteen years of training, living among the absurd magpie scrutinies of wife, children, colleagues, patients, and hostile strangers, most analysts are obliged to be more proper than proper, and their characters, impulses and value judgments become shaped to satisfy the social necessities of their work. The social necessities of their work? The analyst is Gibraltar in a pathless middle-class sea, his guiding torch is lit by money, his triumphs are invariably with plain and miserable patients squashed too early by life, ruined permanently for pleasure, and so burgeoning under the stern authority and human comfort that an expensive person listens to them for two and a half hours a week. But the analyst, this middle-class and usually pampered son, is he the one to make the imaginative journey into the tortured marijuana-racked mind and genitalia of a hipster daring to live on

370

the edge of the most dangerous of the Negro worlds? Or is it not finally a matter of courage, courage not necessarily nor uniquely before violence, but courage to accept telling blows to the ego? For what would the analyst do, and what would become of his tidy, narrow, other-directed little world if he were to discover, and may God help him, that the hipster way out by the lip of danger may conceivably know more of the savor and swing in the damn dialectic of the orgasm than he, the doctor, the educated ball-shrinker who diagnoses all joys not his own as too puny.

HIPSTER AND BEATNIK

A Footnote to
"The White Negro"

Hipster came first as a word—it was used at least as long ago as 1951 or 1952, and was mentioned in the New Directions blurb on Chandler Brossard's *Who Walk In Darkness*. It came up again from time to time, notably in Ginsberg's *Howl* ("Angel-headed hipsters"), and was given its attention in *The White Negro*. Then came *On The Road*, and with Kerouac's success, The Beat Generation (a phrase first used by him many years ago, and mentioned several times in articles by Clellon Holmes) was adopted by the mass-media. Beatnik came into existence a year later, in the summer or fall of 1958, the word coined by a San Francisco columnist, Herb Caen. The addition of "nik" however—"nik" being a pejorative diminutive in Yiddish—gave a quality of condescension to the word which proved agreeable to the newspaper mentality. "Beatnik" caught on. But one no longer knew whether the Beat Generation referred to hipsters or beatniks or included both, and some people to avoid the label of beatnik began to call themselves Beats.

Since there is no authority to order this nomenclature, it is anyone's right to set up his surveyor's marks as he chooses, and I will make the attempt here, for I think there are differences, and they should be noted.

The Beat Generation is probably best used to include hipsters and beatniks. Not too many seem to use the word Beats; it is uncomfortable on the tongue; those who refuse to let it die seem to use it as an omnibus for hipsters and beatniks, a shorthand for saying The Beat Generation. This last term is itself an unhappy one, but since it has entered the language, one may as well live with it. Still, it must be said that the differences between hipsters and beatniks may be more important than their similarities, even if they share the following general characteristics: marijuana, jazz, not much money, and a community of feeling that society is the prison of the nervous system. The sense of place is acute—few care to stay away for long from the Village, Paris, North Beach, Mexico, New Orleans, Chicago and some other special cities. Hipster and Beatnik both talk Hip, but not in the same way—the beatnik uses the vocabulary; the hipster has that muted animal voice which shivered the national attention when first used by Marlon Brando.

Now the differences begin. The hipster comes out of a muted rebellion of the proletariat, he is, so to say, the lazy proletariat, the spiv; nothing given to manual labor unless he has no choice. The beatnik—often Jewish—comes from the middle class, and twenty-five years ago would have joined the YCL. Today, he chooses not to work as a sentence against the conformity of his parents. Therefore he can feel moral value in his goodbye to society. The hipster is more easygoing about the drag and value of a moneyless life of leisure.

Their bodies are not the same. A hipster moves like a cat, slow walk, quick reflexes; he dresses with a flick of chic; if his dungarees are old, he turns the cuffs at a good angle. The beatnik is slovenly—to strike a pose against the middle class you must roil their compulsion to be neat. Besides—the beatnik is more likely to have a good mind than a good body. While he comes along with most hipsters on the first tenet of the faith: that one's orgasm is the clue to how well one is living—he has had less body to work with in the first place, and so his chances for lifting himself by his sexual bootstraps are commonly nil, especially since each medieval guild in the Beat Generation has invariably formed itself on a more or less common sexual vitality or lack of it. The boys and girls available to the average beatnik are as drained as himself. Natural that the sex of the beatnik circles in, and mysticism becomes the Grail —he ends by using his drug to lash his mind into a higher contemplation of the universe and its secrets, a passive act, onanistic; the trance is coveted more than any desire to trap it later in work or art. The beatnik moves therefore onto Zen, the search for a lady ends as a search for *satori*—that using a drug goes against the discipline of Zen is something he will face later.

The hipster has a passing respect for Zen, he doesn't deny the experience of the mystic, he has known it himself, but his preference is to get the experience in the body of a woman. Drugs are a gamble for him, he gambles that the sensitivity of his libido on marijuana will help him to unlock the reflexes of his orgasm. If marijuana and the act take more out of him than he gets back, he is not likely to consider himself in good shape. Whereas a beatnik might. Who cares about impotence if one finds within it the breath of a vision? The beatnik, then, is obviously more sentimental—he needs a God who will understand all and forgive all. The hard knowledge of the hipster that you pay for what you get is usually too bitter for the beatnik. But then, the hipster is still in life; strong on his will, he takes on the dissipation of the drugs in order to dig more life for himself, he is wrestling with the destiny of his nervous system, he is Faustian. The beatnik contemplates eternity, finds it beautiful, likes to believe it is waiting to receive him. He wants to get out of reality more than he wants to change it, and at the end of the alley is a mental hospital.

If a hipster has a fall, it is to death or jail. Psychosis is not for him. Like a psychopath, he is juggling the perils of getting your kicks in this world, against the hell (or prison) of paying for them in the next. The hipster looks for action, and a bar with charge is where he goes when marijuana has turned him on—the beatnik, more at home with talk, can be found in the coffeehouse. The poet is his natural consort, his intellectual whip, even as the criminal, the hip hoodlum, and the boxer is the heart of knowledge for the hipster who ducks the psychotic relations between beatniks as too depressing, a hang-up, they go nowhere which can nourish him. The beatnik is in the line of continuation from the old bohemian, and nowhere near in his tradition to the hipster whose psychic style derives from the best Negroes to come up from the bottom. Yet the beatnik is to the Left of the other, for the hipster is interested in exploring the close call of the Self, and so has to collaborate more with the rhythms and tastes of the society he quit. It is not that the hipster is reactionary, it is rather that in a time of crisis, he would look for power, and in the absence of a radical spirit in the American air, the choices of power which will present themselves are more likely to come from the Right than the moribund liberalities of the Left. The beatnik, gentle, disembodied from the race, is often a radical pacifist, he has sworn the vow of no violence—in fact, his violence is sealed within, and he has no way of using it. His act of violence is to suicide even as the hipster's is toward murder, but in his mind-lost way, the beatnik is the torchbearer of those all-but-lost values of freedom, self-expression, and equality which first turned him against the hypocrisies and barren cultureless flats of the middle class.

For years now, they have lived side by side, hipster and beatnik, white Negro and crippled saint, their numbers increasing every month as the new ones come to town. They can be found wherever one knows to look, in all their permutations and combinations, in what is finally their unclassifiable and separate persons. I have exaggerated some tendencies, and made some divisions, but I have also blurred the spectrum of individuality by creating two types who never exist so simply in the real life of any Village ferment. If there are hipsters and beatniks, there are also hipniks and beatsters like Ginsberg and Kerouac, and across the spectrum like a tide of defeat—rebellion takes its price in a dead year and a deadened land—there are the worn-out beats of all too many hipsters who made their move, lost, and so have ended as beatniks with burned-out brains, listening sullenly to the quick montage of words in younger beatniks hot with the rebellion of having quit family, school, and flag, and on fire with the private ambition to be charged one day so high as to be a hipster oneself.

ADVERTISEMENT FOR "HIP, HELL, AND THE NAVIGATOR"

Richard Stern wrote a preface for this interview, and I can only add that he is modest about his part in it. If I become half-eloquent now and again, some of the credit must go to him. He had the faculty of stimulating me into more or less articulate speech. I was tired when I began the interview, I had had very little sleep for several days, and perhaps for that reason I found myself rushing into a confession of ideas I had never really talked about with anyone before.

Probably the worst fault with the interview is its sincerity— I meant every word I said, and so it has a head-on force and a complete lack of wit. But some of my notions about Hip as a religion are given away here, and so offer a sidelight on the Prologue to my new novel which ends this book.

HIP, HELL, AND THE NAVIGATOR

An Interview with Norman Mailer by Richard G. Stern

The interview took place in my apartment on May 6, this year.* None of the material was rehearsed, no questions were written out or thought about beforehand, and there was no warm-up session except thirty seconds of irrelevant talk which we used for volume control. The tape † itself is mottled with children's voices,

* *1958.*
 † *The tape is available in the Harper Library of the University of Chicago.*

the zoom of a couple of evening planes, and the clink of glasses being put down on coffee tables; and these sounds sometimes form a humorous counterpoint to the interview itself.

Mailer and I had known each other only a week—he'd come to Chicago as a Visiting Lecturer in the Department of English—but we had become good friends, and the interview was to be a continuation of the many conversations we had had during the week. As readers may suspect, it is not quite that. We began by expressing our fear of the tape recorder (not included here), and although Mailer soon seemed to lose sight of the whirring spools, I didn't. Secondly there was the artificial urgency to "produce" something, absent from most conversations. Thirdly, some of Mailer's responses began to throw me: I hadn't suspected the intensity and quality of some of the beliefs he expressed, and I not only reacted—which is natural—but I verbalized the reactions for the machine. My expostulations may be taken as testimony to my surprise, and then as testimony to the final "artificiality" which characterized the interview, my embarrassed consciousness of the role of interviewer, of soliciting gadfly, and occasionally devil's advocate (or God's perhaps). It would be hard for me to gauge the extent of my sincerity here in the interview.

Granted these defects, almost all of them the defects of the interviewer and his technique—or lack of it—the results, it seemed to Mailer and myself, are still worth printing. They take off from some pieces alluded to early in the interview, Mailer's article, "The White Negro: Superficial Reflections on the Hipster," which appeared in the Summer 1957 issue of *Dissent*, the exchanges between Mailer, Jean Malaquais and Ned Polsky which appeared in the Winter 1958 issue of *Dissent*, and the piece by Norman Podhoretz on "The Know-Nothing Bohemians" which is in the Spring 1958 issue of *Partisan Review*. The manner of taking off is one which might lead to this piece being called (in the words of a friend) "The Third Testament." This refers to something I was talking about a few hours after the interview took place. I was saying that the group of youngish American-Jewish writers now coming into such prominence might be said to be composing a new sort of testament, a bizarre theology. Bellow's amazing new novel, *Henderson, The Rain King* (which I've read only in uncorrected typescript), expounds a kind of psychological totemism raised magically into believability, at least into the sort of believability usable in fiction;

Bernard Malamud's *The Assistant* and some of his stories center about a kind of Essene conversion, though friends of mine have called them "really Christian," or rather resentfully, "evangelical"; Salinger's slightly sentimental variety of Buddhism has, in its drive toward greater explicitness, nearly driven him from the writing of that fiction which was primarily distinguished by its ache for belief. Now, Mailer joins this group—and explosively. Although centuries of epic theological and philosophical finagling seem to have passed him by, he is the most explicit "theologian" of all the writers, a kind of Manichaean whose overlooking of his "heretic" predecessors seems not only forgivable, but, considering the quality and urgency of his expression, indispensable.

A final note on the rhythm and authenticity of the interview: Mailer talked generally with rapidity, I with hesitation; Mailer with clarity, I with mumbles. Mailer's speech gets more and more rapid and rises to a pitch of excited engagement in the second half of the tape. All in all, there is a kind of music in the tape, and this is nowhere seen so clearly as when our friend Bob Lucid breaks in with a question, an excellent question, but one which comes as a shock to the "sound-spell." I am not suggesting that this "music" constitutes a unique or even an unusual quality, but it does communicate a rapport and ease which will not show up on the printed page, which must of necessity remain slavish to the words as they were said. For with the exception of those few speeches which are starred, this is essentially the interview as it was transcribed by a stenographer. One can even say it is an accurate copy but for the editing of a few false starts, repetitive mannerisms, and an involuted construction or two. The starred speeches were, however, rewritten, since the original remarks in these places were usually too bare and needed expansion. This was supplied separately by Mailer and myself, each of us agreeing to rewrite our own specific remarks in the off-hand spirit of the dialogue—if the reader does not notice them, that will be appropriate—they were meant to stand out as little as possible.

RICHARD STERN: I've been reading "The White Negro" and a fair amount of other material on the hipster, and I must say that intellectually I resent Hip as much as I can resent anything. Now I wonder about the extent of your allegiance to Hip. Are you using this material for fiction, or are you committed to it as a style of life, one which you want to practice yourself and recommend to others?

NORMAN MAILER: All right, good. I think the difficulty for most people who are at all interested in my work is that I started as one kind of writer, and I've been evolving into another kind of writer. And since we live in a time of enormous insecurity, what generally happens is that this insecurity is reflected in the critical snobberies of the moment. Most serious readers like a writer to be a particular thing. It's important; it's reassuring, somehow. I've noticed that most of the writers one might consider as thin blades, yes? stilettos, dirks, mmm? end up having a sure critical niche. And there have been a few writers like myself taking a particular little journey, and this journey consists of losing all the friends that one's found in the past, and not making enough new ones to make it a profitable venture in and of itself. So, I think if I'm going in this direction, it has to be assumed at least from the outside that I'm serious. Now whether I advocate Hip is another thing entirely.

STERN: The interesting thing about Hip is that Hip shouldn't belong to writers. If you're a genuine hipster you're committed, it seems to me, to a kind of anti-expressionism, Dada, or something like that. You're interested in the quality of the experience itself. If you're a sincere hipster you shouldn't be a writer.

MAILER: As a writer I'm not interested in less expression. What attracts me about Hip is that it's involved with more expression, with getting into the nuances of things.

STERN: More expression or more experience?

MAILER: The two have an umbilical relationship. What makes a novelist great is that he illumines each line of his work with the greatest intensity of experience. One thing about Hip you have to admit is that the hipster lives in a state of extreme awareness, and so, objects and relations that most people take for granted become terribly charged for him; and, living in a state of self-awareness his time slows up. His page becomes more filled. The quality of his experience becomes more intense. That doesn't make for less expression; it makes for greater difficulty of expression. It makes for writing more pages about fewer episodes which is certainly not the quintessence of the inarticulate.

STERN*: O.K. You maintain that there is an easy relationship between having experience and expressing it. It seems to me that the hipster is someone who has a lot of trouble with both experience and expression. His "kicks," his psyche-jogging, might I think be traced to the trouble.

Then there's another thing as far as writing goes. Isn't a novel controlled by some overriding notion, by a kind of fanaticism which organizes a great deal of disparate material? In a sense, a novel is like the mind of a madman: everything—casual looks, street signs, world news reports—is charged with meaning. That's why novelists write about ruling passions like love and ambition, passions which put their mark on all they touch, trivial or major. Now I can't believe that Hip allows for such overriding notions and passions. For the hipster, the cool one, detail is illumined, livid, but for its own sake, unqualified by considerations of any organization, the sort of organization which novels demand. I wonder if such material can be put into fiction.

MAILER: I think it can; and not only that, but I think Hip is particularly illumined by one notion so central and so shattering that its religious resonances and reverberations are going to dominate this coming century. And I think there is one single burning pinpoint of the vision in Hip: it's that God is in danger of dying. In my very limited knowledge of theology, this never really has been expressed before. I believe Hip conceives of Man's fate being tied up with God's fate. God is no longer all-powerful. [Here a phrase was lost to static in the tape.] The moral consequences of this are not only staggering, but they're thrilling; because moral experience is intensified rather than diminished.

STERN: Now that's a fantastic assertion. That really makes me sit up. What is the notion of God behind all this? Do you mean that some kind of personal god is dying with us?

MAILER: Now I only talk about my own vision of it, really, because it's not the sort of thing that you normally talk about with most hipsters. I think that the particular God we can conceive of is a god whose relationship to the universe we cannot divine; that is, how enormous He is in the scheme of the universe we can't begin to say. But almost certainly, He is not all-powerful; He exists as a warring element in a divided universe, and we are a part of— perhaps the most important part—of His great expression, His enormous destiny; perhaps He is trying to impose upon the universe His conception of being against other conceptions of being very much opposed to His. Maybe we are in a sense the seed, the seed-carriers, the voyagers, the explorers, the embodiment of that embattled vision; maybe we are engaged in a heroic activity, and not a mean one.

STERN: This is really something.

MAILER: Well, I would say it is far more noble in its conception, far more arduous as a religious conception than the notion of the all-powerful God who takes care of us.

STERN: And do you take to this conception for its perilous nobility, or do you take to it because you believe in it?

MAILER: I believe in it.

STERN: You believe in it.

MAILER: It's the only thing that makes any sense to me. It's the only thing that explains to me the problem of evil. You see, the answer may well be—how to put it?—that God Himself is engaged in a destiny so extraordinary, so demanding, that He too can suffer from a moral corruption, that He can make demands upon us which are unfair, that He can abuse our beings in order to achieve His means, even as we abuse the very cells of our own body.

STERN: Is it a person's duty to find out whether he's of God's party, whether he's working with God-beneficent or God-maleficent?

MAILER: Well, look, let's go back; let's go back to something much more modest for the moment which I think may tie this up, to a small extent, anyway. You asked me before why Hip is interesting for the novel. Well, up to now, when a novelist treats someone like a drug addict, the Square way is to treat the addict as a poor sociological cripple who is doomed and damned and goes down to his inevitable defeat. In Hip, which has after all to a certain extent come out of drug-taking (it's one of the elements in the growth of Hip) the attitude would be more that if taking drugs gives one extraordinary sensations, then the drug-taker is probably receiving something from God. Love perhaps. And perhaps he is. Let's just entertain the notion as a rational hypothesis which may or may not be true and let's see how far we go with it. If the hipster is receiving love from God he may well be draining some of the substance of God by calling upon this love, you see, which the drug releases. And in draining the substance of God he's exhausting Him, so that the drug-taker may be indulging an extraordinarily evil act at the instant he is filled with the feeling that he is full of God and good and a beautiful mystic. This involves new moral complexities which I feel are far more interesting than anything the

381

novel has gotten into yet. It opens the possibility that the novel, along with many other art forms, may be growing into something larger rather than something smaller, and the sickness of our times for me has been just this damn thing that everything has been getting smaller and smaller and less and less important, that the romantic spirit has dried up, that there is almost no shame today like the terror before the romantic. We're all getting so mean and small and petty and ridiculous, and we all live under the threat of extermination. In contrast, the notions of Hip enlarge us, they make our small actions not necessarily large, but more meaningful. If we pick up a bottle while listening to some jazz and we feel each of our five finger tips in relation to the bottle, the bottle begins to have a kind of form for us and we begin to feel each of our finger tips is receiving a different thing from the shape and the structure of the glass, and we then begin to think that maybe the very structure of this glass could conceivably contain some kind of hell within its constitution, some inorganic frozen state of imprisoned being less being than us. I think it's a more interesting notion than just picking up a bottle and pouring out some whisky.

STERN: It's a very pretty notion.

MAILER: Hip is pretty.

STERN: But it's all action, it's all erectile, isn't it? It's all feeling and taste and touch and smell. Isn't that the trouble with it?

MAILER: The trouble is that it's enormously difficult to return to the senses. We're all civilized, and to return to the senses and keep the best parts of our civilized being, to keep our capacity for mental organization, for mental construction, for logic, is doubly difficult, and there's a great danger that the nihilism of Hip will destroy civilization. But it seems to me that the danger which is even more paramount—the danger which has brought on Hip—is that civilization is so strong itself, so divorced from the senses, that we have come to the point where we can liquidate millions of people in concentration camps by orderly process.

STERN: Every powerful and refining force involves danger and waste. Does this divorce from the senses you talk about justify cashing in two or three thousand years of continuous culture?

MAILER*: Well, your argument is moot. It's too vast for this —for me. But let me try to put it this way. If the divorce from the senses I talk about is becoming a human condition, then by all means, yes, civilization must be cashed in or we will destroy ourselves in the cold insensate expressions of due process of law and atomic radiation. On the other hand maybe this divorce from the senses involves just a small part of my generation, and the Square, in contrast, leads a sensuous life with sufficient contentments to keep him civilized (in the good sense) and equable. It is we—hipsters— who would then be the only ones alienated from our senses. If this be true, then everything I have said is merely an intricate and ingenious rationalization to defend my neurotic . . . perversities, anh? Of course, I don't believe this is true.

STERN: All right, let's grant that it's moot. Now you have a career, a personal career, a career as novelist, and then maybe a career as an apostle of a new creed. Let's leave the last.

MAILER: Yes, let's leave the last.

STERN: Let's even leave the first and just look at the novelistic career. You are a novelist. You conceive of yourself as a novelist, though for the past week you've been saying you don't get much from literature any more. You're looking for something else. But still, you conceive of yourself as a novelist.

MAILER (interrupting): I don't want to be put on record that way. It's more complex than that.

STERN*: All right, let's forget that and concentrate on what all this has to do with you as a practicing novelist. How are these notions going to work for you? I saw them operating in the play version you made of The Deer Park. There you had a prologue in Hell, but I think you will remember I thought the Prologue was extraneous to the play. It was as if a critic had watched the play and said, "Doesn't seem like much until I let you in on the secret: These people are in Hell." Wasn't that something you just "put over" on your material? After you had really treated it, finished with it?

MAILER: Well . . . (sighs) when I was doing The Deer Park as a novel, characters existed on one level. It seemed to me that putting them into Hell deepened the meaning of their moral experience. That the situation of being in Hell and not knowing it is perhaps the first inversion—no, I don't want to say it that way—it is the first dislocation of the moral space. I find it difficult to express these things—they're terribly intangible for me. It's as if the belief that one exists on one level of being, when in fact—if one could ever discover that fact—one exists on another level of being may literally be the human condition. And so, I didn't do it as a casual or superficial thing. It may be that I lacked enough art to make the Prologue work for the play. But I wanted precisely this double state of existence, this existence of a people who are in Hell and did not know it.

STERN: You had a kind of double state in the novel. There it was a natural extension of the fiction, however. You quoted from the memoirs of a French courtier, one who described the rot of Louis Quinze's Court, and I think the idea was to give an extra dimension to the people you were writing about. It was like saying, here's another ash about to fall into the chasm. There you didn't falsify—my opinion here of course—your work, only expanded it. The idea of art seems to me to be to generate emotion from the treated material, not to point out some material and some feeling and say, "Put them together, reader."

MAILER: Well, let me avoid answering you directly. I feel that the final purpose of art is to intensify, even, if necessary, to exacerbate, the moral consciousness of people. In particular, I think the novel is at its best the most moral of the art forms because it's the most immediate, the most overbearing, if you will. It is the most inescapable. One could argue much more easily about the meaning of a nonobjective painting or of music, or whatever. But in the novel, the meaning is there. It's much closer; one could argue about ambiguities, but, because one is using words, it's much closer to the sense of moral commandments, moral strictures. And one gets into a particular thing which is terribly interesting, you begin to explore the interstices of moral reaction—which is the first approach to religious experience for many of us, especially since the organized religions don't begin to cover the enormous and terrible complexities of moral experience. It may be that particular people, working in various religions, individually working with particular people in their parish or whatever may bring some good along with a great deal of harm. But institutionally I believe that the organized religions are morally dead, that their net effect is deleterious, if not hideous and horrible. Organized religion is probably becoming one of the great enemies of our time . . . (reflectively) They're murderers of the senses.

STERN: So, as far as a work of art goes, we can work it out and then shove it into any pew or forum we want, all to exacerbate the moral consciousness. We can write a Prologue in Hell—or, how about a Prologue in Heaven?

MAILER: Oh, it would be more interesting.

STERN: More interesting?

MAILER: But it would be more difficult. That was beyond my grasp.

STERN: So for you, actions themselves are neutral. The novelist delivers and then labels them in any way he wants. The belief here is that the actions themselves won't satisfy the reader; he won't be used up, happily cleared of his emotional clots at the end of the book, but will have something left over, will ache for a balm to be supplied outside the novel. Art exacerbates the moral conscience, and then the moral conscience goes out to vote for the reform ticket, and thus eases the ache the novelist has put in it. The novelist's deposit is to be cashed in the world.

MAILER: Well, ideally, what I would hope to do with my work is intensify a consciousness that the core of life cannot be cheated. Every moment of one's existence one is growing into more or retreating into less. One is always living a little more or dying a little bit. That the choice is not to live a little more or to not live a little more; it is to live a little more or to die a little more. And as one dies a little more, one enters a most dangerous moral condition for oneself because one starts making other people die a little more in order to stay alive oneself. I think this is exactly the murderous network in which we all live by now.

STERN: And this is what the hipster does; he strikes out at others; he's constantly craving for more. He faces the risk of the extinction of his senses, extinction of his being, extinction of his capacity for making distinctions.

MAILER: He does certain things that are very brave in their way; he gambles for one thing with his soul—he gambles that he can be terribly, tragically wrong, and therefore be doomed, you see, doomed to Hell. Which the churchy people don't do at all. They're thinking of nothing but their own nasty little souls which are being maintained for some careful preservation afterward. The hipster is gambling with death and he is gambling with the Hereafter; and he may be wrong.

STERN: And the novelist is gambling with his talent as a novelist.

MAILER: Oh, yeah. Yeah.

STERN: The one talent he's got.

ROBERT LUCID: I can see it with the novelist, but I can't see it with the hipster. This is what kills me. You presume consciousness, you presume purpose, you presume direction on the part of this class—if that's the word—analogous to the novelist. And it seems to me that the whole notion of Hip is, in fact, unconscious, it is mere action.

STERN: I think it was said that the hipster risks his personal being—whatever that may be—and that the novelist risks his talent as a novelist. He does it because he has the choice of living a little more or dying a little more.

LUCID: The point is that the novelist consciously makes decisions and accepts the moral consequences. It seems to me the kind of guy we're talking about as hipster *qua* hipster is a guy who is, in fact, unconscious of risks of this kind, of the profundity . . .

MAILER: Consciously, he may think he's cutting quite a few corners as far as that goes. What I'm postulating in all this—the notion I've been working with all along that's been tacit to my remarks, implicit in my remarks, is that the unconscious, you see, has an enormous teleological sense, that it moves toward a goal, that it has a real sense of what is happening to one's being at each given moment—you see—that the messages of one's experience are continually saying, "Things are getting better," or "Things are getting worse. For me. For that one. For my future, for my past, mmm?" It is with this thing that they move, that they grope forward—this navigator at the seat of their being.

PART 5 Games and Ends

ADVERTISEMENT FOR GAMES AND ENDS

America is a hurricane, and the only people who do not hear the sound are those fortunate if incredibly stupid and smug White Protestants who live in the center, in the serene eye of the big wind. They cannot possibly know what it is like to start your life from the outside and try to reach the center, indeed they do not care to know, not really, not most of them—I sometimes think they would rather see the Republic go over to the Russians than to the discords of the sexual underground. Against these currents from the bottom and the curious sensual qualities of the green plant marijuana which will become for the sixties what the saloon was for the twenties (for yes, I think even the cops will be smoking it, they'll have to, or they will never keep up) against the nihilist waves of the years to come, the Square citadels of Protestantism will feel the future not as waves, but rather as vibrations and static. Since the Protestant is the historical embodiment of the great will which deadened the flesh (in all cruelty and no taste, one must insist that cancer has been their last contribution to civilization), the White Protestant's ultimate sympathy must be with science, factology, and committee rather than with sex, birth, heat, flesh, creation, the sweet and the funky; they must vote, manipulate, control, and direct, these Protestants who are the center of power in our land, they must go for what they believe is reason when it is only the Square logic of the past, and so if a time of apocalypse is on its way, they must finally be against the freedom of the body and the democracy of the flesh, they must go with the Russians rather than the Hip, for the Soviet sense of science and formal procedure will be more attractive to them, or rather less terrifying than the violence of the street fighter, the rebirth of sex, and the rounds of the ball.

In "The White Negro" we began a patrol through the theme of Hip which will continue through the rest of this book. If patrol is a word not without its affectations here, it is accurate nonetheless. In the Philippines we used to go out in the morning and make a rough tour up hills, through rice paddies, over brooks and along the edge of a modest jungle five miles in diameter. When we came back at night, fifteen miles older in the feet, wet twice with rain and sweat, our report on quiet days, and most of them were quiet, came down to more than that there was no enemy activity on our route. It was an extrapolation from very few facts. A village through which we passed had seen no Japanese in days; from the top of a high hill which had a good view of valley we saw nothing move, and the shreds of Japanese equipment we found on the trail were old, and had rotted in the wet. It was practice to assume that since we saw little, there was little, but we never knew, and once in a while we were surprised. In the beginning, I used to wonder at the empty spaces there must be in Intelligence, for the working maps at Headquarters were marked and pinpointed by the reports of patrols such as ours, and it seemed to me that armies moved on masses of half-truth and misinformation. Only years later did I come to realize that most of life was like that, and understanding was neat only for those who were afraid of experience and full of fact.

If we continue on a tour now through new terrain, it will have the life and fatigue of a patrol—there will be no real guides, and little enough of direct explanation, just a few intellectual sights, and more questions than answers. But then one cannot give a lecture on Hip, one must feel it, one must take the part of one's experience which is alive to the subject, and let it take the point. As may be seen later, Hip is never built on the fact, but rather on the nuance, and one enters it properly with the sensuous fear of a patrol.

When a reconnaissance was over, we never remembered what the terrain had been like for every step of the way. There were miles when most of us walked with our heads down, and came back with no more than a dull overlong impression of the clumps and roots in a field of grass. Later, in sleep perhaps, we would give a dramatic line to what we had seen—the high hill we had not climbed would lay its shadow over the route, and the small river hidden by brush whose banks we had avoided took to itself the marrow of a likely mystery; there was a squad leader or two who had a nose for where to take us, and having slept the night on the uncertain conclusions of what he had seen the day before, he would work the structure of an art in his sleep: small facts, experience, and the touch of his instinct would have their unconscious war, and leave him in the morning with a new sense of form which was the record of that psychic war; if he were still a good squad leader and on his nerve, he would take us that morning up the particular hill and along the riverbank we had avoided the day before. It made no sense as a military activity—none of us had the slightest desire to be killed in an action which could not even give a good marble of fact to the ponderous idiots who directed our fate, the squad leader was no more anxious than we were to get knocked off that way, but if he had a bit of the artist in him, and the good ones always did, he would gamble on his perception because it was the only way for him to grow. If he did not take the high hill he would never find out if his suspicion that Japanese might be there was good or wrong, and so whenever he would next have to call on a collaboration between his paranoia and his courage, his instincts would be slack with untested questions. A good squad leader looked for a bit of trouble to keep himself cool, and it was remarkable how seldom one ran into ambush.

Since it is small profit for me to ambush my readers needlessly, or even to push them without proper cause, I have divided the rest of these writings into three sections. The first bears the same relation to a patrol that a rest-camp does to a battlefield; after the full pack of The White Negro and the pieces which followed, I think the reader is entitled to an easy time for awhile. So the short stories, light articles and fragment of a play which begin this part of the book are intended to be entertaining. They are followed by another difficult terrain called Notes Toward A Psychology Of The Orgy which I cannot recommend to everyone, for some of the ideas are too large, and the essays are as cryptic as their title. (They are in fact no more than expanded notes.) The last, "From Surplus Value to the Mass Media" is a forced march on the mind if one is not familiar with Marxist terms. Unhappily it is also, I think, one of the more important short pieces in this book.

Last comes a literary engagement: two poems, a portion of The Deer Park as a play, an expanded perception on Picasso, and an evaluation of many of my contemporaries. So far as I know, this is the first time any of us has talked out in public about his competitors with the same words one might use in the living room. Hence, an *historic document. At the end will come three portions from my new novel which can stand more or less by themselves. To say any more would give the game away, for I should not like to think that the rest of this book is altogether without ambush.*

ADVERTISEMENT FOR "IT"

This was written in 1939, a few days after I came to Harvard. Archibald MacLeish gave an address to our Freshman Class, and as he was talking about the beginning of the Second World War, I jotted down a short story, the shortest story I've ever written.

IT

We were going through the barbed-wire when a machine gun started. I kept walking until I saw my head lying on the ground.

"My God, I'm dead," my head said.

And my body fell over.

ADVERTISEMENT FOR "GREAT IN THE HAY"

I wrote this story in 1950 when I was in Hollywood. The beginnings of The Deer Park *can be seen here.*

Years later I looked for the piece, and could find it nowhere. Then one night Mickey Knox mentioned the title. He had been using "Great In The Hay" for years, he told me, as an actor's bit at parties.

GREAT IN THE HAY

Once there were two producers named Al and Bert. They were both short, they were both bald, they were both married, and they both produced pictures. They even had offices next to one another. Everything about them was so similar that they might have been considered twins if it were not for a difference so great that one never thought of them as being the least alike.

The difference was that the one named Al had the reputation of being great in the hay. In every other respect he was much the same as Bert, whose only reputation for want of something better was that he made a great deal of money.

This irritated Bert. He would call people in, he would talk to them, he would say: "I've known Al for twenty years. We got married within three months of each other, we make the same salary, we've had approximately the same number of big box-office grossers and box-office duds, we're the same height, we're almost the same weight, our looks are similar, and yet Al has the reputation of being great in the hay. Why should he have that reputation?"

It came to bother Bert, it came to bother him colossally. He would ask everyone, and no one would tell him the answer. He came at last to approach it as a business problem. He called in a private detective.

To the detective, he said, "I want you to find out the reason. I don't care how low-down and dirty. The man has a secret, there's a reason why Al is an expert and I'm an unknown. I want you to find that reason."

The detective went out, he scouted around, he compiled a list of names, he ended with a duplicate of the little black book which Al was keeping. To each of the addresses listed went the detective. As he obtained his answers he filed his reports, and when he was done he returned to Bert.

"Your report is wasted money," Bert cried. "You've taught me nothing. You've merely confused me. Let me read to you what they say. It's disgusting."

Bert read from the report. He read what Claudia Jane had to say, and Dianthe, and Emeline, and Fay, and Georgia, and Hortense, and all the others.

"He is the best lover I've ever used," said Claudia Jane, "because he is floppy and lets me throw him around."

"He is magnificent," murmured Dianthe, "he melts my ice. He rides over me, disdains me, leaves me convinced I am a woman."

"He is cute," wrote Emeline, "and all my own."

"A master at sexpertease," stated Hortense, "because I tell you, buster, I'm bored with less."

"Pure," dictated Fay, "and not addicted to the nasty. Love for him is a communion of purity and simplicity which intensifies my hard-won religious conversion."

"He likes to spend money," lisped Georgia, "and I think that's everything, don't you?"

Bert was enraged. "You call this a report?" he shouted at the detective. "It is nothing but a mish-mosh." He threw the sheets into the air. "You go find his secret."

The detective pounded a weary scented beat. His flat shoes trod through boudoirs while he attempted to elicit a gimmick from the mish-mosh. At last the case was closed. There came a morning when to everyone's surprise, Al left a note which read *Every year I have been getting more and more depressed,* and blew out his brains.

Bert could never understand it. When he discharged the detective, he complained with a sigh, "I still don't understand why Al was so great. It's aggravating. I've lived a full life, and I can tell you. All women are the same in the dark. I ought to know."

So the moral of this story may well be: People who live in the dark live longest of all.

1950

ADVERTISEMENT FOR "THE PATRON SAINT OF MACDOUGAL ALLEY"

This story was done about the time I was writing my war stories and The Notebook. *I sent it to the* New Yorker *which turned it down, and then I put it away. Coming across it now, I like the piece for this section, since it is about a Beatnik who arrived too early to know his name.*

THE PATRON SAINT OF MACDOUGAL ALLEY

How can one describe Pierrot? It is impossible to understand him; one may only tell stories about him. Yet with every move he makes, he creates another story, so one cannot keep up. Pierrot is an original; he is unlike anyone else on the face of the earth.

I can describe how he looks. He is now nineteen, and of average height. He has dark hair, regular features, and a very pleasant smile. There are times when he grows a mustache, and there are times when he shaves it off. During those periods when he sports a few hairs beneath his nose, he looks a year or two younger; when he strips it, he is nineteen again. I suspect he will look nineteen a decade from now; what is worse I often have the suspicion that he looked the same when he was born. Pierrot will never change. He is absolutely predictable in the most unforeseen situations.

He is the son of my friend Jacques Battigny, who is a professor of Romance languages at a university in New York, and never were a father and son more related and less alike. Jacques is a gentleman of considerable culture; as a representative French intellectual it is somewhat intolerable to him to pass through experience without comprehending it rationally. He demands order in every corner of his life. It is his cross that Pierrot is the eternal flux.

Father and son are thesis and antithesis. Put another way, Pierrot is Jacques turned inside out, the clothes-dummy of an intellectual. He has all the attributes of the French mind except its erudition; his greatest joy is to approach logically large bodies of experience about which he knows nothing. The first time I met him, Pierrot spoke to me for hours; he mentioned in passing, Marx, Freud, and Darwin; Heidegger, Kierkegaard, and Sartre; Lawrence and Henry Miller; Nietzsche and Spengler; Vico and Edmund Wilson; Jean Genet and Simone de Beauvoir; Leon Trotsky and Max Schachtman; Wilhelm Reich, Gregory Zilboorg, and Karen Horney. There were two hundred other names of varied importance, and I do not believe he used a word which had less than four syllables. Therefore, it took some time for me to realize that Pierrot was an idiot.

In the hours between, he husked my brains. What did I think of Mr. Aldous Huxley? Pierrot would inquire, and long before I had reconstituted my recollections of Huxley's work and delivered them in some organized form, Pierrot was wondering how I evaluated Mr. Thomas Stearns Eliot. It seemed to me that I had never met an adolescent who was more intelligent: the breadth of his queries, the energy of his curiosity, and the quick reception which shone in his brown eyes, were quite impressive. Chaplin and Griffiths, Jackson Pollack and Hans Hofmann, did I like Berlioz and had I heard Benjamin Britten? Pierrot was tireless. Only when the afternoon had passed and my wife felt obliged to invite him for dinner, did I begin to suspect that Pierrot did not contribute as much as I.

A few minutes later in response to a discreet inquiry or two, Pierrot confessed to me with relish that he had never seen a single one of the pictures he mentioned, nor read one of the authors we spoke about. "You understand," he said to me, "it is so depressing. I want to amass the totality of knowledge, and consequently I don't know where to begin." He sighed. "I look at the books on my father's shelf. I say to myself, 'Is it in these books that I will find the termination, or even the beginning, of my philosophical quest?' You understand? What is the meaning to life? That is what obsesses me. And will these books give the answer? I look at them. They are paper, they are cardboard. Is it possible that the essence of truth can be communicated to paper and ink?" He paused and smiled. "Reality and illusion. I think about history, and I wonder, 'Does Marxism take proper account of history?' Someone was telling me to read Engel's *Marriage and The Family*. Would you recommend it? I am very interested in the subject."

He was absolutely tireless. As dinner progressed, as the dishes were washed, the brunt of conversation shifted from my tongue to Pierrot's. He sat with my wife and me through the evening, he discussed his ambitions, his depressions, his victories, his defeats. What did I think of his parents, he wanted to know, and immediately proceeded to tell me. Pierrot's mother had died, and his father had married again. Georgette was ten years younger than Jacques, and Pierrot found this disturbing. "You understand," he said to me cheerfully, "I look for love. I search for it in the midst of my family, and I do not find it. Between Georgette and me there is an attraction, I ask myself whether it is maternal or physical? I should like to bring matters to a head, but I am a virgin, and I should detest it if I could not satisfy her. Is it true that one must serve the apprenticeship of love?" Long before I could have turned an answer, he had forgotten his question. "And then I wonder in the privacy of my thoughts if what I really seek is the conquest of Georgette, or if I am looking for her only to be my mother. I should like her to hold me close. You understand, I am masochistic. I feel so many things." He held his breast. "I am an infant and I am a lover. Which is my nature? Which do I desire to satisfy? You realize, I want to be close to my father, and yet I am repelled by him. It is like psychoanalysis. I think sometimes I wish to live *menage à trois*, but then I decide I am destructive and desire to live in isolation. Is it man's nature to live in isolation? I feel so lonely at times. I wish to communicate. Communication is a problem which interests me. Does it you?"

At one o'clock in the morning, after numerous hints had failed, I was obliged to tell Pierrot that he must go home. He looked at me sadly, he told me that he knew he bored me, he left with an air of such dejection that my wife and I were ashamed of ourselves, and felt we had turned a waif into the streets. The next time I saw his father, I apologized for this, and was cut short.

"Apologize for nothing," Jacques shouted. "The boy is a monster. He has no conception whatsoever of time. If you had not put him out, he would have stayed for a week." Jacques held his head. "I shall certainly go mad. There is nothing to do with him but to be completely rude. Listen to what has happened."

The story Jacques told was indeed painful. Battigny the senior is a lover of books. He loves to read, he declaims on the art of reading, he loves bindings, he loves type, he loves books separately and together. It seems that Pierrot was once talking to a friend of Jacques', a somewhat distinguished professor. The professor, taken with the boy, loaned him a copy of Florio's translation of Montaigne's essays. It was not a first edition, but it was an old one, and of some value, beautifully tooled in leather, and handsomely printed. "Do you know how long ago that was?" Jacques demanded of me. "It was two years ago. Pierrot has kept it in his brief case for two years. Has he ever read a page?" The answer was that he had not. He had merely kept it, and in the course of keeping it, the cover-board had been sheared and the spine exposed. "I screamed at him," Jacques said softly, "it was indecent. I told him it was two years he had kept it, and he told me no, it was only a short period. He cannot comprehend the passage of time. He is always about to dip into the book, to study it here and smell it there. It is shameful.

"It is intolerable," Jacques cried. "He torments me. I have talked to his English teacher at high school. He asks her if he should study *Beowulf*, and he cannot even pass the examinations. I do not care if he does not go to college, I am not a snob about it, but the boy is incapable of doing anything with his hands. He cannot even learn a trade."

I was to discover that Pierrot could not even learn to say yes or no. He was quite incapable of it, no matter to what brutal lengths I pursued him. Once in eating at my house, I asked him if he wished some bread and butter.

"I do not know," Pierrot said, "I ask myself."

"Pierrot, do you want bread and butter?" I cried out.

"Why do you wish me to eat?" he asked dreamily, as if my motive were sinister. "One eats to live, which supposes that life is worth while. But I ask myself: is life worth while?"

"Pierrot! Do you want bread and butter? Answer yes or no!"

Pierrot smiled sheepishly. "Why do you ask me a yes-and-no question?"

One could say anything to him, and he enjoyed it immensely. He had been making advances to my wife for quite some time. No matter how she teased him, scolded him, or ignored him, he persisted. Yet once, when I took a walk with him, he launched into a long description of my virtues. I was handsome, I was attractive, he was stirred by me. And with that he pinched my bicep and said, "You are so strong."

"My God, Pierrot," I said in exasperation. "First you try to make love to my wife, and then you try to make love to me."

"Yes," he said morosely, "and I succeed with neither."

His father finally drove him from the house. He gave Pierrot two hundred dollars, and told him he was to find a job in the city and learn to live by his own labor. Jacques was penitent. "I am so cruel to the boy. But what is there to do? I cannot bear the sight of him. Have you ever watched him work? If he picks up a hammer, he smashes his thumb. He lays down the hammer, he sucks his finger, he loses the hammer, he forgets why he needed it in the first place, he tries to remember, he ends by falling asleep." Jacques groaned. "I dread to think of him out in the world. He is completely impractical. He will spend the two hundred dollars in a night on his bohemian friends."

Only a father could have been so wrong. Pierrot had the blood of a French peasant. The two hundred dollars lasted for six months. He lived with one friend, he lived with another; he lunched with an acquaintance and stayed for dinner. He drank beer in the Village; he was always to be found at Louis', at Minetta's, at the San Remo, but no one remembered when he had paid for a drink. He was pretty enough to be courted, and he had frequent adventures with homosexuals. They were always finding him in a bar, they would talk to him, he would talk to them. He would tell them his troubles, he would confide, he would admit warmly that he had never discovered anyone who understood him so well. He would end by going to the other's apartment. There Pierrot would drink, he would continue to talk, he would talk even as the friend removed his shirt and apologized for the heat. It was only at the penultimate moment that Pierrot would leave. "You understand," he would say, "I want to know you. But I am so confused. Do we have a basis to find a foundation of things in common?" And out he would skip through the door.

"Why do they always approach me?" he would ask in an innocent voice.

I would make the mistake of being severe. "Because you solicit, Pierrot."

He would smile. "Ah, that is an interesting interpretation. I hope it is true. I would love to make my living in an antisocial manner. Society is so evil."

He lived with a girl who was a fair mate for him. She had a tic at one corner of her mouth, and she was a follower of Buddha. The girl was trying to start a Buddhist colony in America. It was all mixed somehow with a theory about the birth trauma which she explained to me one night at a party. The reason armies functioned in combat was because the noise of battle returned the ordinary soldier to the primal state of birth. At such a moment his officers came to represent the protecting mother, and the soldier would obey their will even if it meant death. She was proud of the theory, and snapped at Pierrot when he would attempt to discuss it with her.

"A wonderful girl," he told me once. "It is a most exciting affair. She is absolutely frigid."

It seemed that if he dropped his shoes upon the floor, she would not allow him to approach her. "There is such uncertainty. It recaptures the uncertainty of life. I think about it. People meet. Lives intersect. It is points on a plane. Would you say this is a fit topic for philosophical investigation?"

In the course of events the Buddhist threw him out. At any rate, metaphorically she threw him out. The affair ended, but since Pierrot had no place to live, he continued to stay with her while he looked for another friend to give him a bed. During this period he came to me to ask if I would put him up, but I refused. After making these requests, he would look so forlorn that I hated myself.

"I understand," he said. "One of my friends who is analyzing me by hypnosis has made me see that I exploit everyone. It is the influence of the culture, I would think. I have become very interested in the movements of political bodies. I see that previously I adopted too personal an attitude. What is your opinion of my new political approach?"

"We'll discuss it another time, Pierrot. I'm awfully sorry I can't put you up for the night."

"It is all right," he said sweetly. "I do not know where I shall sleep tonight, but it does not matter. I am an exploiter, and it is only proper that people should recognize this in me." He left with a meek forgiving look. "I shall sleep. Do not worry about me," he said as the door closed.

Five minutes later I was still trying to put the matter from my mind when the doorbell rang. Pierrot was back. All night he had had a problem he wanted to discuss with me, but in the interest of our conversation, it had completely slipped his mind.

"What is it?" I asked coldly, annoyed at having been taken in.

He answered me in French. "*Tu sais, j'ai la chaude-pisse.*"

"Oh, Christ!"

He nodded. He had been to see a doctor, and it would be cleared up. There would be a wonder drug employed.

"Not by one of your friends, I hope?"

No, this was a bona-fide doctor. But he had another problem. The ailment had been provoked by the Buddhist. Of this, he was certain. At the moment, however, he was engaged in an affair with a young married woman, and he was curious to know whether he should tell her.

"You certainly should." I grasped him by the shoulder. "Pierrot, you have to tell her."

His brown eyes clouded. "You understand, it would be very difficult. It would destroy so much rapport between us. I would prefer to say nothing. Why should I speak? I am absolutely without morality," he declared with passion.

"Morality be damned," I said. "Do you realize that if you don't tell the girl, you will have to see the doctor again and again? Do you know how expensive that is?"

He sighed. This is what he had been afraid of. Like the peasant brought slowly and stubbornly to face some new and detestable reality, he agreed dourly. "In that case, I shall tell her. It is too bad."

Lately, I have hardly seen Pierrot. His two hundred dollars has run out, and he is now obliged to work. He has had eleven jobs in four months. I could not hope to describe them all. He has been let go, fired, dismissed, and has resigned. He was an office boy for two days, and on the second day, pausing to take a drink, he placed his letter basket on the lip of the water cooler. Somehow—he is convinced it is the fault of the cooler—the water ran over the papers. In attempting to wipe them, he dropped the basket, and the wet paper became dirty. Signatures ran, names became illegible, and to the fury of the office manager, Pierrot did not attempt to excuse himself but asked instead why Americans were so compulsive about business correspondence.

He also worked in a factory. He was very depressed after the first day of work had ended, and called me up in such a mournful voice that I felt obliged to see him. He was tired, he was disgusted. "I hold a piece of metal in my hand," he said to me, "and I touch it to an abrasive agent. Slowly square corners become round. Eight hours of such work I suffer. Can this be the meaning to existence?" His voice conveyed that he expected to continue the job until the end of time. "I search for my identity. It is lost. I am merely Agent 48."

At this point I rose upon him in wrath. I told him that he had two choices. He could work in order to live, or he could die. If he wished to die, I would not attempt to discourage him. In fact, I would abet him. "If you come to me, Pierrot, and ask for a gun, I will attempt to find you a gun. Until then, stop complaining." He listened to me with an enormous smile. His eyes shone at the vigor of my language. "You are marvelous," he said with admiration.

The very last I've heard is that Pierrot is soon to be drafted. Some of my friends are very upset about this. They say that the boy will be a mental case in a few weeks. Others insist that the army will be good for him. I am at odds with both of them.

I see Pierrot in the army. He will sleep late, curled in a little ball beneath his blankets. He will be certain to miss reveille. About eight o'clock in the morning he will stumble drowsily to the mess hall, his mess gear falling from his hand, and will look stupidly at the cook.

"Oh," he will say, "oh, I am late for breakfast."

"Get out of here," the cook will say.

"Oh, I go." Pierrot will nod. "I deserve to miss a meal. I have been negligent. Of course, I will be out all day on a march, and I will be very hungry, but it is my fault. And it does not matter. What is food?" He will be so unhappy that the cook no matter how he curses will scramble him some eggs. Pierrot will suggest toast, he will induce the cook to heat the coffee, he will engage him in a philosophical discussion. At eleven o'clock, Pierrot will leave to join his training platoon, and at two in the afternoon he will find them. Hours later, at retreat parade, the inspecting officer will discover that Pierrot has lost his rifle.

That will be the beginning of the end. Pierrot will be assigned to K.P. for three days in a row. By the first morning he will so have misplaced and mis-washed the pots that the cooks will be forced to assist him, and will work harder than they have ever worked. By evening the mess sergeant will be begging the first sergeant never to put Pierrot on K.P. again.

The army cannot recover from such a blow. K.P. is its foundation, and when cooks ask to remove men from that duty, it can take only a few days before every soldier in the army will follow the trail blazed by Pierre Battigny. I see the army collapsing two months after Pierrot enters it.

At that moment I hope to influence the course of history. Together with such responsible individuals as I may find, I will raise a subscription to send Pierrot to the Soviet Union. Once he is there, the world is saved. He will be put in the army immediately, and before his first day is over, the Russians will have him up before a firing squad. Then Pierrot will rise to his true stature.

"I ask myself," he will say to the Russian soldiers, "Am I not miserable? Is life not sad? Shoot me."

At this point the Russians will throw down their arms and begin to weep. "We do not enjoy ourselves either," they will sob. "Shoot us, too." In the grand Russian manner, the news will spread across the steppes. Soldiers everywhere will cast away their weapons. America and Russia will be disarmed in a night, and peace will come over the earth.

They will build a statue to Pierrot at the corner of Eighth Street and MacDougal. New generations will pass and spit at him. "He was Square," they will say.

1951

ADVERTISEMENT FOR A LETTER
TO THE NEW YORK POST

This letter gives a bit of importance to a man who has no importance to me, but I put it in for the opportunity to say that I had nothing to do with the making of the movie of The Naked and The Dead, *and my only, if considerable, sin was to sell the book after years of protecting its chastity.*

A LETTER TO THE
NEW YORK POST

On Monday, August 11, Paul Gregory, the producer of the movie, *The Naked and the Dead*, was quoted in Archer Winsten's column as saying this about me:

> Mailer? He's an incorrigible blank. I don't mind temperament. I've never known a talent worth a damn without it. [But there are limits] . . . we're in a restaurant together and he throws the potatoes the whole way across the restaurant. Of course, he'd said he didn't want the potatoes, but there are other ways of getting rid of them. And the lawsuits. You have anything to do with him, you've got lawsuits.

To dispose of the last misstatement first, I have had one lawsuit in all my life—it is one I am having now against RKO and Warner Bros. on matters related to the making of *The Naked and the Dead*.

As for the potatoes—of course not. I've never thrown potatoes in a restaurant, at home, in bed, or at Paul Gregory. Mr.

Gregory and I ate together once (just once), and he may have received a violent impression of me from something I said.

At the time he was trying to buy *The Naked and the Dead* and he kept telling me it was a great, great book, the greatest book he had ever read (which may indeed have been true if he had not read very many books), and when I asked him how he would go about translating this great, great book into a theatrical proposition, he mentioned the name of a soldier who dies in the first 20 pages of the novel, and he added:

"I hear background music playing 'From The Halls of Montezuma.'

"This is off the top of my head, of course, but I hear the Marine hymn and I see the Marine uniform of this boy covered with blood. Norman, am I interesting even your little finger?"

And I answered, "Paul, if you want to interest my little finger, please stop calling these soldiers Marines."

Could it be that this is what Gregory remembers as mashed potatoes flying across a restaurant?

A little later in the evening, for the first and only time in my life, I fainted dead away. Looking back on it, I would suspect the reason was that something honorable had worn out in me, and I knew I was going to sell my book (which I loved so much) to a man who didn't know the difference between the Army and the Marines.

HOW TO COMMIT MURDER
IN THE MASS-MEDIA—A

A few months ago, I was approached by a man who had started to do a broadcast for the Canadian Broadcasting System on the Beat Generation. He had been collecting taped interviews from various people who might be considered figures in the ferment, and on the basis of "The White Negro" he wished to interview me as well. I tried to refuse; I offered the excuse that usually I avoided interviews because there was a tendency to talk away too many new ideas. In that case, he asked, would I merely read some passages from "The White Negro." I said yes.

He came over to my apartment one evening with his tape recorder, and after ten or fifteen minutes of passing conversation, I read a few pages of my words into his microphone. He told me that once the various tapes were put together into a master tape, he would invite me to a party where he would play it.

About a month later, the party took place. I went with my wife and my friend Mickey Knox to a cold-water pad, south of the village, and the scene had three beards to every chin, a lot of wine, some beer, and no whisky. We were late, and the tape (which was more than an hour long) was already in the middle. What I heard of it was good, candid, even informative for a broadcast. On the other hand, it was tendentious. The man who had interviewed me was the narrator, and he was not sympathetic to the Beat, his tacit attitude was closer to his presumably Square Canadian audience than to the men and women he interviewed.

When my voice came on, I had a shock. It is rarely good to hear one's own voice, but I had lived through that years ago, and I was familiar with the sound now, I was even able to listen to myself with a cool ear. What I was hearing now at this party was not my own voice, however. It was high-pitched, shrill, very rapid, and with a clipped staccato beat—I sounded like Hitler. Then the narrator came on: a warm masculine voice. His natural speech had been good, but it was not this good.

It took something to keep silent. As the broadcast went on, I noticed that this contrast of voices continued. All the hipsters and Beatniks were shrill, feminine, nervous and quick—the narrator was the rich radio voice of North America. I knew something had been done to the tape, and the moment the machine was turned off, I went over to the narrator and asked him if the voice on the tape sounded very much like my voice. He looked uneasy. No, it didn't seem the same, he said. I asked the narrator if he had turned up the treble for the others, and the bass for himself, and he seemed honest in his answer that he had only an English field machine which had no such controls.

Finally a girl whispered to me, "Probably his batteries were weak, and he didn't have money to buy new ones." Looking at him through the filter of such small detail, I knew that was part of the explanation, for weak batteries slow the speed of the tape. When such a tape is played at normal speed, the voices turn quick and shrill, like a record on an old-fashioned gramophone whose turntable revolves too quickly. Of course, the narrator had had the leisure to re-record his own voice at the studio, which was why he had sounded good, and now felt guilty. The tape had expressed a sad comedy of vanity and worn-out tools.

I tell this bit of story because it gives a hint of what is done on every broadcast and telecast. On a major network, only subtle improvements or flaws are added by sound engineers to the voice, but since millions are listening, it is fair to assume that a few hundred thousand people are shifted from an instinctive dislike to a small appreciation of the performer. If the super-state of the future arrives, this technique has its obvious uses for brain-washing the populace out of one ideological corral and into another: by good make-up or bad, by bass or by treble, by a camera closing in at bad times, and dollying backward at moments of climax, a man with ideas unhappy for the State may be shuffled to the rear of a debate, and never know how much of him was lost in the adjusted mirror of a television screen. The present-tense will be altered at the instant it comes into being.

Even worse, the history of the past may be warped at the root, by the judgment of our senses. If a new sympathy for Nazism should arise in America, who knows but that the unforgettable voice of Adolph Hitler will be replayed to the ear of a future people, so modified, made so attractive and so *American* that the Fuehrer's tone will be heard in the Twenty-First Century as the Big Daddy voice of all virile and velvety broadcasters.

HOW TO COMMIT MURDER
IN THE MASS-MEDIA—B

Two years ago, I was on television for the first time. It was only a local show for the area of Greater New York, but during that season it had come into prominence. Night after night, from eleven to twelve, Mike Wallace, who conducted *Night Beat,* would take each of two guests through a separate thirty-minute interview. Wallace had a hard personality in those days, he was a little like a young district attorney, dogged, not altogether fair, and with a good ability to force his guests into confessions which were startling to hear over a television set. *Night Beat* was one of the first shows to use an extreme close-up of the face, and when a guest began to perspire the drops were large as camphor balls. One watched the show with the interest of a hunter.

Television, ideally, should have a sadistic edge. The shape of the set and the quality of the image have a clinical effect on the senses. One finds it dull to react to singers or dancers—they seem a little warped as they come out of the machine. On TV, a cold dead nakedness is more stimulating to the eye, and *Night Beat* used to offer that. (Later, Wallace moved to another channel and had a nationwide interview; as everyone expected, his method was stripped of its bite, and his air time became almost as bland and homogeneous as any other half-hour of national entertainment.)

The night I was on Wallace's show proved interesting. I had not been ready for the way it would feel; I suppose I had not expected that the existence of a million invisible people staring at me would seem like the sensuous equivalent of an electric chair. My nerve was under control, but my mind was empty. Each time Wallace would ask a question, I would not know if the next word in my answer would make its appearance on time or not. Yet with it all, I felt as alive as an actor on opening night, and after a while I began to think I was doing very well—my own personality was so charged for me, that I assumed it would be as charged for everyone else. In fact, I was doing only fairly well, and if to my surprise, people complimented me afterward for appearing calm, I also had the leisure over the next few weeks to listen to a recorded tape of that half-hour, and I would wince at how vague my mind had become, and how much I had left unsaid which should have been said. All the same I kept a memory of the program. There had been one exchange which gave me pleasure. It went:

WALLACE: I understand that in a column that you wrote for *The Village Voice,* before the last election, you proposed that Ernest Hemingway run for President, say-

407

ing, "This country could stand a man for President, since for all too many years our lives have been guided by men who were essentially women, which indeed is good for neither men nor women."

MAILER: That's right. I said that.

WALLACE: Were you serious about it?

MAILER: Oh, absolutely.

WALLACE: (*coming in for the kill*) What do you mean by that—"men who were essentially women"? Who among our leaders is so unmasculine that you regard him in that light?

MAILER: Well, I think President Eisenhower is a bit of a woman.

When the show ended five minutes later, my wife came up to me and whispered, "*Well,* we may be dead tomorrow, but it was worth it."

A little did happen. Through various tunnels and channels, I heard that James Hagerty, the President's news secretary, phoned Channel Five the next day to ask for a transcript of the broadcast. (More likely, it was someone in Hagerty's office.) And a day or two later, the same story appeared in Jack O'Brian's column for the New York *Journal-American*. Odds are, the story is true. If I were news secretary to the President, I would do something like that. It succeeds in putting a slight chill on the producer and the other principals of the show, it is a way of saying, "You boys on Channel Five want to keep your nose clean, now don't you?" At any rate, I was not invited again to any show by Mike Wallace. Perhaps I was not a very interesting guest.

A year later, Wallace asked me for permission to print an abridged version of our half-hour in a book he was getting together for Simon and Schuster of selected interviews. I gave permission and forgot about it until I saw the book. It was a handsome affair, a large soft-cover magazine-sized offering called *Mike Wallace Interviews*, and it was low in price, designed for a mass market. Going through its pages, I felt a little like a poor cousin at a rich family dinner. There were full-page photographs of the other principals, and many half-page photographs, shots in action on the show, shots at home—a generous study of some scattered celebrities. I received the smallest picture in the book, and when I saw it, I would have been happier if I had never been invited to dinner. The picture had been taken in

1949, and it showed a young sweaty adenoidal young man in desperate need of a haircut. His eyes glitter, his mouth is getting ready to snarl, and he has a mad look in his eyes. He bears an unmistakable resemblance to a cornered rat. I remembered that picture well, it was the worst picture ever taken of me, and *Time* magazine used it in 1951 next to the Death-To-Norman-Mailer review they did of *Barbary Shore*. The photograph had been taken on a particular afternoon at the Waldorf Peace Conference two years before, back in March 1949, and for a few days I had indeed felt like a rodent, for I was about to leave the Progressive Party. I thought it no longer made sense to talk out against a totalitarian atmosphere in America while locking oneself intellectually into a one-windowed cell which did not permit a view of all that might be worse in Russia. It had taken many months to come to this point, and if not for Jean Malaquais, it might have taken years, but the sum of my doubts had come to decision, and I did not believe in the Peace Conference. For three days I walked around talking to people I knew, trying to buttonhole them, wanting to explain why the Peace Conference could bring no peace, and in the frantic atmosphere of those insane few days, I would be told, "That's nice, Norman. Now will you help us on talking to . . ." and so it went. I had many friends in the Progressive Party, and much had been made of me—it was my simple duty to tell them that if I spoke in public I would lose them forever. But no one could listen to anything. America was at its second peak of anti-Russian hysteria then, and the week before the conference had brought all but open incitements to violence in the New York tabloids. The meetings at the Waldorf-Astoria were surrounded by thousands of pickets restrained by hundreds of police. They had come perhaps out of the dream that the doors of the Waldorf might open to them, and they could smash some motherfucking Reds, loot the silk of that overrich hotel and perhaps drag back to Queens or Staten Island a real live Russian to char over a slow fire on their barbecue pit. At least so it seemed to those of us who were inside the Waldorf, all the well-dressed Progressives and fellow travelers who were come to congregation. Naturally, no one listened to me, and like a log in a jam I was bumped and carried over those three days, to land on the Speaker's dais for the climactic session. Shostakovitch was there—I had seen him back and forth those three days, petrified, or so it seemed, of all Americans, Russians, flash bulbs, reporters, interviewers, airports, perhaps even of life itself, and Alexander Fadeyev sat near me on the dais, a hulking bully-beef of a Russian novelist, bureaucrat even to the articulation of his ham fat hands on heavy thighs, and he's dead now, fallen out of favor and then a suicide. When my turn came to speak, I made some dumb rushing collision of sounds for three minutes, I spoke of monopoly capitalism and state capitalism, and how only socialism could save the world, and America was not close to that, and Russia was not close, and people should not believe in countries and patriotism anyway, and peace conferences like this gave the idea that one could, and so were wrong—and all the while I knew I was betraying the people who had come in some little part to hear me, for this was not what they wanted to hear, and I did not know if I spoke out of new and deep political conviction, or if a part of me was now looking only to get myself free of the Progressive Party and might I be really afraid of the final wrath of those psychically starved hoodlums on the street outside? So there came a point toward the end when I was not too far from weeping, as indeed I had been close to weeping through all of this speech, and to avoid that disaster, I screwed up my face into a snarl, feeling like a miserable and undeserving rat, and then some flash bulbs went off, and I sat down.

The photograph of this instant was used to grace my interview in Wallace's book. There it stands for the record of another moment eight years later when the same young man, now not so young, and with rather a different face, decided he might just as well gamble on his opinion that the President of the United States was a bit of a woman. So it was natural that when I turned the page and came across this old picture which was supposed to be new, I thought, You shits. That's another one I owe you.

ADVERTISEMENT FOR "BUDDIES"

What comes next is the fragment of a one-act play. It runs along for about ten minutes and then breaks off in the middle. I started to write it one afternoon and went along at good speed for two hours. Hardly a word has since been changed. That night, I started to smoke after seven days without cigarettes, went to The Ordeal which is legally called The Ideal Bar and is situated across the street from the White Horse Tavern, quietly went through eight or nine shots of blended whisky, went home at closing, fell into a leaden bombed-out sleep and woke at half-past twelve in the afternoon with the mood of my play shattered beyond repair. I have not been able to find a new thought for it since. That action was as useless as anything I've done in a while, but in any case, the play would probably have run down sooner or later, for to keep its life, the situation would have to become more outrageous with every minute of stage action. Probably it could have been successful only by a major effort. Let us leave what was not done with the dependable remark that good beginnings to plays are easy to write.

BUDDIES, or THE HOLE IN THE SUMMIT

Fragment of a One-Act Play

E

So I see we're alone at last.

K

I'm captivated to be your host.

E

Well, now, that's one of the matters I think we ought to get down to discussing first. You see, formally, that is in the procedural sense, you are not my host. We meet as principals, do we not?

K

Primaries.

E

I don't know if that's the word. Of course, it's very good of you to speak in my language.

K

I detest translators. Judases. We almost had our private war with China because a translator made an error, a disgusting error. He said . . . that I said . . . that a certain Chinkie—you say?

E

Chinaman.

K

Chinaman of Chinese extraction to be precise. Anyway I won't bother to translate it—my mind is too weak—From Chinese to Russian to English. It's too much!—I'd have to be a poet. You like poetry?

E

In my country all the poets wear beards.

K

Yes, yes, your beatniks. We're very proud of them here. We say that you are entering Russia's nineteenth century—America is coming under the spiritual mantle of Dostoyevsky.

E

You Europeans are so damn cultured.

K

Hah, hah! It is our weakness. We are corrupt, cosmopolitan—our minds work in too many places. You Americans, you know how to concentrate. Your steel mills! There is concentration. If you will permit me, that is real culture.

E

Now, we agreed we would not get into dogma.

K

I love you. But you cannot take a compliment.

E

You seem to understand me in a big hurry.

K

You—I mean saying your country, your strong simple primitive country, I mean in the cultural sense, not you. I speak in the general abstract. Look, my friend.

E

Now look, I like you too, but I don't know if we can say we're friends.

K

I love you. If we never speak again, if our meeting of you and me as primary summits comes to zero and nothing, comes to disagreements, lack of cordiahlity, war—yes, let's use the word.

E

I don't even like the sound of that word.

K

You, you do not like the sound of words. You're a Protestant. Forgive me.

E

Absolutely we must keep religion out of this. Your creed and mine cannot mix.

K

Excuse me, we Russians, we're a passionate people, we say what we think—I say to you, if we never see each other again, in my privacy, like when I am talking to myself, I will think of my good and great friend, the President of the United States, E, my darling. Let's get along. Would you like a drink?

E

No, I can't accept a drink. I don't want to offend you, but it was understood that even if we meet in your old capital of Moscow . . .

K

Leningrad is the old capital. This is Moscow, new capital.

E

Damn those fools—they gave me a double-ended fact again.

K

It is all right. We always get a mixup of the capital *chez* your country, that is to say Wall Street and Washington, Washington is your capital right, no I'm wrong, Wall Street.

E

You're being damn good about this, but I want to apologize.

K

Don't. We don't have your feeling about the charm of a charming place. Why the old man . . .

E

You mean . . . S?

K

Yeah, Him. He used to say that we wouldn't have Communism until we could refer to Moscow as 78.7°–121.5°.

414

E

Temperature?

K

No, latitude and longitude. He wanted all cities to have numbers. He was a moron.

E

Isn't that a strong word to use about him, heh, heh?

K

No. The old man never understood love.

E

You think a lot about love.

K

I got to. Russians are lovers. It breaks our heart we read in your press we are barbarians. Nonsense! Roughnecks with tender hearts, nothing worse—who can explain it to your papers?

E

You ought to read what our press says about me. They're not hard only on you—they are sheer hell on everybody.

K

Except the capitalists.

E

Well, let's stay off that.

K

You don't want to talk about nothing interesting. You want to sit down immediately, get to work, it's a mistake. Look, I been looking forward to this meeting.

E

Yes, it's a challenge. Very vital.

K

Vital, vitality, energy, zip—you say?

E

Well . . .

K

Zip—I love that word. Zip, zip. Your country and mine, we are the countries of zip, zip. Power, energy, we talk each other's language. Let's explore each other.

E

You mean our mutual interests.

K

Yes, something of the sort.

E

Well, we can't.

K

What's the matter now?

E

There's a matter, I don't want to say it's substantive or procedural —the hell with that. The fact is you've been guilty—I'm sorry to wreck this most cordial atmosphere, but somewhere, somehow— well the fact is you are not my host and I am not your guest. We meet as equals.

K

We are equals. You are my only equal in the whole world.

E

Well, that's an odd way to put it.

K

I interrupt you, my friend. Forgive me.

E

Yes, well now that we're getting underway, and the unpleasantness is going to be the first going, I mean the rough going—well, I wish you wouldn't interrupt me.

K

I only wish to stimulate you.

E

It distracts me.

K

I'm a bear. I want to hug everything I talk to.

E

Now let me give you something to think about. In the army we got a word for that kind of thing.

K

Thing?

E

That is to say, you want to hug everything you would talk to.

K

Precisely. I'm a lover.

E

Sure you are. But in the army we would say, Old K, he's nothing but a mother.

K

Is that a compliment or an insult?

E

It's an army expression.

K

General—in the coldest way, what is on your mind?

E

You've broken your word to me.

K

I see we are close to another international misunderstanding.

E

You're damn right we are. There's a disagreeable detail we have to dispose of.

K

Yes. You Americans always eat the last course first. What is dessert to us is appetizer to you. Fruit cup with sherbet, if you please.

E

I think you're one of those poets. You talk in parallels all the time.

K

I must. Two straight lines, you and me. Since we will never meet, I must try to make us move at least in parallel.

E

There's that damn European mind again.

K

Have some vodka.

(Starts to pour)

E

Hold it, Mother.

K

All right.

(Puts the vodka down)

Now, I'm ready to listen to your display of your dahmn barbarian American mahnners.

E

My manners be damned. Yours will take no prize either. I'm getting down to cases this instant.

K

Please do.

E

Don't interrupt.

K

I do as I please. You do not wish to be my guest—I cease to be your host.

E

Now hold all those Russian horses—I'm not your guest. We're not meeting in Moscow.

K

Where are we please?

E

That is to say, we are in fact on the soil of Moscow if you will, but technically, by prior arrangement, we are not here, here in the Kremlin.

K

But we are here.

E

Not for the purposes of this meeting. It was agreed that we meet in international territory belonging to no one.

K

Why didn't we choose a hole?

E

We made a hole, goddammit, and you know it. A metaphorical hole right in your Kremlin, by Jesus! So long as I'm here, it don't belong to you.

K

It belongs to God you'll tell me next.

E

It partakes of the spirit of international law.

K

Still, if I left you alone, you'd get lost in this place.

E

Damn all intellectuals. Don't tell me you don't understand the commitments that your man made with my man that we had to meet in Russia or else you would lose face to . . .

K

Don't mention his name.

E

All right. We'd just as soon have you in as him.

K

You bet.

E

Kay. So here we are. Your man promises my man that we meet in

Moscow, anywhere, your soil, and you'll cut an international hole for me and my staff.

K

We did. We had to save your face too.

E

Then face it, buddy. We meet equal to equal. I'm not your guest, you're not mine. You want to pour me vodka, I got to pour you Scotch.

K

You mean alternate drinks?

E

That's what it means being equal to equal. We can't drink unless we mix the drinks.

K

You have no soul.

E

Now, look. I keep telling you. The subject of religion is a boil on my bottom.

K

You're the same as the old man. If you had your way you'd give numbers to cities too.

E

Let's leave all personalities and private opinions to others. Facts. That's what I read for breakfast. Facts are the compost of history. The fact is I'm left buried deep in you-know-what the moment you start serving me vodka, because then I'm just a pawn of a guest and you become my Communist host.

K

You read your own papers too much.

E

They got better syntax than yours.

K

You're thinking of the translations. Judases every one of them.

420

E

You remember that speech you called me a Wall Street lackey?

K

Translation! I said you were a Wall Street podorshka.

E

And how does that improve the situation?

K

Podorshka means a wise kind understanding superior, modest, masterful and faithful old servant who really runs things.

E

That was translated as lackey?

K

Your capitalist press.

E

Good God. It's getting so you can't even trust Grandma Moses.

K

Life is sad.

E

Still you did call me a servant.

K

Do you think we are ready so soon to discuss the class struggle and your relationship to abstract forces?

POSTSCRIPT TO BUDDIES

The idea for this play came from my friend Howard Fertig. He was telling me one night about an idea he had for what could be a major novel if its comic possibilities were ever explored to the end. The two main characters would be the head of the Soviet Union and the President of the United States. Fertig had a conception of the theme which I'll not go into here, because conceivably it is a novel he might write some day.

As we were talking, I said that the situation of two such men closeted with one another would be good for a play. Howard was puzzled by my remark—he had been seeing it as a novel of some delicacy and psychological depth. I proceeded to throw out three or four wild and half-attractive gambits, and since the drinks were fine we had a good time with it.

Next day, after a good sleep, I found myself starting to write some dialogue. What I put together was rather different from Fertig's sense of the possibilities, but I would never have thought of the play if he had not suggested the situation. Before printing it here, I naturally asked his permission, and he was generous in letting me take squatter's rights on his territory.

ADVERTISEMENT FOR "NOTES TOWARD A PSYCHOLOGY OF THE ORGY"

At one time I was going to give this book the title of The Hip and the Square, *and more than once I thought of doing an essay on the subject. Finally, I tried. I began with a list, and then I wrote a dozen pages or so. There were one hundred and thirty items on my list, sixty-five to each column. But in 1,500 words I managed to discuss only four items. It became obvious that the only way to satisfy the title was to write a book. So I gave up the project.*

But I was left with the list, and the fragment of an essay. Later a few other short essays grew from the list. After a while I realized that these were no more than expanded notes for another book which I will doubtless never write (a most ambitious Das Kapital of the psychic economy). To be successful it would have to be long, comprehensive, disciplined and scholarly, and since I lack such gifts of patience, and would wear out the novelist in me by giving my years to such an effort, the choice came down to something so simple as whether to print these cryptic pages or leave them in a file. Obviously, I liked them enough to include them here. Set by themselves, they have their obvious shortcomings, but they were written to go with "The White Negro," and in context with that essay, they form the intellectual core of this book, a primitive foray into the more formal aspects of Hip. To my knowledge no one else has yet attempted this terrain. For that reason I go so far as to call them "Notes toward the Psychology of the Orgy," the last five words being the name of that large work I will probably never dare.

THE HIP AND THE SQUARE

I. The List

Hip	Square
wild	practical
romantic	classic
instinct	logic
Negro	white
inductive	programmatic
the relation	the name
spontaneous	orderly
perverse	pious
midnight	noon
nihilistic	authoritarian
associative	sequential
a question	an answer
obeying the form of the curve	living in the cell of the square
self	society
crooks	cops
free will	determinism
Catholic	Protestant
saint	clergyman
Heidegger	Sartre
sex	religion
wedeln	rotation
the body	the mind
rebel	regulator
differential calculus	analytic geometry
Schrodinger's model of the atom	Bohr's model of the atom
Wilhelm Reich as a mind	Wilhelm Reich as a stylist
Marx as a psychologist	Marx as a sociologist
Thelonious Monk	Dave Brubeck

Hip	*Square*
The **N. Y.** *Herald Tribune*	*The New York Times*
Trotsky	Lenin
Dostoyevsky	Tolstoy
Havelock Ellis	Krafft-Ebing
D. H. Lawrence	Aldous Huxley
Nixon	Dulles
Churchill	Clement Attlee
Inches, feet, yards, and miles	the metric system
alchemists	chemists
hipster	beatnik
call girls	psychoanalysts
the child	the judge
the present	the past and/or the planned future
T-formation	Single Wing
dialectical	linear
anarchists	socialists
barbarians	bohemians
illegitimacy	abortion
Picasso	Mondrian
sex for orgasm	sex for ego
a catlike walk from the hip	a bearlike walk from the shoulder
sin	salvation
physiology	anatomy
manners	morals
doubt	faith
grace	force
murder	suicide
psychopathic	schizophrenic
orgy	onanist
murder or homosexuality	cancer
marijuana	liquor
motorcycle	scooter
reconnaissance	guided tour
to seduce by touch	to seduce by reasoned argument
nuance	fact
to listen to the sound of the voice and take one's meaning from there	to listen to the meaning of the words and obey no other meaning

II. Catholic and Protestant

Reading the list, many were likely to feel that just so soon as some kind of internal order came to present itself for a few of the items, the mind would stumble over a new pair of opposites whose connotations to the reader were the opposite of what he had thought Hip or Square could be. There are of course places where the list is doomed to be private, especially since large words are set in new bearings without qualification at all: I put the Catholic with Hip, the Protestant with Square, yet just a line or two earlier, "free-will" has been dealt to Hip, "determinism" to Square, and after all it is Protestantism which gave freedom of conscience, and so by implication, free will, to the emotional history of the West. But then I should explain that the list is put together by my sense of the present, and this sense tells me that Tillich and the Protestant existentialists to the side, American Protestantism has become oriented to the machine, and lukewarm in its enthusiasm for such notions as heaven, hell and the soul. The Catholic Church can still not divorce itself *as much* from one of the indispensable notions of Hip, that particular one which is now unhappily codified by saying that we have a body (Catholics would say soul) which is growing at every instant of existence into more or into less, and that we begin to die at a disproportionate rate when we are not as brave as we ought to be. (Here Catholics might speak of a lapse from faith or grace). It is not that Catholicism and Hip are congruent in most of their parts, or that many Catholics are likely to become hipsters, it is certainly not an attempt to say that Hip is compatible for the Catholic since it is conceivable that Hip, if it emerges into a new religion, can well end by attacking the Church on Her high private ground of the flesh and the soul—it is rather that it demands less of a shift in the style of the mind for a Catholic to become Hip than a Protestant. Protestantism was never that concerned to capture the private parts of man, Protestantism being not so much a religion as a technique in the ordering of communities, able to accelerate the growth of the scientific spirit while maintaining the discipline of society; put another way, Catholicism was not able to separate the mind from the body. Flesh, the ills of the flesh, thought, and the crippled medieval limits of thought were carried in the womblike vision of the Church through the long gestation of the Middle Ages. Protestantism became the means by which the mind could nose out into a new understanding of the universe while the body remained in the restraints of monogamy, family and the state. It is the probability of probabilities that the unconscious terror of every mind (or Mind) which directed society from our beginnings has been a terror of that orgy which is the consequence to losing the theological and oligarchical direction of society, a fear which may come from our experience of the past, for every culture which divorced itself from the authority and institutions of its society seemed to fall into the mysterious historical backwaters of a disappearance; instinctively our assumption is that the culture disappeared in the orgiastic round of a decadence, a falling away into apathy, pleasure, and lack of restraint which was the breath upon which Nature and/or the Barbarian recovered the scene, digested the culture, and left us with no more than such classic enigmas as the jungle-covered ruins of the Mayan civilization.

That is man's historic fear; literally; it can be said that history was created by man's decision to conquer nature, and the evolution of his institutions may have come out of the need to shape the body and mind into proper parts of a social machine which could move into attack upon the mysteries and powers of his existence. At a price, be it said. The sense of Self was forced to retreat before the sense of the Other, the beholder, the critic, the judge. Man has grown into a brain whose powers of formal connection bear comparison to the mechanically elaborate intellections of a Univac machine, but the body which supports this brain now suffers by a cancerous alienation from the senses. If the orgy has taken on a new if nightmarish attraction to the deadened multimillions of our civilization, its appeal may not be irrational, for the orgy is capable of creating a dramatic parallel to those infantile situations in which the energies of the senses were first jailed in the psychic machines of uncreative social habit. It is no great secret that this drift toward the orgy is warred against (in the underground war of our time) by the managers of our society, who see in its approach a reflection of the rage for violence, for murder, for maiming and for loot which would be the sport of these leaders themselves if they were free. It could be argued that the men who become the real leaders of society have usually arrived to power by an extraordinarily uncommon ability: they are able to sublimate an urge within themselves (far more pressing in its intensity than the obsessions of average men) to defile, to deaden, and to destroy. The fear of license is indeed the fear of the regulators, the managers, the upper classes, the unbeat, for if they were to express themselves exactly as they wished, the orgy would be equal to carnage. Whether the orgy would be equal in fact to the cannibalism of civilization is of course beyond the speculative bounds of an essay—the purpose of this reconnaissance has been to find a few of the reasons present in the mind when Catholicism was put on the side of Hip and Protestantism to the Square.

III. T-formation and Single Wing

A passing effort like this can do no more than offer a few bites of stimulation, and leave a clue to the marks of our new nihilism. Let me move now to the intellectually trivial but specific antagonisms of the T-formation and the Single Wing, where the subject will be at least no larger than its space. I've called the Single Wing Square, and the T-formation Hip, but since not everyone is likely to know the details of the game, I think it best to illuminate this mild thesis with a Martian detachment. Seen from such a distance, football is an orderly combat with legislated rules between twenty-two bodies, eleven to a side. As is true of all wars, it is a study in energy and entropy. Over the years a good coach will liberate a nice concentration of energy in his athletes, more than a poor coach might do with the same material. The coach's talent has to arise then out of a fine if often unconscious instinct for the kind of psychic nourishment his athletes need from him. The entrance, however, into football of the T-formation was a sociological phenomenon—it seemed able to charge bad and mediocre teams as well as good ones. Nearly every school which adopted it began to improve: as coaches were saying then in newspaper interviews, "The kids seem to get more fun out of the new kind of football."

Now, a sociological phenomenon is no more than a psychological flush which is common to many. When the complexities of the T-formation replaced the power of the Single Wing, some greater unspoken satisfaction must have been offered to most players. There is no bad taste equal to commenting on the sexual themes of a national sport, but psychology is granted its medical dispensations, and so I will dare the attempt.

In the Single Wing, the ball is passed from the center to the backfield. Depending on the play and player who gets it, it travels in open air from three to ten feet. Anyone who has ever put on a uniform knows how much attention is given to the football. The offensive line feels at its best in the moment it is waiting for the center to pass the ball. In the instant when the ball goes through the air, a psychic power is removed from the line, they are back to being peons, a working class mining out holes for the upper-class heroes of the backfield, an image which is not so new but is nonetheless real. A lineman ends the game with a feeling that he's done a good day's work or a bad one; a halfback is more likely to live with the scent of a rich few seconds here and a nice movement there. So, backfield and line live in an unhappy class relation, one whose psychic contradictions are unsolvable until the game is changed from the specialization of labor to the round-robin of labor, men playing for a time in the backfield and then going to the line, or vice versa. But for the present, the revolution not having come to football, the T-formation served to narrow the psychic void between backfield and line. In the T, the quarterback crept up behind the center, indeed he moved directly behind him, the two hunched one behind the other like copulating dogs, or let us be brave with the fact, like men in the classic pose of sodomy. The ball instead of being passed was handed back between the legs.

Now, of course football was always oriented around the ass —any game which uses up the power of the male hormone must find a way to counteract the passivities of fatigue. The quick and simple solution of athletes has always been to pat each other on the butt, and it is a practical gesture so far as that goes and seems to do its biochemical work, although a man from Mars might be taken by

429

a small sense of contradiction between our sexual laws and the happy broil with which eighty thousand people will watch the heroes and nonentities of two big teams whack and thump and pat each other's cracks at any moment of crisis on the five-yard line. Not to mention the millions who stare on television. This act of fraternity can be offered as easily in the Single Wing as the T, but since the pat on the bottom is a personal expression, it lacks the formal sanction and so greater unconscious pleasure of an institutionalized ritual. Here is where the T-formation satisfies society and the self. The working-stiffs in the line no longer lose possession of their ball, they hand it back between their legs (the center serving as the I of them), they hand it back, and *bang* the play has started, it has started with a little psychic slap just off the skin of their bottoms, and this gives drive to the lack of drive in their legs, it is the soupçon of a *frisson*, lost in the impact of the immediate play, but the unconscious has been given its tickle or two.

Now, of course, I've made too much of the moment; there are not so many football players who would be aware of what I'm saying, but one's argument must remain that the T-formation is more Hip than the Single Wing because it is closer to the sexual needs of a team, and so liberates more testosterone, just a little more, maybe so little more as it takes to run the length of a football field by five-tenths of a second under eleven seconds rather than four-tenths of a second. But the difference is there, the T-formation is more to the point, and the complications of its reverses and the style of its quarterback may finally count for no more than the prongsmanship and buggery at the seat of its root.

A NOTE ON COMPARATIVE PORNOGRAPHY

Our time is obsessed with sex as blood, as murder, as adultery, orgy, and rape. No one picks up a magazine without coming on such titles as "The Real Menace of Drugs" or "Promiscuity in the High School," "Will Our Divorce Rate Increase?" "Is the Beat Generation a Sexual Revolution?" "Can the Psychiatrist Solve Crime?"

It is boring to go on with the above. Talk of pornography ought to begin at the modern root: *advertising*. Ten years ago the advertisements sold the girl with the car—the not altogether unfair connection of the unconscious mind was that the owner of a new convertible was on the way to getting a new girl. Today the girl means less than the machine. A car is sold not because it will help one to get a girl, but because it is already a girl. The leather of its seats is worked to a near-skin, the color is lipstick-pink, or a blonde's pale-green, the taillights are cloacal, the rear is split like the cheeks of a drum majorette.

Look at the commercials on television. Toothpaste is not sold so much any more by its offer to forestall decay or clean the taste in one's mouth; now its benefits are vague—they seem to have something to do with protecting the mouth against the itch to *fellatio*. For the phallus has come to the supermarket and the drugstore in a thousand hand-sized plastic cylinders which give a spray or a shoot of insecticide, meringue, shaving cream, or roll on out of a deodorant with a ball-shaped tip. The vagina leaves the calling card of her spiral in every third or fourth commercial; she is for the feminine commodities, for face powder and washing machines, she is peace and rest, a salesman for aspirin coiling her spiral into the upset of the stomach and the ache of the brain.

One can of course not be certain it is necessarily bad to live in a country where almost every commodity is festooned with sexual symbol. Under nice circumstances it may not be deadening to vitality. But then we do not have the beginnings of nice circumstance. There is no one of power who has a tongue to say that sex has become the center of our economy, and so the commodities which wall the years of our lives are not going to be presented to us for what they are: machine-made sacraments closer to the consumer than the bread and wine of his Host. Sex comes to us now at the end of a productive process, and it is heavy with biological guilt, for the urge to mate is dying in us and we need the spice of a dead object. The punishing trip to a flesh outside us is beginning to seem less attractive than the machine we buy, the consumer is beginning to leave his desire to mate for the desire to hunt down his happy and faithful fetish.

But to put one's dream of love into the deadness of an object is to drift on the wind of the psychotic. The heart of the insane lives in the wish to move away from life outside oneself, grow God-like in the vault of the brain, and then move on to give the schizophrenic's gift of life to what does not have life and never can (short of that interesting moment when God decides that machines deserve more of His attention than do we).

The bleak drift of a national sex-life which depends on commodity has become so acute that it is possible the raw (that is, pure) works of pornography, the strip-shots, the five-dollar pamphlets, the magazines of the tit, the comic books, and the obscene movies, are less crippling to the mind than the respectable products of the respectable economy: a sixteen-year-old boy closeted in the bathroom with the photo of a prostitute is laying the physical ground of his neurosis—he will pay later in bad reflex, pinched orgasm and nervous guilt, but at least he is not looking for a fetish —on the contrary, he is beginning his search for a mate. If he paralyzes most of his chances by looking for satisfaction to come out of himself, he is at least still staring out—his dream is how climactic it would be to find such a woman in the real.

That much deserved to be said for pornography. It must also be said that pornography gives no preparation for sex. In the pornographic dream, all comings come together, the torso is lithe, the smell is clean, pleasure arrives like manna. What a shock for the sensitive adolescent when he finds the courage to capture his first sex. For good, by times, as it may be, there are dead small corners for which he is not prepared, and responsibility he never knew. Nothing in the life of his fantasy prepared him for tenderness, for war, for the tragic need of sex to move into love or be chilled to something less.

The obscene is sometimes defined as that which is out of joint with nature. It is not the worst definition, and by its measure,

America is an obscene nation. The vast blank walls of our factories and government institutions are a dislocation worked by committee upon the senses. We are a sick country, proliferating cancer into every breath of being, and when one comes to think of the curious tolerance we give to pornography, provided it is a compromise and never too direct, the answer may even be found in the guilty and sluggish unconscious of the authority which manipulates us, for in a dull hopeless worrying way they may sense that the mass-media are leading us toward a national psychosis. Of course, the mass-media can hardly be rooted out of insane ground without killing the psychology of the consumer, and starving the market out of that growth whose nutrient is the heat of the fetish. So from the dumb smog of unhappy compromise come the comic books and the billboards and the clean smut and the smut which is cleaned, and with it all, some airless hope of the authority that real sex will linger on.

But could the dull power of the State, the Law, and the Church allow the artist to explore the dead battleground and small life of sex today? could one ask that the Power be ready to accept the consciousness of close description, the dignity of the explicit? no, that asks for too much. As a nation we are now dedicated to the principle that all men have an equal opportunity to cheat life, and if we die too soon with too little, our senses lost before our leaving, no one to mourn for us but that three-hundred-horsepower chromium cunt in the cement-brick garage—well, death is better for the race than consciousness, thinks the Power, for with consciousness might come a cataclysm of history, a shift from the manipulator to his human material, and then, all horror of the void, what can eternity offer to a defeated power?

FROM SURPLUS VALUE
TO THE MASS-MEDIA

No one can work his way through *Das Kapital* without etching on his mind forever the knowledge that profit must come from loss—the lost energy of one human being paying for the comfort of another; if the process has become ten times more subtle, complex, and untraceable in the modern economy, and conceivably a hundred times more resistant to the careful analysis of the isolated radical, it is perhaps now necessary that some of us be so brash as to cut a trail of speculation across subjects as vast as the title of this piece.

Let me start with a trivial discrepancy. Today one can buy a can of frozen orange juice sufficient to make a quart for 30 cents. A carton of prepared orange juice, equal in quality, costs 45 cents. The difference in price is certainly not to be found by the value of the container, nor in the additional cost of labor and machinery which is required to squeeze the oranges, since the process which produces frozen orange juice is if anything more complex—the oranges must first be squeezed and then frozen. Of course orange juice which comes in quart cartons is more expensive to ship, but it is doubtful if this added cost could account for more than 2 or 3 cents in the price. (The factors are complex, but may reduce themselves as follows: The distributor for cartons of prepared orange juice is generally the milk companies who are saved most of the costs of local distribution by delivering the orange juice on their milk route. While the cost of shipping whole oranges is greater, because of their bulk, than cans of frozen juice, it must be remembered that the largest expense in freight charges is loading and unloading, and the majority of freshly picked oranges have in any case to be shipped by freight to a freezer plant, converted, and shipped again.) What is most likely is that the price is arrived at by some kind of developed if more or less unconscious estimation by the entrepreneur of what it is worth to the consumer not to be bothered with opening a can, mixing the frozen muddle with three cans of water, and shaking. It is probable that the additional 12 or 13

434

cents of unnecessary price rise has been calculated in some such ratio as this: the consumer's private productive time is worth much more to him than his social working time, because his private productive time, that is the time necessary to perform his household functions, is time taken away from his leisure. If he earns $3 an hour by his labor, it is probable that he values his leisure time as worth ideally two or three times as much, let us say arbitrarily $6 an hour, or 10 cents a minute. Since it would take three or four minutes to turn frozen orange juice into drinkable orange juice, it may well be that a covert set of values in the consumer equates the saving of 3 or 4 minutes to a saving of 30 or 40 *ideal* cents of his pleasure time. To pay an extra 12 actual cents in order to save this 40 ideal cents seems fitting to his concept of value. Of course, he has been deprived of 10 actual cents—the extra comfort should have deprived him of no more than 2 of his actual cents. So the profit was extracted here from a disproportionate exploitation of the consumer's need to protect his pleasure time rather than from an inadequate repayment to the worker for his labor. (Such contradictions to this thesis as the spate of Do-It-Yourself hobbies, or magazine articles about the problem of what to do with leisure, are of too serious a nature to dismiss with a remark—it can however be suggested that the general hypothesis may not be contradicted: the man who is bored with his leisure time, or so industrious as to work at handicrafts, can still resent inroads upon his leisure which he has not chosen. Indeed it might be argued that the tendency to be attracted to private labor-saving devices is greatest in the man who doesn't know what to do with himself when he is at home.)

At any rate, if the hypothesis sketched here should prove to have any economic validity, the consequences are worth remarking. When the source of profit is extracted more and more (at one remove or another) from the consumer's at-home working time, the consumer is paying a disproportionate amount for the desire to work a little less in his leisure time. Over the economy as a whole, this particular germ of profit may still be minuscule, but it is not at all trivial once one includes the expenses of the war economy whose costs are paid by taxation, an indirect extraction of leisure time from the general consumer, who then has noticeably less money in his leisure to pursue the sports, occupations, and amusements which will restore to his body the energy he has spent in labor. (To take the matter into its real complexity, the conflicting anxieties of living in a war-and-pleasure-oriented environment opens most men and women to a daily spate of psychic havoc whose damages can be repaired only by the adequate exercise of a *personal* leisure appropriate to each, exactly that leisure which the war economy must impoverish.) By this logic, the root of capitalist exploitation has shifted from the proletariat-at-work to the mass-at-leisure who now may lose so much as four or five *ideal* hours of extra leisure a day. The old exploitation was vertical—the poor supported the rich. To this vertical exploitation must now be added the horizontal exploitation of the mass by the State and by Monopoly, a secondary exploitation which is becoming more essential to a modern capitalist economy than the direct exploitation of the proletariat. If the origin of this secondary exploitation has come out of the proliferation of the machine with its consequent and relative reduction of the size of the proletariat and the amount of surplus value to be accumulated, the exploitation of mass-leisure has been accelerated by the relative contraction of the world market. Through the postwar years, prosperity has been maintained in America by invading the wage-earner in his home. Nineteenth century capitalism could still find its profit in the factory; when the worker was done, his body might be fatigued but his mind could look for a diversion which was relatively free of the industry for which he worked. So soon, however, as the surplus labor of the proletariat comes to be replaced by the leisure-value given up by the consumer, the real expropriator of the wage-earner has to become the mass-media, for if the domination of leisure time is more significant to the health of the economy than the exploitation of the working time, the stability of the economy derives more from manipulating the psychic character of leisure than forcibly subjecting the working class to its productive role. It is likely that the survival of capitalism is no longer possible without the creation in the consumer of a series of psychically disruptive needs which circle about such wants and emotions as the desire for excessive security, the alleviation of guilt, the lust for comfort and new commodity, and a consequent allegiance to the vast lie about the essential health of the State and the economy, an elaborated fiction whose bewildering interplay of real and false detail must devil the mass into a progressively more imperfect apperception of reality and thus drive them closer to apathy, psychosis, and violence. Nineteenth-century capitalism exhausted the life of millions of workers; twentieth-century capitalism can well end by destroying the mind of civilized man.

If there is a future for the radical spirit, which often enough one can doubt, it can come only from a new revolutionary vision of society, its sicknesses, its strengths, its conflicts, contradictions and radiations, its self-created incapacity to solve its evasions of human justice. There is the root of social problem. An injustice half corrected results in no more than a new sense of injustice and suppressed violence in both parties, which is why revolutionary situations are meaningful and liberal situations are not, for liberal solutions end by compromising a society in the nausea of its past and so bog the mass-mind further into the institutionalization of social habits and methods for which no one has faith, and from which one cannot extract the psychic marrow of culture upon which everyone in a civilization must depend. If this revolutionary vision is to be captured by any of us in a work or works, can one guess that this time it will explore not nearly so far into that jungle of political economy which Marx charted and so opened to rapid development, but rather will engage the empty words, dead themes, and sentimental voids of that mass-media whose internal contradictions twist and quarter us between the lust of the economy (which radiates a greed to consume into us, with sex as the invisible salesman) and the guilt of the economy which must chill us with authority, charities for cancer, and all reminder that the mass consumer is only on drunken furlough from the ordering disciplines of church, F.B.I., and war.

SOURCES—A RIDDLE
IN PSYCHICAL ECONOMY

The question: Go through the two passages which follow and see if you can pick the writer who was the source of each selection.

A. In the pages that follow I shall bring forward proof that there is a psychological technique which makes it possible to interpret the unconscious undercurrents of society, and that, if that procedure is employed, every society reveals itself as a psychical structure which has an unconscious direction or conflict of direction which can be detected at any assignable point in the overt activities of social life. I shall further endeavor to elucidate the processes to which the strangeness and obscurity of these unconscious undercurrents of society are due and to deduce from these processes the nature of the psychical forces by whose concurrent or mutually opposing action social conflict, progress and retrogression are generated. Having gone thus far, my description will break off, for it will have reached a point at which the problem of the unconscious undercurrent of society merges into more mysterious and conceivably mystical problems, the solution of which must be approached upon the basis of inner experience of another kind.

B. The unconscious life of those people in whom the conventionally accepted mode of sexual relations prevails, presents itself as an immense accumulation of unsatisfied desires, its unit being a single unrequited desire. Our investigation must therefore begin with the analysis of an unrequited or forbidden desire.

A desire is, in the first place, created by a need inside us toward an entity that by its properties satisfies sexual wants of some sort or another. The nature of such wants, whether for instance they spring from social frustration or from individual physiological necessity, makes no difference. Neither are we here concerned to know how the fulfilled desire satisfies these wants, whether directly as means of gratification, or indirectly as means of improving one's social status.

The answer: If the prose was a trifle strained in those two selections, the fault is mine—I lacked the art to find new words which could fit comfortably into the resonant sentences of the two gentlemen who did not write the above passages, but indeed wrote what comes below.

A′ In the pages that follow I shall bring forward proof that there is a psychological technique which makes it possible to interpret dreams, and that, if that procedure is employed, every dream reveals itself as a psychical structure which has a meaning and which can be inserted at an assignable point in the mental activities of waking life. I shall further endeavor to elucidate the processes to which the strangeness and obscurity of dreams are due and to deduce from those processes the nature of the psychical forces by whose concurrent or mutually opposing actions dreams are generated. Having gone thus far, my description will break off, for it will have reached a point at which the problem of dreams merges into more comprehensive problems, the solution of which must be approached upon the basis of material of another kind.

—*The Interpretation of Dreams*, Sigmund Freud; trans. by James Strachey, Basic Books.

(The selection is the opening paragraph of the work.)

B′ The wealth of those societies in which the capitalist mode of production prevails, presents itself as "an immense accumulation of commodities," its unit being a single commodity. Our investigation must therefore begin with the analysis of a commodity.

A commodity is, in the first place, an object outside us, a thing that by its properties satisfies human wants of some sort or another. The nature of such wants, whether, for instance, they spring from the stomach or from fancy, makes no difference. Neither are we here concerned to know how the object satisfies these wants, whether directly as means of substistence or indirectly as means of production.

Das Kapital, Karl Marx; trans. by Samuel Moore and Edward Aveling, Modern Library Edition.

(Again the selection is from the opening two paragraphs.)

439

LAMENT OF A LADY

        Normally
            I can't come
        And when I can   well then
                for some dim reason
                usually I don't
            Although once I did
                almost

They say Italian men are fine
        wild and mild as wine
And the French   I thought them tired
The Germans   I'm afraid of them
And the English are cultivated to the teeth.

            To tell the sad dreary truth
                it was a Jew
        Almost I came with him
                    almost
                was pissy
                    but sweet

Oh, there's a vogue to the sweet
It's star and far
        smell of drinks in a good bar
                mink
                and a soupçon of stink

        A Jew
        You
        Dear Kike
        I wish you were a dyke.

I GOT TWO KIDS AND ANOTHER IN THE OVEN

There we were,
    a blur,
    a void in the ovoid.
For the ova and the brat
    like their punning formal familiars
    the oven and the bread
    exist in an intellectual relationship
    an arbitrary declaration
    of the will upon the flesh
    so that the flesh body will.

Ah!
    what if . . . it is not like that at all?
    and seed swims into an eternity of closing spaces and dying seas,
        seed so adrenal in the whip of its race
        that the royal procession into cavern
            beyond feminine cavern
            is felt not as majesty
        nor tropical velvets of water
        which murmur for birth
    but in all despair as most desperate night.

Yes.
    what if the seed be already a being? So desperate that it
        claws, bites, cuts and lies,
        burns, and betrays
    desperate to capture the oven, be nectared in yeasterly expansion.

One wins
    upon occasion
    (assuming there is no diaphragm, jelly, condom, pill,
        or coit interrump to gulp up a death on the
        sandy sun-lit beaches of a woman's belly
    wipe goes a sheet like a winter wind)

One wins
> one out of some multi-million other sons and daughters not to
> be born

One wins
> one more there is,

> one more or less incandescent enthusiasm,
> itch of the detumescent present,
> new god, embryonic two-cell
> good at murder.

ADVERTISEMENT FOR THE DEER PARK
AS A PLAY

Some time next year I plan to publish the play of The Deer
Park. *As the script now stands, it is cut to the bone, but it still has
twelve scenes and would take three and a half hours to play.
When I am feeling indecent about it, I think it has a chance to affect
the history of the American theatre. Little of this possibility is
present I would guess in the small extract which is printed here,
but these were the only pages I could find which seemed able to
stand by themselves, and I did want to have a taste of the play in
my collection.*

*For those readers who are familiar with the novel, a confusion
may be present. In adapting the book, I changed a few things: most
noticeably, Eitel and Marion Faye have been in prison before the
play begins and Marion Faye has had a career as an actor. Let it be
also said that the action takes place in Hell, but in the scene, and
extracts from two other scenes, which I've mounted here, that condition is not directly apparent.*

THE DEER PARK

(Scenes two, three, four)

SCENE TWO

Eitel's rented ranch-house in the desert.

Eitel is smoking a cigarette on the patio. He is in his dressing gown. Elena comes out from the bedroom, and enters the living room. She is a near-beauty, but indeed this is misleading for she is not so much beautiful as sexual. Yet her manner is a touch rough, and her voice is not usually one of her assets. Although it is by times rich and musical, all too often the nasalities, the whines, the snarls and the sneers of a poor childhood are restrained with difficulty. At this moment, put together in a strapless evening gown which clashes with her morning hangover, she moves as if she feels unfresh.

"Let's have coffee," Eitel says. When she nods sullenly, he goes on in a manner which is just a touch too animated.

EITEL

After we get a little food in us and feel human, I'll take a drive out to your hotel and bring you some clothing. It'll pick you up.

ELENA

Don't worry about me. I'll get out.

EITEL

I didn't mean for you to get out.

ELENA

(Firmly)
No . . . it's been nice.
(A moment of uncomfortable silence)
But I don't want coffee.

EITEL

We're not saying goodbye to each other so quickly as this.

ELENA

Nothing ever works in the morning.

EITEL

Let's have coffee.
(Hands her a cup)
You'll see. We must have a hundred things to talk about.

ELENA

I don't know if I like to talk. It changes everything.

EITEL

It's true—girls who are dancers usually don't talk a great deal. Were you a good dancer?

ELENA

(Hesitating—over the coffee cup)
Let's say I wanted to be. Once in a while my agent would get me a job for a couple of weeks.

EITEL

You sound modest.

ELENA

I'm conceited. I still think I could have made it if I hadn't met Collie. He wanted me under lock and key in case he had a free hour.

EITEL

So you stopped dancing.

ELENA

Yes, I was kept . . . I'm lazy.
(Sighs)
I'm lazy and Collie is stingy. We were a good pair.

EITEL

You must have brought out the best in each other.

ELENA

The best.
(Depression dampens her)
It was low of Collie to dump me in this town.

EITEL

As a practical matter, what is there to keep you from going back to the city?

ELENA

I don't know anybody in the city.

EITEL

You don't know anybody in the city? You lived there all your life you told me.

ELENA

I don't make friends. Women aren't in a hurry to get along with me —not if they have a man around, and I make most men nervous. The ones I don't make nervous don't like me unless I say yes I can't live unless it's tonight. I didn't get into the kind of thing with most people where I would want to see any of them again. So I don't know anybody in the city.

EITEL

No family?

ELENA

I come from a big family. When they're that big it just takes one fight and then you've had it . . . They found out Collie was keeping me . . . I'd die before I would see them again.

EITEL

You're a proud little girl in your way.

ELENA

I don't care what kind of celebrity you used to be. Don't talk to me so superiorly as if I'm applying for a job.

EITEL

I didn't realize I had such a tone in my voice.

ELENA

Well, you did. You act like an Englishman.

445

I was wondering how you would describe me.

(Her voice reveals emotion for the first time)
I wouldn't talk about you to anyone.
(Eitel looks away, but the question comes)
Why, would you talk about me?

Only if I were being psychoanalyzed.
(He slaps her bottom)

(For the first time, laughs merrily)
I know what you mean. I was always asking my analyst about Collie. I wanted to learn how to make Collie think I loved him.

Did you succeed?

No.

You're finished with the analyst now?

I stopped going.
(A light shines in her eyes for an instant)
I think I used to go out and get into some of the crazy things I did, just so I could be more interesting to my doctor.
(She laughs)
You know, so he'd write me up as a case or something.

(Trying not to wince at her language)
How did Collie take all this?

He'd have forgiven me if I'd let him watch.

446

You think you're better than Collie.

ELENA

Well, I don't know.
(An impish look in her green eyes)
I've done some fantastic things.

EITEL

More fantastic than last night?

ELENA

(Slapping him lightly)
Don't brag.

EITEL

I feel I have something to brag about.

ELENA

Men always do. I think men are . . .

EITEL

Are?

ELENA

Easy to fool.

EITEL

Thank you.

ELENA

Oh, you're good. You know you're good . . . why you're a champion.

EITEL

I'm a professional anyway.
(He smiles)
Beware. You wouldn't want to fall in love with me, would you?

ELENA

(She looks away)
I don't love anybody.

EITEL

Feel on your own?

                        ELENA

Yes.

                        EITEL

Good way to feel.
        (Says the next speech lightly)
Let's stay together for a few days.

                        ELENA

I don't think so.

                        EITEL

Why?

                        ELENA

I'm free of Collie, and I want to see if I can live by myself.

                        EITEL

You're giving the real reason?

                        ELENA

It wouldn't work with you.

                        EITEL

Why not try?

                        ELENA

        (Ironically)
Sure, why not try?

                        EITEL

        (Holds his temper)
Well, you are going to stay in town?
        (Elena nods)
We'll see each other . . . Even every night if it works out that
way.

                        ELENA

Yes, you do what you want, and I'll do what I want.

                        EITEL

Need any money . . . ?

                        ELENA

        (She is at the door which leads from the living room to the
        patio)

I've got enough to get by for a while.

EITEL

Let me warn you that I'm really a very cold man.

ELENA

(She has opened the door)
You're full of emotion. . . .
 (She starts to go out)
   On the last exchange between Eitel and Elena, Marion
   Faye has entered the patio from the street. As Elena
   comes out the door of the living room she runs face to
   face with Marion Faye. He is medium in height or under,
   perhaps twenty-four, good-looking, clean and lithe in his
   movements, catlike.

MARION

 (To Elena—for this moment they are alone on the patio)
Don't go yet.

ELENA

 (Calling Eitel—a little dread in her voice)
You got a visitor.

EITEL

 (Joins them on the patio)
Elena, I'd like you to meet Marion Faye. . . . Marion, this is Elena
Esposito.
 (His poise is marred just perceptibly by Faye's unexpected
 appearance)

MARION

 (Very slowly does he enunciate the words)
Elena Esposito . . .

ELENA

You know my name?

MARION

I've heard about you.

ELENA

 (More quietly)
Well, don't believe what you heard, because I heard about you, too.

449

MARION

Whatever you heard is right.

ELENA

(Intrigued, but retreating)
I think I used to see you in some movies.

EITEL

Marion was a talented actor.

MARION

A talented feature actor.

ELENA

Yes, now I remember. I read about you. You were in a car accident
. . . a girl was with you.

MARION

(Flatly)
She was killed.

ELENA

(Shuddering)
I could never get over something like that.

MARION

You get over it.

EITEL

Marion feels he's paid for it.
(Elena looks puzzled)

MARION

(Flatly)
I was driving my car with a suspended license. They sent me to
Eitel's campus.

EITEL

We were practically cell-mates.

MARION

Except I found prison more stimulating than Eitel.

ELENA

Marion, you're odd.

MARION

I know what I want. Dig?

ELENA

(Offended, she turns to Eitel)
I'll be over at my hotel.

EITEL

Wait for my call.

ELENA

See you tomorrow—as we said.
(Coldly)
Goodbye, Marion.
She Exits.

EITEL

(After Elena's exit)
Why today? I haven't seen you in weeks.

MARION

I heard you were making the rounds with Elena last night. I wanted to see what Collie's girl looked like.

EITEL

Why?

MARION

Collie is a collector. Any girl he keeps for three years is interesting to me.

EITEL

I won't ask you to leave her alone—I don't believe you could move in on her.

MARION

Oh, I could. I could whistle and she would hear it from a mile away. Have a little respect for human experience.

EITEL

The experience of a pimp?

MARION

Charley, I know more than the President of the United States, and
so does a nigger whore.

EITEL

Isn't it possible you exaggerate the benefits of pimpery in order to
conceal from yourself the real cause of your . . . anguish?

MARION

Which is?

EITEL

Panic, homosexual panic.

MARION

Homosexual panic. You're the one to talk.

EITEL

I am. For me, the worst part of prison was the sex. I chose to stay
away from that, from all of that. I didn't see any reason why I
should start at this late date.

MARION

It left you middle-aged, baby.

EITEL

You. When you were in prison you ran amok.

MARION

I used to worry that I was queer. Now, I know I'm only half-queer.

EITEL

Half-queer, and without dignity.

MARION

You have your dignity and you feel . . . amputated.

EITEL

I did. I did until last night.
    (Turns away, speaks almost to himself)

But last night something happened.
(His voice turns just perceptibly)
It was extraordinary.

MARION

Come on, Charley. For fifteen years you couldn't make a picture without being king of the hay, and now you flip over a chick who used to tickle Collie Munshin's little itches.

EITEL

I'd prefer it if you didn't talk about her that way.

MARION

Man, you are laying the foundations of a monumental mistake.

EITEL

When I was younger I gave and I gave of myself. It never meant a thing. Many parts of me were not alive. I was merely using them up. But, today . . . today I know that there is something different in me.

MARION

What talent Elena must have.

EITEL

You could never feel Elena's talent.

MARION

Maybe I wouldn't hear all the jazz you hear, lover, but I could develop her talent. You have to worry whether you have enough to develop her talent.

EITEL

I have more than I ever had.

MARION

You've been a name too long. You're spoiled. Once you could make love to a woman and the sugar of your reputation would make her warm and open before you moved a finger. Now, you're an ex-con who can't get a job and doesn't have any real dough left. And you want to keep a girl who was born to travel in a big league. Hard times ahead, Charley, and maybe I'll just demonstrate it to you.

CURTAIN

EXTRACT FROM SCENE THREE

(After Sergius is gone, Eitel starts to embrace Elena, but she is not responsive. He walks away, and then reveals by his next speech that he is in a state.)

EITEL

Where were you last night?

ELENA

I want to talk to you about that. Your friend called me for a date.

EITEL

Which friend?

ELENA

Marion Faye.

EITEL

You accepted?

ELENA

Well, I didn't think that you and I should see each other every night.

EITEL

So you had a casual date?

ELENA

A little more than that.

EITEL

You mean a lot more than that?

ELENA

Yes.

EITEL

Obviously, I haven't been enough for you.

ELENA

How you talk.

EITEL

Still, you had something left in reserve.

ELENA

You're enjoying this.

EITEL

Elena! Why did you do it?

ELENA

I was curious. I wanted to . . .

EITEL

Don't tell me. I'm an expert on female psychology.

ELENA

You must be an expert on everything . . . I didn't know, and I wanted to find out if . . .

EITEL

. . . if this blossoming of the flesh was something you could cultivate only with me, or whether any old lad would do. Is that it?

ELENA

(Mutters her answer)
Something like that.

EITEL

Something like that. I could kill you.

ELENA

But I want to tell you . . .

EITEL

What?

ELENA

I felt like a statue with him.

EITEL

Only you didn't act like a statue with him.

ELENA

Well . . . I thought of you all the time.

EITEL

You're a pig.

ELENA

(Starts to cry)
You don't care about me. You don't really care. Just your pride is hurt.

EITEL

Elena, how could you do it?

ELENA

You think I'm stupid.

EITEL

What has that got to do with it?

ELENA

When a woman's unfaithful, she's more attractive to a man.

EITEL

You idiot! Stop reciting your lessons!

ELENA

It's not lessons. I know . . .

EITEL

Don't you understand? I think I love you.

ELENA

You don't love me.

EITEL

(Amending it)
I love you.

ELENA

I worship you. It's better with you than it's been with anyone.

CURTAIN

EXTRACT FROM SCENE FOUR

At curtain Elena is alone on stage, tidying the living room. Marion enters from the street door, crosses the patio, and looks in on her. They stare at one another for a moment.

ELENA

Charley isn't here.

MARION

It's you I want to talk to.

ELENA

Marion, we don't have a hell of a lot to say.

MARION

You're a liar. It was all there for me last time, and it was the same for you.

ELENA

Don't tell me what I felt.

MARION

We were making it. There is no other truth. Just that.

ELENA

Just that. I never felt so low in my life as I felt after being with you. It was the gutter. And, now, leave me alone. Charley is the one I want to make it with.

MARION

You act a part with Eitel—a nice pretty ingenue who cares so terribly about her man. Not your scene, baby. You were born to get your kicks. Come live with me.

ELENA

Wow!
        (In a soft voice, of course.)

MARION

As you see, I mean it.

ELENA

I think you do.

MARION

I would need an adding machine to count my old jazz—and you, you're the one I want, you can be the best for me, and I can be the best for you. Because you're wild, baby, you're wild like me.

457

ELENA

You're a pimp.

MARION

Yes. So I could find somebody like you.

ELENA

You disgust me.

MARION

Look, I got deep into you. If you tried and I tried and we didn't make it—I would kill myself.

ELENA

You would kill me.

MARION

Kill you?

ELENA

My father was a small-time hoodlum. I know about murder.

MARION

Yes . . . Maybe I would murder you. You're yellow. You make your nest with a middle-aged man.

ELENA

You think I stay with him because he's good to me and kind?

MARION

He's your nurse.

ELENA

He's my lover.

MARION

I don't believe it.

ELENA

He's my lover . . . I never could use that word before. Not for other men. Not for you. But he's my lover. When he touches me . . .

MARION

. . . you are ready to receive the next touch.

458

ELENA

Crazy.

MARION

And the next touch is not what you thought it would be, but a little more and in a new direction and it opens you.

ELENA

You know about love.

MARION

I know about sex, baby. I feel that for a hundred men and women.

ELENA

And a dog or two.

MARION

Yes, and a dog or two. And you got the dog in you, baby—let's give Eitel that, he turned you on. He turned you on, and he'll leave you. You have no future with Eitel.

ELENA

He loves me.

MARION

Whatever he has, whatever he owns, sooner or later he comes to detest it because it's his, and so it can't be good. He's a snob. Nothing less than a princess could bring him joy.

(Eitel enters from the street. As the patio gate slams, Elena and Marion become silent. Eitel enters the living room—there is silence.)

EITEL

It's pleasant that you came to visit us, Marion.

MARION

You and I are friends.

EITEL

(With a gesture toward Elena)
Friends?

459

MARION

Charley, you've been living long enough to know that when a pal makes it with your girl for a night, she comes back to you enriched.

ELENA

(Laughs mockingly)
Not always, Marion, not always.

MARION

(Stares at her)
We won't go into details. I'll just say, Charley, it's good you came when you did—your girl was getting nervous.

Exit Marion

AN EYE ON PICASSO

For the last fifty years (if one is to take as his point of departure Les Demoiselles d'Avignon) Picasso has used his brush like a sword, disemboweling an eye to plaster it over the ear, lopping off a breast in order to turn it behind an arm, scoring the nostrils of his ladies until they took on the violent necessities of those twin holes of life and death, the vagina and the anus. Up and down the world of appearances he has marched, sacking and pillaging and tearing and slashing, a modern-day Cortez conquering an empire of appearances. It is possible that there has never been a painter who will leave the intimate objects of the world so altered by the swath of his work. The institutional world, the monumental world, the world of skyscrapers and glass-walled banks, of public gardens and functional architecture belong (at their best) to Mondrian, the Bauhaus, and Corbusier. Picasso's conquests range through the constellation of small objects, through ash trays and lamps and crockery and textile designs and the oncoming tendency of women's fashions (swollen bellies, padded hips, lopsided breasts), through green eye make-up and silver nail polish, Greenwich Village jewelry and custom-made peasant shoes with laces on a diagonal, through homosexual haircuts, the coiffures of East Side poodles, and the chromium swaths and steel crimps of the American automobile.

But of course these influences are the superficial victories which come to mind, the sensuous fertilization of those objects and creatures which lend themselves to the sensuous. More profound is a conquest of form so complete that all modern painting including the relative emancipation from form of such artists as Hofmann and Pollock derive from his Napoleonic marches. He is the first painter to bridge the animate and the inanimate, to recover the infantile eye which cannot distinguish between a pitcher and a bird, a face and a plant, or indeed a penis and a nose, a toe and a breast. Tearing through all obsidian flats of surface, the gargantuan anomalies of his figures return us to the mysteries of form. Picasso is the monomaniac of form, showing us a figure which is the proliferation of the breast, the eye as breast, the nose as breast, the chin, and the head, the shoulders, knees, belly, and toes as a harem garden of breasts—or equally a cornucopia of fecal forms, of genitalia, of buttocks, or conversely—for this is the other half of the demonstration—he will reconstruct the topologies of our flesh in geometric cells, until a triangle or a rhomboid will prove his case. Here is a face, he says to us, I have given it the form of the letter *W*, I have placed a triangle for one eye, ignored the nose, compounded a prism of triangles for the mouth, made facets of the neck, and drawn angles for the breasts, and yet it is a person, this one breathes, she has character, a most refractory and stubborn character, but she is there, a lady of triangles, and if the triangle is equal to conveying the mystery of the human figure, then the triangle is a mystery as well, Q.E.D.

For he is also saying that exploration is circular, it moves along the route of the association, and so any exploration of reality must travel not from object to object but from relation to relation. In this sense he is the modern creator of the visual symbol, the father of all advertising art. The symbol is the flag of the empires he has cut out for himself, the symbol is the visual presentation of a nonvisual chain of relations. Picasso's guitar is hips, a waist, and the breast; it is a torso; it is woman; it is an hourglass; it is time; it is sound; it is two opposed waves ∽∽ ; it is the curve of two lovers in the act, it is the act, it is creation.

But of course it is none of these things unless we give to it the links of consciousness, unless we choose to adopt the guitar as a symbol for some all but unperceived relations of sex and time and sound and creation, and in doing so we have done no more than disembowel a Picassan eye, collide infinities against one another in order to leave the corpse of a psychopathic joke, since it is undoubtedly the enthusiasms of the moment rather than an intrinsic and continuing relation which has been attached to the symbol.

So the painter as warrior is conversely an infant, never too long alienated from that other universe out of which he was born—conquistador, warrior, lover, wrestler, the artist as infant is forever learning and relapsing, distinguishing the eye from the ear only to sink back into that ocean of equivalents where an open mouth and a windowpane are interchangeable, and light and sound collide at the edge of the skin.

462

EVALUATIONS—QUICK AND EXPENSIVE COMMENTS ON THE TALENT IN THE ROOM

The only one of my contemporaries who I felt had more talent than myself was James Jones. And he has also been the one writer of my time for whom I felt any love. We saw each other only six or eight times over the years, but it always gave me a boost to know that Jim was in town. He carried his charge with him, he had the talent to turn a night of heavy drinking into a great time. I felt then and can still say now that *From Here to Eternity* has been the best American novel since the war, and if it is ridden with faults, ignorances, and a smudge of the sentimental, it has also the force of few novels one could name. What was unique about Jones was that he had come out of nowhere, self-taught, a clunk in his lacks, but the only one of us who had the beer-guts of a broken-glass brawl. What must next be said is sad, for Jones has sold out badly over the years. There is not a man alive he cannot charm if he chooses to, and the connection of that gift to his huge success made him a slave of our time, for it handcuffed the rebel in him. Like Styron, like myself, like Kerouac, he has been running for President as well as sticking at his work, and it was near tragic to watch the process as he imprisoned his anger, and dwindled without it.

I do not know that one can judge him. His first virtues are an appetite for life and an animal sense of who has the power, and maybe it would have been worse for Jones to deny himself. So he spent years hobnobbing with gentlemanly shits and half-ass operators and some of it had to rub off on him, especially since he had no art for living with his weaknesses, and a blind vanity which locked him out of his faults and took him on a long trip away from anyone whose mind could see into his holes.

The debacle of *Some Came Running* is, however, more of Scribner's fault than his own. They handled him like poltroons. There was no one in the house who had guts enough to say that

Some Came Running was a washerwoman at 1,200 pages, and could be fair at 400. So a little of Jones' very best writing was lost in the dreary wastes and tiresome egotisms of his most accurate if caterpillarish portrait of the Midwest.

Next came *The Pistol*, a dud. More vanity. The God of Sir Jones looking for his nose and wondering about applause.

Yet Jones could do ten bad novels, and I would never write him off, not even if it seemed medically evident he had pickled his brain in the gin. For Jones, like a bull, is most dangerous when almost dead, and with a rebel whiff of self-respect all hell might break loose. If Jones stops trying to be the first novelist to end as a multimillionaire; if he gives up the lust to measure his talent by the money he makes; if he dares not to castrate his hatred of society with a literary politician's assy cultivation of it, then I would have to root for him because he may have been born to write a great novel.

So may William Styron have been born, only I wonder if anyone who gets to know him well could wish him on his way. I will try to be fair about his talent, but I do not know if I can, because I must speak against the bias of finding him not nearly as big as he ought to be.

Styron wrote the prettiest novel of our generation. *Lie Down in Darkness* has beauty at its best, is almost never sentimental, even has whispers of near-genius as the work of a twenty-three-year-old. It would have been the best novel of our generation if it had not lacked three qualities: Styron was not near to creating a man who could move on his feet, his mind was uncorrupted by a new idea, and his book was without evil. There was only Styron's sense of the tragic: misunderstanding—and that is too small a window to look upon the world we have known.

Since then only a remarkably good short novel, *The Long March*, has appeared by Styron. But he has been working hard over the years on a second novel, *Set This House on Fire*, and I hear it is done. If it is at all good, and I expect it is, the reception will be a study in the art of literary advancement. For Styron has spent years oiling every literary lever and power which could help him on his way, and there are medals waiting for him in the mass-media. If he has written a book which expresses some real part of his complex and far from pleasant view of the American character, if this new novel should prove to have the bite of a strong and critical consciousness, then one can hardly deny him his avidity as a politician for it is not easy to work many years on a novel which has something hard and new to say without trying to shape the reception of it. But if Styron has compromised his talent, and written what turns out to be the most suitable big book of the last ten years, a *literary* work which will deal with secondhand experience and all-but-deep proliferation on the smoke of passion and the kiss of death, if he has done no more than fill a cornucopia of fangless perceptions which will please the conservative power and delight the liberal power, offend no one, and prove to be ambitious, traditional, innocuous, artful, and in the middle, breathy and self-indulgent in the beauty of its prose, evocative to the tenderhearted and the reviewers of books, then Styron will receive a ravingly good reception, for the mass-media is aching for such a novel like a tout for his horse. He will be made the most important writer of my generation. But how much more potent he will seem to us, his contemporaries and his competitors, if he has had the moral courage to write a book equal to his hatred and therefore able to turn the consciousness of our time, an achievement which is the primary measure of a writer's size.

Truman Capote I do not know well, but I like him. He is tart as a grand aunt, but in his way he is a ballsy little guy, and he is the most perfect writer of my generation, he writes the best sentences word for word, rhythm upon rhythm. I would not have changed two words in *Breakfast at Tiffany's* which will become a small classic. Capote has still given no evidence that he is serious about the deep resources of the novel, and his short stories are too often saccharine. At his worst he has less to say than any good writer I know. I would suspect he hesitates between the attractions of Society which enjoys and so repays him for his unique gifts, and the novel he could write of the gossip column's real life, a major work, but it would banish him forever from his favorite world. Since I have nothing to lose, I hope Truman fries a few of the fancier fish.

Kerouac lacks discipline, intelligence, honesty and a sense of the novel. His rhythms are erratic, his sense of character is nil, and he is as pretentious as a rich whore, as sentimental as a lollypop. Yet I think he has a large talent. His literary energy is enormous, and he had enough of a wild eye to go along with his instincts and so become the first figure for a new generation. At his best, his love of language has an ecstatic flux. To judge his worth it is better to forget about him as a novelist and see him instead as an action painter or a bard. He has a medieval talent, he is a teller of frantic court tales for a dead King's ears, and so in the years of James Madison's Avenue, he has been a pioneer. For a while I worried about him as a force from the political right which could lead Hip into a hole, but I liked him when I met him, more than I would have thought, and felt he was tired, as indeed why should he not be for he has traveled in a world where the adrenalin devours the blood.

Saul Bellow knows words, but writes in a style I find self-willed and unnatural. His rhythms have a twitch. There were some originalities and one or two rich sections to *Augie March* (which is all I know of his work) but at its worst it was a travelogue for timid intellectuals and so to tell the truth I cannot take him seriously as a major novelist. I do not think he knows anything about people, nor about himself. He has a whacky, almost psychotic lack of responsibility to the situations he creates, and his narrative disproportions are elephantiastical in their anomaly. This judgment is not personal, for we met only once, under easy circumstances, and had a mild conversation which left me neither remembering nor dismembering him as a man.

Since writing the above, I have read his short novel *Seize The Day*. It is, I think, the first of the cancer novels. Its miserable hero, Tommy Wilhelm, leads a life of such hopeless obstacles to the dreams of gentle love trapped in his flesh, that one would diagnose him as already in a pre-cancerous stage. That Wilhelm bursts into tears and weeps before the bier of a stranger in a funeral parlor, in that surprisingly beautiful ending to *Seize The Day*, is the first indication for me that Bellow is not altogether hopeless on the highest level. But before he can begin to command the respect he has been given too quickly by the flaccid taste of these years, he must first give evidence, as must Styron, that he can write about men who have the lust to struggle with the history about them, for it is not demanding to write about characters considerably more defeated than oneself since the writer's ego is rarely in danger of being punished by too much self-perception, and compassion can be poured over one's work like cream from a pitcher.

If one does not request an apocalyptic possibility for literature, then I have been needlessly severe on Bellow, for his work does no obvious harm, but I think one must not be easy on art which tries for less than it can manage, or in the example of Augie March, does something worse, muddles the real and the false in such ambitious copulation that the mind of the reader is debauched. Augie is an impossible character, and his adventures could never have happened, for he is too timid a man ever to have moused into more than one or two cruel corners of the world. But there it is: to simulate a major mood, Bellow must create a world which has none of the psychic iron of society, none of the facts and nuance of that social machine which is geared to catch all but the most adept of adventurers by weakness and need.

When and if I come to read *Henderson the Rain King*, let me hope I do not feel the critic's vested interest to keep a banished writer in limbo, for I sense uneasily that without reading it, I have already the beginnings of a negative evaluation for it since I doubt that I would believe in Henderson as a hero.

Algren has something which is all his own. I respect him for staying a radical, yet I do not feel close to his work. Probably it is too different from my own. If I say that I do not think he will ever do a major work until he overcomes his specialty—that ghoulish and weirdly sentimental sense of humor which is pure Algren and so skitters him away from the eye of his meanings—well, I offer this without the confidence that I see into him. Of all the writers I know, he is the Grand Odd-Ball. Once he took me to a line-up in Chicago, and I could have sworn the police and the talent on the line had read *The Man With The Golden Arm* for they caught the book perfectly, those cops and those crooks, they were imitating Algren. Yet all the while Nelson laughed like a mad tourist from Squaresville who was hearing these things for the first time.

Salinger is everyone's favorite. I seem to be alone in finding him no more than the greatest mind ever to stay in prep school. What he can do, he does well, and it is his, but it is finally not very lively to live on a campus where bully-muscle always beats those who feel but feel weak. I cannot see Salinger soon emerging onto the battleground of a major novel.

Of course, this opinion may come from nothing more graceful than envy. Salinger has had the wisdom to choose subjects which are comfortable, and I most certainly have not, but since the world is now in a state of acute discomfort, I do not know that his wisdom is honorable.

Paul Bowles opened the world of Hip. He let in the murder, the drugs, the incest, the death of the Square (Port Moresby), the call of the orgy, the end of civilization; he invited all of us to these themes a few years ago, and he wrote one short story, *Pages from Cold Point*, a seduction of a father by a son, which is one of the best short stories ever written by anyone. Yet, I am not ready to think of Bowles as a major novelist—his characters are without life, and one does not feel that the author ever lived with them. He does not love them and certainly he does not hate them—he is as bored with his characters as they are bored with each other, and this boredom, the breath of Bowles' work, is not the boredom of the world raised to the cool relations of art, but rather is a miasma from the author. One can never disregard Paul Bowles, however, for whatever his lacks, his themes have been adventurous and pure.

Vance Bourjaily is an old acquaintance and upon occasion we are friends. I thought his first two novels were insignificant, and it seemed to me he stayed in existence because of really nice gifts as a politician. (Since very few people in the literary world have any taste—they are much too tense with fashion—the virtue of being a good literary politician is that one can promote one's own fashion, be put in vogue, and so relax the bite of the snob to the point where he or she can open the mouth and sup upon the message.) But I never understood Bourjaily because I kept expecting him to go Madison Avenue, I was certain he would sell out sooner or later. Instead he did the opposite, wrote a novel called *The Violated*, which is a good long honest novel filled with an easy sense of life and detail about pieces and parts of my generation, a difficult book to do, and Bourjaily did it with grace, and had a few things to say. He is the first of my crowd to have taken a major step forward, and if his next novel is as superior to *The Violated* as was *The Violated* to his early work, he could end up being champion for a while. But I doubt if he could hold the title in a strong field, for his taint is to be cute.

Chandler Brossard is a mean pricky guy who's been around, and he'd have been happier as a surgeon than a novelist, but he is original, and parts I read of *The Bold Saboteurs* were sufficiently interesting for me to put the book away—it was a little too close to some of my own notions. Brossard has that deep distaste for weakness which gives work a cold poetry. I like him as a man but I think there are too many things he does not understand; in common with many of us he is too vain about his strengths, too blind to his lacks, and since he has not had the kind of recognition he wanted and maybe deserved, I get the feeling he has temporarily lost enthusiasm for the race. Yet it would not surprise me if he appeared with a major work in ten or fifteen years, or however long it takes for the rest of the world to become as real to him as Chandler Brossard.

Something of the same may be said of Gore Vidal. He is one of the few novelists I know who has a good formal mind. We spent an hour once talking about my play of *The Deer Park*, and it was the best criticism I ever received from one of my competitors —incisive, detached, with a fine nose for what was slack in the play or insufficiently developed. The best of it was that he took my play on its own terms and criticized it in context rather than wasting our mutual hour in a set of artillery and counterbattery barrages about the high aesthetic of the theatre. Since his remarks were helpful to my play, and he knew they would improve the work, I thought it generous of him and more than decent. Since then I have seen sides of him I thought not so nice, and I do not know that one could call him a friend. I mention this not to comment on Vidal's character but to correct the balance—I do not feel that I owe him a favor, and so my comments on his work may be considered more or less objective.

Not that I have the definitive word to say. While the considerable body of his work (the largest of my generation) still presents no single novel which is more successful than not (at least in those of his novels which I've read), he has developed a variety of styles, and he has continued to experiment. In his essays, where he is at his best, he often brings a brave and cultivated wit to the pomades of the national suet. But in his fiction it seems difficult for him to create a landscape which is inhabited by people. At his worst he becomes his own jailer and is imprisoned in the recessive nuances of narcissistic explorations which do not go deep enough into himself, and so end as gestures and postures. But if Vidal does not lose his will, he could still be most important, for he has the first requirement of an interesting writer—one cannot predict his direction. Still I cannot resist suggesting that he is in need of a wound which would turn the prides of his detachment into new perception.

I've read two stories by Anatole Broyard. They are each first-rate, and I would buy a novel by him the day it appeared.

One writer who was not properly applauded was Myron Kaufmann, whose *Remember Me to God* was one of the most honest novels written since the war. Kaufman is not a fine writer, and his work is perhaps too solid, too sober, and too lacking in innovation to attract quick attention, but he had more to say about the deadening of individuality in the American Jew than anyone I can remember, and of the novels about Jews which I have read, his is easily the best since Meyer Levin's *The Old Bunch*. Kaufmann's talents as a realist are so complete, and his eye for detail is so sharp, that he is bound to become important if he can amass a body of work against the obstacle of writing in a time whose first love is self-deception.

Calder Willingham is a clown with the bite of a ferret, and he suffers from the misapprehension that he is a master mind. He has written what may be the funniest dialogue of our time, and if *Geraldine Bradshaw*, his second novel, had been half as long, it would have been the best short novel any of us did. But it is hard to bet on Calder, for if he ever grows up, where will he go? He lacks ideas, and is as indulgent to his shortcomings as a fat old lady to her Pekinese. This said, it must also be admitted that he is one of the few writers who can make an evening, and once he put me down with the economy of a Zen master. I had just finished *Natural Child*, and happened to run into him at the White Horse Tavern. "Calder," I said, coming on like Max Lerner, "I'd like to talk to you about your book. I liked parts of it and didn't like other parts."

"Nawmin," said Calder. "Could you lend me two bucks? I haven't had breakfast yet."

That Ralph Ellison is very good is dull to say. He is essentially a hateful writer: when the line of his satire is pure, he writes so perfectly that one can never forget the experience of reading him —it is like holding a live electric wire in one's hand. But Ellison's mind, fine and icy, tuned to the pitch of a major novelist's madness, is not always adequate to mastering the forms of rage, horror, and disgust which his eyes have presented to his experience, and so he is forever tumbling from the heights of pure satire into the nets of a murderously depressed clown, and *Invisible Man* insists on a thesis which could not be more absurd, for the Negro is the least invisible of all people in America. (That the white does not see each Negro as an individual is not so significant as Ellison makes it—most whites can no longer see each other at all. Their experience is not as real as the experience of the Negro, and their faces have been deadened in the torture chamber of the overburdened American conscience. They have lost all quick sense of the difficulty of life and its danger, and so they do not have faces the way Negroes have faces—it is rare for a Negro who lives it out to reach the age of twenty without having a face which is a work of art.)

Where Ellison can go, I have no idea. His talent is too exceptional to allow for casual predictions, and if one says that the way for Ellison may be to adventure out into the white world he knows so well by now, and create the more difficult and conceivably more awful invisibility of the white man—well, it is a mistake to write prescriptions for a novelist as gifted as Ellison.

James Baldwin is too charming a writer to be major. If in *Notes of a Native Son* he has a sense of moral nuance which is one of the few modern guides to the sophistications of the ethos, even the best of his paragraphs are sprayed with perfume. Baldwin seems incapable of saying "Fuck you" to the reader; instead he must delineate the cracking and the breaking and the melting and the hardening of a heart which could never have felt such sensuous growths and little deaths without being emptied as a voice. It is a pity, because Baldwin is not without courage. His second novel, *Giovanni's Room,* was a bad book but mostly a brave one, and since his life has been as fantastic and varied as the life of any of my fellow racketeers, and he has kept his sensitivity, one itches at times to take a hammer to his detachment, smash the perfumed dome of his ego, and reduce him to what must be one of the most tortured and magical nerves of our time. If he ever climbs the mountain, and really tells it, we will have a testament, and not a noble toilet water. Until then he is doomed to be minor.

I have a terrible confession to make—I have nothing to say about any of the talented women who write today. Out of what is no doubt a fault in me, I do not seem able to read them. Indeed I doubt if there will be a really exciting woman writer until the first whore becomes a call girl and tells her tale. At the risk of making a dozen devoted enemies for life, I can only say that the sniffs I get from the ink of the women are always fey, old-hat, Quaintsy Goysy, tiny, too dykily psychotic, crippled, creepish, fashionable, frigid, outer-Baroque, *maquillé* in mannequin's whimsy, or else bright and stillborn.* Since I've never been able to read Virginia Woolf, and am sometimes willing to believe it can conceivably be my fault, this verdict may be taken fairly as the twisted tongue of a soured taste, at least by those readers who do not share with me the ground of departure—that a good novelist can do without everything but the remnant of his balls. If to this, I add that the little I have read of Herbert Gold reminds me of nothing so much as a woman writer, well I do not know that I have to be aware now of still another such acquaintance.

There are fifty fine writers who could be mentioned, and the odds are not that the first of us to become major will come from their host. More likely we are to hear from writers altogether unknown, working in silence, here, nowhere and there.† But since I can speak only of people with whose work and/or person I am knowledgeable, I can do no more than tip my hat to such men and boys

---

* *With a sorry reluctance to spoil the authority of this verdict, I have to admit that the early work of Mary McCarthy, Jean Stafford and Carson McCullers gave me pleasure.*

† *The ten episodes from "Naked Lunch," which were printed in Big Table, were more arresting, I thought, than anything I've read by an American in years. If the rest of William Burroughs' book is equal to what was shown, and if the novel proves to be a novel and not a collage of extraordinary fragments, then Burroughs will deserve rank as one of the most important novelists in America, and may prove comparable in his impact to Jean Genet.*

of good repute as William Gaddis, Harvey Swados, Harold Humes, William Humphrey, Wright Morris, Bernard Malamud, John Philips, and all the other respected old and new styles of our piggish time.

I will cease with the comment that the novelists will grow when the publishers improve. Five brave publishing houses (a miracle) would wear away a drop of nausea in the cancerous American conscience, and give to the thousand of us or more with real talent, the lone-wolf hope that we can begin to explore a little more of that murderous and cowardly world which will burst into madness if it does not dare a new art of the brave.

LAST ADVERTISEMENT FOR MYSELF
BEFORE THE WAY OUT

If America is rich in talent, which it is, this wealth seems more than equaled by the speed with which we use up our talent. Years ago, in college, I devoured a book of criticism by Joseph Warren Beach, called American Fiction, 1920–1940; *today, the book would not have to be brought up to date—no one from that generation of major American writers who came before my own has put out work of the first importance since the war, not unless one wishes to assign high seriousness to* The Old Man and The Sea, East of Eden, Fable, The Face of Time, *and the half-dozen monotonously even novels of J. P. Marquand.*

Yet what a generation they were—how much more impressive than my own. If their works did not prepare us for the slack, the stupor, and the rootless wit of our years, they were still men who wrote strong, original novels, personal in style—so many of us were ready to become writers because of the world they opened.

To call the role today is depressing. Wolfe is dead and Fitzgerald is dead; both dead too early; one, a burned-out rocket, the other a gentleman blade who concealed his wounds too long and died lingering over them. Hemingway lost his will to work, or so it seems; Faulkner passed his zenith. Each of them has greatness, and yet neither has written the one novel which would be a monument to his work, and they had gifts on a grand scale.* Dos Passos wrote

---

* *Hemingway's new novel, all these years in the writing since the Second World War, may turn out to be excellent in its way (although I doubt it) but the question to ask will still be whether the* Old Man *says anything which can bother an eight-year-old or one's grandmother. Hemingway seems to have abused his sensitivity and bravery in such a way as to keep his physical courage by indulging his moral sloth. Now at his worst, he adds to the nausea he once cleared away.*

his big work, and none of us has done a novel to come close to it, but the time betrayed him, and he was beached on the dry sands of his political integrity and had to live with the salt water of insufficient recognition. Farrell plowed his broad groove and remained true to himself—he, too, was cheated of a recognition which could match his size, and so he did not have the opportunity to learn about new worlds, and grow; instead he wore down with dignity, and fashion has passed him by. Steinbeck seemed to lose conviction, as well he might—the world became too complex and too ugly for a man who needed situations of Biblical simplicity for his art. And J. P. Marquand, whom Beach saw fit to include, did not do anything new—he just did a lot of very little, and made a gloomy fortune doing it. One must go back to an earlier time, to Dreiser, to Lewis, and to Sherwood Anderson, in order to come across men who wrote across the larger length of their lives and had a career which came close to the limit of what they could do.

America is a cruel soil for talent. It stunts it, blights it, uproots it, or overheats it with cheap fertilizer. And our literary gardeners, our publishers, editors, reviewers and general flunkeys, are drunks, cowards, respectables, prose couturiers, fashion-mongers, old maids, time servers and part-time pimps on the Avenue of President Madison. The audiences are not much better—they seem to consist in nine parts of the tense tasteless victims of a mass-media culture, incapable of confronting a book unless it is successful. The other part, that developed reader in ten with education, literary desire, a library, and a set of acquired prejudices is worse, for he lacks the power to read with a naked eye. His opinion depends on the sluggish and culturally vested taste of the quarterlies, and since these magazines are all too often managed by men of large knowledge and small daring, the writers they admire are invariably minor, overcultivated, and too literary. Small highly polished jewels reflect upon even smaller gems. The light is private, and they would not have it otherwise. Their real delight is in the abysmal taste of the majority, for a broad vein of good taste in American life would wash away the meaning of their lives.

So the strong talents of my generation, those few of us who have wide minds in a narrow overdeveloped time, are left to wander through a landscape of occult herbs and voracious weeds, ambushed by the fallen wires of electric but meaningless situations. Our promotions are often undeserved, our real efforts are understood too late; the first of us to die will have a fine funeral and his literary stock will boom before the wake is wet. If it were not for some new generation coming to life—a generation which might be more interesting than my own, or so I must hope, it would be best to give up, because all desire is lost for talking to readers older than oneself. Defeated by war, prosperity, and conformity, the best of our elders are deadened into thinking machines, and the worst are broken scolds who parrot a plain housewife's practical sense of the mediocre—worn-out middle-class bores of the psychoanalytical persuasion who worship the cheats of moderation, compromise, committee and indecision, or even worse, turn to respect the past.

There was a frontier for my generation of novelists. Coming out of the orgy of the war, our sense of sex and family was torn in two. The past did not exist for us. We had to write our way out into the unspoken territories of sex—there was so much there, it was new, and the life of our talent depended upon going into the borderland. Instead—and it is the old story—we all learned, one from the trap of another, that what was not trimmed from our pages by an editor's nudge was given away in the hagglings of publisher and author, and that which was left, and some of us insisted upon keeping all or almost all of what we had written, was then distorted, shit on, or ignored by the best and worst of the daily reviewers. And in the quarterlies—God's blessing if the works of four or five of us were compared and dismissed by a bright young academic with a small sense of life.

Now it is getting a little better. Some of us will probably be launched on a second wave of recognition (our contemporaries are getting old enough to have a bit of power themselves), but what a waste there has been. John Horne Burns is dead, a nice talent, sexual, not too dishonest, oversweet but tender—the poisonous stupidities of the reviewers toward his last two novels hurried his going, and who knows what could have happened to his talent, for it had the promise of size. The rest of us are older than we ought to be, ten years used up in two or three of war, and another twenty spent in the fourteen years since. When I come to assess myself, and try to measure what chance I have of writing that big book I have again in me, I do not know in all simple bitterness if I can make it. For you have to care about other people to share your perception with them, especially if it is a perception which can give them life, and now there are too many times when I no longer give a good goddamn for most of the human race. I had the freak of luck to start high on the mountain, and go down sharp while others were passing me. So I saw their faces as they learned to climb, and what faces they were! fear first, with avidity up the ass; their steps— snobbery; the peak, power; and their terror—consequence.

Still! There is the fault of others, and the fault of oneself, and I have my debts to pay. Fitzgerald was an indifferent caretaker of his talent, and I have been a cheap gambler with mine. As I add up the accounts, I cannot like myself too much, for I was cowardly when I should have been good, and too brave on many a bad chance, and I spent my first thirty years abusing my body, and the last six in forced marches on my brain, and so I am more stupid today than I ought to be, my memory is half-gone, and my mind is slow; from fear and vanity I paid out too much for what I managed to learn. When I sit down, soon after this book is done, to pick up again on my novel, I do not know if I can do it, for if the first sixty pages are not at all bad, I may still have wasted too much of myself, and if I have—what a loss. How poor to go to death with no more than the notes of good intention. It is the actions of men and not their sentiments which make history—the best sentence I've ever written —but I would hate to face eternity with that for my flag, since I am still at this formal middle of my life a creator of sentiments larger than my work.

Let me finish with a word about the new book, for the Prologue to it ends my collection. By present standards of publishing practice, it will be, if I can do it, an unpublishable work. Since it is likely to take ten years—what with a side-effort or two to pick up some money—I do not have the confidence that you will see it in its completed form, except as an outlaw of the underground like Tropic of Cancer, Ulysses, or Les Cent-Vingt Journées de Sodome. If it is to have any effect, and I can hardly look forward to exhausting the next ten years without hope of a deep explosion of effect, the book will be fired to its fuse by the rumor that once I pointed to the farthest fence and said that within ten years I would try to hit the longest ball ever to go up into the accelerated hurricane air of our American letters. For if I have one ambition above all others, it is to write a novel which Dostoyevsky and Marx; Joyce and Freud; Stendhal, Tolstoy, Proust and Spengler; Faulkner, and even old moldering Hemingway might come to read, for it would carry what they had to tell another part of the way.

NOTE FOR "THE TIME
OF HER TIME"

*In the new novel, "The Time of Her Time" will come some
fifty or a hundred pages after "Advertisements for Myself On The
Way Out." Here, I thought to reverse the order. It seemed more
agreeable to me to end this book with the Prologue.*

THE TIME OF HER TIME

1.

I was living in a room one hundred feet long and twenty-five
feet wide, and it had nineteen windows staring at me from three
of the walls and part of the fourth. The floor planks were worn
below the level of the nails which held them down, except for the
southern half of the room where I had laid a rough linoleum which
gave a hint of sprinkled sand, conceivably an aid to the footwork of
my pupils. For one hundred dollars I had the place whitewashed;
everything: the checkerboard of tin ceiling plates one foot square
with their fleur-de-lis stamped into the metal, the rotted sashes on

the window frames (it took twelve hours to scrape the calcimine from the glass), even parts of the floor had white drippings (although that was scuffed into dust as time went on) and yet it was worth it: when I took the loft it stank of old machinery and the paint was a liverish brown—I had tried living with that color for a week, my old furniture which had been moved by a mover friend from the Village and me, showed the scars of being humped and dragged and flung up six flights of stairs, and the view of it sprawled over twenty-five hundred feet of living space, three beat old day beds, some dusty cushions, a broken-armed easy chair, a cigarette-scarred coffee table made from a door, a kitchen table, some peeled enamel chairs which thumped like a wooden-legged pirate when one sat in them, the bookshelves of unfinished pine butted by bricks, yes all of this, my purview, this grand vista, the New York sunlight greeting me in the morning through the double filter of the smog-yellow sky and the nineteen dirt-frosted windows, inspired me with so much content, especially those liver-brown walls, that I fled my pad like the plague, and in the first week, after a day of setting the furniture to rights, I was there for four hours of sleep a night, from five in the morning when I maneuvered in from the last closed Village bar and the last coffee-klatsch of my philosopher friends' for the night to let us say nine in the morning when I awoke with a partially destroyed brain and the certainty that the sore vicious growl of my stomach was at least the onset of an ulcer and more likely the first gone cells of a thoroughgoing cancer of the duo-denum. So I lived it that way for a week, and then following the advice of a bar-type who was the friend of a friend, I got myself up on the eighth morning, boiled my coffee on a hot-plate while I shivered in the October air (neither the stove nor the gas heaters had yet been bought) and then I went downstairs and out the front door of the warehouse onto Monroe Street, picking my way through the garbage-littered gutter which always made me think of the gangs on this street, the Negroes on the east end of the block, the Puerto Ricans next to them, and the Italians and Jews to the west—those gangs were going to figure a little in my life, I suspected that, I was anticipating those moments with no quiet bravery considering how hung was my head in the morning, for the worst clue to the gangs was the six-year-olds. They were the defilers of the garbage, knights of the ordure, and here, in this province of a capital Manhattan, at the southern tip of the island,

479

with the overhead girders of the Manhattan and Brooklyn bridges the only noble structures for a mile of tenement jungle, yes here the barbarians ate their young, and any type who reached the age of six without being altogether mangled by father, mother, family or friends, was a pint of iron man, so tough, so ferocious, so sharp in the teeth that the wildest alley cat would have surrendered a freshly caught rat rather than contest the meal. They were charming, these six-year-olds, as I told my uptown friends, and they used to topple the overloaded garbage cans, strew them through the street, have summer snowball fights with orange peel, coffee grounds, soup bones, slop, they threw the discus by scaling the raw tin rounds from the tops of cans, their pillow fights were with loaded socks of scum, and a debauch was for two of them to scrub a third around the inside of a twenty-gallon pail still warm with the heat of its emptied treasures. I heard that the Olympics took place in summer when they were out of school and the streets were so thick with the gum of old detritus, alluvium and dross that the mash made by passing car tires fermented in the sun. Then the parents and the hoods and the debs and the grandmother dowagers cheered them on and promised them murder and the garbage flew all day, but I was there in fall and the scene was quiet from nine to three. So I picked my way through last night's stew of rubble on this eighth morning of my hiatus on Monroe Street, and went half down the block to a tenement on the boundary between those two bandit republics of the Negroes and the Puerto Ricans, and with a history or two of knocking on the wrong door, and with a nose full of the smells of the sick overpeppered bowels of the poor which seeped and oozed out of every leaking pipe in every communal crapper (only as one goes north does the word take on the Protestant propriety of john), I was able finally to find my man, and I was an hour ahead of him—he was still sleeping off his last night's drunk. So I spoke to his wife, a fat masculine Negress with the face and charity of a Japanese wrestler, and when she understood that I was neither a junk-peddler nor fuzz, that I sold no numbers, carried no bills, and was most certainly not a detective (though my Irish face left her dubious of that) but instead had come to offer her husband a job of work, I was admitted to the first of three dark rooms, face to face with the gray luminescent eye of the television set going its way in a dark room on a bright morning, and through the hall curtains I could hear them talking in the bedroom.

"Get up, you son of a bitch," she said to him.

He came to work for me, hating my largesse, lugging his air compressor up my six flights of stairs, and after a discussion in which his price came down from two hundred to one, and mine rose from fifty dollars to meet his, he left with one of my twenty-dollar bills, the air compressor on the floor as security, and returned in an hour with so many sacks of whitewash that I had to help him up the stairs. We worked together that day, Charley Thompson his name was, a small lean Negro maybe forty years old, and conceivably sixty, with a scar or two on his face, one a gouge on the cheek, the other a hairline along the bridge of his nose, and we got along not too badly, working in sullen silence until the hangover was sweated out, and then starting to talk over coffee in the Negro hashhouse on the corner where the bucks bridled a little when I came in, and then ignored me. Once the atmosphere had become neutral again, Thompson was willing to talk.

"Man," he said to me, "what you want all that space for?"

"To make money."

"Out of which?"

I debated not very long. The people on the block would know my business sooner or later—the reward of living in a slum is that everyone knows everything which is within reach of the senses —and since I would be nailing a sign over my mailbox downstairs for the pupils to know which floor they would find me on, and the downstairs door would have to be open since I had no bell, the information would be just as open. But for that matter I was born to attract attention; given my height and my blond hair, the barbarians would notice me, they noticed everything, and so it was wiser to come on strong than to try to sidle in.

"Ever hear of an *Escuela de Torear?*" I asked him without a smile.

He laughed with delight at the sound of the words, not even bothering to answer.

"That's a bullfighter's school," I told him. "I teach bullfighting."

"You know that?"

"I used to do it in Mexico."

"Man, you can get killed."

"Some do." I let the exaggeration of a cooled nuance come into my voice. It was true after all; some do get killed. But not so many as I was suggesting, maybe one in fifty of the successful, and one in five hundred of the amateurs like me who fought a few bulls, received a few wounds, and drifted away.

Charley Thompson was impressed. So were others—the conversation was being overheard after all, and I had become a cardinal piece on the chaotic chessboard of Monroe Street's sociology—I felt the clear bell-like adrenalins of clean anxiety, untainted by weakness, self-interest, neurotic habit, or the pure yellows of the liver. For I had put my poker money on the table, I was the new gun in a frontier saloon, and so I was asking for it, not today, not tomorrow, but come sooner, come later, something was likely to follow from this. The weak would leave me alone, the strong would have respect, but be it winter or summer, sunlight or dark, there would come an hour so cold or so hot that someone, somebody, some sexed-up head, very strong and very weak, would be drawn to discover a new large truth about himself and the mysteries of his own courage or the lack of it. I knew. A year before, when I had first come to New York, there was a particular cat I kept running across in the bars of the Village, an expert with a knife, or indeed to maintain the salts of accuracy, an expert with two knives. He carried them everywhere—he had been some sort of hophead instructor in the Marines on the art of fighting with the knife, and he used to demonstrate nice fluid poses, his elbows in, the knives out, the points of those blades capering free of one another—he could feint in any direction with either hand, he was an artist, he believed he was better with a knife than any man in all of New York, and night after night in bar after bar he sang the love-song of his own prowess, begging for the brave type who would take on his boast, and leave him confirmed or dead.

It is mad to take on the city of New York, there is too much talent waiting on line; this cat was calling for every hoodlum in every crack gang and clique who fancied himself with the blade, and one night, drunk and on the way home, he was greeted by another knife, a Puerto Rican cat who was defective in school and spent his afternoons and nights shadow-knifing in the cellar clubhouse of his clique, a real contender, long-armed for a Latin, thin as a Lehmbruck, and fast as a hungry wolf; he had practiced for two months to meet the knife of New York.

So they went into an alley, the champion drunk, a fog of vanity blanketing the point of all his artistic reflexes, and it turned out to be not too much of a fight: the Puerto Rican caught it on the knuckles, the lip, and above the knee, but they were only nicks, and the champion was left in bad shape, bleeding from the forearm, the belly, the chest, the neck, and the face: once he was down, the Puerto Rican had engraved a double oval, labium majorum and minorum on the skin of the cheek, and left him there, having the subsequent consideration or fright to make a telephone call to the bar in which our loser had been drinking. The ex-champion, a bloody cat, was carried to his pad which was not far away (a bit of belated luck) and in an hour, without undue difficulty the brother-in-law doctor of somebody or other was good enough to take care of him. There were police reports, and as our patois goes, the details were a drag, but what makes my story sad is that our ex-champion was through. He mended by sorts and shifts, and he still bragged in the Village bars, and talked of finding the Puerto Rican when he was sober and in good shape, but the truth was that he was on the alcoholic way, and the odds were that he would stay there. He had been one of those gamblers who saw his life as a single bet, and he had lost. I often thought that he had been counting on a victory to put some charge below his belt and drain his mouth of all that desperate labial libido.

Now I was following a modest parallel, and as Thompson kept asking me some reasonable if openly ignorant questions about the nature of the bullfight, I found myself shaping every answer as carefully as if I were writing dialogue, and I was speaking particularly for the black-alerted senses of three Negroes who were sitting behind me, each of them big in his way (I had taken my glimpse as I came in) with a dull, almost Chinese, sullenness of face. They could have been anything. I had seen faces like theirs on boxers and ditch diggers, and I had seen such faces by threes and fours riding around in Cadillacs through the Harlem of the early-morning hours. I was warning myself to play it carefully, and yet I pushed myself a little further than I should, for I became ashamed of my caution and therefore was obliged to brag just the wrong bit. Thompson, of course, was encouraging me—he was a sly old bastard—and he knew even better than me the character of our audience.

"Man, you can take care of yourself," he said with glee.

"I don't know about that," I answered, obeying the formal minuet of the *macho*. "I don't like to mess with anybody," I told him. "But a man messes with me—well, I wouldn't want him to go away feeling better than he started."

"Oh, yeah, ain't that a fact. I hears just what you hear." He talked like an old-fashioned Negro—probably Southern. "What if four or five of them comes on and gangs you?"

We had come a distance from the art of the *corrida*. "That doesn't happen to me," I said. "I like to be careful about having some friends." And part for legitimate emphasis, and part to fulfill my image of the movie male lead—that blond union of the rugged and the clean-cut (which would after all be *their* image as well)— I added, "Good friends, you know."

There we left it. My coffee cup was empty, and in the slop of the saucer a fly was drowning. I was thinking idly and with no great compassion that wherever this fly had been born it had certainly not expected to die in a tan syrupy ring-shaped pond, struggling for the greasy hot-dogged air of a cheap Negro hashhouse. But Thompson rescued it with a deft little flip of his fingers.

"I always save," he told me seriously. "I wouldn't let nothing be killed. I'm a preacher."

"Real preacher?"

"Was one. Church and devoted congregation." He said no more. He had the dignified sadness of a man remembering the major failure of his life.

As we got up to go, I managed to turn around and get another look at the three spades in the next booth. Two of them were facing me. Their eyes were flat, the whites were yellow and flogged with red—they stared back with no love. The anxiety came over me again, almost nice—I had been so aware of them, and they had been so aware of me.

2.

That was in October, and for no reason I could easily discover, I found myself thinking of that day as I awoke on a spring morning more than half a year later with a strong light coming through my nineteen windows. I had fixed the place up since then, added a few more pieces of furniture, connected a kitchen sink and a metal stall shower to the clean water outlets in the john, and most noticeably I had built a wall between the bullfight studio and the half in which I lived. That was more necessary than one might guess—I had painted the new wall red; after Thompson's job of whitewash I used to feel as if I were going snow-blind; it was no easy pleasure to get up each morning in a white space so blue with cold that the chill of a mountain peak was in my blood. Now, when I opened my eyes, I could choose the blood of the wall in preference to the ice slopes of Mt. O'Shaugnessy, where the sun was always glinting on the glaciers of the windows.

But on this particular morning, when I turned over a little more, there was a girl propped on one elbow in the bed beside me, no great surprise, because this was the year of all the years in my life when I was scoring three and four times a week, literally combing the pussy out of my hair, which was no great feat if one knew the Village and the scientific temperament of the Greenwich Village mind. I do not want to give the false impression that I was one of the lustiest to come adventuring down the pike—I was cold, maybe by birth, certainly by environment: I grew up in a Catholic orphanage—and I had had my little kinks and cramps, difficulties enough just a few years ago, but I had passed through that, and I was going now on a kind of disinterested but developed competence; what it came down to was that I could go an hour with the average girl without destroying more of the vital substance than a good night's sleep could repair, and since that sort of stamina seems to get advertised, and I had my good looks, my blond hair, my height, build, and bullfighting school, I suppose I became one of the Village equivalents of an Eagle Scout badge for the girls. I was one of the credits needed for a diploma in the sexual humanities, I was par for a good course, and more than one of the girls and ladies would try me on an off-evening like comparison-shoppers to shop the value of their boy friend, lover, mate, or husband against the certified professionalism of Sergius O'Shaugnessy.

Now if I make this sound bloodless, I am exaggerating a bit —even an old habit is livened once in a while with color, and there were girls I worked to get and really wanted, and nights when the bull was far from dead in me. I even had two women I saw at least once a week, each of them, but what I am trying to emphasize is that when you screw too much and nothing is at stake, you begin to feel like a saint. It was a hell of a thing to be holding a nineteen-year-old girl's ass in my hands, hefting those young kneadables of future power, while all the while the laboratory technician in my brain was deciding that the experiment was a routine success— routine because her cheeks looked and felt just about the way I had

485

thought they would while I was sitting beside her in the bar earlier in the evening, and so I still had come no closer to understanding my scientific compulsion to verify in the retort of the bed how accurately I had predicted the form, texture, rhythm and surprise of any woman who caught my eye.

Only an ex-Catholic can achieve some of the rarer amalgams of guilt, and the saint in me deserves to be recorded. I always felt an obligation—some noblesse oblige of the kindly cocksman—to send my women away with no great wounds to their esteem, feeling at best a little better than when they came in, I wanted it to be friendly (what vanity of the saint!). I was the messiah of the one-night stand, and so I rarely acted like a pig in bed, I wasn't greedy, I didn't grind all my tastes into their mouths, I even abstained from springing too good a lay when I felt the girl was really in love with her man, and was using me only to give love the benefit of new perspective. Yes, I was a good sort, I probably gave more than I got back, and the only real pains for all those months in the loft, for my bullfighting classes, my surprisingly quiet time (it had been winter after all) on Monroe Street, my bulging portfolio of experiments—there must have been fifty girls who spent at least one night in the loft—my dull but doggedly advancing scientific data, even the cold wan joys of my saintliness demanded for their payment only one variety of the dead hour: when I woke in the morning, I could hardly wait to get the latest mouse out of my bed and out of my lair. I didn't know why, but I would awaken with the deadliest of depressions, the smell of the woman had gone very stale for me, and the armpits, the ammonias and dead sea life of old semen and old snatch, the sour fry of last night's sweat, the whore scent of overexercised perfume, became an essence of the odious, all the more remarkable because I clung to women in my sleep, I was one Don John who hated to sleep alone, I used to feel as if my pores were breathing all the maternal (because sleeping) sweets of the lady, wet or dry, firm or flaccid, plump, baggy, or lean who was handled by me while we dreamed. But on awakening, hung with my head—did I make love three times that year without being drunk?—the saint was given his hour of temptation, for I would have liked nothing more than to kick the friendly ass out of bed, and dispense with the coffee, the good form, my depression and often hers, and start the new day by lowering her in a basket out of my monk-ruined retreat six floors down to the garbage pile (now blooming again in the freshets of spring), wave my hand at her safe landing and get in again myself to the blessed isolations of the man alone.

But of course that was not possible. While it is usually a creep who generalizes about women, I think I will come on so heavy as to say that the cordial tone of the morning after is equally important to the gymkhana of the night before—at least if the profit made by a nice encounter is not to be lost. I had given my working hours of the early morning to dissolving a few of the inhibitions, chilled reflexes and dampened rhythms of the corpus before me, but there is not a restraint in the world which does not have to be taken twice—once at night on a steam-head of booze, and once in daylight with the grace of a social tea. To open a girl up to the point where she loves you or It or some tremor in her sexual baggage, and then to close her in the morning is to do the disservice which the hateful side of women loves most—you have fed their cold satisfied distrust of a man. Therefore my saint fought his private churl, and suffering all the detail of abusing the sympathetic nervous system, I made with the charm in the daylight and was more of a dear than most.

It was to be a little different this morning, however. As I said, I turned over in my bed, and looked at the girl propped on her elbow beside me. In her eyes there was a flat hatred which gave no ground—she must have been staring like this at my back for several minutes, and when I turned, it made no difference—she continued to examine my face with no embarrassment and no delight.

That was sufficient to roll me around again, my shoulder blades bare to her inspection, and I pretended that the opening of my eyes had been a false awakening. I felt deadened then with all the diseases of the dull—making love to her the night before had been a little too much of a marathon. She was a Jewish girl and she was in her third year at New York University, one of those harsh alloys of a self-made bohemian from a middle-class home (her father was a hardware wholesaler), and I was remembering how her voice had irritated me each time I had seen her, an ugly New York accent with a cultured overlay. Since she was still far from formed, there had been all sorts of Lesbian hysterias in her shrieking laugh and they warred with that excess of strength, complacency and deprecation which I found in many Jewish women—a sort of "Ech" of disgust at the romantic and mysterious All. This one was medium in size and she had dark long hair which she wore like a Village witch in two extended braids which came down over her flat breasts, and she had a long thin nose, dark eyes, and a kind of lean force, her arms and square shoulders had shown the flat thin muscles of a wiry boy. All the same, she was not bad, she had a kind of Village chic, a certain snotty elegance of superiority, and when I first came to New York I had dug girls like her—Jewesses were strange to me—and I had even gone with one for a few months. But this new chick had been a mistake—I had met her two weeks ago at a party, she was on leave from her boy friend, and we had had an argument about T. S. Eliot, a routine which for me had become the quintessence of corn, but she said that Eliot was the apotheosis of manner, he embodied the ecclesiasticism of classical and now futureless form, she adored him she said, and I was tempted to tell her how little Eliot would adore the mannerless yeasts of the Brooklyn from which she came, and how he might prefer to allow her to appreciate his poetry only in step to the transmigration of her voice from all urgent Yiddish nasalities to the few high English analities of relinquished desire. No, she would not make that other world so fast—nice society was not cutting her crumpets thus quickly because she was gone on Thomas Stearns Eeeee. Her college-girl snobbery, the pith for me of eighty-five other honey-pots of the Village aesthetic whose smell I knew all too well, so inflamed the avenger of my crotch, that I wanted to prong her then and there, right on the floor of the party, I was a primitive for a prime minute, a gorged gouge of a working-class phallus, eager to ram into all her nasty little tensions. I had the message again, I was one of the millions on the bottom who had the muscles to move the sex which kept the world alive, and I would grind it into her, the healthy hearty inches and the sweat of the cost of acquired culture when you started low and you wanted to go high. She was a woman, what! she sensed that moment, she didn't know if she could handle me, and she had the guts to decide to find out. So we left the party and we drank and (leave it to a Jewish girl to hedge the bet) she drained the best half of my desire in conversation because she was being psychoanalyzed, what a predictable pisser! and she was in that stage where the jargon had the totalitarian force of all vocabularies of mechanism, and she could only speak of her infantile relations to men, and the fixations and resistances of unassimilated penis-envy with all the smug gusto of a female commissar. She was enthusiastic about her analyst, he was also Jewish (they were working now on Jewish self-hatred), he was really an integrated guy, Stanford Joyce, he belonged on the same mountain as Eliot, she loved the doers and the healers of life who built on the foundationless prevalence of the void those islands of proud endeavor.

"You must get good marks in school," I said to her.

"Of course."

How I envied the jazzed-up brain of the Jews. I was hot for her again, I wanted the salts of her perspiration in my mouth. They would be acrid perhaps, but I would digest them, and those intellectual molecules would rise to my brain.

"I know a girl who went to your bullfighting school," she said to me. She gave her harsh laugh. "My friend thought you were afraid of her. She said you were full of narcissistic anxieties."

"Well, we'll find out," I said.

"Oh, you don't want me. I'm very inadequate as a lover."

Her dark hard New York eyes, bright with appetite, considered my head as if I were a delicious and particularly sour pickle.

I paid the check then, and we walked over to my loft. As I had expected, she made no great fuss over the back-and-forth of being seduced—to the contrary. Once we were upstairs, she prowled the length of my loft twice, looked at the hand-made bullfighting equipment I had set up along one wall of the studio, asked me a question or two about the killing machine, studied the swords, asked another question about the cross-guard on the descabellar, and then came back to the living-room–bedroom–dining-room–kitchen of the other room, and made a face at the blood-red wall. When I kissed her she answered with a grinding insistence of her mouth upon mine, and a muscular thrust of her tongue into my throat, as direct and unfeminine as the harsh force of her voice.

"I'd like to hang my clothes up," she said.

It was not all that matter-of-fact when we got to bed. There was nothing very fleshy about the way she made love, no sense of the skin, nor smell, nor touch, just anger, anger at her being there, and another anger which was good for my own, that rage to achieve . . . just what, one cannot say. She made love as if she were running up an inclined wall so steep that to stop for an instant would slide her back to disaster. She hammered her rhythm at me, a hard driving rhythm, an all but monotonous drum, pound into pound against pound into pound until that moment when my anger found its way back again to that delayed and now recovered Time when I wanted to prong her at the party. I had been frustrated, had waited, had lost the anger, and so been taken by her. That finally got me—all through the talk about T. S. Eliot I had been calculating how I would lay waste to her little independence, and now she was alone, with me astride her, going through her paces, teeth biting the pillow, head turned away, using me as the dildoe of a private gallop. So my rage came back, and my rhythm no longer depended upon her drive, but found its own life, and we made love like two club fighters in an open exchange, neither giving ground, rhythm to rhythm, even to even, hypnotic, knowing neither the pain of punishment nor the pride of pleasure, and the equality of this, as hollow as the beat of the drum, seemed to carry her into some better deep of desire, and I had broken through, she was following me, her muscular body writhed all about me with an impersonal abandon, the wanton whip-thrash of a wounded snake, she was on fire and frozen at the same time, and then her mouth was kissing me with a rubbery greedy compulsion so avid to use all there was of me, that to my distant surprise, not in character for the saint to slip into the brutal, my hand came up and clipped her mean and openhanded across the face which brought a cry from her and broke the piston of her hard speed into something softer, wetter, more sly, more warm, I felt as if her belly were opening finally to receive me, and when her mouth kissed me again with a passing tender heat, warm-odored with flesh, and her body sweetened into some feminine embrace of my determination driving its way into her, well, I was gone, it was too late, I had driven right past her in that moment she turned, and I had begun to come, I was coming from all the confluences of my body toward that bud of sweetness I had plucked from her, and for a moment she was making it, she was a move back and surging to overtake me, and then it was gone, she made a mistake, her will ordered all temptings and rhythms to mobilize their march, she drove into the hard stupidities of a marching-band's step, and as I was going off in the best for many a month, she was merely going away, she had lost it again. As I ebbed into what should have been the contentments of a fine after-pleasure, warm and fine, there was one little part of me remaining cold and murderous because she had deprived me, she had fled the domination which was liberty for her, and the rest of the night was bound to be hell.

Her face was ugly. "You're a bastard, do you know that?" she asked of me.

"Let it go. I feel good."

"Of course you feel good. Couldn't you have waited one minute?"

I disliked this kind of thing. My duty was reminding me of how her awakened sweets were souring now in the belly, and her nerves were sharpening into the gone electric of being just nowhere.

"I hate inept men," she said.

"Cool it." She could, at least, be a lady. Because if she didn't stop, I would give her back a word or two.

"You did that on purpose," she nagged at me, and I was struck with the intimacy of her rancor—we might as well have been married for ten years to dislike each other so much at this moment.

"Why," I said, "you talk as if this were something unusual for you."

"It is."

"Come on," I told her, "you never made it in your life."

"How little you know," she said. "This is the first time I've missed in months."

If she had chosen to get my message, I could have been preparing now for a good sleep. Instead I would have to pump myself up again—and as if some ghost of the future laid the squeak of a tickle on my back, I felt an odd dread, not for tonight so much as for some ills of the next ten years whose first life was stirring tonight. But I lay beside her, drew her body against mine, feeling her trapped and irritable heats jangle me as much as they roused me, and while I had no fear that the avenger would remain asleep, still he stirred in pain and in protest, he had supposed his work to be done, and he would claim the wages of overtime from my reserve. That was the way I thought it would go, but Junior from New York University, with her hard body and her passion for proper poetry, gave a lewd angry old grin as her face stared boldly into mine, and with the practical bawdiness of the Jew she took one straight utilitarian finger, smiled a deceptive girlish pride, and then she jabbed, fingernail and all, into the tight defended core of my clenched buttocks. One wiggle of her knuckle and I threw her off, grunting a sound between rage and surprise, to which she laughed and lay back and waited for me.

Well, she had been right, that finger tipped the balance, and three-quarters with it, and one-quarter hung with the mysteries of sexual ambition, I worked on her like a beaver for forty-odd minutes or more, slapping my tail to build her nest, and she worked along while we made the round of the positions, her breath sobbing the exertions, her body as alive as a charged wire and as far from rest.

I gave her all the Time I had in me and more besides, I was weary of her, and the smell which rose from her had so little of the sea and so much of the armpit, that I breathed the stubborn wills of the gymnasium where the tight-muscled search for grace, and it was like that, a hard punishing session with pulley weights, stationary bicycle sprints, and ten breath-seared laps around the track. Yes, when I caught that smell, I knew she would not make it, and so I kept on just long enough to know she was exhausted in body, exhausted beyond the place where a ten-minute rest would have her jabbing that finger into me again, and hating her, hating women who could not take their exercise alone, I lunged up over the hill with my heart pounding past all pleasure, and I came, but with hatred, tight, electric, and empty, the spasms powerful but centered in my heart and not from the hip, the avenger taking its punishment even at the end, jolted clear to the seat of my semen by the succession of rhythmic blows which my heart drummed back to my feet.

For her, getting it from me, it must have been impressive, a convoluted, smashing, and protracted spasm, a hint of the death throe in the animal male which cannot but please the feminine taste for the mortal wound. "Oh, you're lucky," she whispered in my ear as I lay all collapsed beside her, alone in my athlete's absorption upon the whisperings of damage in the unlit complexities of my inner body. I was indeed an athlete, I knew my body was my future, and I had damaged it a bit tonight by most certainly doing it no good. I disliked her for it with the simple dislike we know for the stupid.

"Want a cigarette?" she asked.

I could wait, my heart would have preferred its rest, but there was something tired in her voice beyond the fatigue of what she had done. She too had lost after all. So I came out of my second rest to look at her, and her face had the sad relaxation (and serenity) of a young whore who has finished a hard night's work with the expected lack of issue for herself, content with no more than the money and the professional sense of the hard job dutifully done.

492

"I'm sorry you didn't make it," I said to her.

She shrugged. There was a Jewish tolerance for the expected failures of the flesh. "Oh, well, I lied to you before," she said.

"You never have been able to, have you?"

"No." She was fingering the muscles of my shoulder, as if in unconscious competition with my strength. "You're pretty good," she said grudgingly.

"Not really inept?" I asked.

"*Sans façons,*" said the poetess in an arch change of mood which irritated me. "Sandy has been illuminating those areas where my habits make for destructive impulses."

"Sandy is Doctor Joyce?" She nodded. "You make him sound like your navigator," I told her.

"Isn't it a little obvious to be hostile to psychoanalysis?"

Three minutes ago we had been belaboring each other in the nightmare of the last round, and now we were close to cozy. I put the sole of my foot on her sharp little knee.

"You know the first one we had?" she asked of me. "Well, I wanted to tell you. I came close—I guess I came as close as I ever came."

"You'll come closer. You're only nineteen."

"Yes, but this evening has been disturbing to me. You see I get more from you than I get from my lover."

Her lover was twenty-one, a senior at Columbia, also Jewish —which lessened interest, she confessed readily. Besides, Arthur was too passive—"Basically, it's very comprehensible," said the commissar, "an aggressive female and a passive male—we complement one another, and that's no good." Of course it was easy to find satisfaction with Arthur, "via the oral perversions. That's because, vaginally, I'm anaesthetized—a good phallic narcissist like you doesn't do enough for me."

In the absence of learned credentials, she was setting out to bully again. So I thought to surprise her. "Aren't you mixing your language a little?" I began. "The phallis narcissist is one of Wilhelm Reich's categories."

"Therefore?"

"Aren't you a Freudian?"

"It would be presumptuous of me to say," she said like a seminar student working for his pee-aitch-dee. "But Sandy is an eclectic. He accepts a lot of Reich—you see, he's very ambitious, he wants to arrive at his own synthesis." She exhaled some smoke in my face, and gave a nice tough little grin which turned her long serious young witch's face into something indeed less presumptuous. "Besides," she said, "you are a phallic narcissist. There's an element of the sensual which is lacking in you."

"But Arthur possesses it?"

"Yes, he does. And you . . . you're not very juicy."

"I wouldn't know what you mean."

"I mean this." With the rich cruel look of a conquistador finding a new chest of Indian gold, she bent her head and gave one fleeting satiric half-moon of a lick to the conjugation of my balls. "That's what I mean," she said, and was out of bed even as I was recognizing that she was finally not without art. "Come back," I said.

But she was putting her clothes on in a hurry. "Shut up. Just don't give me your goddammed superiority."

I knew what it was: she had been about to gamble the reserves which belonged to Arthur, and the thought of possibly wasting them on a twenty-seven-year-old connoisseur like myself was too infuriating to take the risk.

So I lay in bed and laughed at her while she dressed—I did not really want a go at things again—and besides, the more I laughed, the angrier she would be, but the anger would work to the surface, and beneath it would be resting the pain that the evening had ended on so little.

She took her leisure going to the door, and I got up in time to tell her to wait—I would walk her to the subway. The dawn had come, however, and she wanted to go alone, she had had a bellyful of me, she could tell me that.

My brain was lusting its own private futures of how interesting it would be to have this proud, aggressive, vulgar, tense, stiff and arrogant Jewess going wild on my bottom—I had turned more than one girl on, but never a one of quite this type. I suppose she had succeeded instead of me; I was ready to see her again and improve the message.

She turned down all dates, but compromised by giving me her address and the number of her telephone. And then glaring at me from the open door, she said, "I owe you a slap in the face."

"Don't go away feeling unequal."

I might have known she would have a natural punch. My

jaw felt it for half an hour after she was gone and it took another thirty minutes before I could bring myself back to concluding that she was one funny kid.

All of that added up to the first night with the commissar, and I saw her two more times over this stretch, the last on the night when she finally agreed to sleep over with me, and I came awake in the morning to see her glaring at my head. So often in sex, when the second night wound itself up with nothing better in view than the memory of the first night, I was reminded of Kafka's *Castle*, that tale of the search of a man for his apocalyptic orgasm: in the easy optimism of a young man, he almost captures the castle on the first day, and is never to come so close again. Yes, that was the saga of the nervous system of a man as it was bogged into the defeats, complications, and frustrations of middle age. I still had my future before me of course—the full engagement of my will in some go-for-broke I considered worthy of myself was yet to come, but there were times in that loft when I knew the psychology of an old man, and my second night with Denise—for Denise Gondelman was indeed her name—left me racked for it amounted to so little that we could not even leave it there—the hangover would have been too great for both of us—and so we made a date for a third night. Over and over in those days I used to compare the bed to the bullfight, sometimes seeing myself as the matador and sometimes as the bull, and this second appearance, if it had taken place, in the Plaza Mexico, would have been a *fracaso* with kapok seat cushions jeering down on the ring, and a stubborn cowardly bull staying in *querencia* before the doubtful prissy overtures, the gloomy trim technique of a veteran and mediocre *torero* on the worst of days when he is forced to wonder if he has even his *pundonor* to sustain him. It was a gloomy deal. Each of us knew it was possible to be badly worked by the other, and this seemed so likely that neither of us would gamble a finger. Although we got into bed and had a perfunctory ten minutes, it was as long as an hour in a coffee shop when two friends are done with one another.

By the third night we were ready for complexities again; to see a woman three times is to call on the dialectic of an affair. If the waves we were making belonged less to the viper of passion than the worm of inquiry, still it was obvious from the beginning that we had surprises for one another. The second night we had been

495

hoping for more, and so got less; this third night, we each came on with the notion to wind it up, and so got involved in more.

For one thing, Denise called me in the afternoon. There was studying she had to do, and she wondered if it would be all right to come to my place at eleven instead of meeting me for drinks and dinner. Since that would save me ten dollars she saw no reason why I should complain. It was a down conversation. I had been planning to lay siege to her, dispense a bit of elixir from my vast reservoirs of charm, and instead she was going to keep it *in camera*. There was a quality about her I could not locate, something independent —abruptly, right there, I knew what is was. In a year she would have no memory of me, I would not exist for her unless . . . and then it was clear . . . unless I could be the first to carry her stone of no-orgasm up the cliff, all the way, over and out into the sea. That was the kick I could find, that a year from now, five years from now, down all the seasons to the hours of her old age, I would be the one she would be forced to remember, and it would nourish me a little over the years, thinking of that grudged souvenir which could not die in her, my blond hair, my blue eyes, my small broken nose, my clean mouth and chin, my height, my boxer's body, my parts—yes, I was getting excited at the naked image of me in the young-old mind of that sour sexed-up dynamo of black-pussied frustration.

A phallic narcissist she had called me. Well, I was phallic enough, a Village stickman who could muster enough of the divine It on the head of his will to call forth more than one becoming out of the womb of feminine Time, yes a good deal more than one from my fifty new girls a year, and when I failed before various prisons of frigidity, it mattered little. Experience gave the cue that there were ladies who would not be moved an inch by a year of the best, and so I looked for other things in them, but this one, this Den-of-Ease, she was ready, she was entering the time of her Time, and if not me, it would be another—I was sick in advance at the picture of some bearded Negro cat who would score where I had missed and thus cuckold me in spirit, deprive me of those telepathic waves of longing (in which I obviously believed) speeding away to me from her over the years to balm the hours when I was beat, because I had been her psychic bridegroom, had plucked her ideational diddle, had led her down the walk of her real wedding night. Since she did not like me, what a feat to pull it off.

In the hours I waited after dinner, alone, I had the sense—which I always trusted—that tonight this little victory or defeat would be full of leverage, magnified beyond its emotional matter because I had decided to bet on myself that I would win, and a defeat would bring me closer to a general depression, a fog bank of dissatisfaction with myself which I knew could last for months or more. Whereas a victory would add to the panoplies of my ego some peculiar (but for me, valid) ingestion of her arrogance, her stubbornness, and her will—those necessary ingredients of which I could not yet have enough for my own ambition.

When she came in she was wearing a sweater and dungarees which I had been expecting, but there was a surprise for me. Her braids had been clipped, and a short cropped curled Italian haircut decorated her head, moving her severe young face half across the spectrum from the austerities of a poetess to a hint of all those practical and promiscuous European girls who sold their holy hump to the Germans and had been subsequently punished by shaved heads —how attractive the new hair proved; once punished, they were now free, free to be wild, the worst had happened and they were still alive with the taste of the first victor's flesh enriching the sensual curl of the mouth.

Did I like her this way? Denise was interested to know. Well, it was a shock, I admitted, a pleasant shock. If it takes you so long to decide, you must be rigid, she let me know. Well, yes, as a matter of fact I was rigid, rigid for her with waiting.

The nun of severity passed a shade over her. She hated men who were uncool, she thought she would tell me.

"Did your analyst tell you it's bad to be uncool?"

She had taken off her coat, but now she gave me a look as if she were ready to put it on again. "No, he did not tell me that." She laughed spitefully. "But he told me a couple of revealing things about you."

"Which you won't repeat."

"Of course not."

"I'll never know," I said, and gave her the first kiss of the evening. Her mouth was heated—it was the best kiss I had received from her, and it brought me on too quickly—"My fruit is ready to be plucked," said the odors of her mouth, betraying that perfume of the ducts which, against her will no doubt, had been plumping for me. She was changed tonight. From the skin of her face and the glen of her neck came a new smell, sweet, sweaty, and tender, the smell of a body which had been used and had enjoyed its uses. It came to me nicely, one of the nicest smells in quite some time, so different from the usual exudations of her dissatisfied salts that it opened a chain of reflexes in me, and I was off in all good speed on what Denise would probably have called the vertical foreplay. I suppose I went at her like a necrophiliac let loose upon a still-warm subject, and as I gripped her, grasped her, groped her, my breath a bellows to blow her into my own flame, her body remained unmoving, only her mouth answering my call, those lips bridling hot adolescent kisses back upon my face, the smell almost carrying me away—such a fine sweet sweat.

Naturally she clipped the rhythm. As I started to slip up her sweater, she got away and said a little huskily, "I'll take my own clothes off." Once again I could have hit her. My third eye, that athlete's inner eye which probed its vision into all the corners, happy and distressed of my body whole, was glumly cautioning the congestion of the spirits in the coils of each teste. They would have to wait, turn rancid, maybe die of delay.

Off came the sweater and the needless brassière, her economical breasts swelled just a trifle tonight, enough to take on the convexities of an Amazon's armor. Open came the belt and the zipper of her dungarees, zipped from the front which pleased her not a little. Only her ass, a small masterpiece, and her strong thighs, justified this theatre. She stood there naked, quite psychicly clothed, and lit a cigarette.

If a stiff prick has no conscience, it has also no common sense. I stood there like a clown, trying to coax her to take a ride with me on the bawdy car, she out of her clothes, I in all of mine, a muscular little mermaid to melt on my knee. She laughed, one harsh banker's snort—she was giving no loans on my idiot's collateral.

"You didn't even ask me," Denise thought to say, "of how my studying went tonight."

"What did you study?"

"I didn't. I didn't study." She gave me a lovely smile, girlish and bright. "I just spent the last three hours with Arthur."

"You're a dainty type," I told her.

But she gave me a bad moment. That lovely flesh-spent smell, scent of the well used and the tender, that avatar of the feminine my senses had accepted so greedily, came down now to no more than the rubbings and the sweats of what was probably a very nice guy, passive Arthur with his Jewish bonanzas of mouth-love.

The worst of it was that it quickened me more. I had the selfish wisdom to throw such evidence upon the mercy of my own court. For the smell of Arthur was the smell of love, at least for me, and so from man or woman, it did not matter—the smell of love was always feminine—and if the man in Denise was melted by the woman in Arthur, so Arthur might have flowered that woman in himself from the arts of a real woman, his mother?—it did not matter—that voiceless message which passed from the sword of the man into the cavern of the woman was carried along from body to body, and if it was not the woman in Denise I was going to find tonight, at least I would be warmed by the previous trace of another.

But that was a tone poem to quiet the toads of my doubt. When Denise—it took five more minutes—finally decided to expose herself on my clumped old mattress, the sight of her black pubic hair, the feel of the foreign but brotherly liquids in her unembarrassed maw, turned me into a jackrabbit of pissy tumescence, the quicks of my excitement beheaded from the resonances of my body, and I wasn't with her a half-minute before I was over, gone, and off. I rode not with the strength to reap the harem of her and her lover, but spit like a pinched little boy up into black forested hills of motherly contempt, a passing picture of the nuns of my childhood to drench my piddle spurtings with failures of gloom. She it was who proved stronger than me, she the he to my silly she.

All considered, Denise was nice about it. Her harsh laugh did not crackle over my head, her hand in passing me the after-cigarette settled for no more than a nudge of my nose, and if it were not for the contempt of her tough grin, I would have been left with no more than the alarm to the sweepers of my brain to sweep this failure away.

"Hasn't happened in years," I said to her, the confession coming out of me with the cost of the hardest cash.

"Oh, shut up. Just rest." And she began to hum a mocking little song. I lay there in a state, parts of me jangled for forty-eight hours to come, and yet not altogether lost to peace. I knew what it was. Years ago in the air force, as an enlisted man, I had reached the light-heavyweight finals on my air base. For two weeks I trained for the championship, afraid of the other man all the way because I had seen him fight and felt he was better than me; when my night came, he took me out with a left hook to the liver which had me conscious on the canvas but unable to move, and as the referee was counting, which I could hear all too clearly, I knew the same kind of peace, a swooning peace, a clue to that kind of death in which an old man slips away—nothing mattered except that my flesh was vulnerable and I had a dim revery, lying there with the yells of the air force crowd in my ears, there was some far-off vision of green fields and me lying in them, giving up all ambition to go back instead to another, younger life of the senses, and I remember at that moment I watered the cup of my boxer's jock, and then I must have slipped into something new, for as they picked me off the canvas the floor seemed to recede from me at a great rate as if I were climbing in an airplane.

A few minutes later, the nauseas of the blow to my liver had me retching into my hands, and the tension of three weeks of preparation for that fight came back. I knew through the fading vistas of my peace, and the oncoming spasms of my nausea, that the worst was yet to come, and it would take me weeks to unwind, and then years, and maybe never to overcome the knowledge that I had failed completely at a moment when I wanted very much to win.

A ghost of this peace, trailing intimations of a new nausea, was passing over me again, and I sat up in bed abruptly, as if to drive these weaknesses back into me. My groin had been simmering for hours waiting for Denise, and it was swollen still, but the avenger was limp, he had deserted my cause, I was in a spot if she did not co-operate.

Co-operate she did. "My God, lie down again, will you," she said, "I was thinking that finally I had seen you relax."

And then I could sense that the woman in her was about to betray her victory. She sat over me, her little breasts budding with their own desire, her short hair alive and flowering, her mouth ready to taste her gentleman's defeat. I had only to raise my hand, and push her body in the direction she wished it to go, and then her face was rooting in me, her angry tongue and voracious mouth going wild finally as I had wished it, and I knew the sadness of sour timing, because this was a prize I could not enjoy as I would have on first night, and yet it was good enough—not art, not the tease and languor of love on a soft mouth, but therapy, therapy for her, the quick exhaustions of the tension in a harsh throat, the beseechment of an ugly voice going down into the expiation which would be its beauty. Still it was good, practically it was good, my ego could bank the hard cash that this snotty head was searching me, the act served its purpose, anger traveled from her body into mine, the avenger came to attention, cold and furious, indifferent to the trapped doomed pleasure left behind in my body on that initial and grim piddle spurt, and I was ready, not with any joy nor softness nor warmth nor care, but I was ready finally to take her tonight, I was going to beat new Time out of her if beat her I must, I was going to teach her that she was only a child, because if at last I could not take care of a nineteen-year-old, then I was gone indeed. And so I took her with a cold calculation, the rhythms of my body corresponding to no more than a metronome in my mind, tonight the driving mechanical beat would come from me, and blind to nerve-raddlings in my body, and blood pressures in my brain, I worked on her like a riveter, knowing her resistances were made of steel, I threw her a fuck the equivalent of a fifteen-round fight, I wearied her, I brought her back, I drove my fingers into her shoulders and my knees into her hips. I went, and I went, and I went, I bore her high and thumped her hard, I sprinted, I paced, I lay low, eyes all closed, under sexual water, like a submarine listening for the distant sound of her ship's motors, hoping to steal up close and trick her rhythms away.

And she was close. Oh, she was close so much of the time. Like a child on a merry-go-round the touch of the colored ring just evaded the tips of her touch, and she heaved and she hurdled, arched and cried, clawed me, kissed me, even gave of a shriek once, and then her sweats running down and her will weak, exhausted even more than me, she felt me leave and lie beside her. Yes, I did that with a tactician's cunning, I let the depression of her failure poison what was left of her will never to let me succeed, I gave her slack to mourn the lost freedoms and hate the final virginity for which she fought, I even allowed her baffled heat to take its rest and attack her nerves once more, and then, just as she was beginning to fret against me in a new and unwilling appeal, I turned her over suddenly on her belly, my avenger wild with the mania of the madman, and giving her no chance, holding her prone against the mattress with the strength of my weight, I drove into the seat of all stubbornness, tight as a vise, and I wounded her, I knew it, she thrashed beneath me like a trapped little animal, making not a sound, but fierce not to allow me this last of the liberties, and yet caught, forced to give up millimeter by millimeter the bridal ground of her symbolic and therefore real vagina. So I made it, I made it all the way—it took ten minutes and maybe more, but as the avenger rode down to his hilt and tunneled the threshold of sexual home all those inches closer into the bypass of the womb, she gave at last a little cry of farewell, and I could feel a new shudder which began as a ripple and rolled into a wave, and then it rolled over her, carrying her along, me hardly moving for fear of damping this quake from her earth, and then it was gone, but she was left alive with a larger one to follow.

So I turned her once again on her back, and moved by impulse to love's first hole. There was an odor coming up, hers at last, the smell of the sea, and none of the armpit or a dirty sock, and I took her mouth and kissed it, but she was away, following the wake of her own waves which mounted, fell back, and in new momentum mounted higher and should have gone over, and then she was about to hang again, I could feel it, that moment of hesitation between the past and the present, the habit and the adventure, and I said into her ear, "You dirty little Jew."

That whipped her over. A first wave kissed, a second spilled, and a third and a fourth and a fifth came breaking over, and finally she was away, she was loose in the water for the first time in her life, and I would have liked to go with her, but I was blood-throttled and numb, and as she had the first big moment in her life, I was nothing but a set of aching balls and a congested cock, and I rode with her wistfully, looking at the contortion of her face and listening to her sobbing sound of "Oh, Jesus, I made it, oh Jesus, I did."

"Compliments of T. S. Eliot," I whispered to myself, and my head was aching, my body was shot. She curled against me, she kissed my sweat, she nuzzled my eyes and murmured in my ear, and then she was slipping away into the nicest of weary sweet sleep.

"Was it good for you too?" she whispered half-awake, having likewise read the works of The Hemingway, and I said, "Yeah, fine," and after she was asleep, I disengaged myself carefully, and prowled the loft, accepting the hours it would take for my roiled sack to clean its fatigues and know a little sleep. But I had abused myself too far, and it took till dawn and half a fifth of whisky before I dropped into an unblessed stupor. When I awoke, in that moment before I moved to look at her, and saw her glaring at me,

I was off on a sluggish masculine debate as to whether the kick of studying this Denise for another few nights—now that I had turned the key—would be worth the danger of deepening into some small real feeling. But through my hangover and the knowledge of the day and the week and the month it would take the different parts of all of me to repair, I was also knowing the taste of a reinforced will—finally, I had won. At no matter what cost, and with what luck, and with a piece of charity from her, I had won nonetheless, and since all real pay came from victory, it was more likely that I would win the next time I gambled my stake on something more appropriate for my ambition.

Then I turned, saw the hatred in her eyes, turned over again, and made believe I was asleep while a dread of the next few minutes weighed a leaden breath over the new skin of my ego.

"You're awake, aren't you?" she said.

I made no answer.

"All right, I'm going then. I'm getting dressed." She whipped out of bed, grabbed her clothes, and began to put them on with all the fury of waiting for me to get the pronouncement. "That was a lousy thing you did last night," she said by way of a start.

In truth she looked better than she ever had. The severe lady and the tough little girl of yesterday's face had put forth the first agreements on what would yet be a bold chick.

"I gave you what you could use," I made the mistake of saying.

"Just didn't you," she said, and was on her way to the door. "Well, cool it. You don't do anything to me." Then she smiled. "You're so impressed with what you think was such a marvelous notch you made in me, listen, Buster, I came here last night thinking of what Sandy Joyce told me about you, and he's right, oh man is he right." Standing in the open doorway, she started to light a cigarette, and then threw the matches to the floor. From thirty feet away I could see the look in her eyes, that unmistakable point for the kill that you find in the eyes of very few bullfighters, and then having created her pause, she came on for her moment of truth by saying, "He told me your whole life is a lie, and you do nothing but run away from the homosexual that is you."

And like a real killer, she did not look back, and was out the door before I could rise to tell her that she was a hero fit for me.

ADVERTISEMENT FOR "DEAD ENDS"

One of the characters in the novel will be a rich poet (the plump Episcopalian prep school instructor of the Prologue) who is obsessed with the thesis that men become homosexual in order to save themselves from cancer. Seduced by Marion Faye into taking drugs, some common, some rare, he writes a Haiku:

> The pricks are falling
> like dead grass in the dead air.
> The night will not end.

Marion laughs. "I wish I knew a rich poet who wasn't queer."

The poem "Dead Ends" is written by the homosexual later that night in vision of his unrequited love for Marion. Because he is still out on drugs, the poem is not equal to his severe professional standards, and in the morning he tears it up.

DEAD ENDS

Cancer? they said. What do you know about cancer?

That the cause is so simple we dare not look.

Nothing is simple but a simple mind,
  said my host
    and they laughed at his wit
      which was tone
      to their ears
     for the essence of the urbane
     is the well-burnished god of oneself
     glowing like a brass heart
     in the fireplace of manner.

Still, I said, *if you will allow me*
    to insist on a theme
     which irritates your laughter
 I would submit that the simple
  subtends the complex
  in such a way
    that the complex may never comprehend the simple.

Existentialism bores me, said the host.
   As you know, my passion is precise.
  I say you take advantage of my house
   and flaunt the magic of the simple
    because your mind retains no longer
    those indispensable acids of the scholar,
    the lacework, trace, and dry-point of knowledge.

Deny, you do, the elegance of hard fact
        when you disrupt the line
        of modern conversation
        which depends upon the cruel eye of Vesalius
        to restore our grace.
Anatomy
        is the crystal of the real,
                the concrete,
                and the observable,
                a diamond's point
                        fouled
        in your web of association
        and alliteration—
                those oozy plumbings of
        Physiology
                which bog our mind
                in the unverifiable hypotheses
                of process.
You boast, he said,
        that the cause of cancer is simple
        and I say you will set in montage
        a play of tricky lights
        which will create two mysteries
        where before there was one.
You tax the brain
        with idle connection
        squander its store of the royal, the close,
                and the uncreated
        You are the apostle
        of the insane!
And there were cheers
        from those who listened.
For the company was alert
        and enjoyed their careers
                as the bright, the cold, and the quick.

No, hold! I said, hold in what you say
        before we lose all conversation forever
        between your mind and mine.
For I am, yes, an apostle of the insane

if we can agree that
> *the*
>> *navigator*
>> *of our brain, our spirit, our seed—*
>> *is almost dead.*

Already too much, shouted the host.
I loathe an empty word.

In the logic of retreat, said I even louder,
> *when the body and mind are sick*
>> *(in their cups of*
>>> *cowardice and despair and defeat*
>>>> *and hatred which never breathed*
>>>>> *the air of open rage)*
> *then we are left only to choose our disease*
>> *for by the sick of logic*
>> *the choice is closed to suffer*
>>> *psychosis*
>>>> *or take one's odds*
>> *that the insanity from which we flee*
>> *will not hunt the boredom of our cells*
>>> *into the arms*
>>> *of the arch-narcissist*
>> *our lover, the devil,*
>>> *whose ego is iron*
>>> *and never flags*
>>> *in its wild respect*
>>> *for cool power.*
> *Narcissism,* I say, *yes, narcissism*
>> *is the cause of cancer*
> *Cancer comes to those who*
>> *do not love their mate*
>> *so much as they are loved*
>> *when they look at themselves*
>>> *in the mirror.*

2

And when they went to silence
For like a prophet I had touched

the open corner of a nightmare's wound
Then I could speak in the small dead voice
Of a man for whom power came too late
      and
    Yes, I told them:
        whoever comes so close
        as to breathe upon his mirror
        conceives a world so rich
          alone
          and murderous to Time
        that the Divine Economy
        can suffer all luxuries of
        hell greed stink and waste; all
        but the love of a man for himself.
Such love destroys the sleep of God.

Or, better, smiled the host, why not say:
    Our weary Father cannot sleep
      for fear
      that our first act
     upon achieving Him
     would be
     to cut
     His throat.
    So he bribed the devil with cancer
    The queer of the diseases.

I kiss your feet
I kiss your hand
I think you're grand
I think you're Mad,
    cried a camp.

May I go on, said the host:
    Consciousness is the breath
     with which we breathe
     our sickness away—and if we fail . . . well
    Mortal illness is a vehicle
     returning us to the dream
     from which we came
    a transit from one life
    to the wordings of the next.

No, I cried, *No!*
　　Disease is now extreme—
　　　a failure to speak
　　　from some part of flesh
　　　　to some other part,
　　　　a failure
　　　　to dare a pain
　　　which may not cease.
For what we do not dare to feel
　　returns then as waste and routine
　　　　to the depths of the flesh,
　　the twitch of habit
　　　　as
　　the self returns to the self
　　　　no lover found
　　　beyond our pleasure-loving skin
　　　to warm the cold hole
　of Time
　　　outraged in her chastity
　　　guarded in that prison
　　　of endless mirrors
　　　　which repeat
　　　in cold silver
　　　　upon
　　　blinded glass
　　　　the polished sliver of nerve
　　　　the petrified shriek
　　　　of death adoring her youth
　　　that frictionless coupling
　　of flesh upon glass
　　　　which is the old age of love
　　　　when love is the love
　　　　　of oneself
and connection
　　to the body of others
　　　　is a convict's riot
　　　　of movement
　　　　　within
I loved myself too much
Gave the dead end away

Till you have lack in your courage
And will leave me to the
orgy of the unalive
who is ourselves
when we are beautiful
in the glass.

The devil have mercy on your fright.
You are rationalizing the night,
        laughed the host.
    If you were not square as the archangel
    I could have told you:
            Cancer comes from
                television
                filter cigarettes
                air conditioning
                foam rubber
                the smell of plastic
                deodorant
                wit that fails
                antibiotics
                the mirror, yes,
                and all other attempts
                of the sucker esprit
                to get something
                    for no.
                Now go,
                    said my host,
                I have been able to mother
                    the body of another
                    and sweet is the feel
                    that the timeless hour of love
                    is the first breath
                    of the sweet bitch Time.

But I found my wit before the door
        and turning said
You mean, Find mother
        in the clutch of another
Your life is a hole
And cancer is the death of the hole.

And if hole upon
          hole
     is the dead of poetry
     as a scheme in rhyme
     well fail me never
          dear wit
     cancer is the boredom
     where sound cannot be.

ADVERTISEMENTS FOR MYSELF ON THE WAY OUT

Prologue to a Long Novel

1.

To be forced to admire what one instinctively hates, and to hate all which one would naturally love is the condition of our lives in these bad years, and so is the cause beneath other causes for our sickness and our death. If some of you will understand immediately what I mean, I still must think of the others who are to take the trip with me: that mob of readers whose experience of life is as narrow as it is poor, and worse if the truth be told—they are picking up this book because they have heard it is good for the bathroom and so may palliate their depression; this book! my tale of heroes and villains, murderers and suicides, orgy-masters, perverts, and passionate lovers, my lust to capture Time.

For those readers courage is required. My passion is to destroy innocence, and any of you who wish to hold to some part of that warm, almost fleshly tissue of lies, sentimentality, affectation and ignorance which the innocent consider love must be prepared instead for a dissection of the extreme, the obscene and the unsayable.

The mark of a philosopher is that he puts his name to his work, he wants his ideas to carry the connotation of the syllables (those primitive sounds) which make up the armature of his character. So, properly, I should introduce myself here, and indeed I would, if I were able, but my name eludes me and at present would slip by without meaning to you—I am virtually married to Time unless she has already divorced me (of which indigestible statement, more explanation later) and so my name alters as Time turns away from me, and it is not all that natural to explain who I am. Let it go. Only a dreary mind cannot bear mystery.

Yet I do not know if I should evade your questions. The most murderous emotions are aroused when we cannot find the word to fit the particle, and murder (in favor of which I will find some arguments) still has the disadvantage of distracting the attention. Since I wish the various intelligences who take the trip with me to finish with stimulation to their brains and sweet for their bodies, I must necessarily take into account that the duller minds among you cannot support the luxury of listening to a voice without a face unless you are handed some first approximation to my state. I will therefore suggest it is possible I am a kind of ghost, the ghost of exhausted passion—but I prefer to believe this is completely untrue. How much less disagreeable to be some breath in the caverns of the unconscious of one of the figures in this unnatural mystery, or indeed to be the consciousness brought into being by the relations and mutilations of the exceptional characters I will introduce.

Only to say this is to deny it, for if I am the creature of relationship, I must be not so much consciousness as corporeal, containing a blastopore whose nucleic proteins limn a signature, the given first half of my destiny. Yes, I must be the breath of the present-present, a point of size swimming in my unglimpsed mother's first freshets of amniotic fluid, an embryonic two-cell, me, engaging no less than the fluid consciousness of a God, His comprehension still in mine, as I believe is true of all beings not yet born but budding in the belly. So I could be an embryo eight instants old, a work of gestation away from light and noise and pain, and yet knowing more than I will ever know again because I am part of Him. (Or is it Her?)

But to step without benefit of clergy onto the moot worms of theology is to lose our ground. The dock of our embarkation is the mystery of my eye and to whom or what it belongs: am I ghost, embryo, intellect, wind of the unconscious, or some part of Him or Her or Hem or Hir?—but there it is—Hem or Hir—a bona fide clue; only the Devil would ever boast of being thus intimate with the Divinity. So, through this work, at the best of times between us, when we are even laughing together, there should remain a reservation, a polite terror that the illumination is furnished by the Prince of Darkness, and the color of my light is satanic.

Of course, I could be as easily the old house in which the end of this story takes place (what resonances are contained in the studs, the joists, and the bowed floor planks of an old house). I could be a tree—there is a tree outside this house, an unusual maple whose bole divides into four trunks only a few hands from the ground, and whose branches in the leafless winter articulate the noble forms of the nerve paths of a brain as one might see them in the surgically drafted plates of one of those sturdy grisly nineteenth-century handbooks on medical practice. There is even a garden, a most delicate garden—we are near the sea—and the flowers in summer have that rare electric vivaciousness which comes from salt air, sandy soil, and fertilizer laced up overrich with artificial nectar and mead. Flowers have always been sinister to me when they are lovely—they seem to share the elusive promise of a woman who is beautiful and whose voice is too perfect—one never knows if she is the avatar of a dream or some masterwork of treachery, she is so different from ourselves.

If I make such a comparison, it is obviously quite unnatural to me that I should share my existence with a flower, yet I advance the hypothesis in the interest of being comprehensive, and because the possibility is perversely appealing: where better could a demon hide himself than in the vulva of a garden bloom—if some pleasure-snatcher plucks the stem (have you ever heard *that* cry of pain?) the ex-flower can poison the house before it withers away. Yes, one does well to fear plants—once, out of an ill-timed overabundance of energy and boredom I kicked over a giant mushroom. It was five inches across the head, and I could have sworn it gave a venomous cry of rage as death came to it—"You bastard," I heard it say; such a vile fate for that exceptional mushroom, skull-like in its proportions and bold in size. I was sorry. Not every mushroom grows with such lust, and I had violated a process perhaps centuries in the chain. So from fear I mention the flower as well as the tree, and while whispering that vegetative life repels me more than not, I would add my bow to nature—I could be of the ocean and the sand dunes, that primal marriage of the little stones and the vast water—I could be of them, but I hope not; certain embraces are too monumental and so become dull. To say that the oceans of the world are but one tear of God's compassion is a metaphor so excruciatingly empty that the flatulence of a celibate must have been its first wind. But to believe that God like man can suffer occasionally from diarrhea is an infectious thought which stimulates all but the churchly and the vicious.

I will leave the oceans then, I will leave the flowers and the bees and the trees, reminding you that the extraordinary can hide in the meanest maggot, and will reduce myself as an interesting speculation to the dimensions of a dog. There is a hound in this book, brought to a climactic party we are soon to talk about, a poodle dog, Standard, pedigree, A.K.C., descended by his dam from a line of Westchester champions, his sire merely certified, and like all large poodles who have gained the attention due a rich pervert, he is an incredible dog. I know him so well that I cannot evade the last hypothesis—I could be that dog, for the vision of our life which is soon to disrupt your brain is in part a dog's view: a dog has no more than to meet another dog on the street, smell the hindquarters, and know whether friendship is possible, which well may be why dogs are invariably gloomy.

Enough. It would be unseductive to boast of how I will probably travel from the consciousness of one being to the emotions of another—a house, a tree, a dog, a cop, a cannibal, all equal to my hunter's eye and promiscuous ear.

2.

There is a master pimp in our presence who is a candidate for the role of hero (his rivals for your vote, a television celebrity and a psychoanalyst) and for a time some years ago, this pimp, whose name is Marion Faye, dabbled at the edges of painting (giving for excuse the observation that such study might enrich his conception of the pornographic photography by which he then was making his living). Faye was a poor painter, but he had a love affair which went on for several weeks with the form of the spiral, and it was a matter of no mean significance to him that the valve of a snail shell as seen through his microscope (Zeiss, 2,000 Deutschmarks, oil immersion, binocular eyepiece) was a spiral galaxy of horny cells whose pigmentation had the deep orange of a twilight sun. Staring into the eye of the snail valve, he would wonder what heats of emotion had breathed into its red—he was of course on drugs at the time—and afterwards, giving his marijuana-refreshed eyes to the whorls on the ball of his thumb and the tips of his fingers, he found the spiral again, and he had that thrill of fright so common to medieval alchemists, psychics, drug addicts, and perhaps available to a few of you: that exquisite terror of sensing oneself at the edge of secrets no other being has been brave enough to invade. For there it was: the tips of the fingers were for touch, as indeed was the snail valve (obliged to close at the lick of danger) and so for touch were all the other natural spirals he knew—he was by profession an accomplished familiar to the intricate double helix in the vaginal expansion, and the other holes of women, and for that matter, men; so he accepted the logic of his intuition: the natural spiral, wherever it appeared, was the mark for a complex of feeling, and if parts of the night sky disported in a spiral, there was sensation behind them, light years of space vibrating with sensuality and anguish, desiring . . . ? But this was another question, too vast. Temporarily he gave up the investigation—in truth the form of his thought was also spiral: he would have to make that all but circular voyage through experience before he would came back to contemplate the spiral again.

Which perhaps is why I have chosen this way to introduce so active a man as a master pimp. If one is interested to begin to understand one's own life, the first of the useful axioms is that genius appears in all occupations, and as a pimp, Marion Faye was a genius. The proof is that he made a million dollars in a few years. Just how is a matter of such interest that it will later concern us in great detail, for one can explore such minutiae only by discovering the psychic anatomy of our republic.

Good. He was a millionaire, and still young, and he owned several houses in different parts of the country and one in Acapulco, and he had his private plane which he flew himself, and various cars, accouterments, servants, jewelries, larders, and investments. Not to mention several going businesses and the two endowed lovers who attended him, man and women. He had done this all in a few years, after coming out of prison without a penny, and he was of course not nearly satisfied, at least not at the moment I describe. Like all men who are Napoleonic in their ambitions and wide as the Renaissance in their talents, he had instincts about the nature of growth, a lover's sense of the moment of crisis, and he knew, perhaps as well as anyone alive, how costly is defeat when it is not soothed by greater consciousness, and how wasteful is the profit of victory when there is not the courage to employ it. So he knew the danger of inertia (if one does not grow, one must pay more for remaining the same), and for months there had been a decision he was unable to make: as had happened before, he felt his powers leaving him. His strength came from decision and action, he was religious (in a most special way to be sure), he was superstitious with the most sophisticated of superstitions, but as a practical matter he believed in the reality of Hell, and he had come to the point in his life, as he had foreseen in terror many a time, when the flux of his development, the discovery of the new beauties of his self-expression, depended on murdering a man, a particular man, perhaps as exceptional as he, a man who could hardly fail to be aware that his own development, as opposed to Marion's was also at an impasse which could be breached equally, if in the opposite direction, by the murder of Marion Faye who once had been his friend.

It was a problem, then, and one of no mean proportions. The tension to murder is as excruciating as the temptations to confess when on a torture rack. So long as one holds one's tongue the destruction of the body continues, the limbs and organs under question may be passing the last answer by which they can still recover, and if one is going to confess eventually it is wiser to do it soon, do it now, before the damage is irrevocable. So with the desire to murder. Each day we contain it a little of that murder is visited upon our own bodies, the ulcers seat themselves more firmly, the liver sickens, the lungs wither, the brain bursts the most artful of our mental circuits, the heart is sapped of stamina and the testicles of juice—who knows? this may be indeed the day when the first of the exploited cells takes that independent and mysterious flip from one life into another—from the social, purposive, impoverished, and unspeakably depressing daily life of an obedient cell, to the other life, wild-life, the life of the weed or hired gun, rebel cell growing by its own laws, highwayman upon the senses, in siege to the organs, rife with orgiastic speed, the call of the beat drumming its appeal to the millions of cells, for if other-life is short, it is wild as well, and without work. Yes, to hold murder too long is to lose the body, hasten that irreversible instant when the first cell leaps upon the habit of stale intelligence and gives itself as volunteer to the unformed cadres in the future legions of barbarian and bohemian.

Of course, murder is never simple for old thieves. Old thieves have tired balls, and if Marion Faye often thought with distant pride that he was one of the few to have climbed beyond the killing precipice of manners, morals, the sense of sin and the fear of germs, he knew how much he had paid—yes, he had lost a part of his gift, he had drained the more extraordinary pleasures of his balls, dulled the finer knives of his brain, and left himself prey to such inertias of exhaustion as he was experiencing in these weeks before he sent out the invitation to the party in the old house at Provincetown, the party which was properly to come off in calculated murder.

3.

It is time now to say a little about this house and where it is situated. The peninsula of Cape Cod is perhaps eighty miles long, and bent in its middle like the knotty, no longer agreeable arm of an old man who once was strong. To the forearm and hand of this coast is given the name of The Upper Cape, and it is pleasant land if one's humor is mournful—wind-swept, with barren moors, lonely dunes, deserted ponds and stunted trees; its colors are gray and dun and the foliage is a dull green. Off the arterial highway with its savage excremental architecture of gas stations, chromium-paneled diners, souvenir traps, fruit stands, motels, blinker lights, salt-eroded billboards, all in cruel vision-blunting pigments, in contrast to this arterial highway garish in its petrifactions of the overextended American will, the side roads are quiet, hardly more than lanes, with small mouse-gray salt-box houses inhabited for the most part by retired Protestants, decent, lean, spare and stingy, gray themselves for the most part with a mouse gray.

There is no excess of life in the fall and winter, and it is country which can be recommended for the solitary—the lonely walks on sandy trails pass by cranberry bogs whose thorny undergrowth is violet in color against the lavender hues of the dunes when the sky is gray. Near Provincetown there are a few miles of empty sand between the bay and the ocean which have the sweep of the desert—the dunes rise into small hills and fall away to valleys where one could believe oneself lost in the Sahara—I have heard of people who wandered about in circles over one dune and down another, never reaching the ocean and never finding the bay, at least not for hours. There are few places on the eastern seaboard where one could bury a man as easily and leave one's chances so to nature, for the wind could leave the corpse under twenty feet of fill, or as easily could discover the cadaver before the cells were cold.

Beyond this desert, at the tip of the Cape, in the palm of the almost closed hand, is one of the last great fishing villages of the world, the place called Provincetown, in winter 3,000 population I suppose, its situation one of the most easterly promontories of the

Atlantic coast. Three miles long and two streets wide, the town curls around the bay on the skin of the palm, a gaudy run with Mediterranean splashes of color, crowded steep-pitched roofs, fishing piers and fishing boats whose stench of mackerel and gasoline is as aphrodisiac to the sensuous nose as the clean bar-whisky smell of a nightclub where call girls congregate.

It was in Provincetown the Puritans landed and held to a starving bivouac for three months before they broke the encampment and moved on to Plymouth Rock. They were without food and besides there was the spiral to wear them down: the Cape from the wrist to the fingers curls like a snail shell, the harbor an eye of water in the center, and one's sense of direction is forever confused. Without looking at the sun one could not point across the bay in the proper direction to Boston, Portugal, or the shores of Barbary. It is a place which defies one's nose for longitude and latitude, a cartographer's despair and a Puritan's as well. (The character of narrow intense faith is rectilinear in conception, which is why the clitorine cove in the façade of most New England churches is triangular or icepick steeple in its form rather than obeying the feminine Catholic arch of almost equally narrow Gothic faiths.)

The house Marion purchased was on a sand dune behind the last hill overlooking the town, and it was isolated, especially in fall and winter, reached by a sandy road which dipped down one dune and up another to give a view of rolling furze, rain water ponds, and the ocean and beach of the back shore. In bad weather the wind was a phenomenon, a New England wind of the lost narrow faiths which slashed through open doors, tempted shutters loose from their catch and banged them through the night, vibrated every small pane in every Cape Cod window and came soughing out of the sky with the cries of storm water in its vaults—on such nights the hundred years of the house were alive with every murderous sleep it had ever suffered: it was the kind of house in which the dogs barked insanely in bad weather, and the nurse could not rest, and the baby awoke in hysterical terror at one in the morning while the mother would feel dread at the hundred rages of her husband restless beside her in marriage sleep, and the house shifted and swayed to the wind like a ship in North Atlantic seas, yes it seemed to contain every emotion which had died a frustrated death in its rooms and walls through a hundred New England winters, each ghost of emotion waiting to seize the storm feelings of the present; it was a house which had the capacity to set free, one upon the other, the dank sore-rotted assassins in the dungeons of a family's character. A storm at the wrong time came on with the horror that this was the night— and indeed there had been one killing there, an unexplained nineteenth-century crime, an old ship captain's widow who had worn a rectangular trough in the planks on the widow's walk at the ridgepole center of the steep roof. She was found dead on a late February night after three days of rain, the wind howling like a wounded shrew.

Now I know it is not in the mode of our pompous obliteration-haunted years to encourage such pathetic fallacies as the animism of the wind and an old house, but since (be I ghost, *geist*, demiurge, dog, bud, flower, tree, house, or some lost way-station of the divine, looking for my mooring in the labial tortures and languors of words) be I whatever, it must be evident that I am existentialist and would propose that when the wind carries a cry which is meaningful to human ears, it is simpler to believe the wind shares with us some part of the emotion of Being than that the mysteries of a hurricane's rising murmur reduce to no more than the random collision of insensate molecules. Yes, if I were to meet that saint with the body of an ox, St. Thomas Aquinas, a gentleman with whom I agree about very little, I would still be obliged to nod in obligation to his exceptional phrase, "the authority of the senses," exactly because I now feel the frustration of a wind which knows so much and can tell your ears so little. As our century moves toward its death, and the death of all of us, so our senses die first, and who has ears to hear the wind when the smoke of mutual hatred is thick on commuter trains, and the subway rails of an evening's television batter into stupidity the sense of the sensual, leaving us null and dumb to the almost ineffable sounds which touch beyond the vanity, the will, the force and the imprisonment of the ego, grim and God-murdering ego, champion of the practical, peasant divinity of the Reformation, that Faustian burgher who built our mills of steel on the stern, the palpable, and the self-evident notion that through a point only one line can be drawn parallel to a given line, when already we are traveling through the non-Euclidean present of space-time. Sooner than we think, lo, the line parallel to the given line will prove to be nothing other than the same line once around the route in the expanding spiral of Being.

And as yet I have said hardly a word about Time.

4.

But if through a given point, a line is drawn parallel to a given line, and proves to be nothing other than the same line, why then we have abstracted a first theorem on the nature of Time: that lines in parallel represent a function of the natural unwinding of Time (its onanistic tracings) when Time left to its own resources is excited into action neither by murder nor love, and so remains in step to the twitching of a clock. Such is passive Time, Time on its way to death; but Time as growth, Time as the excitations and chilling stimulations of murder, Time as the tropical envelopments of love (even if murder is lusty in the chest and love a cold sweat on the hip), Time is then the hard of a hoodlum or the bitch on her back looking for the lover whose rhythm will move her to the future.

But this conjunction is too soon complex and blurs the attention—let us leave it, let us fall away again to the cold palpable house of Marion Faye in the back sands of Provincetown, this sea-salted building which first gave me the thesis that houses are polar in their nature, tending to be boudoirs or churches. This purchase, if we are to agree in what we see, was a church of a house with an enormous two-story cathedral of a living room in dark overstained walnut, the dining room, kitchen, pantry and servant quarters built into what had been the cellar, and the bedrooms, studies, studios, and sun rooms clustered like white-guanoed barnacles, cubicles of rooms all over the top and sides of this two-story chapel with its Gothic arched windows and sombre light. Marion Faye bought it in the hour he saw it—it was a bargain—so big, so chill, so impractical—one had to go down to the cellar to make a sandwich—so gloomy, so sonorous, so sepulchral that it was church for him, and all his other houses (with the exception of the town house, a complex affair) were no more than boudoirs for his pleasure, doll houses in liege to the attractive childhood he had never spent except for some rare bitch-perfumed hours with his mother.

Yes, this was a house for rare occasions, and he visited it seldom, and never in summer when Provincetown was a whore's trunk of frying hot dogs, boat excursionists from Boston, battalions of the gay and regiments of the hip—he saved it for rare weekends in fall and winter, and so far as most people knew, it was not even his house—he had given it on virtually permanent loan to the most extraordinary of his former call girls, a tall dignified Negress with a velvet sensuality who had made her fortune in company with Marion, and now—her various investments concealed—was a rich hostess of no small reputation in many parts of New York, her parties indeed so well run that her net of fine jazz captured the best of intellectual stimulation—what little there was in that dying electric city. This Negress, who had through her career a series of names (the last, by which people now knew her, being Cara Beauchamp) had found in herself a set of exquisitely parallel personalities like hand-worked nesting tables, and so had avoided the hermetic fate of many call girls and almost all prostitutes—she had dissolved that cyst of character, that prison of nonperceptive muscles which maroons even a high-grade whore in self-pity, hysteria, and loathing for her material. No, this one was fluid, she had a touch of accommodation for all perverse duties, blown into a not uncool flame by her fortune in studying with a master. So she was capable of using her encyclopedic knowledge of the colliding congesting rhythms in the bodies of the strangers she met; and the shyest poor parcel of a man, a distinguished physicist let us say, ashy, halfway to the grave, with a dull gray suit and black scuffed shoes dulled to gray, and a pallor of face whose equivocal good health was yellow, and whose oncoming death was gray, was capable still of appealing to her: somewhere in his habit-haunted body and far-departed mind, somewhere in his racked frame which had all the animal magnetism of a catatonic worm (chill and bitter-smelling in its parts) there was a piston of will which would (all whore-patience and art properly applied) give her a memorable night even if the poor will-driven gentleman were half into the grave afterward with the outrage to his sedentary heart. So here was a man who could give her a furious pleasure, for an evening at least, and therefore meeting him at the door to her party, accepting the introduction from her good friend and favorite psychoanalyst (who will become for us a figure of obsessive interest later on) (he had introduced the physicist as an old college friend), she dipped into her enormous reserves of relaxed sensuous attention, took an immediate plot of the physicist's clang-riddled nerves, and came back with a tight formal smile and the suggestion of a feminine will-driven tic at the corner of her own eye (if she thus momentarily debased her beauty, she was seizing the opportunity to relax the muscles of her eye and make a friend—on the whole a profit for our hostess). Indeed she succeeded; the physicist liked her—he liked her even more when late in the evening and pleasantly if quietly—in his way—hysterically drunk with the blending of the tongues, the reentrate cool jazz of the combination for the night—four homosexual Negroes in horn-rimmed glasses—and the murderous ambiguities of such varied honey-wild pussy as paraded at that party, the physicist had the fair opportunity to discuss physics with the remarkable knife-eyed intelligence of the face in *café au lait* who had greeted him at the door. I choose their conversation to repeat because it is essential to our mystery, and if you find it bizarre you must recognize that we hover at the edge of an orgy of language, the nihilism of meaning fair upon us.

"Isn't modern physics to the square side?" she asked of him.

A true language of indeterminate functions, he was thinking, an expression of the off-phase waves of the Negro masses. "Oh, no, not at all, not really," he said. "After all, Einstein was no square."

"I could die that he is dead—so hoped to meet that man," Cara Beauchamp said, "he was hip—a funny man." She sighed for the dead. "But, like I mean, *procedurally*—aren't you physicists nowhere with Time?"

"Nowhere—the philosophical groundwork is lacking I suppose."

"Yes, you don't make the scene." She restrained her force and added softly, "Like Time is when you connect."

"It doesn't exist in between?" He had answered easily, pleased at how well he had picked up this contextual field, but then he repeated it, "Time does not exist when it make no . . . connections?" Perhaps he was too drunk, but there was an old physicist's terror in the beauty of the thought. My God, maybe she's on to something, he was thinking.

"Well, it don't exist, and yet it does."

"Time rests as potential?" he asked, excitement in his dry sad voice, "rests there until the gap is jumped to Time dynamic."

"Yeah—potential and dynamic—that's Time. It dies if it don't connect," and for an instant she was as fond of him as a mother learning from her child. For the rest of her life she had two new words, and what words they were. Through all her unconscious were flexings of cellular pleasure—so much of her experience was rushing to the higher plateau of more precise language.

Actually she had been not altogether inspired in this conversation. She still had the masculine mind of a whore or a hostess—she was a businessman—she searched for synthesis, the big view, and her ideas on Time had come from Marion. Finally she was a salesman—she cannibalized the salvageable from the junk of old conversations to put together some speed for the pitch of her conversation.

She could hardly have done otherwise. She came from a poor Harlem family, late-migrated to New York from the North Georgia line, and her mother had run a cheap Georgia brothel (three girls) and sold heroin in New York until the arithmetic of cutting the ounces wore her down. Cara was the first child in the family to be able to read and write with less difficulty than it took to load a trailer truck. Yet she now had the pride that they all came to her parties, the hothouse haul from Madison Avenue, advertising men and television people laughing at homey house jokes about the sick, curling themselves around a Martini or a model like ivy which slides over ubiquitously from vertical support to vertical support; there was the subtle cream of Negro entertainers from certain particular bistros at the moment not out of favor with Cara Beauchamp, there was a sprinkling from the theatre (those flamboyant timid people), there was a gossip columnist who exercised the discipline not to print a word of what he saw, one or two of the most overrated and/or berated young writers in America would be there, and one fashion photographer, not to mention the pads of Harlem and the cellars of the Village, painters (a growing collection of Abstract Expressionists on her walls), pimps and pushers (those who had proved the most talented of her childhood companions), musicians, a labor leader (yes, there was one) and a banker. It had taken her months but a lawyer who was a friend had induced him to come, and Cara found enough in common to draw him back—her ideas about the personality of those investors with some credit rating whom an exurban bank, proud of its personal touch, might allow to kite a check for twenty-four hours so intrigued the banker as a merger of psychological nuance with fiduciary practice that he returned once or twice. Yes, there was a horde: movie stars who left early, promoters, producers, occasional professional athletes, surgeons, psychiatrists, councillors, pot-heads (discreet to be sure), hoodlums (who could contain themselves), college girls, poetesses . . . the apocryphal story was of her middle-aged Irish elevator operator who became so used to her odd visitors that even a plump

Episcopalian prep school instructor, wearing his go-to-New-York homburg, hand in hand with a sloe-eyed Arab boy who looked like an untamed pet on the prowl from the Casbah gave the elevator man no pause: only a brace of bull-dykers ever did him in—a famous actress in a sailor's peajacket and a gargantuan blonde in pink mink went up together sipping away from long platinum cigarette holders at sticks of Turkish hashish until the smell of sugar and death made the elevator operator so high with the smoke of contact that he was as stone on the return down, and for the first time in thirteen years he dug into the hanging of his cage and floated it on loverly skill to the lobby with the awesome anticipatory joy of the first lunar explorer to kiss the tail of his rocket onto the acned skin of the moon.

So, there it was, the home of Cara Beauchamp, a ten-room co-operative apartment and circus overlooking the East River of the fifties, with a collection of guests almost every Saturday night whose intellectual and physical connections were accelerating Time, and weighting the charge of future acceleration. No wonder that Cara gave it up for a month each year and disappeared into Provincetown where she had nothing more than a few close friends and entertainers to visit out the nights in Marion Faye's private church. Yes, she needed her *schule* as she called it, and she liked the surf-soothing hurdy-gurdy of this fishing town so poorly considered for even her social purposes that hardly anyone she knew was found there.

But I must interrupt, for one pretense I can maintain no longer. I notice that I wander back and forth, speak of the pages which follow, and yet, even as I have the illusion that I put words together at a desk, and the little actions I describe have already happened to me, or to others, still I do not know who I am nor where I am, nor even if literally I write. Yet, just so soon as I suggest that I am without particular embodiment I feel bubbles of laughter at the peculiar present tense of my consciousness which sees into the past, is recovering the future, and yet does neither, for perhaps I scramble the order of Time in order to retrieve the order of form from what is formless and yet over-real. Like the easily distractible feather of attention in the gales of infancy, I move from dread to light amusement to metaphysical certainty, and yet away again as if no one is so real to me as the consciousness which leads me now, but for a moment probably, to the breath of my narrative, and I feel

525

certain—I know not exactly why—that it was after this party, after the conversation between Cara Beauchamp and the physicist, that Marion called for the proper tuition to his instruction and made his demand: Cara was to give a weekend party in Provincetown for a select two dozen from their acquaintance, the guests to be flown up and back by chartered plane, and this in the middle of November when the New York season was on, and the weather in Province-town was bound to be bad.

"Marion," she had answered, "explain what you're doing."

His extraordinary face (one of the handsomest cleanest most sensual faces ever cut from a block of boyish ice) smiled back in arch thought at her. "I feel in the mood for a party that will go on for a while." Then he yawned, and his groin in remonstrance for this thespian's triumph of the casual, gave him a cruel pinch of a grip. He was empty again, the charge was down, he was moving into the late middle-age of some men's middle-thirties, a Dorian Gray whose secret portrait was fleshed within, painted by the out-rages he had exacted of a hundred thousand nerves. He knew the prescription to reverse the process on the portrait, it was the last of the nostrums and it had worked once before; it was murder. Brave murder. Brave murder gave the charge of the man one killed. Time potential and Time dynamic—it was the grand connection, and the dead man's Time because one's own Time, his energies regenerated the dead circuits of one's own empty-balled Time, and one moved away with greater strength, new nerves and a heavier burden. For the balance (that natural grasp of moral justice which the old murder-tempted God still retained—should one hope so?) would be laden even more on the side of Hell, and Marion knew what would await him in Hell, the onanisms of connectionless Time, the misery of the lone chance in one out of the billion of billions to be born again. Hell, where his nerves (those advance intimations of a flesh-terrifying fire, electric in its cold) would un-wind their unspeakable tension with the infinite slowness of nerves become Time in its death, the spiral spinning a blind spider's path, the dreams collapsed, the empire lost, and the fate of the world as well. That was the worst; that was his vanity; that he alone held the vision to save the world—if he failed, his agony would be all the greater for what a rage would be the rage of God. "Am I ready to die?" he asked, listening to the answer the portrait might give him, and the portrait said *no* with a murmur of dread. The balance of his deeds was dark to Marion, and from the God-like eye with which he contemplated himself he knew he was still not Godly enough—it was beyond his vision whether the force of his life upon others had accelerated new love into the agonized fatigues of Time, or had worn Time closer to her hag-ridden dreams of the destiny that failed because it arrived too late, of the new conception which never reached the womb.

5.

The invitations went out, were accepted by almost everyone, the plane was chartered—two flights proved necessary—and the party took place. It is with some hesitation, and the awareness I have betrayed certain premises of your interest, that I must now confess I will not be able to describe this party in rousing detail until we have taken a wide and still unforeseeable circuit of the past. Indeed, it would probably be a disservice of the first order to insert ourselves too brusquely into the dance of deceptions, seductions, perversions and passions which the party whipped into being, the riot of new relationship an unlashed acceleration of the Time of the ladies and gentlemen present. To be successful a party must become more than was intended for it, and I can give you the mean contentment that by my measurement the party was not boring: it had an artist's assortment of those contradictory and varied categories of people who made up the obdurate materials of new sociological alloy in the heat-forge of a ball at Cara Beauchamp's. What gave this party an added attraction, an unconscious verve, was that there were guests who were not altogether what they appeared to be, a Russian spy for one, avid to snap up the friendship of our physicist, a spy of such importance that an agent of the FBI was also present, each of these gentlemen carefully furnished with a false life which was not his own. To complicate matters, there were two other operators with portfolio from the police: one, a narcotics agent, unfortunately addicted himself; another from the vice squad of New York City—what completed the circle was that the detective from the vice squad believed himself close on the proof that Marion Faye had murdered another detective from the vice squad some years before, which in fact was true, but what was unknown to any of these policemen (although the agent from the FBI smelled hints of the possibility) was that the Russian spy, suffering from the mitotic tension latent in the psyche of all spies, had not been content with a double life, but indeed had divided a part of himself again; certain of his more desperate and unprofessional activities in this country had spilled him into the broth of blackmail which nourished the vice squad detective who had been killed; Marion, in taking care of this precise act, had discovered the profession of the spy and so was able to use him for purposes which were by now related to his program for the party—if all of this seems complicated, I can only say that it is but a superficial counterfeit of the real complexities which involved a dozen other guests as well, including Shawn Sergius (born perhaps as Sergius O'Shaugnessy), the only creative personality ever to dominate television, and Dr. Joyce, the psychoanalyst, who had become so overextended beyond his humane means, and had so compromised his career, his profession, and his intimate honor that he was contemplating suicide long before he came to the party.

Indeed a suicide did take place (I do not yet know whether it was the doctor), it was followed by murder, a murder inflamed into fury by exactly that suicide, the suicide preceded by an orgy, the orgy by a series of communions in the act of coitus, both natural and illegal, by sodomists who dictated their characters upon weaker flesh, and copulations which failed as well as fornications which captured pure smell of the fact and left the lovers fluxed with the rhythms and reflexes of one another. It was a ball. There were two dead bodies when all was done, and on one of them the town police found a notebook which contained a list, a peculiar list, for it included everyone, and yet there were more items on the list than people present, and titles applicable to more than one, as if some of the guests contained several categories within themselves. I give it as it was scribbled down, a most appetizing menu:

a queer
a cop
a crook

a Negro
a war hero
a movie star

an athlete
a dope addict
a socialite

a fisherman
an analyst
a call girl

a whore
a businessman
a mother
a father

a child
a sibling
a television entertainer
a politician

a writer
a painter
a jazzman
a rapist

a Timeless wonder (originally a man but altered to a facsimile
of woman)

(There was a line drawn here)

a physicist
a doctor

a taxicab driver
an assembly-line worker
a poodle

a police dog
a boxer
servants

(and another line drawn here)

a ghost (God?) (from the hole—he?)
a house
a tree
a pact
a cemetery

a bug
a flower
a rat
a cow
a horse

an insane man

a storm
a plane
an executioner

a bullfighter

One could do worse than to read this list again. I wonder if in the history of our republic there has been a party equal in montage: a movie star and a rat, a rapist and a war hero, a psychoanalyst and a call girl, poodle and assembly-line worker, child and sibling, an executioner and a ghost, a cemetery and a television entertainer; yes, it is like one of those new games which trap psychology and sociology in a three-dollar cardboard box—"Theatre" it could be called, for one chooses one's role: be a whore, a physicist, a jazz musician, a queer—how dreary is our republic that so few people would buy the game.

A bloody aye! What is to be said of the dead body? How extraordinary a man—if it was a man—to compile such a schedule of personality when he must have known how close he was himself to being taken to the cleaners'—that quick phrase which contains the notion that death purifies.

But death does not purify says my Reason, death dissipates: our consciousness radiates away from ourselves as the cellves deteriorate (forgive the pun, but we speak of death), we slip away—wastefully, unheard but for the night air, our emotions, sneaks, smells, terrors, titillations, thoughts, projects, plans, and—if we have died too late—the dull blanketing gas of our boredom all enter the air, are breathed by others and exhaled away again—perhaps we have influenced the million light years of their imagination by a millimeter. The fats, the blood, the muscles and the bone sink into the earth again (if we are so fortunate as not to stifle in a deluxe hermetic crypt) yes, with the pores of a pinewood box, we give of

530

our poor soured flesh to the wistful cemetery grass—in a century or two perhaps they will let the cows enter there to eat and make the milk and give the meat which will permit one distant relative of a molecule, ten hundred dynasties of family removed, to slip into a human body again. A few of our cells may make the transmigration from our body, which is gone, to the body of another—all that was us reduced to a molecule whose minor deviations from the classical form of the giant protein chain recapture (as do all deviations from classical form) some wry shrunken ion's head of the contradictions and possibilities which were once a man, general of the armies of his cells, Deus to his body-universe.

And is that all? a sacred cow ("I dig the Hindu bit," said Marion once) our best poor bridge to make it back, no matter how cruelly reduced, to the life of those beings who have the power—all too unconsciously—to shift the changing beat of Time? Or is there more?

And if I say I think there is, I turn the key into the category of my own secret, for as some of you may have sensed by now, the list I offered up to your amusement is from me, and I am, oh yes, now I know who I am or was, I am the dead man on the floor, for so I am, yes (what a pure moment of grief at all that has not been done), I am in the endless deliberate instant of the vision given by death, the million dying spasms of the radiating consciousness of words, this last of me, wailing within, turbulent with the terror that I no longer know where I am, nor if there are voices to hear me and answer back. I am off finally, departed on the demented journey whose first echoes I knew in those overpromiscuous moments of malice, license, promise and horror at the heart of a cocktail party when, too drunk with the knowledge of what courage was demanded of me, and what little I had, I used to close my eyes, sitting in the saviorship of a chair, and I would give up the ghost of ego-erect will, and let the vertigo of the liquors suck me away, a far long way in those few instants when I was spinning out with a rapidity to match the salacious pace of our revolving earth, and I was one with something other until the wife or the mistress or whichever latest embodiment of the royal bitch was at my elbow, nudging me back, feminine fingers of fury at spineless disappearing man wrenching me with procreative determination clean up to the living so I would hear:

"Are you all right?"

"I was thinking of something," I would say, "and I like to think with my eyes closed," but that was the lie of appearances to share between us, a bread of false flour, forcibly refreshing me back to my determinations, back to the party after the long swoon away.

But now I go, the vortex does not stop, the winds of the whirlpool—God's gyre again?—are heavy with consequence, and I sink or do I fly? all vectors gone, while in my center, clear as the icy eye of cocaine, I race toward a point of judgment, my courage and cowardice (my masculine thrust and retreat from the avaricious energy-plucking hairy old grotto of Time) trailing behind me in that comet of connotations which is the past topologically reversed by the vision of *now*, as if in recovering the past I am chasing after the future, so that the past, the net of the name-giving surface-perceiving past, is my future again, and I go out into the past, into the trail of the cold eye of past relationship, the eye of my I at home in the object-filled chaos of any ego I choose, at least for this short while between the stirrup and the ground, for in an instant—will it be eternally long? like some cell at the crisis of its cellvish destiny, I race into the midnight mind, the dream-haunted determinations of that God of whom I was a part, and will He choose me to be born again? have I proven one of his best? am I embryo in some belly of the divisible feminine Time, or is the journey yet to make? Or worst of all am I?—and the cry which is without sound shrieks in my ears—am I already on the way out? a fetor of God's brown sausage in His time of diarrhea, oozing and sucking and bleating like a fecal puppy about to pass away past the last pinch of the divine sphincter with only the toilet of Time, oldest hag of them all, to spin me away into the spiral of star-lit empty waters.

So I approach Him, if I have not already lost Him, God, in His destiny, in which He may succeed, or tragically fail, for God like Us suffers the ambition to make a destiny more extraordinary than was conceived for Him, yes God is like Me, only more so.

Unless—spinning instead through the dark of some inner Space—the winds are icy here—I do no more than delude myself, fall back into that hopeless odyssey where libido never lingers, and my nature is nothing other than to search for the Devil while I carry with me the minds of some of you.